one life to live

THE BANNER

LLANVIEW, PENNSYLVANIA

47319   Copyright exclusive to The Banner   75 cents beyond 75 ...
except in P...

Bizarre Baby Switch

Full Text
view Wit

Does It Rev

By K...

Llanview - April 16, Th... ewspaper has come into pos... e full text of the Sun... nterview with Carlo Hesser, ... nterest of the citizens of ... will print that interview in its ... brick house at 11th and Mapl... y his wife, ... former Tr... eir daught... ashington r... employme...

ording to diplomats ...ls.

...dinista decision to a ...taly's new Parliamen ...media magnate Silvi... ...med virtually certain ...rm a government, aft ...redictable ally agre... ...e effort.

...ouncement Sunday by ...i, the leader of the N... ...e, that his party would ... ...ernment, though subjec... ...ditions, appeared to pa ...r President Oscar Luig ...Scalfaro to pick Mr. Berlusconi, ...though most politicians agree that

the rebels, who are known as contras, intended to keep up military attacks until a cease-fire has been negotiated.

JOHANNESBURG, Nov. 9 — Th... Zulu leader, Chief Gatsha Buthelez... said today that he would welcome talk... African National Congress veteran, o... with Govan A. Mbeki, the newly free...

less than 65 feet long, the measure im-

LLANVIEW, April 14 - . At seven ... he sites, the chemical was found a ... evels of 3,000 to 6,000 parts per milli... in the soil, with the highest concentra... tion found at Grantville, Pa.

Earlier Tests Faulty

Earlier this year the agency re... ported that it found significan... amounts of PCB's in water wells i... Lambertville, N.J. However, th... agency found that the testing proc... dures had been faulty and it dete... mined there were no detectable leve...

Ch... have black strider... armed ... said h... leader...

The ... not pa... ment's ... tion u... leased...

Pres... that he ... to pris... must b... ing a ... Party ...

ing PC... the cou... includi... River, that are contaminated by the chemical.

Some chemical industry officials conten... have b...

Imp...

Sena... Democ... man o... vironn... called... tive st... many...

One... rebel o... The ... Cardin... the re... was th... media... been h... the reb... Govern... Mr. ...

...Most of the ...ns," it not... ...ement, the ...te the degr... ...PCB's, dic... ...s at each ...soil and dis...

The age... ...t 49 of the ...f cleanup. ...r. Bush has ...of numero... ...icials and ...nly this t... ...clined to ... ...hite House ...d by critic... ...ade.

...dged his ...unforeseer ...stances could force another c...

The bill would ban the use o... tin, or TBT, on most recreatio... ...nents of the bill say tho... ...a great deal of time i... ...s, where the chemical ... ...damage shellfish. Scie... ...le is known about the c... ...on humans who eat ...hellfish. ...des forbidding TBT pai... ...th non-aluminum hulls ...an 65 feet long, the me... ...Perales spoke of assis... ...cipients and prevent ...egnancies. Children i... ...l, live "in a parallel v... ...along with ours, but ... ...nt."

...said that those arres... ...who the police felt we... ...the prejudicial activ... ...ay.

...e was no indication ... ...ould be held, but som... ...ey would probably ...

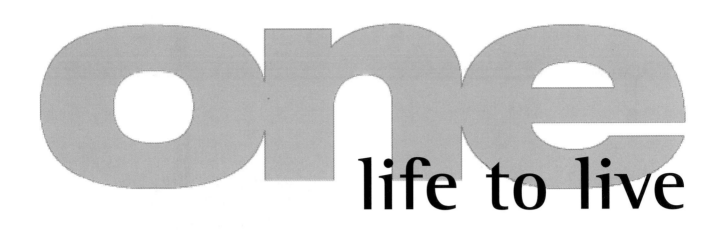

one
life to live

*Thirty Years
of Memories*

GARY WARNER

abc

daytime
press

HYPERION

NEW YORK

THE WILD SWAN

OFFICIALS TRACK ALTERNATE ROUTES FOR ALL
COMMUTERS AS TRANSIT STRIKE LOOMS...P. 23

WIN WITH
THE SUN

THE SUN
BOARD SEEKS USE
FOR WINDE...
SCHOOLS MAY B...
LIMIT PLANNED...

Rodi's
TAVERN
LLANVIEW PA

Gary Warner is the author of *All My Children: The Complete Family Scrapbook* and *General Hospital: The Complete Scrapbook.*

 For information address: Hyperion, 114 Fifth Avenue, New York, New York 10011.

Library of Congress Cataloging-In-Publication Data

Warner, Gary
One life to live : thirty years of daytime drama / by Gary Warner—1st ed.
p. cm.
ISBN 0-7868-6367-6
1. One life to live (Television program) I. Title
PN1992. 77. 048W37 1998
791.45`72—dc21 CIP
97-32728

BOOK DESIGN BY CLAUDYNE BIANCO BEDELL

FIRST EDITION

10 9 8 7 6 5 4 3 2 1

On March 17, 1971, my entire life changed. That was the day that I became Victoria Lord and moved to Llanview. Never did I dream that I would still be there twenty-seven years later.

Since my first day on the set, I have always felt that Llanview is a living, breathing community housed within a stone building on West 66th Street in New York City. We've had a most extraordinary collection of characters who have lived in or visited our town. Some came for a short while; others, like me, found a good home and stayed. But Llanview is not just made up of actors; it is also home to all the writers, directors, producers, designers, all the people who put up our houses and hospital rooms and offices and parks every day, and then pack them up at night. It is made up of those who take care of us, dress us, and make us look good, those who enable you to see and hear us, those who type the scripts and make the phone calls; all those whose job it is to see that our town and our lives run smoothly every day.

I have a brain full of memories of Llanview; of actors and actresses I've worked with and enjoyed, of favorite plots, of mishaps, and tricks we've played on each other, of all the wonderful times I have spent there.

This book contains all the stories and people who have made Llanview what it is; a history that lives in my mind and my heart. I hope you will enjoy it as much as I have.

Erika Slezak

Erika Slezak

Contents

Acknowledgments

I never could have distilled thirty years of daytime excellence into one book without the assistance of these generous individuals—

My thanks to Agnes Nixon for allowing me unlimited access to her scripts and breakdowns from *One Life to Live*'s early years—and, of course, for creating this landmark daytime drama three decades ago.

My special appreciation to former Executive Producer Maxine Levinson, who gave me my first job at ABC Daytime. I learned and absorbed so much in the years I had the pleasure of working under her auspices. I am pleased to salute her with this thirtieth anniversary tribute to *One Life to Live*.

I applaud Executive Producer Jill Faren Phelps's entire production staff at *One Life to Live*, most especially Margo Husin, who lent her vast knowledge and historical perspective to the making of this book. Margo, who has been with *One Life to Live* for more than twenty years, proved to be an indispensable resource.

My special appreciation to stage manager Ray "Ray Jay" Hoesten, for his incredible memory, and to *One Life to Live*'s design team, Roger Mooney and John Kenny. For their valuable assistance, thanks to Ron Carlivati, David Coleman, Howie Zeidman, and Jennifer Rosen.

I wish to acknowledge several key ABC Daytime executives—President Pat Fili-Krushel, Angela Shapiro, Gail Silverman, Nina Silvestri, Molly Fowler, Randi Subarsky, and Harriet Abraham, for their assistance in the compilation of this book. In addition, I extend my appreciation to staff members Danielle Zeitlen, Rosalie Macaluso, Jennifer Kriegel, Sue Johnson, Michele Vicario, Sharon Spaeth, and Marilyn Orrico.

My thanks to the ABC Public Relations Department: Sallie Schoneboom, Monica Neal, *One Life to Live* publicist Nancy Sherman, and from ABC Online: Joanne Berg, Tim Lund, and Ravi Chandran.

As you take pleasure in the hundreds of photographs in this book, please join me in giving thanks to Ann Limongello, ABC's resident on-set photographer and archivist. Not only did Ann shoot the majority of photos contained herein, but she went beyond the call of duty in the behind-the-scenes preparation of this book. My thanks not only to Ann, but to the entire ABC Photography Department, most especially Jill Yager, Peter Murray, Brent Peterson, Michelle Mustacchio, Ann Ferrell, Ida Mae Astute, and dare I forget our esteemed "video-grabber," Maria Melin?

This book could never have been written without the support of my research assistants. Donna Hornak, who retired from ABC after more than twenty years of service, afforded me her own intimate knowledge of the medium, and her extraordinary organizational skills. She deserves credit for assembling the comprehensive list of actors and their roles at the end of the book. I also thank Patricia Hornak for her contributions.

I am fortunate to have had Andrea Rothstein working with me on this project. She handled hundreds of details, and watched thousands of hours of tapes in order to transcribe many of the scripted passages contained in the book. Thank you, Andrea, from the bottom of my heart.

I extend my appreciation to Susan Williamson at the Annenberg School for Communication, Bob Christie at the National Academy of Television Arts and Sciences, and journalists Al Rosenberg, Kathy Henderson, Carolyn Hinsey, Robert Schork, and Connie Passalacqua for their generosity. Special thanks also to Daniel J. Tichio, Jr., Patricia Eboli, Amie Baker, Harry Yazidjian, and Jane Elliot.

I extend my admiration to Doris Quinlan, *One Life to Live*'s first producer, for her insights.

My gratitude to the publishing team at Hyperion—my talented editor, Gretchen Young, her assistants, Jennifer Lang and Jennifer Morgan, and Claudyne Bedell and her superb design team.

Introduction

Years ago, when *One Live to Live* was first germinating in my mind, Saul Alinsky addressed a television conference at the Aspen Institute. This renowned social activist and front-line fighter in the war against poverty and injustice posited that until diverse human beings better understand and respect one another, we can never live in harmony and peace on this planet.

By definition, all television entertainment shows have a mandate to *entertain*. If they fail at that, they go off the air. But isn't an expansion of mental horizons a key ingredient of entertainment? I believe this deeply.

Therefore, Saul Alinsky's challenge struck me as uniquely applicable to a daytime serial whose stories are spun over 260 contiguous episodes a year. His words also resonated to my childhood in the distressingly segregated South of the late 1930s and 40s, and to all the other ethnic, religious, and socio-economic prejudices I had encountered along life's journey, many of which I was probably thoughtlessly guilty myself.

Thus came into focus the basic mission of *One Life to Live*: to fashion stories about richly diverse people as their lives intertwined, as they interacted with one another. . . . To explain the hopes and hardships, the goals, fights, and failures that are ultimately shared by all mankind no matter how disperate their lifestyles.

And so were born the Polish Wolek family; the wealthy Victor Lord with his daughters Victoria and Meredith; Jewish David Siegel, married to Irish-Catholic Eileen Riley; and the supposedly Italian actress Carla Benari who, it was learned five months later, was actually Clara Gray, daughter of the beloved African-American Sadie Gray.

It goes without saying that the success of these characers and their stories depended quite as much on the enormus talents of the actors as on the writing. This has held true ever since, as fine writers have fashioned timely, compelling stories played by superlative talent: The wealthy Buchanans, the struggling Hispanic Vega family, and the African-American Gannon brothers. The other indispensable component, of course, is you, the viewers who responded to these life-affirming plots and whose loyalty has kept *One Life to Live* on the air for thirty years. . . . To you and the wonderful producers, directors, and company teams through the years go my sincerest respect and admiration.

I salute you all.

Agnes Nixon

Part One

*A*fter the death of his wife, Eugenia, Victor Lord threw himself into grooming his daughter, Victoria, to eventually take over the reins of his publishing empire.

1968 ~ 1972

*D*octor . . . Larry . . . Wolek. . . . "

The words rolled off Anna's tongue. She was so proud of her kid brother Larry, who had overcome his humble beginnings to graduate at the top of his class. Now, the youngest Wolek sibling was embarking upon a bold new career as a psychiatric intern at nearby Llanview Hospital.

The three Wolek children—Anna, Vince, and Larry—were raised in a tiny apartment in the lower-middle-class section of Llanview, Pennsylvania. When their parents died, Anna, a woman of great will, courage, and patience, had to be both a mother and sister to her two brothers. She toiled long hours as a cutter in a Philadelphia garment firm, but this did not stop her from doing the work that needed to be done in the Wolek home at night. Vince worked equally hard as a long-distance trucker, joining his sister to scrape up enough money to allow Larry to fulfill their collective dream. The American dream!

Though he had been interning only a few short months, Larry already possessed a rare insight, an intuitive understanding of people and behavior. Llanview Hospital's Assistant Head of Housekeeping, Sadie Gray, the Woleks' longtime across-the-hall neighbor, beamed with pride as she watched Larry go about his rounds. For the past few years, Larry had been like a son to her. But nothing could ever fill the void in Sadie's heart left by the disappearance of her own daughter, Clara, who had run away nine years earlier at the age of fifteen. Clara Gray hadn't been heard from since.

Soon after beginning his internship, Larry met Meredith Lord, a sweet and shy young volunteer, in the hospital courtyard. Meredith fell instantly in love with Larry, much to the displeasure of her overbearing father, publishing tycoon Victor Lord, the richest man in Llanview. Stuffy Mr. Lord considered Larry Wolek to be little more than "fortune-seeking riffraff." Larry's brother, Vince, was equally disdainful of Meredith, constantly calling her "that rich society snob."

Victor pushed Meredith into an engagement with a man he believed was more fitting of her social standing. But Meredith confided in her older sister, Victoria, that she didn't love Dr. Ted Hale, even if he was heir to one of Philadelphia's Main Line families. She much preferred sharing a cozy afternoon in the hospital courtyard with Larry than attending a society party with Ted.

Meredith enjoyed her afternoon chats with Larry. Alone in the courtyard, she opened up about the pain she felt over never having known her mother, Eugenia, who passed away soon after giving birth to her. Meredith grew up frail and sickly, but now for the first time in her life she felt strong—strong enough to go against her father's wishes and break up with Ted Hale!

In July 1968, Meredith broke her engagement. In *One Life to Live*'s first episode—July 15, 1968—Dr. Ted Hale took a deadly fall down the fourth-floor fire escape landing, and the Llanview Police immediately charged Larry Wolek with his murder.

Larry and Ted had been having an argument, part of which was overheard by a nurse, Karen Martin, and Larry's fellow intern, Price Trainor. Though Larry insisted to the police that Ted simply lost his footing and fell, Karen told another story. She told the police that Larry and Ted had been arguing about Meredith. She claimed to have heard Larry threaten Ted! Larry vehemently denied this accusation—but he was lying. He *had* threatened Ted! But only after Meredith's spurned fiancé threatened to tell her a terrible secret. Ted knew something that Larry desperately wanted to keep from Meredith. Ted knew that Meredith was dying.

Ted Hale had stumbled across Meredith's confidential medical records and discovered that she was terminally ill with a malignant blood disease.

"Break up with Meredith now, or I'll go down and tell her the truth," Ted coldly ordered Larry while standing on the fire-escape landing. He never had the chance to reveal his secret. As Ted turned away from Larry, he tripped and fell down the steps to his death.

Larry Wolek risked his promising career and compromised his personal reputation to keep Meredith from discovering the terrible truth about her failing medical condition. Keeping the reason for his altercation a secret, even from his lawyer, Dave Siegel, Larry stood trial and was nearly convicted of murder. However, in a closed-door session, the truth eventually came out and Larry was freed. The court records were sealed, sparing Meredith the news that she only had a precious few months to live. Larry Wolek hoped to spend every last minute with the woman he loved.

One day, while being treated at Llanview Hospital for what she was told was anemia, Meredith suddenly vanished. Soon after, Larry received a letter from her ending their relationship. She didn't love him, Meredith claimed.

Nurse Karen Martin was more than willing to offer Larry

Dr. Larry Wolek's growing affection for rich Meredith Lord caused an uneasy friction in both families. Larry's brother, Vince, wrongly considered Meredith a "snob," while her father, newspaper magnate Victor Lord, saw Larry as "fortune-hunting riffraff."

JOE
When are you going to start having a life of your own?

VIKI
I do have a life! I have a very full life—I have my work, which I enjoy very much, and—

JOE
And you have Daddy and Daddy has you—

VIKI
Don't say that! Joe, please, I don't want to talk—

JOE
You're right. It's no good talking about it. (He kisses her, hard. She resists at first, then responds.)

Despite her father's strong opposition, wealthy Victoria Lord fell for the charming Joseph Francis Riley, a hard-drinking reporter from the wrong side of Llanview's tracks. Viki was torn between her budding love for Joe and her need to please her father, and the strain caused a radically different consciousness, Niki Smith, to emerge.

$\mathcal{T}$ruck driver Vince Wolek landed in jail when he unwittingly helped his Mob-tied girlfriend, Millie Parks, transport drugs across state lines.

CARLA RETURNS HER ENGAGEMENT RING TO DR. JIM CRAIG 1969

Carla Benari couldn't bring herself to tell her lovesick fiancé Jim Craig that she was living a lie. Not only was Carla an African-American trying to pass for white, she had fallen in love with a black doctor, Price Trainor.

JIM
Why are you doing this?

CARLA
Because you were right when you told me I wanted to marry you for the wrong reasons.

a shoulder to cry on. For months, she had loved Dr. Wolek from afar—and this was her chance to grab him! When Meredith returned several weeks later, she spurned Larry's overtures to get back together. Bewildered, he wept in Karen Martin's open arms.

Unbeknownst to Larry, Meredith had overheard the truth about her deadly blood disease. Not wanting to burden Larry, she ran away to San Francisco, then sent him the "Dear John" letter. It pained her deeply to walk away from Larry, but in her heart Meredith truly believed she was doing the right thing. Burying her private anguish and concealing her true affections, Meredith pushed Larry toward Karen. Though Larry did not love Karen Martin, he treasured their friendship, and felt a certain obligation to her when she saved his life.

Early in the winter of 1969, Larry had been napping in a hospital storeroom when a fire suddenly broke out. With the heat of the flames beating down on her, Karen crawled through the storeroom, bravely risking her life to rescue the unconscious Dr. Wolek.

For weeks, Larry's face, burned in the fire, remained wrapped in bandages. Nurse Karen Martin stayed by his side throughout the ordeal, listening as her feverish patient called out Meredith's name in his sleep. Upon his recovery, Larry gave in to Karen's seductive overtures and made love to her. All the while, the forlorn doctor still yearned to be with Meredith, who continued to deny him.

Miraculously, Meredith's condition improved dramatically in 1969, prompting Larry's heart to leap with the hope that they could be together again. Though she was in remission, Meredith continued to resist Larry, not wanting to give him false hope. Eventually, she gave in, and admitted her love. Larry rejoiced at the news! He and Meredith were back together at last. But not for long—just days later, Karen broke the news to Larry that she was pregnant with his child.

Karen gave Larry twenty-four hours to decide. If he didn't marry her, she would "destroy" their baby. Not wanting Karen to have an illegal abortion, Larry, devastated, sacrificed his own happiness and entered into a loveless marriage with Karen Martin.

Meredith found solace with a young man she met in the park. Being the good and trusting soul that she was, Meredith insisted that the man—who suffered from amnesia—come home with her until his mystery could be solved. She gave him the name Tom Edwards—Edwards being the name of her cat! Meredith immediately acknowledged that she and Tom shared a common bond. He didn't seem to have a past, and she might not have a future.

Tom fell madly in love with Meredith, and before long they were engaged to marry. Victor took an immediate liking to the young man, treating him like a son. In fact, Victor Lord *had* a son—one that he had never met. Years earlier, Victor had a wartime affair with a woman named Dorothy Randolph. For years, Victor had searched in vain for the child she gave birth to, who was now a grown man.

Even after Karen Martin Wolek miscarried, and she and Larry separated, Meredith was still determined to go through with her marriage to Tom Edwards. After all, Tom had been such a dear friend in her time of need, she felt obliged to become his wife. However, Tom could see that the love between Larry and Meredith was too strong to be broken by even matrimonial vows. Gallantly, he released Meredith from her promise. Finally, Larry and Meredith were free to marry!

At Llanfair, the sprawling eighteenth-century home of the Lord family, Meredith's sister, Victoria, was thrilled to learn of the reconciliation. Only five years older than Meredith, Viki had always assumed a motherly role toward the sister she affectionately called "Merrie"—though she didn't tell her father how happy she was about Larry and Meredith's reconciliation. Victoria Lord had always placed her blustery father on a pedestal. In Viki's eyes, "Father" could do no wrong. Strangely, she remembered nothing of her mother's death, and felt an uneasy sense of dread every time she tried to recall her passing. "Why?" she wondered. "Why can't I remember anything?"

Upon Eugenia's death, Victor Lord had thrown himself into his work, concentrating on grooming Victoria to take over the reins of his family-owned newspaper, *The Banner*. Without a son to follow in his footsteps, Victor put his eldest daughter through years of strict training and emotional pressure, so that she would be prepared to carry the mantle. But how could Viki live up to the impossibly high standards of the Lord name?

As executive assistant to the publisher, Victoria Lord poured all her energies into *The Banner*, thereby pleasing her father. Though a strikingly beautiful young woman, she had little time, or inclination, for romance. Since her father would certainly disapprove of any young man she would have dated, she had long repressed any desire to become involved in a romantic relationship.

Meredith implored Viki to break the ties to their father and to avail herself of the opposite sex. Most men were intimidated by the cold,

(cont.)

JIM
But I told you I didn't care what the reasons were.

CARLA
It wouldn't be fair to you. Don't make it harder than it is. I can't marry you.

JIM
How do you know, Carla? In six months, you may not feel the same. Carla, is there something you haven't told me? Are you in love with someone else?

Diversity
1968

When Agnes Nixon created One Life to Live, *she introduced not only the wealthy, aristocratic Lord family, but also the less fortunate Polish-American Woleks and the Irish-American Rileys, as well as a multitude of other culturally and economically diverse characters. In 1968, Anna Wolek often shared her troubles with her neighbor, Sadie Gray, who lived across the hall in their apartment building.*

businesslike Victoria. Except one. He was *The Banner*'s star reporter, Joseph Francis Riley, a charismatic fellow from—like his best pal, Vince Wolek—the "wrong side of the Llanview train tracks."

Joe and Viki clashed often as they worked side by side at *The Banner*. Eventually, though, he wore down her resistance. Joe stirred feelings in Viki that she had never experienced before. She was falling in love, much to the consternation of her father, who vehemently disapproved of the budding romance. Victor did everything in his power to separate his daughter from this hard-drinking, hard-living cad. Viki was terribly torn between loving this charming and sexy man, and pleasing her always-demanding father. This internal dilemma caused her to have splitting headaches. To complicate matters, Viki began receiving a series of threatening notes, calling for her to end her relationship with Joe. Who could be sending them? The answer lay deep in Viki's psyche.

In the fall of 1968, a bubbly gal named Niki Smith began making nightly appearances at Ernie's, a seedy waterfront bar. Several regulars noted, but discounted, the fact that this fun-loving floozy bore a strong physical resemblance to heiress Victoria Lord. If they only knew the truth: Niki *was* Viki!

Suffering from a split personality, the normally reserved Viki donned a wig, slapped on a ton of makeup, and painted the town red as her flashy alter ego. To Vince Wolek, Niki Smith was the perfect woman. The minute he set eyes on her, he was in love! Vince told his best pal Joe Riley all about his zesty encounters with the vibrant bombshell in places like Ernie's and another seedy hot spot, The Cave. Eventually, Vinnie's heart was broken when he learned the truth, that Niki did not exist at all. Selflessly, he told Viki of Niki's existence, and with the support of her friends and family, she sought treatment with Llanview Hospital's Chief of Psychiatry, Dr. Marcus Polk. As the "Niki" episodes slowly waned, Viki went ahead with plans to marry Joe Riley. However, on their wedding day in late June of 1969, Niki Smith suddenly returned in the middle of the ceremony and fled the church—with an overjoyed Vince Wolek at her side!

DEVIOUS NURSE KAREN
MARTIN TENDS TO
INJURED LARRY WOLEK
1969

KAREN
It's best that you never
know that Meredith still
loves you. Oh, Larry, my
darling, I will make you a
good wife. It is going to
happen. I love you so
much. I want you so
much. I can make you
love me. You say her
name in your sleep, but
that doesn't matter.
When you wake up, you'll
say mine.

General Hospital's Dr. Steve Hardy journeyed from Port Charles to Llanview to
consult on Meredith Lord's malignant
blood disease. Here, Dr. Hardy confers
with Dr. Jim Craig, Victoria Lord, and Joe
Riley.

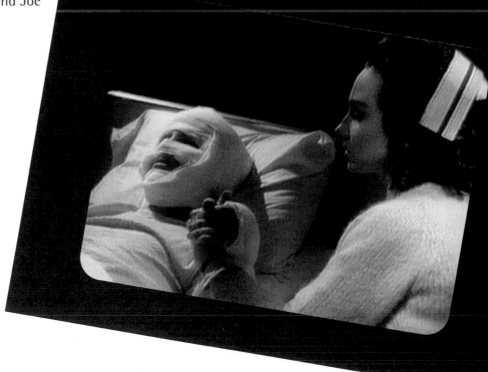

PREJUDICE
1969

Through the unique format of soap opera, One Life to Live *enabled viewers to examine their prejudices in a way no other medium could.*

In October 1968, Carla Benari was introduced as a struggling white actress who became engaged to a white doctor, Dr. Jim Craig—then gravitated toward his handsome black colleague, Dr. Price Trainor.

As they sped toward the state line, Vince realized that he probably didn't have any friends left back in Llanview. But he didn't care; he had Niki. She was back! But not for long. When Vince insisted that she marry him immediately, Niki panicked. Pushed into a matrimonial corner, Niki's only escape was to allow Viki to emerge. She returned home, reunited with Joe, and took major leaps to overcome her split personality. Viki finally remembered writing the threatening notes, then recalled the one memory from her distant past that she had blocked out.

With Dr. Polk's guidance, Viki remembered seeing a terrible argument between her parents at the top of the steep spiral staircase at Llanfair. Victor, raging with anger, confronted his wife with his suspicion that her unborn child had been fathered by another man. Eugenia suddenly lost her balance and plummeted to the bottom of the steps. To five-year-old Victoria, it may have appeared that her father pushed her mother to her death. Soon after, Eugenia Lord gave birth to a tiny little girl, Meredith, then quietly passed away.

Seemingly free at last of the inner turmoil that had driven her psyche to fragment, Viki married Joe, this time without an uninvited appearance by Niki Smith. Tears rolled down the cheeks of Joe's sister, the former Eileen Margaret Riley, who admiringly watched the proceedings with her loving husband, Dave Siegel, and their teenage twins, Timmy and Julie. Even Anna Wolek, who had loved Joe from afar since they were kids playing in the streets of Philly, was happy that Joe had finally found peace and happiness with his beloved Viki.

*D*r. Jim Craig, Llanview Hospital's newly arrived Chief of Staff, was baffled by the case of a patient, aspiring actress Carla Benari. Miss Benari seemed to suffer from the early stages of cirrhosis of the liver, a condition possibly brought on by malnutrition. Dr. Craig, a widower with a teenage daughter, Cathy, took more than a professional interest in Carla's case. He was intrigued by Miss Benari, whom he believed had an emotional problem that may have been contributing to her medical malady.

Jim Craig soon fell in love with his pretty young patient. Carla responded affirmatively when Jim tenderly asked her to marry him. Why shouldn't she? Though they had only known each other a short time, he offered her an abundance of security, warmth, and companionship. But deep in her heart, Carla knew that she didn't love him, and this troubled her. Was she willing to settle for a man she didn't love?

Dr. Craig assigned Carla's case to Dr. Price Trainor, an idealistic black intern, who immediately butted heads with his new patient. Months passed, and Carla realized that there was an exciting chemistry in the air every time she was near Dr. Trainor. "It's a chemistry that makes us fight every time we encounter each other!" she finally told him. Price knew exactly what it was—love—but he felt guilty and ashamed to have fallen in love with a white woman.

Carla took a job as Dr. Jim Craig's secretary and settled into life in Llanview. One day, Carla paid a surprise visit to Anna Wolek, a friend she had met at Llanview Hospital. As she knocked at the door, Sadie Gray opened the door of her apartment across the hall.

"I'm sorry, miss. The Woleks aren't home. Can I take a message for you?"

Carla turned in response—but stopped cold when she saw Sadie. There was a long, awkward moment of awareness, then recognition, followed by mutual shock. Finally, the words came in a whisper.

"Clara!" uttered Sadie.

"Mama!" responded Carla.

Carla Benari was really Clara Gray, the daughter who'd broken Sadie's heart when she walked out of her life as a teenager. Carla, a fair-skinned black woman, had been passing herself off as white while trying to get her acting career off the ground. Sadie listened in astonishment to the details of her tale, then challenged Carla to face the shameful reality of what she had done.

"When you ran away from here nine years ago, you didn't only turn your back on me, you turned your back on all of us," said Sadie. She tried to make her daughter deal with the fact that she was engaged to a white doctor but in love with a black one.

Baring her soul, Carla explained to Sadie that she hadn't asked to be born with lighter skin than many other black people. She revealed the pain and embarrassment she felt for "not looking black enough." Finally, Carla unloaded all her pent-up hostility on Sadie as she recalled the pain of her lonely childhood.

(cont.)

Months passed before viewers (who had by now made an emotional investment in the character of Carla) discovered she was black. Only then was it revealed that Carla was a black woman. Because she could not get a job, she'd changed her name to Carla Benari, claimed Latin heritage, and passed for white. As One Life to Live *examined the searing tragedy of prejudice, the controversial nature of the story prompted one Texas station to drop the show like a hot potato.*

"I sat and I ate my lunch all alone in that empty house, and all the time I knew that somewhere across town you were fussing over somebody else's children," explained Carla. "When I came home from school I was filled up with all kinds of things that I wanted to tell you, but you weren't there to tell. And when you finally came home, you were so damn exhausted that you didn't have that much time for me. You had used up everything that you had to give on strangers that I didn't even know."

Eventually, Sadie and Carla came to an understanding. Through their frank talks, Carla came to the realization that she could never be anything but what she really was. Carla ended her engagement to Jim, and broke the news of her true heritage to Price, who was angry. Proud of his heritage, Price bitterly rejected Carla because she had rejected her race. Eventually, Price and Carla contemplated marriage, much to the displeasure of Price's snobby mother, Grace, who arrogantly peered down her nose at her son's choice for a wife. Grace Trainor didn't feel that Carla, the daughter of a hospital housekeeper, was the right kind of woman for her precious Price.

"There's so much more to being 'right' for each other than love," Grace haughtily told the son she kept under her thumb. Though very much in love with him, Carla resented Price's inability to think for himself. When Grace arranged for Price to take a fellowship in Edinburgh, the young doctor was faced with a dilemma. Should he stay in Llanview with Carla, or accept the great honor bestowed upon him by Edinburgh University in Scotland? Carla wrote him a note telling Price that "I just won't decide for you. Since it's your life . . . it has to be up to you."

Carla left town for a week, returning to learn that Price (mistakenly believing that Carla, by her passivity, wanted him to avail himself of the opportunity) had gone to Scotland. Heartbroken, she accepted comfort from Bert Skelly, the prominent black district attorney and congressional candidate who became the new man in her life.

Jim Craig never thought it could happen again, but soon after his breakup with Carla, he fell in love—with Anna Wolek! After Anna joyously married Jim, she suddenly found herself dealing with the reality of a rebellious teenage daughter growing up in a volatile time: the 1960s. Cathy Craig resented Anna's sudden intrusion in her life. Disobedient by nature, Cathy turned to drugs. At first, the troubled young girl forged blanks from her father's prescription pad to get drugs for herself. Later, she sought out a pusher to provide the pills to satisfy her growing addiction. After discovering what she was up to, Jim didn't want to deal with the reality of Cathy's problems. But it was Cathy who finally persuaded her father to take her to New York City's Odyssey House to help in her recovery.

*A*s the drug problem in Llanview grew worse, reporter Joe Riley began an investigative series in *The Banner*. Joe's probing worried his new wife Viki, who feared for his safety. Vince Wolek, a truck driver, inadvertently became a partner in crime when he became romantically involved with Millie Parks, who was secretly working with mobster Artie Duncan in the drug trade. According to Artie's scheme, Millie was to get Vince to unknowingly transport drugs across state lines. Eventually, Millie's love for Vince, and her guilt over what she had done, enabled her to go to the authorities. Soon after, Artie's dead body was discovered in Vince Wolek's apartment. As the evidence stacked against him, Vince was charged with murder.

With Vince locked behind bars, Joe Riley began his own private mission to prove the innocence of his longtime friend. Joe's investigation during the summer of 1970 took him across the country to California. Viki waited anxiously for her husband to return from his dangerous quest. As the days passed without word from Joe, Viki's fear grew. Then, news came from the coast. Joe's car had careened off a cliff and was found amongst the rocks and surf. Though his body was not recovered, the authorities concurred that Joe Riley could never have survived the deadly plunge.

Devastated by the loss of her beloved husband, Viki's only joy came when Vince Wolek was cleared of Artie Duncan's murder. The case was resolved when Cathy Craig remembered that she had killed the drug-dealing mobster in self defense, then blocked out the tragic incident. Viki shared her grief with Joe's sister, Eileen Siegel, who was dealing with her own teenage problems at home.

(cont.)

NIKI
Just as soon as I can get out, honey. And I will get out again. Oh, Viki tries to pretend I'm not getting to her, but I know I am 'cause that's when she gets those headaches. Promise me you won't tell anybody about me.

VINCE
I promise, Niki. I promise.

𝒩ewspaperman Steve Burke was the kind of mature and stable gentleman Victor Lord always hoped that his daughter Victoria would marry. After Joe Riley's "death," Steve encouraged a devastated Viki to move on with her life. Working side by side at *The Banner*, they got off to a rocky start, but eventually they fell in love and shared a quiet marriage—though Viki could not stop longing for her beloved Joe.

Eileen and Dave Siegel were dismayed when their daughter Julie moved in with her older boyfriend, former football hero Jack Lawson. Head over heels in love with Jack, Julie yearned to get married. But Jack, always the cad, had other ideas—and other women! When Julie finally realized that her lover was less than faithful, she nearly suffered a nervous breakdown. During this difficult period in her life, she met a new man, Dr. Mark Toland. Mark, a Llanview Hospital intern with a captivating Texas twang, quickly captured Julie's heart. They married in 1971, but Dr. Toland soon discovered that his new wife, still emotionally scarred by her breakup with Jack, was frigid. In time, his patience wore thin. The Toland marriage was in big trouble!

Larry and Meredith Wolek could not have been happier in their new marriage. By 1972, Larry had changed his medical interest from psychiatry to internal medicine and was actively treating the less fortunate citizens of Llanview in the hospital's free clinic. By offering the best possible aid to those who couldn't afford it, Larry was paying back society for the support that his family and friends had given him in medical school.

To complete her happiness, Meredith decided she wanted a baby. Larry, sensitive to her blood condition, which was still in remission, did not think it wise for her to get pregnant. But Merrie was so adamant, so convincing in her desire, that Larry gave in. Soon, twins were on the way!

Meredith spent much of her pregnancy in bed, under strict medical supervision. Sadly, one of the twins was stillborn. The other, a boy named Dan, was born healthy and robust. After the tragedy, Meredith became deeply depressed. Larry sought the counsel of a celebrated psychologist, Dr. Joyce Brothers, to help his troubled wife come to grips with her fears.

In the year following Joe's death, a new man, Steve Burke, entered Viki's life. Victor Lord brought the veteran newspaperman in to serve as *The Banner*'s new executive editor. Steve was the kind of levelheaded, conservative man that Victor had always envisioned for his daughter. The manipulative Mr. Lord schemed to throw Steve and Viki together—with disastrous results. Steve, more than a decade older than Viki, found himself profoundly attracted

THE MARCY WADE MURDER CASE
1972

Viki Riley nervously stood by while her fiancé, Steve Burke, stood trial for the first-degree murder of Viki's Banner assistant, Marcy Wade. Steve was represented by Llanview's top trial attorney, but with all the evidence stacked against him, Steve's future looked bleak. Fortunately, a mystery man found key evidence, Marcy's purse, and anonymously delivered it to Steve's attorney, Dave Siegel. The purse, containing a threatening note in Marcy's handwriting, was all that was needed to set Steve free. The mystery man turned out to be Viki's believed-dead husband, Joe.

*D*RUG ADDICTION
1970
One Life to Live *became the first regularly scheduled program to heed a White House request, made in April 1970, to use commercial entertainment to carry a warning on drug use to viewers. The following June, the soap began showing actual group therapy sessions of teenage addicts at Odyssey House in New York. The idea of using real addicts in a television program belonged to Agnes Nixon, creator of* One Life to Live, *who saw it as "a natural outgrowth of our program." In the story, teenager Cathy Craig stole her father's prescription blanks and forged them to get drugs for herself. When her father, Dr. Jim Craig, found out about it, he took her to Odyssey House.*

to her quiet charm and captivating beauty. Still deep in mourning, Victoria Lord Riley initially chafed at Steve's efforts to take her on a date; but after many months, she finally returned Steve's feelings, and they planned to marry.

Vince Wolek, along with Joe's sister Eileen, was appalled at Viki's decision to remarry. They had refused to give up hope that Joe was gone. Both bristled when Viki signed the papers declaring Joseph Francis Riley legally dead. Though she was set to marry Steve, Viki continued to have nightmares that Joe was alive. Pushing the doubts from her mind, she plunged ahead with wedding plans.

Vince and Eileen's objections were not the only obstacles in the way of Viki's happy future with Steve. Steve's brilliant young secretary, Marcy Wade, secretly carried a torch for her boss. Intensely jealous, Marcy grew to hate Victoria Lord. She couldn't let that "whimpering little duchess" marry her beloved Steve! Learning of Viki's problems with a split personality, Marcy developed a devious plan to get Steve for herself.

Marcy schemed to drive Viki over the edge by making her believe that Niki Smith had returned. She even went so far as to don a wig and show up at Ernie's to offer conclusive proof to Viki that her alter ego had returned. However, Marcy's skillful scheme backfired. Viki's deep troubles over the Niki matter actually brought her closer to Steve!

Slipping deeper into psychosis, Marcy added a murderous tangent to her evil plan. If all went right, she intended to kill Vince Wolek and frame Niki Smith for the crime. However, before she could carry out the plan, Steve discovered the depth of Marcy's deception and confronted her outside a warehouse on the docks of the Llantano River. Marcy, dressed in her Niki Smith disguise, pulled a gun on Steve, then craftily announced a change in plans.

"It won't be Vinnie that Viki thinks she killed. It will be you!" she cackled maniacally. Realizing he was about to die, Steve took a chance. He lunged for the gun. During the subsequent struggle, Marcy dropped her purse. A vagrant suddenly appeared, grabbed it, and ran. Just then, the gun went off—and Marcy fell to the ground, dead.

Lieutenant Ed Hall of the Llanview Police Department launched an investigation into Marcy's death. Though Steve proclaimed his innocence, Lieutenant Hall developed his own theory: that Steve and Marcy were having an affair behind Viki's back, and that when Marcy planned to blow the whistle on him, Steve killed her.

Viki watched in horror as her fiancé was charged with first-degree murder. With all the evidence stacked against him, Steve's future looked bleak. Only Marcy's black patent-leather purse, containing an incriminating note saying that Niki Smith planned to kill Vince Wolek, could save him. But where could it be?

On the waterfront, a mysterious, unshaven man who had read accounts of Steve's plight located the missing purse in the belongings of another vagrant named Charley. Now this stranger held the evidence that could exonerate Steve Burke. The man was Joe Riley!

Suffering from a potentially fatal brain aneurysm, Joe stumbled into a local Llanview diner and passed out. He was befriended by Wanda Webb, a tough-talking waitress with a huge heart. Wanda tenderly nursed Joe back to health, and fell in love with the handsome stranger in the process.

Fearing that he was going to die, Joe did not want to make his presence known to his loved ones. But he had to do the right thing and get the purse to the authorities. So he surreptitiously sent the purse to his brother-in-law—Steve's lawyer, Dave Siegel—and the evidence gained Steve Burke's acquittal.

Anguished and very weak, Joe gathered the strength to leave Llanview, sticking around long enough to lurk in the bushes at Llanfair to watch Viki marry another man. Steve and Viki, blissfully happy, left on their honeymoon, just as Joe collapsed and was rushed to Llanview Hospital.

The news of Joe Riley's amazing return delighted the residents of Llanview, especially his devoted sister Eileen. Joe pleaded with Eileen, Jim, and Victor Lord not to notify Viki, but in his weakened condition he could not fight the inevitable. After a delightful honeymoon, Steve and Viki returned to Llanview to be greeted by the startling news about Joe. Viki promptly fainted; upon recovering, she raced to Llanview Hospital in time to catch Joe and Wanda slipping out a side door.

Standing in the hospital corridor, Viki and Joe stared at each other for what seemed like an eternity. As she whispered his name, Joe took a step forward, then collapsed at her feet. His life or death would soon be determined by a delicate operation to repair the aneurysm in his brain. Joe regained consciousness, and at the sight of Viki, his will to live surfaced. He decided that one day they would be together again. Joe's operation was successful, but now Viki was faced with an intense dilemma: which husband should she choose—Joe or Steve?

(cont.)

The unwritten and unrehearsed sessions, featuring Cathy and eight ex-addicts, were edited and integrated into the program over the course of the summer. The response, says Ms. Nixon, was "mind-boggling. ABC had to hire four extra secretaries to handle the mail. I think it got a message across, and I hope that people did take a little more interest in helping the young people of that time."

$\mathcal{L}$ieutenant Ed Hall always got his man—but in 1973, he put aside his police work to doggedly pursue the woman he loved, Carla Gray.

1973~ 1975

Joe Riley made a full recovery from brain surgery and prodded Viki into choosing between her two men.

"I know that whatever decision you make, it will be the right one—sure as my name's Joe Riley," he tenderly told her. "I'll still love you—as I always have and always will—and I'll understand."

Viki admitted to herself, and her loved ones, that she cared equally for Joe and Steve, but since she was Steve's wife now, her duty was to him. Still, she could not get Joe out of her mind. As the weeks passed, Viki's resistance to Joe increasingly wore down, until fate finally intervened. While covering an avalanche in the mountain community of Mt. Jefferson during the winter of 1973, Viki and Joe found themselves staying at the same hotel. Working together again, the old chemistry came bounding back!

"To the greatest reporting team since Matthew, Mark, Luke, and John!" said Joe as he toasted his ladylove with a flute of champagne. As the snow fell gently outside their window, Joe and Viki shared a night of laughs, memories, and dancing. As they slowly swayed to the music of a toy carousel music box, it was as if the years between them no longer existed. As the music ended, Joe and Viki sank down onto the bed and made love.

The next morning, Viki, torn by her love for Joe and her sense of duty to Steve, informed Joe that their night together had not changed things. She could not leave Steve.

"I want us to be friends, Joe. I really do," she gently told him. But after their night of passion, Joseph Riley was not about to let the woman he loved walk out of his life. A bitter argument ensued, causing Viki to flee

Dr. Mark Toland seemed to all to be a decent and caring husband to his wife, Julie Siegel. Little did Julie know that her beloved Mark was spending his spare time playing doctor with his fellow Llanview Hospital staffer, Dr. Dorian Cramer. After pushing Dorian down a flight of stairs, Mark fled to South America. Upon his return to Llanview, the dastardly doc was murdered!

the hotel in tears. She jumped in her car and recklessly drove off—straight into an accident!

The car crash left Viki comatose for months. When she was finally transferred back to Llanview Hospital, doctors determined that Viki was suffering from a "psychogenic" coma. Because of the dilemma she faced, Viki did not want to wake up! It wasn't until her sister Meredith pleaded with her to open her eyes that Viki finally emerged from her coma.

Upon her recovery, Viki stuck to her original plan and returned to Steve. Joe, crushed by her rejection, poured all his energies into assisting Cathy Craig with her first novel. Cathy, now an attractive, truly liberated woman, was Joe's savior during this difficult period. Although he was still very much in love with Viki, Joe allowed himself to be seduced by Cathy.

As the months passed, Viki realized that the joy she once shared with Steve was long gone. A personal tragedy in 1973 helped Viki realize that she should end her marriage to Steve. Two ruthless thieves, Earle Brocke and Ben Howard, broke into Llanfair in search of Victor Lord's priceless art collection. When their robbery went awry, the two thieves held Meredith and her brother-in-law Vince hostage in the Woleks's garage apartment. Days passed as the police, led by Lt. Ed Hall, negotiated with Brocke and Howard for the safe release of the hostages. As negotiations broke down, Meredith and Vinnie attempted a last-ditch escape. During the confusion, the police broke in, and Meredith slipped and hit her head on the floor. Larry watched in horror as an ambulance rushed his beloved Merrie to the hospital, where his fellow doctors determined that the blow to her head had caused a massive cerebral hemorrhage.

Meredith serenely accepted her fate. Knowing she was dying, Merrie peacefully whispered to Viki to let Larry know how happy he had made her. After saying her final good-byes to her loved ones, Meredith Lord Wolek gently left this world. Llanview mourned the untimely passing of this sweet angel who had graced their presence for such a short time.

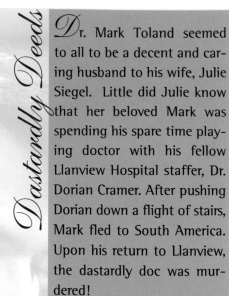

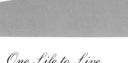

Now a police officer, Vince Wolek went beyond the call of duty when he befriended rebellious street urchin Joshua West. The troublesome bad boy chose to follow a straight and narrow path under the guidance of his adoptive parents, Ed and Carla Hall.

Meredith's death made Viki realize how precious true love can be. More than ever, she knew that her heart was with Joe. Finally, she mustered the courage to ask Steve Burke for a separation. Though furious at first, Steve finally relented and agreed to let her go. He remained in Llanview, enjoying a short-term relationship with Cathy Craig, before accepting a new position as a foreign correspondent for *The Banner*. At long last, Joe and Viki could be together!

Viki hurried to the Caribbean to finalize the end of her marriage, but upon her return, she was faced with terribly shocking news: Cathy Craig was pregnant with Joe's baby! Cathy had kept her impending motherhood a closely guarded secret. When Joe found out, he offered to marry her. Cathy refused his generous offer, insisting that she was a modern woman who could raise her child alone. Quietly, Viki and Joe overcame the shock and remarried in a simple ceremony in New York City.

Wanda, who had loved Joe from afar, soon found happiness with his best friend, Vince Wolek. Much to the delight of the residents of Llanview, Vince, now a cop, made the wisecracking waitress his bride.

Vince's friend, Lt. Ed Hall, found himself a wife when he married Carla Gray, who had ended her relationship with former DA, current Congressman Bert Skelly. Ed and Carla's new marriage was immediately put to the test when they adopted a rebellious young street urchin, Joshua West.

Dave Siegel did not live long enough to see any of his friends tie

*N*urse Susan Barry and Dr. Larry Wolek tended to a celebrated patient—Victor Lord—when the tyrannical newspaper magnate was admitted to Llanview Hospital after suffering a heart attack.

the knot. Sadly, Llanview's much-admired attorney passed away from a massive heart attack. His widow Eileen turned to painkillers to numb her grief.

Eileen eventually sought treatment from Llanview Hospital's newest staff member, Dr. Dorian Cramer. Cool and aloof, Dorian moved into a big house near Llanfair with her neurotic younger sister Melinda, who had once been a promising piano prodigy. Sadly, Melinda's budding career was cut short when a fall from a horse left the timorous girl with a paralyzed left arm. When they learned of the accident, Dorian and Melinda's parents hired a small plane to fly to Melinda's side. Sadly, they never made it. The plane crashed, killing the senior Cramers. The series of tragedies devastated Dorian, who had lost her other sister, Agatha, to pneumonia at the age of thirteen. Melinda was her only family—and Dorian became unduly devoted to fulfilling her troubled sister's every need.

Saddled with guilt, Melinda encouraged her workaholic sister to find a husband. But Dorian just didn't see a permanent man in her future.

"You won't let yourself date because you have to take care of me!" argued Melinda. Though the thoroughly unpleasant Dorian wasn't looking for a husband, she did have a notorious history of stealing married men away from their wives. Her handsome fellow doctor, Mark Toland, became an easy target. Despite ongoing therapy, Mark's wife Julie still had sexual problems that left their marriage on shaky ground. Mark, unfulfilled and frustrated with Julie's frigidity, found what he needed in Dorian Cramer's bed.

Dorian rented a small apartment where she carried out her private fantasies with Mark. Eventually, Melinda stumbled upon Dorian's secret and became furious because she had developed a crush on Mark, too! Melinda Cramer was fed up with living in her sister's shadow. She dreamed up a vicious plot to stab the lovers in their "love nest." Emerging from her hiding place, she lunged for Mark. The blade sliced open his hand, but he managed to subdue his attacker. In the aftermath of her failed scheme, Melinda slipped into catatonia. Dorian, guilt-ridden but relieved that her secret was still safe, shipped Melinda away to a mental institution in Hartford.

*I*n the spring of 1975, Cathy Craig gave birth to a girl, Megan Riley Craig. Just days later, Cathy panicked when her precious baby stopped breathing! Doctors determined that Megan suffered from a congenital heart defect passed on by her father, Joe Riley. Though the baby underwent a corrective surgical procedure, neither Cathy nor Joe were told the dreadful news: Megan would never live past adolescence.

Viki pleaded with Larry not to tell Joe that he had given Megan her fatal ailment—and that any child they might have could suffer the same fate. Knowing Joe would never allow his wife to have children if he knew of the hazards, Viki vowed to keep the news from him.

*A*fter Meredith's death, Larry Wolek buried himself in his work at Llanview Hospital. At one point, he fell in love with one of his patients, a young woman named Rachel Wilson. Rachel, the former secretary to *The Banner*'s Washington correspondent John Douglas, fell critically ill with Hodgkin's disease. Larry spent hours at her bedside, urging Rachel not to lose her will to live. Even when her health took a turn for the worse, Larry refused to give up hope. He grew so obsessed with Rachel Wilson that Dr. Jim Craig was compelled to remove him from the case. Rachel confided to her nurse, Susan Barry, that she wanted to die—and she hoped Larry would help her end her life.

One day, after an argument with his lover, Dorian, Dr. Mark Toland gave Rachel her medication—unaware that Dorian had already administered the required dose of potassium chloride. In her haste, Dorian had failed to initial the patient's chart. The accidental overdose killed Rachel. Mark quickly realized what had happened and joined with Dorian to cover up their negligence.

Larry was arrested, and accused of what the police deemed a mercy killing. Dr. Wolek stood trial and was found guilty of murder. As

$\mathscr{T}$he roots of the bitter rivalry between Viki and Dorian can be traced to events that took place in 1975. Down but not out, Dorian got her claws into Viki's father, Victor Lord. Viki tried to warn her father that Dorian was an opportunist, but to no avail. Mr. Lord was charmed by his cold-blooded new doctor.

he languished in jail, the relationship between secret lovers Mark and Dorian went sour. Dorian, riddled with guilt, went to Mark and threatened to tell Jim the truth about Rachel's death. In a panic, Mark bolted—and as Dorian chased after him she stumbled and took a terrible fall down the stairs.

For weeks, Dorian lay in a coma, while Mark skipped town. After six weeks, Nurse Barry noticed that the comatose Dorian had begun mumbling:

"Larry . . . potassium chloride . . . Mark . . . the initials."

Susan raced to the authorities and told of this breakthrough, which she believed could be beneficial to Larry. Eventually, Dorian emerged from the coma, and confessed her negligence in court. Her testimony set Larry Wolek free. Dorian was fined and suspended from Llanview Hospital, and blamed Viki—a hospital board member—for the decision. She vowed to get revenge on the high-and-mighty Victoria Lord Riley.

But Dr. Dorian Cramer quickly found work—as the private physician-in-residence for Llanview's most prominent citizen, Victor Lord, who had suffered a heart attack that confined him to bed.

Viki resented Dorian's presence in her family home, and sought to convince her father to remove her from the premises. But Victor was adamant in his defense of Dorian—and it was readily apparent that he was charmed by her bedside manner. Dorian was equally beguiled by Victor's money, which afforded her the opportunity to get her mentally ill sister Melinda the finest medical care.

Before long, Victor shocked everyone by revealing that he had made Dorian his wife! The thought sickened Viki. Dorian, her stepmother? How could this be? Despite her abhorrence, Viki could do nothing. Dorian Cramer was now Dorian Lord—mistress of Llanfair!

With his health failing, Victor Lord renewed his quest to find the long-lost son he had fathered during a wartime liaison. Where could he be? Mark Toland knew! While hiding out in South America, Mark discovered information about Victor's son and planned to use it to his own advantage. He slipped back into Llanview and attempted to blackmail the greedy Dorian, who did not want Victor's heir to muck up her plans to inherit the Lord fortune.

Dorian persuaded Mark to change his blackmail plans by giving him a juicy bit of news. Dorian had recently gotten hold of the information that Joe Riley had passed on a congenital heart problem to his daughter Megan—and that Viki was keeping the information from him! Mark's eyes lit up with dollar signs. He proceeded to blackmail Viki, who confided her dilemma to Larry. Dr. Wolek urged Viki to tell Joe the truth, but his words fell upon deaf ears. Viki was determined to spare Joe and pay the money. However, before Viki could drop the money at Mark

It was a rocky ride, but cop Vince Wolek and waitress Wanda Webb finally made it all the way to the altar in 1975. First, Vinnie was shot and wounded in the line of duty, then developed measles just days before the ceremony!

Toland's motel room, someone shot and killed him!

Mark's killer turned out to be a drunken Susan Barry, whose unrequited love for Larry drove her to desperate lengths. Mistakenly thinking Larry and Viki were having a motel-room affair, Susan purchased a gun and set out to shoot the lovers. Arriving at the motel, she encountered Mark. In a besotted haze, Susan mistook Mark for Larry and shot him dead—then blocked out the incident.

Months later, when the horrible memories came flooding back, Susan ran blindly into the street and was struck down by a motorcyclist. Viki was horrified by this terrible turn of events, but she breathed a sigh of relief. The secret she was keeping from her husband, Joe, was safe—for now.

*A*round this time, a mysterious man named Tony Harris showed up. Tony had come to Llanview bearing photos of the Lord family, and although it wasn't revealed at first, the handsome young man was Victor's long-lost son! Eventually, Tony and Victor shared an emotional reunion, which only made Dorian deeply jealous and resentful. To keep Victor from writing Tony into his will, Dorian successfully schemed to turn the two men into bitter enemies. Thanks to her evil machinations, Victor and Tony were constantly at each other's throats!

Tragedy struck when Cathy's daughter, Megan, was killed in a car accident. The baby had been having a respiratory attack and Viki, who had been baby-sitting for her, rushed to get her to the hospital. While pulling out of the driveway of her carriage house, Viki's car skidded and crashed. Megan was killed, and for many weeks Viki languished in a deep coma. Upon her recovery, she vowed to get pregnant without telling Joe the inherent risk it posed to their child. But Cathy, convinced that Megan's death was not an accident, vowed revenge on Victoria Lord Riley!

*E*ileen Siegel's spirits brightened when her son, Tim, came home from law school. Eileen was proud of her handsome son, who was planning to follow in the footsteps of her late husband. But once home, Tim broke the stunning news to his mother that he had dropped out of school. While working as a construction worker at Llanview Hospital, Tim became instantly smitten with a beautiful young nurse, Jenny Wolek. Jenny, a distant cousin to Vince, Anna, and Larry, had come to Llanview in the spring of 1975. She was equally charmed by Tim, and grateful for the attention he lavished upon her. However, Jenny could not act upon her feelings because she was a novice nun about to take her final vows!

Over the summer of 1975, Tim helped Jenny with volunteer work at a local Llanview nursing home. She felt comfortable with him. In time, that comfort turned to love . . . and heartache. Jenny, torn between her feelings for Tim Siegel and her commitment to God, decided to forego her final vows and marry the man she loved. But first she agreed to honor her commitment to aid the innocent earthquake victims in the war-torn South American country of San Carlos.

With a sweet kiss, Tim said good-bye to his bride-to-be as she flew away to South America. Soon after, he learned that several nuns had been killed in an explosion in San Carlos. Tim was horrified. Would he ever see his beloved Jenny again?

$\mathcal{L}$lanview Hospital's new staff psychiatrist, Will Vernon, had his hands full with his first patient, Cathy Craig. Devastated by the news that she would never be able to have more children, Cathy lost touch with reality, then kidnapped Viki's newborn son, Kevin.

1976

*T*im Siegel waited anxiously for news of Jenny's fate. Had she been one of the nine nuns killed in war-torn San Carlos? Soon, word came: Jenny was injured, but alive! Suffering from malaria, Jenny was confined to the ICU unit at Llanview Hospital. Accompanying her back to the States was a doctor—Jenny's dear friend, Peter Janssen.

Tim could not help but notice the strong bond between Jenny and Peter. Despite his concerns, Tim knew in his heart that Jenny loved him, and upon her recovery they stepped up their plans to marry. The wedding plans met with stiff resistance from Tim's mother, Eileen, and Jenny's hotheaded cousin, Vince.

Eileen Siegel managed to convince the young lovers to put off the wedding until June; but Jenny changed her mind and moved the date up when she began waking nightly in a cold sweat with the frightening feeling that something terrible was going to happen to her!

The revised plans met with plenty of opposition—especially from Vince Wolek. One day in mid-March, Vince and Tim had a confrontation in the hospital cafeteria. Both men lost their tempers, but Tim decided to walk away to avoid a physical confrontation. Turning on his heel, Tim headed for the nearest stairwell, with Vince in hot pursuit. Vince stopped Tim, and the argument resumed again. Tim had taken all he could stand. When his anger exploded, Tim swung at Vince, who ducked out of the way. Tim lost his balance, fell down the stairs, and suffered head and internal injuries.

Fearing deep down in her soul that Tim would not survive, Jenny decided that they should marry immediately in the intensive care unit. Jenny, with tears in her eyes, held her beloved's hand as they were pronounced man and wife. Tim forced away the pain that wracked his weakened body, and smiled with joy knowing that Jenny was finally his wife!

Within hours, his condition took a turn for the worse. The following afternoon, Tim Siegel died in Jenny's arms. Tim's passing took an emotional toll on his widowed mother, Eileen Riley Siegel. Joe Riley was a source of strength for his sister during the difficult weeks after the accident that took Tim's life. Privately, Joe was shaken by his nephew's death, coming so closely on the heels of his own daughter Megan's untimely passing. Overwhelmed with grief, Joe finally broke down. Seeing her husband's tears tore Viki apart. More than ever she felt responsible for the death of Joe's only child, but soon his feelings would be buoyed by some incredible news: she was pregnant!

After months of pain, Viki was on the road to a complete recovery from the crippling injuries she'd sustained in the car crash—thanks inadvertently to her new stepmother, Dorian Cramer Lord. To upstage Viki, Dorian had secretly planned a party in her own honor at Llanfair. The wicked Dorian wanted to show everyone that she was now the lady of the manor and mistress of Llanfair, a role always held by Viki. But Dorian had another secret. She had removed Viki's mother's portrait from its place of honor over the fireplace in the library and had replaced it with a huge painting bearing her own likeness. Dorian eagerly anticipated the moment when Viki would walk into the library and see the new portrait.

Walking with a cane, Viki limped into the party and was, as expected, visibly shaken upon seeing Dorian's portrait hanging regally in the Lord library. Viki, always the quintessential lady, refused to give Dorian the satisfaction of seeing her anger. Instead, she quietly excused herself, and went upstairs to seethe in private with Joe by her side. When Viki was ready to return to the party, she stood at the top of the stairs with her cane, about to descend. Looking to embarrass Viki, Dorian brought everyone into the foyer to watch. Defiantly, Viki handed Joe her cane. Looking Dorian straight in the eye, she slowly and elegantly came down the stairs—as the guests burst into applause! Dorian's faint smile belied the humiliation she felt in every pore of her body.

Meanwhile, Viki was thrilled at the prospect of motherhood. She wanted so much to give Joe another child. And yet, she still could not bring herself to tell Joe the terrible truth, that their child could possibly be born with the same heart defect that had afflicted Megan.

The feud between Victor Lord and his son Tony grew more heated in the new year, especially when Tony announced his plans to build a "swinging" singles bar on the same road that led to Llanfair. Unbeknownst to Victor,

Dorian (conspiring with her husband's protégé, Matt McAllister) was doing whatever she could in her own clever way to widen the breach between father and son. At the same time, she persuaded Victor to change his will, making her the primary beneficiary.

In time, though, Dorian's efforts began to fail. Sensing his own mortality, Victor's hostility toward Tony began to wane. Despite Dorian's tricks, father and son tentatively reached out to each other.

Tony began a romance with Cathy Craig, and as their relationship grew more serious, Cathy began to suspect that there was more than met the eye to Tony's long-ago relationship with one of the new editors at *The Banner*, Pat Kendall. She was right!

Ten years earlier, Pat and Tony had engaged in a sizzling romance in Rio de Janeiro. Though she was now a married woman (whose husband was missing and presumed dead), Pat Kendall was clearly still in love with Tony Lord. Thus, she was disheartened to learn that Tony had asked Cathy to marry him. Rather than go to him and confess her feelings, Pat avoided Tony. Meanwhile, Tony could not avoid the fact that Cathy, still emotionally wounded by the death of her baby, was beginning to lose touch with reality. When she learned that Viki was pregnant, Cathy grew psychotic with rage.

In the spring, Pat brought her nine-year-old son, Brian, to live with her in Llanview. Brian, a bright and charming boy, was the joy of Pat's life. He had been raised right by his mother and her husband, Paul Kendall, a radical political activist who had gone underground in the turbulent early 1970s and was now presumed dead. Only Pat knew the truth: that Brian was Tony's son!

Unable to bear the anguish a moment longer, Pat told the whole truth to her friend, Viki, who helped her make a major decision. She resolved to fight for Tony! However, on the day Pat intended to speak to him, she discovered that Tony and Cathy had gone to a neighboring state to get married! Emotionally shattered, Pat realized that there was no longer any hope for her to be with the man she loved.

(cont.)

VIKI
Kevin? Kevin Lord Riley?

JOE
How do you like it?

VIKI
Oh, I love it—and I love you. Oh, Joe, God's in his heaven.

WHO KILLED VICTOR LORD?
1976

Could Dorian Lord have killed her husband, Victor Lord? That's the question her stepdaughter Viki Riley began asking moments after Victor's death in June 1976. Viki steadfastly refused to believe, despite his history of heart problems, that her father died of natural causes. Instead, she suspected Victor's wealthy widow, Dorian, of having done him in. Despite Viki's claims, the authorities could not find evidence to prove Dorian's guilt—and as a result she was never charged with any wrongdoing.

As Tony slowly began to mend his relationship with his father, Victor, Dorian grew more incensed. She didn't want Victor to leave this "bastard" a penny of his vast fortune! Fearing that a father/son reunion would end her chances of inheriting the Lord fortune, Dorian stepped up her campaign against Tony. When Tony realized what she was doing, he went straight to Victor to tell him of his wife's treachery. Later, Victor lashed out at Dorian. Confronted with her lies, Dorian was forced to admit that she'd known before anyone else that Tony was Victor's son. The shock of this revelation proved too much for Victor; on April 30, 1976, he crumpled to the floor of the Lord library. Llanview's most powerful figure had suffered a massive stroke that left him unable to speak.

Determined to keep her husband from recovering, Dorian sprang into action. She succeeded in having Victor moved from the hospital back to Llanfair. Her devilish aim was to isolate him as much as possible from his children and thereby reduce the chances of them finding out about the climactic fight that had led to his stroke.

Soon, a second stroke sent him back to the hospital. As his strength slipped away, Victor struggled to speak to Viki. It became obvious, much to Dorian's distress, that he had something very important to tell his daughter. Sadly, Victor Lord didn't survive long enough to tell the truth about Dorian. Under very mysterious circumstances, Victor Lord died in June.

Llanview was stunned when Victor's will was read aloud and Dorian, rather than Viki, was given control of the estate. Tony received nothing! With a strong power base from which she could now operate, Dorian swiftly moved to take over the various operations of the Lord family empire. At the same time, she set her sights on a new conquest—Viki's husband, Joe Riley! And she believed that she had just the ammunition she needed, for she had stumbled upon Viki's secret. Armed with the news that Megan had died of a hereditary heart problem inherited from her father, Dorian "accidentally" told Joe—and all hell broke loose.

Dorian's well-timed slip of the tongue left Joe devastated, and led to the first serious breach in Viki and Joe's marriage. They eventually reconciled and nervously looked forward to the birth of their baby.

Tony, who had been finding his marriage to Cathy rough going at best, now did all he could to keep his deranged wife from coming completely off the spool. Along with her father, Jim Craig, Tony was able to convince Cathy to seek help with Llanview Hospital's new Chief of Psychiatry, Dr. Will Vernon, who had recently arrived in Llanview with his wife Naomi and their two children, Brad and Samantha. Psychoanalysis did not seem to help Cathy. She lied to Tony, telling him she was pregnant when she hadn't even taken a pregnancy test! Cathy Craig was rapidly losing her mind.

In September, Viki went into premature labor and gave birth to a son—Kevin Lord Riley! Joe and Viki were overjoyed to learn the wonderful news that their son did not have the heart defect that had afflicted Megan. The weeks following Kevin's birth were the happiest Joe and Viki had ever experienced—until the October day they discovered their newborn son was missing. Cathy had kidnapped little Kevin!

Lt. Ed Hall was put in charge of the investigation. Weeks, then months, passed, without word from Cathy. Joe pleaded publicly for Cathy to return the child. Dorian (who was in the midst of a studied campaign to revamp her image) put up reward money. Eventually Cathy was apprehended, but the baby was nowhere to be found! Cathy, more delusional than ever, had no memory of ever marrying Tony. Worse, she had no memory of ever taking Kevin!

Pat's support throughout this crisis made Tony realize how much she still meant to him. One night in mid-November, Pat and Tony gave in to their feelings and made love. Afterward, Pat pulled back, knowing that Tony had to give his full attention to Cathy if she ever was to make a full recovery. Riddled with guilt, Pat tearfully prepared to leave Llanview forever. But fate intervened when, just as she made final plans to depart with Brian, the boy fell ill with a potentially fatal case of bacterial meningitis.

$\mathcal{B}$rad Vernon cared deeply for sweet Jenny Siegel—and so did his very-married father, Will. While wooing the widowed ex-nun, "Brad the cad" continued to carry on a secret affair with a former girlfriend, Lana McClain.

After months of mourning the loss of her beloved Tim, Jenny met a young man who made her smile again. And he was handsome, too! He was Brad Vernon, the son of Will and Naomi Vernon. Jenny was touched by Brad's sweetness and sincerity. Brad, who once dreamed of being a tennis pro, had suffered a severe knee injury that kept him from ever realizing his lofty goals. Brad began romancing Jenny—and two-timing her, too, with Lana McClain, a local Llanview waitress.

At first, Brad's only reason for pursuing the flame-haired waitress was to get her into the sack. Lana, sympathetic and naive, genuinely cared for Brad, and mistakenly thought he felt the same way.

Brad's parents, Will and Naomi, were going through their own personal hell. The Vernon marriage had never been the same since Will's affair nine years earlier, which led Naomi to attempt suicide. Now, Naomi Vernon's fears had returned. She began to suspect that Will was having an affair with his nurse, Jenny—the very same young woman who was dating their son. Seeing Jenny as a threat to her own marriage, Naomi began pushing her toward Brad.

Late in the year, there was a major turning point in Brad and Jenny's relationship. It dawned on Brad that the sweet Jenny wasn't like all the other girls he had been with. She was different. She was a virgin. And he was falling in love with her!

Vince and Anna Wolek were thrilled with Larry's decision to open his own private medical practice. They were less than thrilled about his private life! Much to his siblings' chagrin, Larry began an affair with his second cousin—Jenny's sister, Karen. Karen Wolek was everything that sweet Jenny was not. Karen was flashy, pushy, and ambitious. Raised by a family of modest means, Karen wanted to live the high life—and she saw Larry as her meal ticket. The first step in her master plan was to get him to join the country club, for the sake of improving his practice, of course. The second step was to get Larry to marry her. The third was to sweet-talk Larry into giving her the biggest, most expensive engagement ring in Llanview's local jewelry store. Each conquest proved easy for the beguiling Karen. It was just a matter of time before wedding bells would be ringing!

$\mathcal{F}$our years after Meredith's death, Larry Wolek found happiness again with his second cousin, Karen. Soon after their engagement, the bride-to-be ran into friction from Larry when he refused to honor her extravagant request to throw "the biggest, most lavish wedding that Llanview has ever seen!"

1977

*M*onths passed, and in early 1977, there was still no word about Joe and Viki's missing baby son, Kevin. By now, Joe was convinced that they would never see Kevin again, but he didn't dare share his fears with Viki. To numb the pain, Joe began drinking heavily and found excuses to spend more time at the office. Finally, when he came home drunk one night too many, Joe and Viki got into a major battle, and old wounds were reopened. Joe reminded Viki of how she had withheld the truth about Megan's heart condition from him for so long. Viki bitterly countered with the accusation that none of the present misery would have happened if Joe had not become involved with Cathy Craig, the demented young woman who had kidnapped Kevin.

Dorian did everything in her power to widen the growing schism between the Rileys. The last straw came when Joe stayed out and a furious Viki discovered that he had gone on a drinking binge, then spent the night at Dorian's home, Llanfair. This incident, coupled with Joe's loss of faith that their son was alive, made Viki feel abandoned in every way. She asked Joe to move out. The unthinkable had happened—Viki and Joe's marriage had shattered.

*W*ith each passing day, Cathy's memory became a little clearer. Eventually, she provided the authorities with enough information to locate the woman with whom she had left baby Kevin. In a dramatic and poignant moment, the woman, Mrs. MacGruder, handed Kevin over to Viki. Tears flowed as she clutched her precious son in her arms for the

TWO-TIMING BRAD DUMPS NAIVE LANA 1977

Sweet Lana McClain desperately loved cad Brad Vernon, and he conned her into thinking he felt the same way about her. But all he really wanted from Lana was one thing—sex. All the while, he was two-timing Lana by dating the virginal Jenny Wolek. Forced to choose between the two young women, Brad tried to let poor Lana down gently.

BRAD
I can't see you anymore.

LANA
What are you talking about?

BRAD
Look, Lana, I like you. I like you a lot. But I've got to get my life straightened out. I'm not being fair to you.

first time in months. Viki Riley vowed never to give him up again. Never!

Joe was nowhere to be found during this emotional mother-son reunion. That same night, he had been in a barroom brawl, hit his head, and was hospitalized with a concussion. Upon learning that Kevin had been returned, Joe was overcome with guilt. In an emotional scene, he begged for Viki's forgiveness and another chance for their marriage. Though the wounds were still deep, Viki accepted Joe's request and they reunited.

All the while, Dorian lurked in the background, undaunted by the Riley reconciliation. Not for a moment had she given up her dream of eventually luring Joe from Viki. One afternoon, Dorian stumbled upon Joe passed out at his desk. He wasn't drunk this time. Dorian discovered that for weeks Joe had been having headaches and periods of blurred vision. Behind Viki's back, Dorian took Joe to New York for tests, which revealed some inconclusive brain irregularities . . . possibly a tumor! Dorian convinced Joe that, until his problem could be properly diagnosed, it would be best to keep the information secret. Dorian insidiously worked her wiles on Joe, convincing him that it would be too much of a strain on Viki if he were to reveal the terrible news that something was wrong with him.

Weeks passed as Dorian tried unsuccessfully to use Joe's secret as the fuel to destroy his marriage to Viki. Finally, Joe decided he could not keep quiet any longer. In a panic, Dorian knew that once Joe told Viki her own chances of winning him would be lost. But what could she do now? Dorian's opportunity came when Joe had another seizure at Llanfair and passed out. While he was unconscious, Dorian made a wreck of the room and tore her own dress. Then, when Joe came to, she managed to convince him that he was the one who had done all the damage in the room. Joe was terrified! Was he now capable of violence? Could he in some way harm Viki or, heaven forbid, Kevin? Fearing for the safety of his loved ones, Joe persuaded Viki to take Kevin away to their cabin in the mountains.

While Viki was away, Dorian pushed ahead with her evil efforts to get the vulnerable Joe into bed. She might have succeeded had it not been for the clever thinking of Dr. Peter Janssen, who stumbled upon Joe during a seizure and finally managed to get the whole story out of him. Dorian was frustrated when Peter persuaded Joe to face Viki and tell her everything. Viki listened in horror as Joe explained that he might be fatally ill. Trying to get over the initial shock, Viki grew closer to her beloved Joe than she had ever been. Together, they went to New York, where a second CAT scan revealed the grim news—Joe had a brain tumor.

In a touch-and-go operation at Llanview Hospital, the tumor was carefully removed. To Viki's relief, it turned out to be benign. As Joe recovered, he made sure that the tumor wasn't the only thing cut from his life. He had finally succeeded in cutting Dorian Lord out of his life, too!

*A*s Cathy recovered from her mental illness, the kidnapping charges against her were dropped. To aid in her recovery, Tony promised Pat that he would do the right thing; return to Cathy and resume their marriage, at least until she was strong enough to face life on her own. By now, Pat had told Tony the incredible news that Brian was their son. Brian's illness had been the deciding factor in making Pat realize that Tony had a right to know the truth. However, both decided that it would be too traumatic to tell the boy the truth now, or even in the foreseeable future. During his recovery, Brian stubbornly had been refusing to give up his memory of his "father," Paul Kendall. The big revelation would have to wait.

Tony reluctantly went home to Cathy, but unnerved his wife by refusing to sleep with her. He yearned to be with Pat, who felt the pain of separation with every breath she took. Fortunately, Cathy, through counseling sessions with Dr. Will Vernon and deep discussions with her dear friend, Larry Wolek, arrived at the conclusion that her situation with Tony was hopeless. Healthy at last, she gave him his freedom. The stage was set for Tony and Pat to finally be together.

Realizing they would have to take their relationship one step at a time, Tony and Pat gently told Brian about their wedding plans, and that their marriage would in no way erase or harm his memory of Paul Kendall. Brian lashed out, announcing that he hated Tony!

On the eve of their wedding, Tony was critically injured in an automobile accident. Pat was barely over the shock of Tony's accident when she discovered that her husband, Paul Kendall, was not dead after all! Paul's return proved to be the beginning of a stormy emotional dilemma for Pat. Upon Tony's recovery, she broke the news to him that she had decided, for Brian's sake, that Paul would be moving back home.

Within weeks, Tony and Pat began an affair behind Paul Kendall's back. One night, young Brian stumbled across his mother and Tony in an embrace. The incident proved traumatic for the boy, who kept

(cont.)

LANA
Brad, I love you.

BRAD
Yes, I love you, too, but, uh, it's not the same thing.

LANA
Please don't leave me.

BRAD
You deserve someone better than me, and that's all there is to it.

PAT AND TONY

When her believed-dead husband Paul suddenly reappeared, Pat Kendall wrestled with a difficult dilemma. For the sake of her son Brian, should she make a go of her loveless marriage—or should she follow her feelings and stick with her true love, Tony? Pat elected to reunite with Paul, while enjoying dangerous liaisons with Tony. Paul remained oblivious to their affair, but not young Brian. When the boy spied Pat and Tony in a tender embrace, he bitterly rejected them both.

what he saw a secret from everyone. With enormous hostility, Brian turned against his mother, telling her he hated her more than Tony! Only Brian's therapist, Dr. Will Vernon, was able to ascertain the truth, but Brian swore Will to secrecy.

Early in 1977, no one was happier than Karen Wolek, who spent her every waking moment planning every last detail of the wedding to end all weddings. She wanted the biggest, most lavish affair that Llanview had ever seen. Her plans went smoothly until a week before the wedding, when a shady newcomer from her past showed up in Llanview. His name was Marco Dane. Karen was mortified to see Marco, who had been her lover when both were living in a commune out west. Marco! This low-life loser could destroy everything she'd gained! As she feared, Marco threatened to blow the whistle on Karen.

Marco Dane was one of the few people who knew that Karen Wolek had once been involved in an embezzlement scheme and spent six months on probation. If Larry found out about her past, he would never agree to marry a lying criminal like Karen. Karen confronted Marco, demanding that he leave town immediately. However, this sprite-from-the-wild-side wasn't going anywhere! He sadistically baited Karen, mysteriously refusing to divulge his plans. A chill ran down Karen's spine when Marco whispered that he planned to attend the wedding ceremony, and make his move when the priest got to the part where he says, "If anyone can show just cause why these two people should not be joined together in holy matrimony. . . ." Terrified, Karen went ahead with the wedding, and as planned, Marco showed up—but rather than stop the wedding, he remained strangely quiet!

When the newlyweds returned from their honeymoon, Karen immediately returned to her old ways: sleeping late, not caring for Larry's son Danny properly, and spending much too much money. She cultivated a friendship with Dorian Lord, who became instrumental in helping Karen make elaborate plans for the new house Larry bought for her—plans which Larry and Karen obviously could not afford. Also during this time, Marco Dane got a job with Dorian as a handyman and errand-runner.

Karen quickly became bored with married life, and despite Larry's urging, she refused to change her profligate ways. At the same time, Larry began spending more and more time with hospital volunteer Cathy Craig. Their relationship deepened, though neither Larry nor Cathy were consciously aware yet of their mutual attraction. One day, a plumber, Gus, came to fix the pipes in the new Wolek house. When he flirted with Karen, she flirted right back—and enjoyed it. So much she slept with him.

Later, when she was in a local boutique, Karen tried on an expensive dress, one that she obviously could not afford on the budget Larry had given her. An older, obviously wealthy man stood in the background and admired her. He was Talbot Huddleston, a pillar of the community. Huddleston presented Karen with a tantalizing offer: he would buy her the dress if Karen agreed to have lunch with him. Karen accepted, but their rendezvous included more than just lunch. After a meal and a few glasses of wine, Karen returned to Huddleston's hotel room, where they made love. Before long, Karen was indulging her champagne tastes by having sex with a variety of men, in exchange for extravagant gifts of jewelry and clothing.

Karen wasn't the only Llanview resident keeping secrets. A sweet and seemingly innocent newcomer, Becky Lee Hunt, had come to Llanview to seek fame as a country and western singer. Becky Lee fell in love with Viki's young cousin, Richard Abbott, who was working as a reporter for *The Banner*. Richard suspected that there was some element of mystery in Becky's recent past, and he was determined to find out what she was hiding.

Dr. Will Vernon was also keeping a secret from everyone. Working side by side with Jenny, Will found himself falling in love. Naomi began to suspect that her husband harbored strong feelings for this young woman, who was dating their son Brad. Naomi saw Jenny as a threat to her marriage, and did everything in her power to push Jenny and Brad together. One night, while working late at the hospital, an anguished Will confessed to Jenny that he was in love with her. His powerful confession left Jenny consumed with guilt. She simply could not be responsible for the dissolution of the Vernon marriage. Her voice quivering, Jenny told Will that she could no longer work for him. She asked to be reassigned.

Every time Naomi Vernon saw Jenny and Will together, she was thrown into a panic. Naomi could see, just from the way that Jenny looked at Will, that she was in love with him, even if Jenny didn't know it herself. As the weeks passed, Jenny became more and more troubled by the fact that Will and Brad were both in love with her. Frightened to death that her continued presence might destroy the Vernon family, Jenny decided to go away to a retreat to seek spiritual guidance. While she was away, Naomi embarked upon a desperate plan designed to get Will to come back to her. She attempted suicide by swallowing an overdose of barbiturates but never intended to die. Naomi had every intention of having Brad find her in time. But Brad, never dreaming what his mother was up to, was busy two-timing Jenny again with Lana McClain. While Brad seduced Lana, his mother overdosed and died.

Naomi's death destroyed the Vernon family. Overcome with guilt,

*D*uring the summer of 1978, Viki suddenly found herself faced with the formidable task of raising a teenager! Upon the death of her mother, Irene, Viki's goddaughter, Tina Clayton, came to Llanview and quickly became an innocent pawn in Marco Dane's evil blackmail scheme.

Jenny decided that she would no longer see Brad *or* Will. In the aftermath of his mother's death and Jenny's rejection, a tortured Brad began to fall apart. He turned to Lana McClain for comfort, and led the naive girl to believe that he loved her. Even after Brad managed to reconcile with Jenny, he continued to see Lana on the side. Meanwhile, Jenny could see that Will was still in love with her. She decided that the only way to free herself of the overwhelming guilt was to marry Brad! Her decision to marry him astonished Brad, who was about to receive an even bigger shock: Lana was pregnant with his child! The news panicked Brad, who tried everything in his power to convince Lana to have an abortion.

With Jenny and Brad's wedding rapidly approaching, Lana sank into a state of deep depression, numbing her pain with liquor and pills. Terrified that she would spoil his wedding, Brad went to see Lana. He froze upon learning from a blindly drunk Lana that she intended to deliver a letter to Jenny the next day—the day of the wedding! She had, prior to Brad's arrival, made herself some hot milk, into which she had dissolved two sleeping pills. In a panic, Brad began searching Lana's apartment for the letter. When Lana became agitated, he gave her the milk, unaware it contained a deadly dose of drugs. Brad found the letter and destroyed it. In a move intended to pacify Lana, he gave her his mother's ring, telling her it could be redeemed for a lot of money. As Lana fell asleep, Brad retrieved an airline ticket and cash he had given her in the hope that she would leave town. Just as he was about to leave, Brad became aware that Lana wasn't moving. When he tried to rouse her, he discovered to his horror that she was dead!

In total panic now, Brad wiped the place clean of fingerprints and rushed out, spending the rest of the evening setting up an alibi for himself. He managed to convince his teenage sister, Samantha, to lie for him: and at the inquest she testified that Brad spent the night with her. Also during the inquest, Marco Dane (who had visited Lana earlier in the evening) tried to implicate Brad. Still, Jenny maintained complete faith in her fiancé, and to prove it, she asked Brad to marry her immediately. Then Jenny took the stand, and sent everyone in the courtroom—especially Will—into shock by announcing that she and Brad were man and wife. The police, led by Lt. Ed Hall, suspected that there was foul play in Lana's death, but were unable to prove it. Brad was exonerated of any wrongdoing.

*S*till stinging from the death of her son Brian, the breakup of her romance with Tony, and the dissolution of her marriage to Paul, Pat changed her name from Kendall to Ashley and opted to start her life over again. She was instantly flattered when rich financier Adam Brewster came a-courting!

1978

uring the winter of 1978, Pat Kendall decided the time was right to tell her son Brian that Tony Lord was his natural father. With her husband Paul's approval, Pat sat Brian down in the Kendall living room, and with great sensitivity, broke the news. Still, Brian took the news badly. He lashed out at his mother. How could Tony be his father? He hated Tony! Blinded by tears, he raced out the door and into the street. At that very moment, Karen Wolek was a passenger in a car driven by her favorite "patron," Talbot Huddleston. In the midst of an argument with Karen, Talbot did not see the boy crossing his path. The car struck and killed Brian instantly. To avoid scandal, Huddleston sped away from the accident scene.

The relationship between Tony and Pat deteriorated quickly in the weeks after their son's death. They attempted to communicate, but the old wounds between them had reopened. Paul proved to be a source of strength to Pat during the difficult early weeks of 1978. He gently helped her come out of her shell. She, too, provided support to Paul when two former radical underground enemies, Bonnie Harmer and Herman Cantrell, escaped from federal prison and showed up in Llanview intent on executing the man whose testimony had put them behind bars. In a showdown, Paul was shot, and Jim Craig, Joe Riley, and Jenny Vernon were held hostage in the hospital before the criminals were apprehended and sent back to jail.

Brad went through hell knowing that Jenny could have died in the hostage siege. The crisis made him realize, for the first time, how much he truly loved Jenny. In a moving moment with his father Will,

WHO KILLED MARCO DANE? 1978

Blackmail was Marco Dane's middle name during the fall of 1978. For months, Marco had been threatening to release doctored, naked photographs of Viki's teenage ward, Tina Clayton. To protect Tina's reputation, Viki was prepared to give in to his demands and pay the $50,000 he demanded. At the last minute, she changed her mind and headed to Marco's modeling agency to tell him she wouldn't pay. To her shock, Viki found Marco—dead!

Brad vowed that if Jenny survived the ordeal, he would make a clean breast of it and confess all his transgressions, beginning with the biggest secret of all: the fact that he was present in Lana's apartment on the night she died. When Jenny was safely returned, Brad stayed true to his word and made a full confession of his sins to a stunned Jenny.

Jenny realized that her whole marriage to Brad was based on a lie! Despite Brad's promises to live the straight life from now on, Jenny decided their marriage was over. In desperation, Brad made one final grandstand play designed to elicit Jenny's sympathy and force her to change her mind. After checking with a lawyer and learning that if he went to the authorities and came clean he could get off with a very light sentence, Brad turned himself in and was given a three-month jail sentence. On his last day of freedom, Brad made one final plea for Jenny to hold off on the annulment until after he served his time. Jenny went on a retreat to ponder Brad's seemingly sincere request.

After serving his three-month prison sentence, Brad Vernon came home to learn that Jenny was sticking to her decision to obtain a papal annulment from the church. Brad, now more embittered than ever, was determined to get even with her in any way he could. Soon after his release, he got a job as an all-around flunky for a newcomer, the mysterious millionaire Adam Brewster.

Brad's younger sister, Samantha, developed a teenage crush on an older man—Tony Lord. Realizing that Sam was becoming emotionally attached to him, Tony gently but straight out told her that he didn't love her as she loved him. Deeply hurt by Tony's rejection, Samantha ran from Tony's place in tears. Dr. Pamela Shepherd, Will Vernon's new fianceé, followed Samantha into her car and tried to calm her down. Sam drove off with Pam in the car—and had a terrible accident. Pam died in the crash, and Sam suffered severe facial burns that left her with the possibility of disfigurement. Guilt-ridden, Tony presented Sam with an engagement ring and prepared to marry her, regardless of how her facial surgery turned out.

Jenny's heart went out to Brad in the days after Samantha's tragic accident. Ever compassionate and giving, Jenny offered Brad the comfort he so desperately needed. Once again, Jenny returned to this man who had brought her so much pain.

After divorcing Paul Kendall, Pat resolved to start her life over. Reverting to her maiden name, Ashley, she poured her energies into her new TV talk show on Llanview's local station, WVLE-TV. She was flattered by the attention paid to her by millionaire Adam Brewster, who hid from Pat the fact that he suffered dangerous epileptic seizures. Only Adam's faithful assistant, Gretel Cummings, was aware of the serious nature of his illness.

*S*nobby and ambitious Edwina Lewis, a new writer working for Dorian's *Lord Press*, came to Llanview and set her sights on Becky Lee Hunt's man, the wealthy Richard Abbott. Despite Edwina's seductive efforts, Richard asked Becky to marry him. Faced with losing Richard, Edwina took off for North Carolina to do a little digging into Becky's past. There she learned that Becky's real name was Jackson, not Hunt. What could she be hiding?

Back home in Llanview, Richard received a tantalizing offer from *The Banner*'s editor, Joe Riley, to head up the newspaper's European Bureau. Just as Richard and Becky were about to leave for Europe, a redneck named Luke Jackson showed up in Llanview. Luke was Becky Lee's husband! Edwina viewed Luke's presence as a godsend. He was the one way that she could keep Richard from leaving Llanview.

One night, Luke brutally beat Richard, leaving him with a fractured skull. Luke was apprehended and sent to jail—but before long he escaped and plotted to get his final revenge on Becky Lee for leaving him. In the resulting shootout, Ed Hall was hit and rushed to Llanview Hospital, where he was operated on by Dr. Jack Scott. Dr. Scott performed a delicate operation to remove a bullet lodged near Ed's heart. Carla was grateful to the gruff, no-nonsense Dr. Scott, who began to show more than a passing interest in Ed's wife.

Within weeks, Ed was out of the hospital and on the road to recovery. Carla began spending more and more time at the hospital with Jack, her new boss. Sitting at her desk during the day, she tried to shake off the fantasies she was having about her handsome employer. Their simmering relationship reached an important turning point when Jack asked Carla to accompany him to a medical convention in the Virgin Islands. Ed (who was obviously jealous) opposed the idea. Carla, believing that it was important that she go for professional reasons, left with Jack. However, when they reached the Caribbean, the physical attraction that had long been brewing between them finally came into the open. When Jack kissed Carla, she responded! In the aftermath, Carla was devastated and guilt-ridden. Rushing back to Llanview and Ed, Carla had an immediate meeting with Chief of Staff Jim Craig and requested that she be allowed to quit her job with Jack and go to work for Larry. However, a simple change of jobs did not mean she could stop thinking of and fantasizing about Jack Scott. Ed, back at work, began to sense that his wife was pulling away from him.

*I*n the aftermath of the near-tragedy with Luke Jackson, Becky and Richard married in a loving ceremony held at Joe and Viki's carriage

(cont.)

At first, the Llanview Police suspected that Tina's boyfriend, Greg Huddleston, was the culprit, but before long, Viki was charged with the crime. Viki was ultimately found innocent when hooker Katrina Karr emerged from a coma and fingered Greg's father, Llanview businessman/ pervert Talbot Huddleston. In a remarkable twist of fate, it was later revealed that Marco had not died after all on the night of December 15, 1978. His twin brother Mario, in the wrong place at the wrong time, actually took the fatal bullet.

KAREN AND MARCO

Karen Wolek rued the day that her old lover Marco Dane showed up in Llanview and proceeded to make her life miserable. Mischievous Marco's timing could not have been more dangerous—he arrived just days before Karen was to marry Dr. Larry Wolek. Though he didn't break up the wedding, Marco soon demanded a piece of Karen's prostitution profits. Always platonic, their connection continued for five more years, perhaps because both Karen and Marco thrived by living on the edge. Together, this dangerous duo shared dreams of glory that usually led to trouble, not triumph.

house. Following the wedding, they left Llanview for a fresh start in Europe.

Dorian Lord proved that she was as mean-spirited as ever when her sister Melinda returned after having spent several years in a mental institution. When Dorian noticed that Melinda and Dr. Peter Janssen were gravitating toward each other, she immediately took steps to undermine their relationship. Dorian wanted Peter all for herself!

In the past, Melinda would have succumbed to Dorian's evil schemes. But Melinda was healthy now—and feisty, too! She stood up to her hated older sister, and gave Dorian the comeuppance she had so long deserved. A defeated Dorian could do nothing as Melinda and Peter eloped.

Sadly, soon after the marriage, signs of Melinda's disturbed behavior returned. Believing that she must prove herself to Peter so that he would have the same respect for her that he had for Jenny, Melinda decided to resume her career as a concert pianist. Practicing day and night, she nearly drove Peter insane with her compulsive playing. Her hopes were dashed when, in her big audition, she failed to impress the world-famous Bruno Weston. Melinda lied to Peter, and Marco Dane discovered the charade—and threatened to expose her.

The blackmailing of Melinda was just one of many nefarious Marco Dane schemes perpetrated on the citizens of Llanview in 1978. Having discovered Karen's afternoon romps with married men (who, in return, showered her with lavish gifts), Marco wanted a piece of the action. He forced Karen into becoming one of his "freelance hookers." Although she at first refused his demands, Karen was forced to accept when Marco threatened to spill the beans to her husband, Larry.

Karen no longer enjoyed her "love in the afternoon." She reluctantly slept with various men, paid Marco his cut, and prayed that her upstanding husband would never discover her dreadful secret.

During this time, Viki's lifestyle changed dramatically when her childhood friend Irene Clayton returned to town to tell Viki that she was dying. Irene asked Viki to take care of her sixteen-year-old daughter, Tina. When Irene died, Tina arrived—and suddenly Viki was facing the daunting challenge of raising a teenager! One day, Viki was surprised to see Marco Dane and Karen Wolek together in the lobby of the seedy Wallington Hotel. She confronted Karen, who broke down and admitted the truth: she was a hooker. Believing that Karen was sincere in wanting to quit "the life" and be a good mother to Danny and wife to Larry, Viki confronted Marco and threatened to ruin him if he didn't leave Karen alone. Marco bowed to Viki's threats, but vowed to somehow get even with her someday. Before long, he had found the instrument to even the score—Tina!

Over the summer of 1978, Marco opened a local modeling agency and slowly and carefully won the confidence of sweet and innocent Tina Clayton, who was working at a local pizza parlor and seeing a nice boy named Greg Huddleston. (Greg's father was Talbot Huddleston—Karen's lecherous first john.) Marco hatched his scheme. He plotted to take modeling photographs of Tina and superimpose those shots over the nude body of another model. To get even with Viki, Marco would show the world that Tina was a pornographic model!

Greg Huddleston, sensing Tina's attraction to the slimy Marco, ordered him to stay away from his girlfriend or Greg would kill him! Greg's father, Talbot, also ordered Dane to back off from Tina or pay the price. As Marco carried out his insidious scheme, he never dreamed he would come to like Tina himself! Feeling sorry for the sweet girl, Marco abandoned his dummied photograph scheme and instead began to gaslight Viki into thinking that her split personality, Niki Smith, had returned.

One day, Viki again confronted Marco about his role in Tina's life. Wanting to get Viki off his back, Marco countered by showing the nude photographs of "Tina" to her. Marco threatened to circulate the scandalous photos unless Viki paid him off. After anguishing for days, Viki went to Marco's health club with $50,000—though she was determined not to hand it over to him. To her shock, Viki found Marco's dead body! Thinking fast, she took Tina's photos from the file cabinet and hurried out.

For a time Greg Huddleston was held in custody as the prime suspect in Marco's murder. But when the police learned that the murder weapon was pawned by one Niki Smith, Greg was released and Joe, aware now that the circle was closing around Viki, went to Pine Valley (home of ABC's *All My Children*) to retain the services of attorney Paul Martin. By the end of 1978, both Joe Riley and Paul Martin feared that an indictment against Viki was only a matter of time.

Karen was finally free of Marco! At home, her life with Larry (now Chief of Staff at Llanview Hospital) was never better. Furthermore, Karen knew that her friend, hooker Katrina Karr, had seen Marco the day he died. Could she have killed Marco Dane? Karen's greatest fear was that Viki would be blamed for something that Katrina actually had done.

*M*ELINDA AND PETER

When Melinda Cramer fell in love with Dr. Peter Janssen, she found out just how dangerously detestable her sister Dorian could be. Dorian pulled out all the stops to keep Melinda and Peter apart, even lying to her sister that she and Peter were lovers. Worse, Dorian threatened to have the recently cured Melinda returned to a mental institution. Despite the dangers posed by Dorian, Melinda and Peter ran away and got married.

$\mathcal{I}$n October, Viki Riley kept vigil at her beloved Joe's bedside as he peacefully passed away.

1979

Nineteen seventy-nine began on a horrifying note for Viki Riley when a grand jury handed down an indictment against her for the murder of Marco Dane. Attorney Paul Martin entered a plea of "not guilty" on her behalf, and Llanview's most sensational murder trial began in early February.

Anxious to help Viki in any way she could, Karen Wolek searched day and night for her hooker friend, Katrina Karr, whom she believed knew who killed Marco. Unfortunately, Karen made the mistake of telling this to Talbot Huddleston. Talbot feigned great concern that Viki Riley might be suffering an injustice. However, his real concern was that Katrina Karr might have seen him commit the crime. Talbot Huddleston killed Marco Dane!

Viki's trial began in February, and from the outset the prospect of acquittal looked bleak, primarily because of her desire to protect Tina. The prosecution, led by Llanview's brilliant DA, Herb Callison, built a strong case against Viki. After a month of damaging testimony, Callison dropped the biggest bombshell of all into the proceedings by calling a surprise witness—Marco Dane's twin brother, Dr. Mario Corelli. Dr. Corelli, who practiced medicine in Colorado, introduced damaging letters Marco had written to him about how Viki had threatened him.

The trial of Viki Riley reached a thrilling climax when Karen Wolek took the stand for the defense. Karen had finally found her old friend from "the life," Katrina Karr. In exchange for money she needed for drugs, Katrina gave Karen the combination to a post office box, which Katrina claimed contained information revealing the identity of Marco Dane's killer. When Karen went to the post office to get the information, she discovered to her horror that Talbot Huddleston had beaten her to it. To further complicate matters, Karen learned that the previous night Katrina had been run down by a car and was now lying comatose in Llanview Hospital. Karen correctly guessed that Talbot was the killer—and prepared to break the news in court.

But when Karen took the stand, she was savagely cross-examined by DA Callison, who forced her to reveal the whole sordid truth of her life as a hooker! Larry listened in stunned silence as his wife revealed that she had been turning tricks when he thought she was at home.

Later that day, word came from the hospital that Katrina had come out of her coma and named Talbot as the killer. This revelation was enough to exonerate Viki—but for Karen the damage had been done. The whole world now knew of her secret life as a hooker, and her marriage to Larry appeared to be doomed.

In the weeks after Karen's painful confession, Dr. Larry Wolek discovered that there were those—Dorian and her allies—who would visit his wife's sins upon him. Dorian led a vicious campaign to have Larry ousted as Chief of Staff of Llanview Hospital. At long last, Dorian felt she had a way to even her score with Larry and his dear friend, Viki. As Larry's replacement, Dorian ordained her old friend and mentor Dr. Ivan Kipling, a move that the ambitious and cutthroat Dr. Kipling strongly favored.

Karen also encountered severe difficulties finding a job. In despair, she nearly returned to the street again. Ironically, it was Dr. Mario Corelli who dissuaded her from going back to "the life." Karen's fortunes took a turn for the better when, after several weeks of separation, Larry decided to make a last attempt to salvage their marriage. However, word that a Larry/Karen reconciliation was in the works quickly spread to Dorian, who used it to revive her endless vendetta against Larry. At Dorian's urging, the hospital board voted to ask Larry for his resignation. Larry decided to fight the board's decision, but Dorian's actions succeeded in making Karen come to the conclusion that she would always be Larry's albatross.

$\mathcal{J}$oe Riley could not believe his ears when Viki broke the news that she was pregnant with their second child. Sadly, Joe passed away before his wife gave birth to their son, Joey.

What do you want from me? You want blood? You want me to say that I'm lower than the lowest piece of scum? You want more filth? You want more slime? You want more names? I'll give you another name, Talbot Huddleston!

He was my first john, he was the first of a string of so many men I don't even remember their names. Now . . . now, are you satisfied?

With great sadness, Karen decided to divorce Larry, who found comfort with Faith Kipling, the warmhearted wife of the cold-blooded Llanview Hospital doctor, Ivan Kipling. Faith was every bit as sweet as Ivan was sour—and she and Larry (and his son Danny) struck up a special bond.

$\mathcal{D}$r. Mario Corelli settled in Llanview, where he devoted hours to his new job at the Llanview Hospital Free Clinic. In time, Karen discovered an amazing truth: Mario was really Marco. Marco Dane! He wasn't dead after all!!!

Karen forced Marco to tell what really happened on December 15, 1978, the night he was supposedly murdered. It seemed that Marco had returned to his health club and was horrified to discover the dead body of his brother Mario. He then made the instant decision to exchange identities with the corpse!

Marco implored Karen to keep his secret, telling her that he'd been "born again." After considerable soul-searching, Karen decided to protect Marco on one condition—that he immediately stop practicing medicine. Marco had no choice but to agree to her terms.

The one bright spot in Karen's life was her sister, Jenny. She was delighted to be pregnant with Brad's baby. Unbeknownst to Jenny,

JOE TELLS VIKI HE IS
DYING
1979

VIKI
Well then, it's very serious
then, isn't it?
Is it another aneurysm, do
you have to be operated
on again?

JOE
No, it's not an aneurysm,
and there will be no operation. I have a brain
tumor.

VIKI
Oh God.

JOE
It's inoperable. There isn't
anything that anybody
can do. I only have a few
months, at the most.

though, Brad was back on the road to ruin. This time, he had developed a compulsion for gambling. With his losses mounting, Brad resorted to desperate measures by stealing Jenny's key to the hospital's pharmacy and giving it to a mobster named Brick. In exchange, Brick agreed to wipe out Brad's debts. When Brick and an accomplice tried to rob the pharmacy, they were caught by Dr. Jack Scott, who was shot and paralyzed in the violent exchange.

The shooting of Jack Scott represented another major step in the volatile marriage of Ed and Carla Hall. Prior to the shooting, Ed had decided he'd had it with Carla's vacillation over Jack. Asking Carla for a divorce, Ed moved into Ina Hopkins's boarding house. When Jack was hospitalized, Carla was finally able to articulate her love for him. Upon his recovery, Carla was more than a little shocked when Jack told her that he had no intentions of marrying her. It seemed that he was more interested in an affair than in marriage. However, Jack finally decided that he was too much in love to lose Carla.

In the fall of 1979, Carla married Jack in what marked a low point in Ed Hall's life. Fortunately, Ed was able to rely on the friendship of soulmates Katrina Karr and Karen Wolek during this difficult time. The marriage of Carla and Jack did not last long. Realizing that he was a scoundrel, Carla divorced Dr. Scott and eventually left Llanview to study law.

Karen Wolek grew deeply concerned about her sister's pregnancy. Complications forced Jenny to check into the hospital for several weeks. Feeling guilty that Brad was home alone without her, Jenny asked Karen to look after him. Karen knew that Brad had no love for her, but whatever Jenny wanted, Karen would do.

Brad and Karen clashed at first, but eventually Brad became fascinated by his sexy sister-in-law. The fascination grew into obsession. One night, Brad tried to seduce Karen. When he got physical, Karen put up a struggle, and Brad became enraged. What began as seduction suddenly turned to rape.

In the aftermath of the rape, Karen was left in a state of trauma and outrage. Brad ordered her to keep her mouth shut, and the device he used to keep Karen quiet was Jenny's well-being. Karen knew she couldn't reveal a word about the rape because if Jenny were to find out, it would all but destroy her. Mired in guilt and depression, Karen agreed to Brad's demands.

But Larry began his own detective work trying to discover the cause of his wife's distress, which led him to the realization that Brad raped Karen. In a rage, Larry beat Brad to a pulp! The news spread quickly, and it was only a matter of time before Jenny put all the pieces together and finally arrived at the whole horrible truth herself.

Jenny threw Brad out of their apartment, telling him that she never wanted to see him again. In court, a dejected Brad Vernon agreed to a plea bargain; for the lesser charge of assault, he was sentenced to three months in prison.

The gruesome revelation that Brad raped Karen proved to be traumatic for Jenny, leading to the premature birth of her tiny baby by Cesarean section. When Karen and Marco visited the nursery where Jenny's baby lay next to Katrina Karr's newborn, something terrible happened. Jenny's baby suddenly went into cardiac arrest and died before their eyes! In a panic, Karen came up with an incredible plan: They would switch babies! Marco argued that it would be wrong and insane to do such a thing. However, when a grim Karen told him that switching the babies was the price she asked for silence about his own switched identity, Marco relented and did the deed.

Katrina fell into a deep depression when she was told that her baby died. Jenny took baby Mary home, never suspecting that the precious little girl belonged to another woman. As for Karen and Marco, they felt severe pangs of guilt about their deed, but neither was aware that Katrina's sense of loss would one day haunt them all.

*D*orian's sister Melinda sank deeper into psychosis in 1979. When her paranoia reached new heights, she checked herself into the Compton Clinic. Before leaving Llanview, Melinda begged Peter to wait until she was mentally healthy again and could return to him. Peter agreed, though he was clearly falling in love with Jenny Vernon.

*J*enny's sister-in-law, Samantha Vernon, was overwhelmed when Tony Lord proposed marriage to her. However, she came to realize that Tony had only agreed to marry her out of guilt over her near-fatal car accident, and at the last moment, she called off the ceremony.

*P*at Ashley finally discovered what her lover, Adam Brewster, tried to hide—the fact that he suffered from a severe case of epilepsy. With the secret out in the open, Pat married Adam, unaware that he was concealing another heinous secret from her. Adam, who was broke, masterminded (with Dorian's financial backing) a shady arms deal with the notorious Torrentino regime in war-torn San Carlos. When Pat discovered that

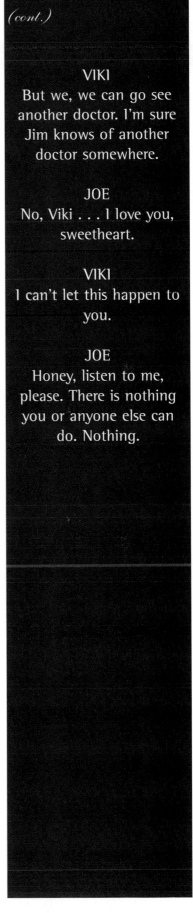

(cont.)

VIKI
But we, we can go see another doctor. I'm sure Jim knows of another doctor somewhere.

JOE
No, Viki . . . I love you, sweetheart.

VIKI
I can't let this happen to you.

JOE
Honey, listen to me, please. There is nothing you or anyone else can do. Nothing.

*D*YING JOE INTRODUCES
VIKI TO HER FUTURE
HUSBAND, CLINT
1979

JOE
Sorry, sweetheart, we got
to drinking and talking,
and time just got away.

VIKI
Yes, I'm very aware of the
fact that you've been
drinking

(To Clint)
and if I have you to thank
for that, sir, or if you are
under the impression that
you can continue the
party here, I'm terribly
sorry, you cannot.

Adam had put all moral considerations aside in order to get his financial empire back in order, she quickly had their new marriage annulled.

For comfort, Pat turned to her TV producer, Dick Grant. In Pat's presence, Dick was a cheerful, charming, very outgoing gentleman. However, he had developed a psychotic crush on her. When Samantha Vernon discovered that Dick had transformed his tiny apartment into a photo-covered shrine to Pat, he kidnapped her, then Pat, before the police apprehended him.

In the aftermath of the near-tragedy, Samantha turned to Jim Craig's nephew, Mick Gordon, a world-champion speed skater, who had his heart set on winning a gold medal in the 1980 Olympics. However, Mick's hopes were dashed when he broke his legs in a tragic small-plane crash. Mick's overbearing mother, Fran, blamed Samantha for shattering her son's Olympic dreams, and she was willing to go to any lengths to keep Mick and Sam's love from being consummated.

In the fall of 1979, Pat's look-alike sister, Maggie Ashley, arrived from England. Though she appeared to be polite and shy, it became apparent that Maggie harbored a deep resentment for her pretty blond sister.

*V*iki Riley received some joyous news when she discovered she was pregnant with her second child. The only source of consternation in Viki's life was provided by her ward, Tina. Having been spurned by Mario

Corelli, Tina had taken up with a rather undesirable young crowd, which included an unsavory motorcyclist named Jud.

In the fall, Viki's husband, Joe, began suffering severe headaches and dizzy spells—all the classic signs of a recurrence of the brain tumor that had nearly killed him several years earlier. When Joe learned from his doctors, Jim Craig and Ivan Kipling, that he had only a few weeks left, he faced his fate with the same stoic courage he had shown previously. Over Jim's objections, Joe elected not to break the news to Viki until he had gotten all his affairs in order.

Knowing he had precious little time left, Joe treated Viki to a wonderful wedding anniversary. Together, they celebrated their son Kevin's third birthday. Though Joe tried his best to hide his illness, Viki began to be aware of his headaches and became increasingly concerned about him.

With time running out, Joe handpicked his successor as editor of *The Banner*. He sent for the editor of a small but prestigious newspaper in Arizona: Clint Buchanan.

Joe ultimately had no choice but to break the news of his impending death to Viki, who went into deep shock. As his days dwindled down to a precious few, Joe did everything within his power to shower love upon his one and only true love, Viki. Joe beseeched Viki to move on with her life after he was gone. He urged her to find someone else, someone to love who would love her in return.

On the afternoon of Wednesday, October 3, 1979, Joseph Francis Riley died of a massive brain tumor. Viki courageously accepted Joe's death, as he would have wanted. She poured her energies into working with Clint at *The Banner*, and fending off a takeover attempt by her arch-rival, Dorian Lord.

Clint braced himself for the arrival of his Texas family. An entourage of friends and relatives arrived including his father Asa's girlfriend Mimi King, his right-hand man Chuck Wilson, nephew Rafe Garretson, and country singer Johnny Drummond. The one face Clint was happy to see was his high-strung younger brother, Bo, who had been browbeaten by his domineering father. But not Asa! Clint had been estranged from his "pa" for years, and was clearly agitated at the prospect of Asa Buchanan's imminent arrival. Quickly, Clint understood that Bo had been sent on a mission by Asa: to get Clint to return to the family fold.

Clint dated both Pat and Maggie Ashley—but only found himself interested in Pat. Maggie made a play for Clint, who rebuffed her. However, Pat, unwilling to hurt her sister any more than Clint already had, refused to have anything to do with him. As the year came to an end, Maggie hatched a plan to steal Pat's identity. By impersonating Pat, Maggie could have Clint all to herself!

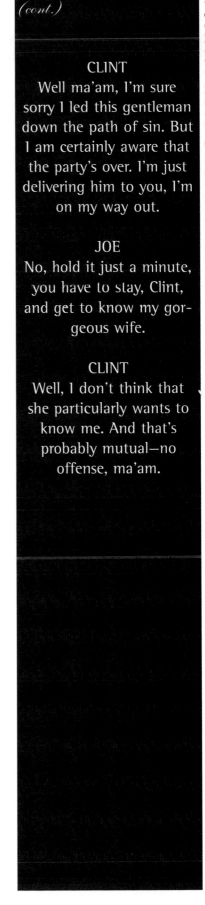

(cont.)

CLINT
Well ma'am, I'm sure sorry I led this gentleman down the path of sin. But I am certainly aware that the party's over. I'm just delivering him to you, I'm on my way out.

JOE
No, hold it just a minute, you have to stay, Clint, and get to know my gorgeous wife.

CLINT
Well, I don't think that she particularly wants to know me. And that's probably mutual—no offense, ma'am.

*H*omesick for his native Texas, millionaire Asa Buchanan bought a massive estate, Southampton, and turned it into a little bit of the Lone Star State. Here, Asa corralled his sons, Bo and Clint, and right-hand man Chuck Wilson, at his birthday bash for soon-to-be ex-girlfriend Mimi King, and future wife Samantha Vernon.

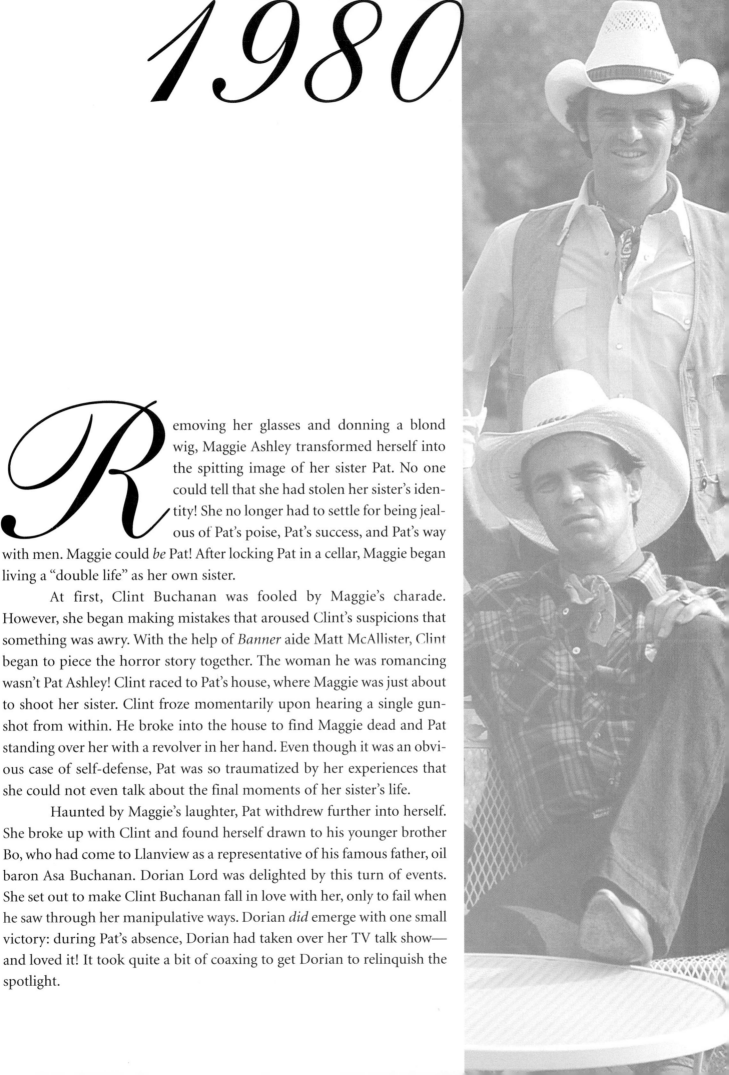

1980

Removing her glasses and donning a blond wig, Maggie Ashley transformed herself into the spitting image of her sister Pat. No one could tell that she had stolen her sister's identity! She no longer had to settle for being jealous of Pat's poise, Pat's success, and Pat's way with men. Maggie could *be* Pat! After locking Pat in a cellar, Maggie began living a "double life" as her own sister.

At first, Clint Buchanan was fooled by Maggie's charade. However, she began making mistakes that aroused Clint's suspicions that something was awry. With the help of *Banner* aide Matt McAllister, Clint began to piece the horror story together. The woman he was romancing wasn't Pat Ashley! Clint raced to Pat's house, where Maggie was just about to shoot her sister. Clint froze momentarily upon hearing a single gunshot from within. He broke into the house to find Maggie dead and Pat standing over her with a revolver in her hand. Even though it was an obvious case of self-defense, Pat was so traumatized by her experiences that she could not even talk about the final moments of her sister's life.

Haunted by Maggie's laughter, Pat withdrew further into herself. She broke up with Clint and found herself drawn to his younger brother Bo, who had come to Llanview as a representative of his famous father, oil baron Asa Buchanan. Dorian Lord was delighted by this turn of events. She set out to make Clint Buchanan fall in love with her, only to fail when he saw through her manipulative ways. Dorian *did* emerge with one small victory: during Pat's absence, Dorian had taken over her TV talk show—and loved it! It took quite a bit of coaxing to get Dorian to relinquish the spotlight.

PARIS, FRANCE
1980

In One Life to Live's first journey across the Atlantic, Bo Buchanan flew to Paris to surprise Pat Ashley. The couple celebrated their blossoming love amidst the scenic wonders of France during the spring of 1980.

"JACKIE COURTNEY AND I WERE THE ONLY TWO ACTORS TO GO TO PARIS. WE DIDN'T TAKE ANY MAKEUP ARTISTS, OR HAIR AND WARDROBE PEOPLE. SO JACKIE AND I WOULD GRAB OUR COSTUMES OUT OF AN OLD STATION WAGON EVERY MORNING. BELIEVE ME, IT WAS HARD WORK—NOT EXACTLY CHAMPAGNE AT MAXIM'S."

ROBERT S. WOODS
(BO BUCHANAN)

When Pat Ashley entered his life, Bo Buchanan was in the midst of a torrid affair with his father's mistress, Mimi King. It was not a difficult conquest. Mimi, thinking her days with Asa were numbered, managed to seduce Bo.

Richard Abbott returned to Llanview with his new wife, Becky Lee, who had signed with the Buchanan Enterprises recording label. Becky was thrilled when the Buchanans booked her into the Grand Ole Opry. At the same time, she discovered that she was pregnant—and could lose the baby if she encountered any undue stress. Driven by her childhood dream, Becky kept the news from Richard and went to Nashville, where her singing was a triumph. Later, backstage at the Opry, Becky collapsed and lost her baby. Although Richard's bitterness threatened the marriage, Clint managed to patch up the Abbotts, for the time being, at least.

In February 1980, Asa Buchanan finally blew into Llanview for the first time and immediately assailed his son Bo for his incompetence. Almost immediately, Clint and Asa were at war! Asa hired young Samantha Vernon to work for him. Sam, who was living with skater Mick Gordon, became instantly enchanted with her new lifestyle—a world of money and, more importantly, power. Asa was equally impressed by Samantha, but he was more interested in her youth and her body than her business expertise. So captivated by Asa and his charisma, Sam did not see that her best friend, Tina Clayton, was seducing Mick! At the same time, sexpot Tina was also waging a campaign to attract Bo's protégé, country-and-western singer Johnny Drummond.

When Samantha found out about Mick's affair with Tina, she threw him out of her loft, then threw herself into her work with Asa. He gave her a lavish twenty-first birthday bash in his mansion, Southhampton. The party, complete with a rodeo, dancing girls, and a whole barbecued steer, climaxed with Asa (determined to maintain his youthful, macho image) parachuting from a plane! Upon landing, Asa injured his knee and was flown to Llanview Hospital for surgery.

Bo flew to Paris to surprise Pat Ashley. When he checked into Pat's hotel, Bo was spotted by Pat's new friend, an elegant middle-aged woman, Nicole Bonard. When Nicole spotted Bo, she recognized him instantly. Bo was her son! Nicole Bonard was actually Asa's wife, Olympia Buchanan. Many years earlier, when Bo and Clint were children, Olympia had an affair with ranch hand Yancey Ralston and became pregnant. During an argument, Olympia killed Yancey. When Asa found out, he had Olympia banished to Europe, telling his children that their mother had died.

Now, years later, Asa saw a photo of Nicole and Pat in Paris taken by Bo and went into a state of shock! If she were to resurface, he feared, Nicole could not only ruin his empire, but destroy his relationship with his sons and Samantha Vernon. Asa's fears were partially realized when Nicole told Pat that "Bo is not a true Buchanan." Before Pat could find out what her cryptic comment meant, Nicole Bonard was gone!

To keep Nicole in check, Asa had her flown to Llanview, where he imprisoned her in an eerie, dark mansion, Moor Cliffe. Asa hired his nephew, Rafe Garretson, to watch over her, telling the naive young man that Nicole was insane. Troubled by Nicole's pleas for freedom, Rafe questioned the unusual circumstances, but was told by Asa's aide, Chuck Wilson, to do his job and trust his Uncle Asa.

As Bo and Pat fell in love and got engaged, Asa did his darndest to break them up. Asa Buchanan hated strong, independent women like Pat Ashley so much that he forced his own mistress, Mimi King, to try and seduce Bo. She followed Bo to Nashville (where Becky Lee and Johnny Drummond were performing at the Grand Ole Opry) and attempted—unsuccessfully—to lure him into bed. As the year went on, the relationship between Bo and Asa grew more bitter and competitive, until Bo finally opted to leave the family fold and start his own company, Lone Star Records. Bo was determined to beat his daddy at his own game!

*D*uring this period, the father that Tina had never known—Ted Clayton—arrived in Llanview intent on reconciling with his daughter. However, Ted wasn't Ted at all! He was Tom Clarkson, a recently released inmate who was about to try and con Viki out of her fortune, and Tina out of her inheritance. Suave "Ted" made himself indispensible to the widow Riley, who had just given birth to her second son, Joseph Francis. In her arms, Viki held proof of her and Joe's great love. Sadly, there was no Joe to walk in the room to share her joy. Ted Clayton was determined to fill that void in Viki's life. He set out to get control of her emotions . . . and her money.

Before long, Ted pitted himself against Clint Buchanan, who had taken more than a professional interest in Viki, his publisher at *The Banner*. When Ted learned that Clint was about to propose marriage to Viki, he stepped up his plan by masterminding the kidnapping of Tina. His goal was not only to get his hands on the ransom, but to make himself indispensable to Viki. When Tina was safely returned home, Ted proposed marriage to Viki. Flustered but touched by his request, Viki opted for time to consider the offer.

*K*aren Wolek grew nervous every time Katrina Karr visited Jenny and her baby girl, Mary. By now, Katrina had begun dating a handsome beer-truck driver, Marcello Salta, who made her see that she was a wonderful, worthy person. As for Jenny, with Brad finally out of her life (he was serv-

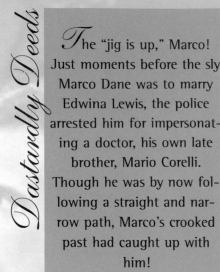

*T*he "jig is up," Marco! Just moments before the sly Marco Dane was to marry Edwina Lewis, the police arrested him for impersonating a doctor, his own late brother, Mario Corelli. Though he was by now following a straight and narrow path, Marco's crooked past had caught up with him!

ing time in Statesville Prison for raping Karen), she turned to her friends for support. Most of all, she found herself drawn to Dr. Peter Janssen. In the spring, Jenny and Peter declared their love for each other, but they faced an uphill battle. Peter needed a divorce—and his wife Melinda, whom Dorian had declared mentally incompetent, was not about to give him one. Also, Jenny was determined to remain true to her marriage vows and not sleep with Peter until she obtained an annulment from Brad.

When baby Mary became ill with a minor blood disease and needed a transfusion, Peter realized from her blood type that Jenny could not be her mother. One look at the footprints and Peter saw that Mary Vernon was Katrina's baby, not Jenny's. Karen had switched babies! Tormented by his discovery, Peter promised Karen that he would not reveal the truth to Jenny.

*M*arco Dane was finding it harder and harder to impersonate his dead brother, Mario Corelli—especially after falling in love with Edwina Lewis. Edwina demanded total honesty, which Marco simply couldn't provide. At the same time, he was having a tough time fending off Dorian Lord's attempts to prove that "Mario" was really Marco. When the stress of leading dual lives proved too much, Marco developed selective amnesia. To her horror, Karen Wolek witnessed cool and calm Mario turn into wild-eyed Marco—and not turn back! Karen hid her Jekyll-and-Hyde pal in a sleazy motel, then had him committed to a sanitarium.

Mario's dependence upon Karen made Larry jealous. As the gap in their relationship widened once again, Larry turned to Ivan Kipling's estranged wife Faith for companionship. Karen, who still loved Larry with all her heart, grew jealous of his friendship with Faith Kipling.

Ivan was a brilliant brain surgeon with a host of secrets. Among them was the fact that he was the natural father of Edwina Lewis, who despised him. Kipling

*W*hen Dorian saw an opportunity to become Pennsylvania's new First Lady, she grabbed it! In 1980, Ms. Lord romantically wooed Llanview's ambitious DA Herb Callison while skillfully steering his successful campaign for governor. Herb won—but was forced to resign when it was uncovered that he and Dorian had engaged in illegal campaign activity.

also had a very secret, very personal fetish: He liked to frequent prostitutes and dress them in sexy lingerie before having sex with them. Ivan shuddered when he saw Karen Wolek for the first time. She had been one of his hookers—and could expose his perverted obsession.

Determined to protect his secret, Ivan set a trap for Karen, asking her to meet him in a deserted building. Kipling intended to kill her! In the ensuing struggle, Karen took a terrible tumble down a flight of stairs. Just as Ivan was about to finish her off, two vagrants entered the building, forcing him to flee. Karen was rushed to the hospital in a coma. Ivan, as chief neurosurgeon, was put in charge of her case! He called for immediate surgery, where he planned to kill her—this time for sure! The moment arrived when Ivan decided to make the "fatal mistake" that would end her life, he changed his mind. His pride in his profession and his devotion to the Hippocratic oath prevented him from killing Karen on the operating table.

In the aftermath of the surgery, Ivan injected Karen with drugs to keep her silent for as long as possible. Reconciling with his wife, he coerced Faith into becoming his accomplice. They injected a drug into Karen's IV that would cause her respiratory system to collapse. In thirty minutes, Karen Wolek would be dead. However, Jenny's prompt action saved her sister—and the Kiplings managed to elude the authorities and escape to South America.

*M*arco decided that the only way to avoid going crazy was to marry Edwina and leave town for good. Once he and Edwina left Llanview, thought Marco, he could live a stress-free, peaceful life as Mario Corelli. The Corelli/Lewis wedding promised to end tensions that had been building since Mario's "attacks" began. Karen, who was enjoying some rare happiness with Larry, would finally be free of the man who had given her so much grief over the years.

On the morning of the wedding, Dorian was more convinced than ever that Mario was an imposter. She took evidence to Edwina's apartment, determined to save her friend from making a terrible mistake. Edwina refused to listen to her or to even look at Dorian's so-called evidence. Determined not to let Marco Dane escape, Dorian pulled enough strings to get an indictment against him, and he was arrested in his wedding suit just before the marriage took place and was charged with impersonating a doctor.

Edwina, in a state of shock, broke all ties with Marco. He went to jail, refusing to even see Karen, hoping to weaken the suspicion that she was his coconspirator. Of course, Larry knew enough to assume that Karen had to have aided and abetted Marco. When questioned, Karen told Larry the truth. She knew that she had violated not only her promise of honesty, but also Larry's own morality and his ethics as a doctor. Larry, caught between his love for Karen and his duty, asked Karen for time to let them both consider what had happened. The following day, Karen, guilt-ridden and not wanting to hurt Larry and his son Danny anymore, packed her bags and moved into Ina Hopkins's boarding house. Eventually, Marco and Edwina reconciled, and married in a touching, private ceremony.

*A*fter her breakup with Clint Buchanan, Dorian sank her claws into Llanview's ambitious DA, Herb Callison. With Dorian's guidance and financial support, Herb won a close election for governor in the fall. Unbeknownst to him, Dorian had obtained a huge illegal campaign contribution from Asa Buchanan in exchange for his winning a state highway contract from the new governor. Unfortunately, Herb had promised the same highway deal to a local mobster, Irwin Keyser. It was only a matter of time before news of these dishonest maneuvers began to leak to the press. At year's end, Dorian made final plans to become the First Lady of Pennsylvania—just as whispers of "scandal" were heard in the inner circles of Llanview.

When counterfeiter Ted Clayton put out a contract to kill Marco Dane and Karen Wolek, the dynamic duo narrowly avoided death by jumping onto a moving train to elude the hit men. Karen escaped the ordeal unscathed, but Marco was less fortunate, having sustained a bullet wound to the arm.

1981

*D*orian Lord was too involved with her wedding plans to do more than deny the rumor that her intended husband, Governor Herb Callison, had received illegal campaign contributions from millionaire Asa Buchanan. On the day of the wedding, the newly elected Lt. Governor Ed Hall, convinced of Herb and Dorian's guilt, faced his conscience and resigned from office. Dorian immediately did her best to shore up Herb's backbone. She refused to let him resign in disgrace!

However, with the evidence mounting against him, Herb had no choice but to relinquish the governorship. Dorian's dream, and Herb's career, collapsed. In disgrace, Herb Callison took a lowly position as public defender.

During this trying period, Dorian discovered that she needed her sister Melinda as much as Melinda had always needed her. Nevertheless, Melinda was on her way back to the Compton Clinic after having threatened Jenny Vernon with a letter opener. Her insane act meant further postponement of Jenny and Peter's wedding. A dejected Peter realized that he could never get a divorce from Melinda until she was mentally fit. On her last night in Llanview, Melinda overheard a secret conversation between Peter, Marco, and Karen that would send her further into madness. Melinda heard them talking about the notorious baby switch in which Marco and Karen switched Jenny's dead baby with Katrina's little girl.

*P*at Ashley had to wonder what had happened to Nicole Bonard, the friend she'd met in Paris. She kept remembering Nicole's final, cryptic

Nicole Bonard, really Olympia Buchanan, was hell-bent on getting revenge against ex-husband Asa for keeping her imprisoned in a spooky mansion while he arranged to marry young Samantha Vernon. In June 1981, Nicole finally escaped, managed to buy a gun, and showed up at Asa and Sam's wedding. However, just before making a deadly move, Asa's nephew Rafe appeared and whisked her away.

words to her that Bo was "not a true Buchanan." Where could she be? Pat hired Ed Hall, now a private detective, to help her find her missing friend.

Asa was holding Nicole (who in truth was Asa's first wife, Olympia) in Moor Cliffe, the estate next to Llanfair. During the early weeks of 1981, Asa finally got young Samantha Vernon to agree to marry him. At the same time, Asa's nephew, Rafe, developed a genuine fascination for Sam, who had no idea that the handsome young man she visited at Moor Cliffe was a Buchanan!

As Asa and Sam prepared to marry, Nicole escaped from her makeshift prison and plunged a knife into Asa's shoulder. The knifing did not seriously injure Asa, who quickly fabricated a story to explain his injury. On Asa's wedding day, Nicole escaped again, bought a gun, and hid in the church as the guests arrived. With gun in hand, Nicole prepared to stop the wedding. However, at the last second, Rafe appeared and silently subdued the raving woman. With Chuck Wilson's assistance, Rafe dragged Nicole out of the church and back to Moor Cliffe.

The wedding continued without incident. However, all hell broke loose at the reception when Becky Lee's ex-husband, Luther Jackson, crashed the festivities. Drunk and hostile, he blamed Sam for destroying his marriage to Becky, then pointed a gun at Asa. In the ensuing struggle, a shot rang out—striking Dr. Peter Janssen, who was rushed to Llanview Hospital for emergency surgery.

As the days passed, Peter's condition worsened and, fearing he would die, he wanted to confess his part as conspirator in the baby switch. Karen convinced Peter to confess to a priest. Suspicious of Peter's actions, Brad secretly placed a voice-activated tape recorder in Peter's hospital room—and learned the startling truth that Marco and Karen had switched Jenny's dead baby with Katrina's healthy child in the hospital nursery. Armed with the news, Brad threatened to tell Jenny, but found that he could not hurt the woman he still loved with this dreadful secret.

Even on Jenny and Peter's wedding day, Brad could not bring himself to stop the ceremony. With Karen as maid of honor and Larry as best man, Jenny Vernon became Mrs. Peter Janssen.

Katrina, whose engagement to Marcello Salta came unglued when he discovered on the eve of their wedding that she had once been a hooker, comforted Brad. Katrina revealed to him that she suspected that he was the father of her dead baby, the result of an evening they'd spent together at the Wallington Hotel nearly three years earlier.

$\mathcal{B}$ecky Lee and Richard's marriage fell apart in 1981 when Becky Lee realized that she loved her singing partner, Johnny Drummond. Richard left town, and Johnny left his new flame Tina in the dust, and hurried into a romance with Becky Lee.

$\mathcal{T}$he Ted/Viki/Clint triangle lost a side when Clint decided not to pursue a relationship with Viki. Clint sensed, correctly, that Ted Clayton was duping Viki. Despite Clint's words of warning, Viki was happy with Ted, blissfully unaware that he was actually the head of a counterfeit ring centered in Llanview.

Detective Vince Wolek, hot on the trail of the ringleader, paid a terrible price upon discovering that Ted was a counterfeiter. To silence Vince, Ted administered a poison through a ring on his finger. The deadly dose took an hour to work. Vince, not knowing he was dying, came to Karen and his wife Wanda, then collapsed! His last words were, "Tell Viki . . ." Before he could finish the sentence, Vince died. Doctors ruled that a heart attack caused his sudden death.

The untimely death of the affable Vince Wolek deeply affected the people of Llanview. Viki was extremely upset, though Ted did his best to "comfort" her. Anna and Jim Craig tried to console Wanda in her time of grief. In mourning, Wanda devoted her energies to Llanview West, her new country-and-western nightclub. In a moving memorial service, Larry paid tribute to the brother who was responsible for him becoming a doctor.

More than almost anyone, Karen felt the pain of Vince's death. If she had gone with Vince on the night of his death as he had wanted, he might still be alive. Determined to befriend Steve Piermont, a member of the counterfeiting ring who she knew could lead her to his boss, Karen pretended to return to hooking! Within days of Vince's death, Karen was prowling the Wallington Hotel—scene of so much heartache in the past—insisting to all that she was back in "the life." Larry, who was now showering his kindness and honesty upon Asa's much-maligned former mistress Mimi King, was one of many who was skeptical of Karen's sudden regression.

Suspicious of Karen's motives, Ted asked Viki to find out what was going on. However, before she could provide him with answers, Viki left with Clint to attend a publisher's conference in New York. Alone in New York, Clint and Viki shared candlelit dinners and long walks together. By the end of the trip, they realized what their friends had known for months—they were in love. When Viki returned to Llanview, she resolved to break off her relationship with Ted. But she never had the chance!

With the assistance of a chemist, Ted Clayton spiked Viki's sherry with a debilitating drug that put her under his control. During Viki's drug-induced spell, Ted successfully instilled fear and indecision about

With her sister Karen as maid of honor and Dr. Larry Wolek as best man, Jenny Vernon became Mrs. Peter Janssen. Jenny's ex-husband Brad threatened to disrupt the ceremony but backed off at the last second, allowing Jenny to enjoy the day.

her relationship with Clint. While Clint was in Texas with Pat Ashley investigating her contention that the missing Nicole Bonard was actually his mother, Ted continued administering the mind-altering drug to Viki. Through a number of manipulatory acts, he finally convinced her to marry him! Upon his return, Clint realized the extent of Ted's machinations. He warned Viki that she would be making the biggest mistake of her life by becoming Mrs. Ted Clayton. For the time being, Clint's words of warning went unheeded.

Karen Wolek put on the performance of a lifetime as she convinced everyone—including counterfeiter Steve Piermont—that she had returned to her wild ways. She got Piermont to give her a job as a runner for the ring. Marco, ever shrewd, was the first to guess that Karen was actually trying to finish what Vince Wolek started. Steve blackmailed Marco into joining the ring, threatening to harm Edwina if he should balk. Edwina began wondering about Marco's mysterious appointments. His secret involvement proved a destructive element to his new "marriage." Before long, a sad Edwina asked Marco to move out.

Ted, fearing exposure, ordered Steve to put a contract out on Karen and Marco. Steve was faced with a dilemma. Having grown fond of Karen Wolek, Steve pleaded with her to run away. If she didn't extricate herself from the counterfeiting ring, she would be facing almost certain death. Karen refused and went ahead with a counterfeit money drop—but not before confiding in Ed Hall (now a captain of the Llanview Police) of her involvement.

In a shoot-out in a deserted railroad yard, Marco was wounded in the arm, but he and Karen were able to get away from the gunmen by running onto a bridge, then jumping onto a moving train. Ed arrested Steve Piermont, pleading with him to turn state's evidence against Ted Clayton.

*D*eeply concerned that Viki was in grave danger, Clint took action. Arriving at Viki's carriage house, Clint pleaded with Viki to come away with him. When she resisted, Clint picked Viki up over his shoulder and bodily carried her away to her cabin in the mountains. When Ted learned of their whereabouts, he showed up and poisoned Clint—just like he'd done to Vince Wolek! At Llanview Hospital, doctors saved Clint's life by administering an antidote. To Viki and Tina's horror, Ed Hall captured Ted and arrested him.

As he was being carted off to jail, Ted resolved to bring Marco Dane and Karen Wolek down with him. When Karen and Marco realized they were being framed, they went on the run. They knew that Steve Piermont was the only one who could clear their names. To track him down, they joined a carnival run by Steve's family. To complicate matters, Marco and Karen were stunned to discover that Ted Clayton had escaped from jail!

A young girl named Cassie Howard arrived in Llanview and took an unusual interest in Dorian Lord and her husband Herb Callison. Lying about her age, the teenager got a job as a receptionist at the Llanview Health Club, then began making cryptic phone calls to her grandmother in California. After a few days, the youngster received devastating news—her grandmother was dead. Dorian was stunned when Cassie finally revealed her secret: she was her daughter! Stunned, Dorian refused to believe this amazing pronouncement. Cassie was upset by her mother's rejection.

Alone with Herb, Dorian admitted that she had given birth to a daughter while she was in medical school. Herb listened as Dorian explained that, on September 11, 1966, she had given birth to her boyfriend David Renaldi's baby. One day, Dorian came home to discover

*K*atrina Karr finally put her sordid past behind her when she met her perfect match, beer-truck driver Marcello Salta. Their blissfully innocent romance came to an abrupt halt when, on the night before their wedding, Marcello discovered her deep secret—his bride-to-be had once been a hooker!

that David had taken off with their baby, Cassie. David, a concert pianist, went to live with his mother in California, then left Cassie behind and went off to Europe.

In time, Dorian and Cassie agreed to face this new relationship one step at a time. To win over her daughter, Dorian threw a special surprise party for Cassie, attended by everyone who was anyone in Llanview.

*I*n the fall, Tony Lord came back to Llanview, where he met and became instant friends with Bo Buchanan. Tony's former flame, Pat, was otherwise occupied. Through a series of events, Pat and Clint correctly surmised that Asa was keeping Nicole Bonard prisoner somewhere in Llanview. But not for long! Nicole escaped, and plotted to get even with the husband who had ruined her life. With glee, she decided to hatch her revenge scheme at Asa's upcoming Masquerade Ball honoring his new wife, Samantha Vernon Buchanan.

When the evening of the ball finally arrived, Nicole wasn't the only uninvited guest hiding behind a mask. The evil Dr. Ivan Kipling, who had fled to South America the previous year, had returned to Llanview to wreak havoc once again.

Nicole donned her mask and an exact copy of Samantha's dress, then proceeded to lock Sam in a walk-in freezer. Slipping into the party, Nicole confronted Bo, telling him the incredible truth that she was the mother he never knew—and she'd been kept imprisoned in a sanitarium for years by Asa. She pleaded with Bo to shoot Asa. Bo, mesmerized by this incredible revelation, headed back to the ball. He might have actually carried out Nicole's deadly request had he not been intercepted by Clint and Pat. Nicole stunned the assembled guests by pulling off her mask and revealing that she was Olympia Buchanan—very much alive!

Meanwhile, Asa hurried to rescue Samantha from the locked freezer. Having heard Nicole's story, Sam was furious! She refused to accept Asa's lies for another minute. Sam coldly told Asa that she was leaving him, for he had deceived her for the last time.

Asa's nightmare was far from over. Nicole wanted him dead. When she got Asa alone, the first Mrs. Buchanan pulled out a pistol and shot her ex-husband! Samantha rushed to Asa's side and grabbed for the gun. In the struggle, Nicole tripped on the balcony. As Sam reached out to save her, Nicole lost her footing and plummeted to the ground below. In the aftermath, Samantha told Asa that (having been manipulated for the last time) she must leave him.

Bo visited his mother in the hospital. In excruciating pain, she spoke three final words to her son—"Pat . . . your father . . ."—before dying. Confused, Bo confronted Pat, who was compelled to tell him the shocking news that Asa Buchanan was not his real father. Bo was stunned to learn that his real father was the late Yancey Ralston.

Bo bitterly vowed to make Asa pay dearly for the sins he had perpetrated on his family!

$\mathcal{F}$ramed for a 1981 crime they didn't commit, fugitives Marco Dane and Karen Wolek found refuge in a carnival, where they made a four-legged friend.

o's whole life had been a lie! He was deeply hurt by the news that Asa was not his real father. Embittered and vengeful, Bo declared war on Asa Buchanan. First on his agenda, he renounced the Buchanan name, declaring that his new name was Bo "Ralston."

Pat Ashley became jealous when Bo began dating Georgina Whitman, a bright and beautiful scientist who had come to town with Pat's old flame, Tony Lord. Tony and Georgina were on a top-secret project involving solaramite, a rare metal-mineral that they hoped could be mined, processed, then used as a cheap alternative to oil fuel. They struck pay dirt, discovering huge stores of solaramite under the Llanfair and Moor Cliffe mansions. Before long, Bo teamed up with Georgina and Tony and engaged in a bitter battle with Asa and *his* new partner, Dorian Lord, who had recently separated from husband Herb Callison.

Georgina developed a vacuum extractor to mine solaramite, but the plans for the high-tech machinery turned out to be faulty. The device was dangerous! Bo raced to warn Asa, who had stolen the plans and built the machine, but he wouldn't listen. Asa pulled the switch that began the machine's operation, and the two men narrowly escaped death when the device exploded in a burst of flames. Later, Bo risked his own life when he agreed to test-drive a car fueled by solaramite. The car exploded, and this time Asa pulled Bo from the flames!

Still, the near tragedies failed to reconcile Bo and Asa; the two stubborn men remained estranged. Bo's romance with Georgina fizzled,

**CLINT EVICTS LLANFAIR'S
RESIDENT "SERPENT,"
DORIAN LORD
1982**

*Dorian Lord finally lost
her battle to keep Llan-
fair . . . but not before
trying every trick in the
book. When she tried
to convince Clint she
couldn't get out of bed, he
got her to move—by
tossing a snake at her!*

CLINT
Good. You know, out
West I spent some time
with the Indians. Some of
their remedies are truly
amazing. There's this one
remedy where you spend
an entire hour in bed
with a rattlesnake. They
claim it will cure almost
anything. Ha! (He throws
a rubber snake in Dorian's
bed—she jumps.)

DORIAN
Ahhhhh! It's a fake snake.
You monster! You
monster!

too, and she left Llanview to join a California firm that was building the first manned space vehicle to Mars.

One couple who found romance was Pat Ashley and Tony Lord. After much coaxing, Pat came to accept Tony's adventurous lifestyle and married the man she loved in a beautiful wedding ceremony. When an opening in *The Banner*'s Middle East Bureau came about, Pat refused to stand in her husband's way.

Bo's quest to discover his "Ralston" roots took him to Louisiana, where he met his Aunt Euphemia. The eccentric old woman harbored a secret grudge against the long-lost relative who popped up on her doorstep. Euphemia was less than cordial to Bo, but her nephew Drew, a med student, seemed quite eager to come to Llanview. What Bo didn't realize was that Drew had strict instructions from the Ralston clan to bring down the Buchanan empire and restore the Ralston fortune. But once in Llanview, Drew seemed an unwilling participant, and he developed a fascination for Samantha.

Soon a second Ralston—Delila—showed up in town. The beautiful young woman, who worked in a rodeo, was not a participant in her mother Euphemia's plan to sabotage the Buchanans. In fact, Delila had been estranged from her family for years. Before long, she found herself a Buchanan of her own: Asa! The old coot was instantly enchanted by Delila's beauty, sex appeal, and her endless ability to surprise him. Bo grew resentful and jealous as Asa continued his efforts to hook Delila. To take his mind off his gorgeous cousin, Bo turned his attention to single singer Becky Lee Abbott.

When Ted Clayton escaped from jail, Tina wasn't surprised. By now, she knew that this man who claimed to be her father was as slippery as they came. However, Tina was in for the shock of her life when she encountered a smartly dressed woman in an art gallery. Suddenly, the woman whipped off her wig. It was Ted in disguise! Before he could harm Tina, Capt. Ed Hall shot and killed him. Tina, traumatized by the horrible events, left town to start a new life.

After Ted's death, Marco and Karen finally were able to clear their names in the counterfeiting scheme. Steve Piermont was sentenced to a short jail term for his role in the illegal operation. As for Viki, Ted was gone, but the path was still far from clear for romance with Clint Buchanan. Viki wanted some time to herself, and that drove a love-struck Clint Buchanan crazy! At *The Banner*, Clint found it exceedingly difficult to work beside the woman he loved, without any positive feedback from her. What to do? Resign, that's what!

With great sadness, Viki accepted Clint's decision to take a new job as executive editor at *The Banner*'s chief competitor, *The Chronicle*.

The battle lines were drawn. Llanview's press war took on new fury when Clint lured prize-winning reporter Edwina Lewis away from *The Banner*. Working side by side, Clint and Edwina began a torrid affair.

For the first time in years, Dr. Larry Wolek was content and happy. Divorced from Karen, Larry eagerly anticipated marrying his new love, Mimi King. Just before the wedding, Larry met up with the renowned Dr. Hugo Wilde—who was actually his mortal enemy, Ivan Kipling! Kipling coldly informed Larry that he was about to atone for his sins. Larry screamed in horror as he realized that Ivan was about to perform surgery on him.

Larry awoke with no memory of what had taken place in the operating room. He was unaware that Ivan was now controlling his every move through a device implanted in his brain. Returning to Llanview, Larry never showed up for his own wedding. Mimi, who was left standing at the altar, was devastated. Instead of marrying Mimi, Larry had gone straight to Karen, telling her that he still loved her dearly. Karen did not know what to make of her "changed" ex-husband. Before long, Ivan's ultimate aim became apparent: he wanted to capture Karen Wolek and was using Larry to do his bidding!

Ivan and his assistant, Astrid Collins, came to Llanview to keep tabs on Larry and Karen. Moving into Timberdark Farm on the outskirts of town, they befriended Dorian's young daughter, Cassie. When Capt. Ed Hall grew suspicious of the strange activities at the farm, he showed up at Timberdark—only to have Dr. Kipling implant a device in his brain, too!

Finally, Ivan apprehended his real prey, Karen Wolek. Luring her to Timberdark, he issued an ultimatum to her. If she agreed to come away with him to his South American jungle paradise, then he would leave instructions for the removal of the implants from Ed's and Larry's brains. If not, the devices would soon dissolve, killing both of them! Karen had no choice but to agree. Reluctantly, she boarded a plan with Dr. Kipling, as Marco arrived in the nick of time to rescue Larry and Ed.

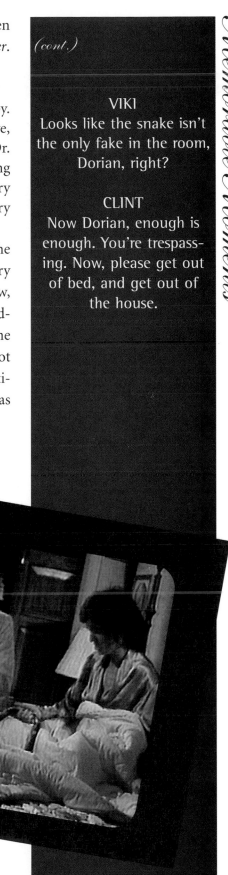

(cont.)

VIKI
Looks like the snake isn't the only fake in the room, Dorian, right?

CLINT
Now Dorian, enough is enough. You're trespassing. Now, please get out of bed, and get out of the house.

JENNY IS FORCED TO GIVE HER DAUGHTER BACK TO KATRINA
1982

Jenny Vernon was stunned to discover that her precious Mary, whom she had raised from birth, was not her daughter. Three years earlier, Marco and Karen had switched Jenny's dead baby with Katrina's living baby. When the baby switch was exposed, Jenny, with her heart breaking, had no other choice but to part with little Mary.

JENNY
Mary, Katrina is going to take you to Florida. Remember how much fun you had there the last time, remember that? Wouldn't it be fun to go back there again? And when you get back, you can tell me all about it, okay? Now I want you to give me a big hug, and a big kiss. And, Mary, I want you to be a good girl. Will you be a good girl for me? I love you so much!

After piecing together the clues, Marco, Jenny, and Larry (recovered from the operation to remove his implant) arrived in Ivan's "paradise," located deep in the jungles of San Carlos. When bandits attacked Marco, Larry alone continued the search for Karen, who had no choice but to "marry" Ivan in a bizarre wedding ceremony at his lavish plantation. Just before he tried to consummate their "marriage," Karen escaped into the jungle!

Ivan and his guards gave chase, but Larry heroically rescued Karen in the nick of time. Grateful to see him, Karen raced into Larry's open arms and they shared a passionate reunion. But the nightmare was far from over. Together, Karen and Larry faced numerous perils in the jungle, but their strong and renewed love prevailed. Ivan's turncoat assistant, Astrid, made her own escape and joined them in a hazardous flight downriver. In a climactic chase, Ivan caught up with the escaping trio. In a life-and-death fight on the river bank, Larry prevailed, sending the demented Dr. Kipling to the crocodiles.

*B*ack in Llanview, Marco Dane turned his attentions to a new career: show biz! Marco directed a murder-mystery movie, *Blood Moon*, which he shot on location in Llanview. Marco was especially enthused about the script, based on the Hatchfield Murders, an actual event that had occurred in Llanview fifteen years earlier.

Joining Marco in the new enterprise was his long-estranged younger brother, Gary Corelli, who was making a play for Cassie Callison's affections. However, Cassie was playing the field, dating both Gary Corelli and wealthy Kyle Dickinson.

Soon, life imitated art on the set of *Blood Moon* when the lead actor, Rudy Lavasso, was murdered! It was obvious to all that the killer wanted *Blood Moon* shut down! Marco and Capt. Ed Hall set a trap to catch the killer. However, their plan went awry when Marco's ex-wife, Edwina, saw a gunman about to shoot him. Edwina threw herself in front of Marco and took a near-fatal bullet. The killer turned out to be Kyle Dickinson, the son of the culprit in the actual Hatchfield murder case. Kyle held Cassie hostage, then Dorian, before being apprehended and locked away.

*A*fter nearly three years, Marco and Karen's notorious baby switch came one step closer to being revealed when Dorian received a letter from her institutionalized sister, Melinda, stating that Mary Vernon was really Katrina's baby, not Jenny's. Dorian, unaware of the implications, showed the letter to Marcello Salta. In a rapid series of events, Marcello told Larry, who confronted Karen and forced her to reveal her part in the baby switch. To protect Jenny, Larry vowed to keep the switch secret. But Marcello didn't!

When Marcello told the news to a stunned Katrina, she demanded proof. Larry tried to convince Kat that what Marcello had told her was a ridiculous rumor. She then confronted Marco, who feigned surprise at the incredible tale. Karen, however, could no longer hide the truth from her dear friend. With her back against the wall, Karen confessed. Katrina wanted

*F*rom the mid-1970s through the mid-1980s, Brad Vernon wreaked more havoc than anyone else in Llanview. Brad's most heinous act of treachery occurred in 1979 when—with his wife Jenny in the hospital—he sexually assaulted her sister, Karen.

SILVER SPRINGS, FLORIDA 1982

The diabolical Dr. Ivan Kipling kidnapped Karen and took her to his South American hideaway in 1982. One Life to Live *only journeyed as far as the Florida Everglades (which stood in for the jungles of South America) to shoot the climactic conclusion to the story.*

"I ENJOYED THE TIME WE WENT ON LOCATION TO FLORIDA—ESPECIALLY WHEN LARRY RESCUED HIS WIFE, KAREN. IT WAS THE ONLY TIME I SAVED ANYONE ON THE SHOW! OF COURSE, I'VE SAVED PEOPLE THROUGH MEDICAL MEANS, BUT I'D NEVER BEEN A REAL HERO BEFORE. IT FELT WONDERFUL!"

Michael Storm
(Dr. Larry Wolek)

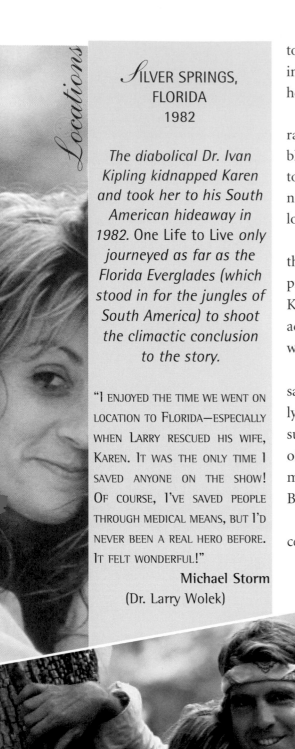

to tell Jenny at once, and Marcello tried in vain to make her wait. He insisted that if anyone should tell Jenny, it should be the man she loved—her husband, Peter Janssen.

Peter agonized over the moment that was finally at hand. He raced home from the hospital to face Jenny before she learned the terrible truth from Katrina. But Peter never made it! Just as Katrina was about to reveal the baby switch to Jenny, the Llanview police arrived with grim news: Peter had been killed in a car accident. In view of Jenny's horrible loss, Katrina said nothing further about the baby switch.

Peter's death had momentarily stopped Katrina from revealing the truth to Jenny. In the weeks after, Brad convinced Kat to stay silent by proposing marriage to her. He promised that, if she married him, then Katrina would be little Mary's stepmother, and would see her often. Kat accepted Brad's proposal, and the secret was finally safe once again. Or was it?

Jenny's lingering suspicions drove her to steal the key to Brad's safe-deposit box and there she found the audiotape that Brad had secretly made of Peter confessing the switch to a priest. The bombshell disclosure stunned Jenny—but it did not destroy her. The shocking knowledge of the baby switch turned Jenny into a woman who would take desperate measures to keep her child. With renewed inner strength, she returned Brad's tape and kept the discovery to herself.

Jenny's hopes shattered when she encountered Katrina in the cemetery while paying a sorrowful visit to her real baby. Seeing Jenny in tears, Katrina realized that she finally knew the truth. Katrina was faced with a dilemma. Should she fight for her baby in the courts, or marry Brad and be Mary's stepmother? Ever the cad, Brad answered the question for Katrina when she caught him proposing to Jenny!

Sadly, Jenny realized she must give her daughter to Katrina to prevent the pain Mary would suffer in a courtroom custody battle . . . and to keep Marco and Karen from going to prison. In a tearful, poignant moment, Jenny handed over the girl she loved with all her heart to Katrina.

Meanwhile, the implications of the baby switch reverberated throughout Llanview. Most of all, Dorian Lord demanded in a televised editorial that the perpetrator of the crime be brought to justice. When the District Attorney's office began harassing Jenny, Viki (who now knew the truth) countered with her own angry editorial, in which she stated that she knew for a fact Jenny was innocent. She would only say that this information came from a privileged source of information. Before a grand jury, Viki refused to name her source and was sent to jail!

Of all people, Viki's rival, Clint Buchanan, worked endless hours to obtain her release. In the process, he and Viki grew close again, and with bars between them, Clint proposed. When Viki's prison vigil came to an end, she and Clint became man and wife. They married in a beautiful autumn ceremony held at Viki's family home, Llanfair, which the newlyweds moved into after having Dorian evicted!

Karen and Larry decided to hold off on their own wedding plans until the baby-switch crisis cooled. Their stormy reunion was threatened by the return of Steve Piermont, who had recently been released from jail. Steve began his romantic pursuit of Karen by sending her flowers. Then, while Larry was on the night shift, he sneaked into her bedroom and watched her sleep. Karen protested violently that he had to stop harassing her. But Marco, who knew Karen best, keenly observed that Karen's failure to tell Larry about Steve indicated hidden passions that she refused to admit— even to herself. Marco's insights were right on target. While Larry was away at a medical conference, Steve visited Karen, and they kissed passionately. In vain, Karen tried to resist, but she finally succumbed to his dynamic presence.

Throughout the fall of 1982, Karen tried to banish the fantasies she was having about Steve from her mind. For solace, she fled to a country inn in Nantucket, but when Steve followed, Karen couldn't resist his allure. During a stormy night, they made love in a shack on the beach.

Back in Llanview, Karen discovered that a contract had been put out on Steve by the Mob. Trying to help him, she became a target, too! Steve pleaded with Karen, telling her that they would die unless they left town immediately. Karen was perplexed. While stalling for time, Steve was shot and seriously injured. Together they fled town.

Larry tracked Steve and Karen back to Nantucket, where Karen was forced to make the painful choice between the two men who loved her. With great difficulty, she chose Steve, because his need for her was greater. While a dejected Larry journeyed back to Llanview, Steve and Karen headed for Canada to start a fugitive life.

$\mathscr{H}$erb Callison adopted Dorian's daughter Cassie and remained her dearest friend and closest confidant throughout his stormy marriage to her mother. When Herb walked out on Dorian in 1983, he took Cassie with him!

1983

For months, Asa Buchanan worked hard to win back Bo's love. But Bo, having discovered that Asa was not really his father, wanted nothing to do with the man he used to call "Pa." Now, early in the winter of 1983, Asa had stumbled upon an incredible secret—Bo really *was* his son after all. The shocking revelation, which came in the form of a letter from Delila's Aunt Twyla to Bo, provided indisputable proof that Yancey Ralston was sterile. There was no way he could have sired Bo.

The news thrilled Asa. But when he went to tell Bo, Asa couldn't help but notice the developing closeness between his son and Delila. Asa realized that revealing the secret would send Delila directly into Bo's arms. And Asa wanted Delila for himself! He clearly understood that Delila and Bo were in love, but, believing they were kin, they had been fighting the mutual attraction. To keep Delila under his thumb and in his bed, Asa kept his mouth shut. More cunning than ever, Asa eloped with Delila. A forlorn Bo turned his attentions to Becky Lee Abbott, who was painfully aware that he was seeing her on the rebound.

In February, Asa and Brad were taking his new sailing vessel for a trial run in Florida. As they ventured out on the high seas, disaster struck. A gasoline leak in the boat's engine caused the craft to explode, and Asa and Brad were thrown into the raging waters. Violent waves separated them, and Brad was certain that Asa was lost forever.

The news of Asa Buchanan's drowning sent shock waves through Llanview. In his will, Asa divided the bulk of his fortune between Bo and his new wife Delila. In the will, Bo was perplexed by Asa's reference to "my

BO INTERRUPTS ASA'S WEDDING TO DELILA
1983

BO
Didn't you forget to ask anyone if they had any objections, speak up? Because I got a whole lot of reasons these two shouldn't be getting married.

ASA
Shut up, boy! You get out of here, or I'll throw you out of here.

BO
Delila, you don't love him.

ASA
Now you stop telling her how to feel, you deal with your own crazy feelings.

DELILA
Stop it. Stop it. Listen! Would you listen to me! Bo, I made a choice. Nothing you can say or do is going to change it. I love Asa. I love Asa. I said it. Now that's it.

dear son." Brad provided the stunning answer to Bo's question when he revealed the secret. Bo, shocked to learn he was a Buchanan after all, was deeply enraged that Asa had kept the truth to himself, knowing that Delila might not marry him if she knew that Bo was not her cousin.

Of course, Asa wasn't dead at all! Certain there was a conspiracy to assassinate him and that Bo and Delila were having a love affair, Asa had instructed Brad to sneak him back to Llanview. While Asa and Brad implemented their plan, Bo and Delila's brewing passions finally overtook them. They made love, promising themselves they would marry after a respectable period of time. Little did they realize that Asa's return was imminent.

At the memorial service honoring Asa, who should show up but the "dead man" himself! To Bo and company, Asa's resurrection was as shocking as his death. Seeking to reclaim what was his, Asa set out to keep Delila away from Bo. Confused and incapable of coping with all that had happened, Delila was faced with a dilemma: which Buchanan would she choose?

In spite of her love for Bo, Delila felt honor-bound to remain with her husband. But Clint and Bo worked together to change Delila's mind. They knew that they could win over Delila by branding Asa as a liar. After Delila heard the truth that Asa knew all along—that he was Bo's father, but had lied so that he could win her for himself—she left the old man. Stricken, angry, and stubborn, Asa vowed revenge on all those who had betrayed him.

Bo rejoiced in the discovery that he was finally free to be with Delila. However, there were complications. Bo had recently made love to Becky Lee—and now she was pregnant! Becky Lee confided the news to Drew Ralston, then Larry Wolek, but chose not to tell Bo because she knew he was in love with Delila. For now, Becky Lee would be content with single motherhood.

A chance encounter at the gynecologist's office led Delila to discover Becky Lee's delicate condition. Alarmed that she would tell Bo she was carrying his baby, Delila pressed for a fast divorce from Asa and a hasty marriage to Bo. In May, Delila Ralston became Mrs. Bo Buchanan in a ceremony held at Llanfair.

*B*rad Vernon continued to romance his ex-wife Jenny, who was otherwise occupied consoling Larry Wolek after Karen's painful departure. Jenny became so convinced that Brad had changed his evil ways that she consented to marry him again! Brad, realizing that he had accomplished a minor miracle in winning Jenny away from Larry, strove to keep the slate clean so that she would never be disappointed in him again. Dancing around Asa's machinations, however, made the assignment quite difficult for him, so he quit to open a new hotel, the Vernon Inn.

*S*uspicious of Becky Lee, Asa forced her to admit that she was pregnant with Bo's baby. Becky knew that Asa would try to use this knowledge to destroy Bo and Delila's marriage. Before she would allow that to happen, Becky Lee threatened Asa, informing him that if he revealed her pregnancy to Bo, he would never lay eyes on his grandchild.

For the moment, Asa's hands remain tied. The thought of another Buchanan offspring filled him with joy. Asa offered to support Becky Lee and her baby if she would let him raise the child, but she refused because she had accepted a proposal of marriage from a benevolent soul, Drew Ralston, whose own romance with Samantha Vernon Buchanan had fizzled. However, on their wedding day, Drew was shot and killed in a botched robbery at the florist shop where he was buying Becky Lee's bouquet.

Becky Lee vowed to name her baby Drew after the valiant young man who had given his life for her. After Asa promised that he would not expect her to sleep with him, she agreed to become his wife. Asa firmly believed that she would, in time, come to love him.

ECHO AND CLINT

Celebrated photographer and international jet-setter Echo DiSavoy arrived in Llanview and immediately set her sights on a very married Clint Buchanan. Despite his deep feelings for his wife, Viki, Clint could not resist the sultry blond countess. They shared a wet and wild time before capping off their dangerous liaison in bed. If only Clint realized that Echo was hell-bent on destroying his marriage as payback for his suspected role in the long-ago death of her mother.

Becky Lee wrote a letter to Bo, explaining that her baby was his. Leaving the letter in Viki's car, with instructions that it was only to be read upon the event of her death, Becky Lee married Asa. As for Delila, she returned from her honeymoon only to learn she was sterile. Certain that Bo would leave her when he learned that she could not give him what he wanted most in the world, Delila concocted an incredible lie, telling Bo she was carrying his baby. Caught up in a web of lies, Delila finally admitted her deceit to Bo, whose heart went out to his barren wife.

Unforeseen kidney problems made the final stages of Becky Lee's pregnancy treacherous. After the birth of her son, Drew, her condition worsened. Fearing she would die, an anguished Asa told Bo the truth: he was the father of Becky Lee's baby! Bo was overjoyed to have what he had wanted most in the world—a son.

Feeling neglected, Delila began an affair with the disreputable Anthony Makana. In rapid time, Bo filed for divorce from Delila, though she managed to convince him to postpone his plans to end their marriage. To make himself forget his wayward wife, Bo turned his attentions to his newly acquired football team, the Llanview Cougars. Little did he know that the notorious Anthony Makana had paid the Cougars star player, Alec Lowndes, $30,000 to throw a big game. Alec, who was dating the much-older Carla Hall (who had returned to Llanview after obtaining her law degree) changed his mind, and actually became the hero of the game! After suffering an injury, Alec was saddened by the discovery that he could never play football again. A jealous Ed Hall watched from afar as his ex-wife Carla comforted the ailing athlete. Though still in love with Carla, Ed poured his energies into a relationship with Courtney Wright, the Cougars' press agent.

Unable to accept the demise of her marriage to Bo, Delila decided to lose herself in dance. *Exotic* dance! She accepted a job at Wildlife, a new-wave disco run secretly by Anthony Makana and his partner Laurel Chapin. As the spotlight entertainer, doing erotic and sensational dances for the appreciative clientele, Delila abandoned all concern for her reputation as Mrs. Bo Buchanan. As she danced, Delila was unaware that a secret admirer had come to watch her perform. It was Brad Vernon!

Brad had stumbled on the club quite by accident after a serious fight with Jenny. Their relationship came to an abrupt end when Brad learned that Katrina was taking a job in Florida and intended to take Mary with her. Anonymously, he mailed a news clipping about Kat's hooker past to her prospective employer. Kat lost the job, and when Jenny discovered Brad's ruthless act, she ended their engagement—and this time their breakup was forever!

Another long-standing romance came to an abrupt end when Pat Ashley received the sorrowful news that her husband Tony had been killed while on a dangerous assignment in war-torn Lebanon. Viki and Clint offered what consolation they could, but Llanview only brought Pat painful memories. Working for her archenemy Dorian Lord at WVLE didn't help much, either. With a fond farewell to her loving friends, Pat left town to accept an exciting new job at a Chicago TV station.

*M*arco Dane was busy with two new jobs—running a legitimate health club by day, and a fly-by-night modeling agency, Dreamfaces, by night. For a while, he led a double personal life, too, juggling romances with both Samantha and Edwina. Marco struggled valiantly to prevent the two women from discovering his deception.

The Countess Echo DiSavoy, a world-renowned photographer, arrived in Llanview along with her brother Giles Morgan. Echo moved into the garage apartment at Llanfair, and set out to implement a mysterious plot against the very-married Clint Buchanan. Clint found her hauntingly familiar, but could not understand why she stirred such feelings in him. Clint became so drawn to Echo that one day he kissed her. Days later, they made love. In the afterglow, Clint's memory flashed to Gizelle, a woman he had known years earlier. Clint struggled to remember more. Who was she? He knew that Gizelle looked exactly like Echo, but that's all he could recall.

Echo knew all too well why she resembled this mystery woman from Clint's past. Gizelle was her dead mother! Firmly believing that Clint was responsible for Gizelle's fall from a bridge to her death, Echo wanted revenge. She planned to fake her own death and frame Clint for the crime. Echo carefully followed the plan that Giles masterminded for her . . . with one exception. She never expected to fall in love with Clint! Still, at Giles's urging, she followed through with the scheme by luring Clint to an old Llanview bridge, engaging him in a bitter brawl, then jumping to her "death." Dorian Lord, who witnessed the encounter from afar, declared in court that Clint had pushed Echo!

Viki and Marco tracked down the very-much-alive Echo, who confessed her deception under oath during Clint's pretrial hearing. When Clint was set free, Echo and Giles moved out of Llanview, leaving Viki and Clint to reconstruct their damaged marriage.

Handsome and suave David Renaldi had charmed Viki in order to get the job as conductor of the prestigious Llanview Philharmonic. David, however, went out of his way to avoid meeting Dorian. After his job was secure and his contract signed, David consented to see her. The rage Dorian displayed when she was finally face-to-face with him confused everyone. Only David knew the reason for this apparent hatred— he was the man who had walked out on her years earlier, taking their baby daughter Cassie with him!

David made an uneasy peace with Dorian, then struck up an easy friendship with Jenny Janssen. Soon, Cassie returned from school in Europe and, to Dorian's dismay, she was charmed by her newfound father, and vice versa. This, of course, only served to enrage Dorian further. In an effort to protect her daughter, Dorian had a legal document drawn up for David to sign. It stated that, in the event of Dorian's and Herb's demise, David would not attempt to obtain Cassie's inheritance for himself. This move infuriated David, who declared that he would never turn his back on his daughter again.

Danger followed David Renaldi to Llanview when it was revealed that this talented concert pianist had once been a spy! Years earlier, David had been involved in an underground railroad of sorts, smuggling terrorist rebels out of foreign countries. When David's old organization recruited him again, he refused adamantly. But before long, David Renaldi found himself lured back into a life of illegal espionage. He was risking his life, and that of his loved ones, by playing secret agent again.

David's actions aroused Dorian's suspicions. Soon, Dorian was recruited by the government to aid in their plan to trap and stop David. However, it turned out that the government agents who enlisted Dorian were frauds! Eventually, David and Dorian grew close again as they teamed up to assist the FBI in capturing the dirty-dealing bad guys.

David was cleared of all charges, but Dorian found herself in hot water—at home! Furious at Dorian for her lies, Herb, who had only recently reconciled with his wife, walked out again, this time taking Cassie with him! Although this saddened her, Dorian realized that she would prefer to share her life with David. However, her plans were stopped in midstream upon discovering that David had begun a romance with Jenny. Once again, Dorian was alone!

When her relationship with Marco went sour, Edwina immersed herself in a short-term romantic relationship with his younger brother, Gary.

$\mathcal{G}$etting married proved more difficult than David and Jenny ever imagined. When they first tried to tie the knot in February 1984, the unexpected arrival of David's "other" wife Liat threw the wedding into chaos!

1984

*L*lanview eagerly anticipated the 1984 marriage of Jenny Janssen and David Renaldi. And no one awaited the wedding with more zest than Brad and Dorian—because they were plotting to stop it! Brad had discovered, through one of David's contacts in the underground, that the groom-to-be had once married a woman and brought her to the United States, thus helping her escape oppression in a Southeast Asian country. Although David's marriage to Liat Reynolds was annulled shortly after her escape to the United States, a clerical error prevented it from being official. Dorian and Brad brought Liat to Llanview, and on the day of Jenny and David's wedding, she appeared at the church to make a startling announcement: *she* was Mrs. David Renaldi and the wedding must not take place! After stopping the wedding, Liat left town as quickly as she had arrived.

Another complication threatened David's happiness with Jenny. Laurel Chapin, terrified by the growing investigation into her partner Anthony Makana's shady activities, paid a visit to Dorian. The two women struggled at the top of the staircase in Dorian's duplex, then suddenly Dorian tripped and tumbled down the stairs!

David was the first to discover Dorian's unconscious body. For days, she lay in a coma. Upon regaining consciousness, Dorian (suffering from temporary paralysis) discovered that Jenny might be willing to give David another chance, so she stepped up her own scheme against the lovers. Dorian proceeded to tell Jenny a vicious lie, claiming that *David* was the one who'd pushed her down the stairs. Only if Jenny refused to

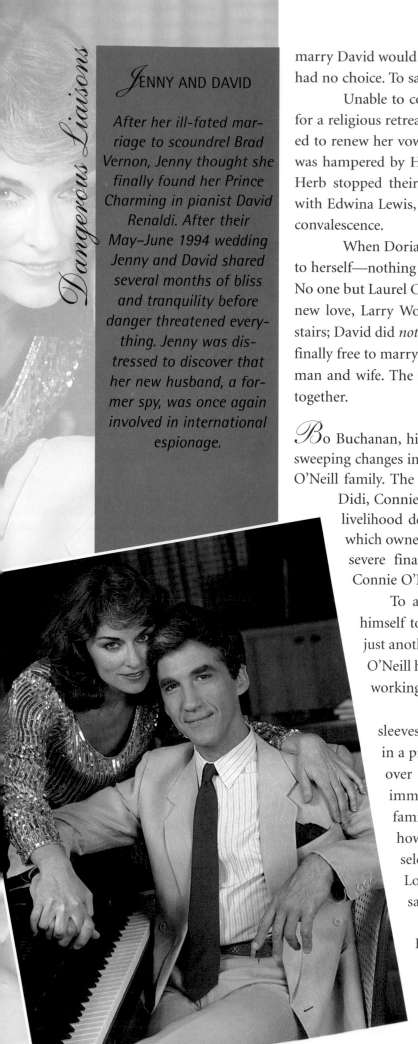

JENNY AND DAVID

After her ill-fated marriage to scoundrel Brad Vernon, Jenny thought she finally found her Prince Charming in pianist David Renaldi. After their May–June 1994 wedding Jenny and David shared several months of bliss and tranquility before danger threatened everything. Jenny was distressed to discover that her new husband, a former spy, was once again involved in international espionage.

marry David would Dorian keep this information from the police. Jenny had no choice. To save David, she had to break up with him.

Unable to cope with the sorrow of her breakup, Jenny left town for a religious retreat. Convinced that she could trust no one, she decided to renew her vows as a nun! Dorian's subtle scheme to seduce David was hampered by Herb, who realized that he was still in love with her. Herb stopped their divorce proceedings, ended his budding romance with Edwina Lewis, and moved into Dorian's duplex to help during her convalescence.

When Dorian regained the use of her legs, she kept the big event to herself—nothing and no one could stop her mission to seduce David. No one but Laurel Chapin, who after being hit by a car and healed by her new love, Larry Wolek, confessed the truth that Dorian fell down the stairs; David did *not* push her! With no obstacles in their path, Jenny was finally free to marry her man! On June 1, 1984, Jenny and David became man and wife. The newlyweds looked forward to a long and happy life together.

Bo Buchanan, his marriage to Delila in a shambles, sought to make sweeping changes in his life. He found just what he needed in Llanview's O'Neill family. The O'Neills—patriarch Harry and his three daughters, Didi, Connie, and Joy—were proud working-class people whose livelihood depended on their work at the Lord-Manning plant, which owners Viki and Clint were considering closing because of severe financial problems. The plant workers, led by feisty Connie O'Neill, hated the Lords and Buchanans.

To avoid conflict because of his name, Bo introduced himself to the O'Neills as Bill Brady, an unemployed laborer, just another working stiff. In rapid time, "Bill" moved into the O'Neill home and found irresistible comfort in this unknown working-class world.

Continuing his masquerade, Bo rolled up his sleeves and took a job at the plant, assisting Harry O'Neill in a proposal to save the place by having the workers take over the failing enterprise. Away from the plant, Bo immersed himself in the fabric of the close-knit O'Neill family and fell in love with eldest daughter, Didi. Didi, however, was engaged to marry the plant's legal counselor, Mark Pemberton, who was secretly draining Lord-Manning funds and committing heinous acts of sabotage at the plant.

Toiling day after day in the Lord-Manning plant, Bo clandestinely investigated several acts of apparent sabotage that took place. Mark ran scared. Feeling the noose tightening around his neck, he pressured Didi to elope with him. Just then, Didi found out that "Bill" was a phony! The stunning discovery that her "friend" Bill Brady was really a Buchanan propelled her to run away with her fiancé. In the nick of time, Bo discovered Mark's crimes, but the lawyer escaped, then took Viki hostage in hopes of leaving the country with her. Posing as Clint, Mark took Viki to the airport, but the real Clint arrived in time to struggle with Mark and prevent him from detonating a plastic explosive that he had brought with him. Didi, safe and secure, planted a big kiss on Bo's lips! Bo and Didi were in love!

The crisis over, "Bill Brady" returned to his old identity and faced new challenges. Harry, hurt by Bo's masquerade, ordered him to move out of the O'Neill house. Thinking that Bo still loved Delila, Didi began to believe that she and Bo were not meant for each other after all. Desperate to prove his feeling for Didi, Bo took two important steps. First, he told Delila that their divorce plans were still on. Second, he abducted Didi against her will and whisked her away to New York. In the Big Apple, Bo introduced Didi to a fantasy world that only the very rich could buy! For a moment, it seemed that she could happily live the dream forever.

When Bo and Didi got engaged, Asa teamed up with Delila to try to break them up. They brought Didi's first lover, Brian Beckett, from Tucson to Llanview. Brian was determined to win Didi back from Bo, and began his stay in town by giving Bo a black eye! Didi's sister, Connie, took a job at the Vernon Inn, and before long, she was engaged to the hotel's owner, Brad—blissfully unaware that he was facing financial collapse.

After failing in scheme after scheme designed to destroy Bo and Didi's relationship, Asa finally gave up. Brooding, he refused to attend their wedding. Instead, he packed up Becky Lee and baby Drew and flew to Arizona. Unfortunately, their private plane ran into foul weather and the Buchanans were forced to parachute to the ground before the pilot made a crash landing. Asa and Drew survived the night in an abandoned building, but where was Becky Lee? Asa searched high and low for his wife—but she was gone! Back in Llanview, the disaster forced Bo and Didi to postpone their wedding.

Was Becky Lee Buchanan really dead? Not at all! Suffering from amnesia, she was working as a waitress in a New Mexico tavern. Calling herself "Maria Hathaway," Becky Lee developed a close relationship with the short-order cook, Jesse Wilde. Meanwhile, Asa offered a $100,000 reward for information leading to her safe return. A greedy couple, Lou and Evelyn Maddox, discovered her whereabouts, but they demanded a cool million dollars for her safe return!

𝒩ow Llanview's Assistant District Attorney, Carla Scott rekindled her old love for ex-husband Ed Hall. However, their budding romance suffered irreparable damage when Carla was forced to indict Ed in the murder of mobster Herve Boudin.

In a lighter vein, Marco Dane discovered that his wacky, redheaded secretary, Maxie McDermott, had been lying to her mother for several years. Complete with phony press clippings, Maxie had convinced her mother that she was a successful, famous singer who lived in a mansion and was engaged to marry none other than Marco himself. The silly scheme backfired when Maxie's mother called to say she was moving to Ireland to live out her remaining years—but first wanted to stop in Llanview to see her daughter, the star. With Marco's help, Maxie pulled off the scam, convincing her mother that she was a singing sensation!

Samantha Vernon ended her short-term relationship with mobster Anthony Makana when she realized that she really loved Asa's nephew, police officer Rafe Garretson. Rafe and Samantha were married at the Crown Casino Hotel in Atlantic City, but the ceremony was interrupted when mobster Herve Boudin suddenly raced through the reception room. He had just murdered Leo Coronal, kingpin of an important Philadelphia crime family.

Leo's grandson, Rob Coronal, witnessed the shooting, fled the scene, and escaped to Llanview, where he took refuge in the deserted Atheneum Theater. There he met and fell hopelessly in love with Cassie Callison. Cassie, fed up with her mother's manipulations, had recently left home. When Dorian threw her a grand party for her eighteenth birthday, Cassie angrily burned her mother's gift—a check for one million dollars—and made a public declaration of her independence. She was equally enchanted with Rob!

Rob Coronal was the son of mobster Alessandro Coronal, who had changed his name to Alex Crown and gone straight, buying a string of legitimate hotels. After the death of his father, Leo, Alex was approached by Mob leader Descamedes. The organization wanted him to replace Leo Coronal as head of the Coronal crime family. Alex was reluctant, preferring a normal life for his son Rob.

Alex had raised Rob alone after his wife, Laurel Chapin, had died in childbirth. Now, years later, Alex discovered to his amazement that she was alive! Laurel was equally amazed to learn that her son, who was stolen from her at childbirth by Leo Coronal, was hiding out somewhere in Llanview. Together, Alex and Laurel tracked down Rob, who had disappeared after the shooting in Atlantic City. They shared a touching, but tentative, reunion.

Samantha Vernon had also caught a glimpse of the killer, Herve Boudin. Newly married and blissfully happy, Sam tried to dispel her doubts and fears that Boudin would kill her, too. Sadly, Sam's fears came true when Boudin shot her at the Vernon Inn health club.

Brad and Rafe, who were at the club, responded quickly and dis-

THE MURDER OF HARRY O'NEILL
1985

The opportunistic Mitch Laurence plotted to shoot Clint Buchanan in cold blood and then frame Viki's alter ego Niki Smith for the crime. However, when Mitch's scheme went awry, kindly Harry O'Neill was gunned down by accident as Niki, dazed by drink, looked on in horror.

Mitch had a foolproof alibi, so Tina went on trial for the murder. Only Niki Smith could save her—but she had turned back to Viki after the shooting and had no recollection of the event! On the witness stand, Tina's lawyer, Pete O'Neill, relentlessly grilled Viki, forcing Niki to reemerge and clear Tina.

covered Sam floating facedown in the hot tub. At the hospital, Dr. Larry Wolek pronounced Sam brain-dead—and told Rafe some amazing news. Sam was pregnant when she drowned. To the surprise of many, Delila offered to bear Sam's unborn baby. Rafe agreed and doctors swiftly performed an embryo transplant from Sam's womb to Delila's. When the procedure was completed, Dr. Will Vernon sadly turned off the machines that were keeping his daughter alive. Rafe, destroyed at the loss of his new bride, took a leave of absence from the police force to search full time for Sam's killer.

Carla Scott, now Llanview's Assistant District Attorney, was having a difficult time in the romance department. Her boyfriend, retired football hero Alec Lowndes, suffered from a lack of self-worth after a knee injury ended his career. Alec was forced to accept a job from the slimy Anthony Makana and reluctantly became official greeter at Makana's nightclub, Wildlife.

At police headquarters, Carla began spending lots of time reminiscing with her ex-husband, Capt. Ed Hall, about the wonderful times they shared during their marriage. Ed cared deeply for his ex-wife, but was busy romancing Courtney Wright. Realizing that she didn't love Alec, Carla made a decision: She left the football star and moved in with her mother, Sadie Gray. Sadie took every opportunity to drop discreet hints about how Ed and her daughter should renew their relationship.

Before long, it was like old times for Ed and Carla! They terminated their respective relationships with Courtney and Alec and rekindled the old sparks again. However, Ed and Carla's renewed love suffered greatly when Ed was forced to kill mobster Herve Boudin in self-defense.

Boudin's daughter Michelle (who came to live with David and Jenny) claimed she saw Ed shoot her father in cold blood. When no gun was found on the dead man, Ed was suspended from the police force pending a grand jury investigation into the case. Carla, the newly elected District Attorney, faced the dismal task of presenting the case against him in court.

With Rafe Garretson's help, it was dis-

*S*amantha Vernon took delight in the amorous advances of the slick Anthony Makana, but when she began to suspect that he was tied to the Mob, she broke off their relationship and married incorruptible cop Rafe Garretson.

covered that Michelle had hid her father's gun after he was shot and lied about Ed firing his pistol at an unarmed man. Ed breathed a hefty sigh of relief when the charges against him were dropped. The following year, Ed was dealt another blow when Carla left Llanview for greener pastures—a judgeship in Arizona.

*A*t year's end, blue-blooded Dorian Lord began an unlikely romance with blue-collared Harry O'Neill, who quickly had trouble dealing with his flamboyant paramour. Dorian, ashamed of her snobbish behavior, apologized to Harry. He accepted her willingness to change, however, and their budding romance intensified.

*V*iki received a shock when, out of the blue, Tina returned to town with startling news. While reading her late mother's diary, she had discovered that Ted Clayton was not her father after all. Armed with this incredible discovery, Tina was moving back to Llanview to find her real daddy. Let the games begin!

(cont.)

JUDGE
I asked you, Mrs. Buchanan, are you all right?

VIKI
I'm not Mrs. Buchanan. What are you people talking about? Wait a minute. What is this? Is someone trying to pin a rap on me? Wait a minute. You! You want me to tell everybody how Harry was killed? My God, it only happened a few minutes ago. Arrangements haven't been made for the funeral and for everything.

JUDGE
Ms. Smith, we understand how upset you are.

VIKI
(remembering what happened)
Harry came in and he didn't even know what hit him. He just, he didn't even see me. He just fell. He [Mitch] ran away. He killed my Harry. He killed the man I loved, and then he just ran away.

*W*hile searching for his missing wife Becky, Asa received much-needed moral support from his old friend, Lucinda Schenk.

1985

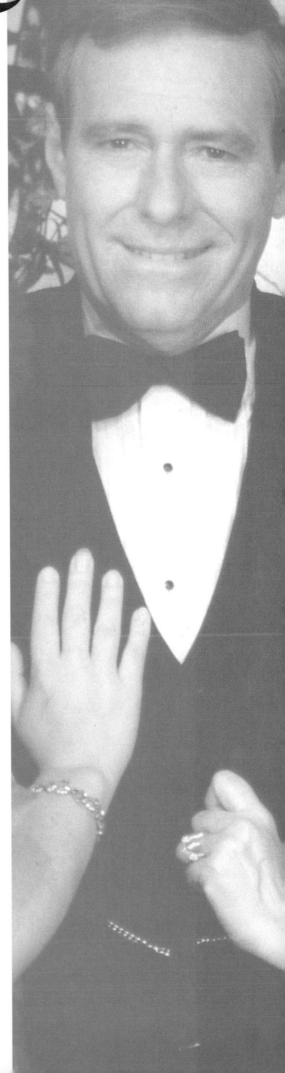

*N*ineteen eighty-five began on a strange note for Becky Lee Buchanan, who was now living in New Mexico and suffering from amnesia. Struggling to discover her real identity, Becky Lee agreed to go with her friend Jesse Wilde to his home in Avery, Tennessee, where she joined him and his sister Clover in the operation of their family tavern. Clover grew to resent Becky, who was straying further from her desire to find out her true identity because she was falling in love with Jesse! Working side by side, Becky Lee and Jesse became lovers.

*B*ack home in Llanview, Asa grieved over his missing wife—and took out his frustrations on the world. He immediately dropped his oil prices in an attempt to destroy his competition. His greatest threat seemed to come from fellow oil baron Lydia Farr, an American living in Venice, who was determined that Asa would not ruin her. Before long, both Asa and his adversary, Lydia, found themselves prisoners together in Venice—having been kidnapped by Lydia's devious partner, Peter Russo. Imprisoned together, Asa and Lydia became squabbling combatants.

Hearing of his father's kidnapping, Bo flew to Venice to rescue him, but was astonished to find sexy government agent Jinx Rollins working on the case, too. When Didi found out that Bo was with Jinx, she was jealous and angry, not believing Bo's claim that their friendship was innocent. Jinx's jealous boyfriend, Marco, followed them to Venice, and joined in the search for Asa. Also, a beautiful Italian waif, Giulietta Fellini, grew instantly fascinated by Bo, and offered her own knowledge of the city as an aid to the rescuers. Marco and Bo rescued Asa, who was stunned to discover that Becky Lee had returned to Llanview!

*J*esse Wilde, who had stumbled upon Becky Lee's true identity, loved her too much to keep it a secret forever. Along with Jesse, Becky returned to Llanview and her memory remained clouded until she saw her baby boy, Drew. As she cuddled Drew, Becky Lee's memory came flooding back. Now, which man would she choose: Asa or Jesse? Faced with this troubling dilemma, Becky Lee realized that she cared deeply for Asa, but she truly loved Jesse. Sadly, Asa turned Drew over to Becky Lee, who started her happy new life in Tennessee.

*B*o returned from Venice to find Didi unsure if she wanted to marry him. Certain that Bo was having an affair with Jinx, Didi ended their relationship.

Rafe Garretson became a new daddy in 1985. Delila, who had become Rafe's and his late wife Samantha's surrogate mother, gave birth to a baby daughter. Delila handed the precious child over to Rafe, who named her Sammi in honor of his late wife.

Bo's fun-loving buddy from his days in Vietnam, Michael James "Woody" Woodward, came to Llanview. Woody arrived in a helicopter, and announced he was in Llanview to make a movie, *Backfire*, starring Bo's and Asa's old flame, Mimi King. Bo quickly found himself caught in the middle as he watched Woody make time with his old pal Mimi, who was fast becoming something more than a pal to him. Woody turned out to be an agent working for the National Security Bureau, investigating the Buchanans.

More than anything, Bo missed his beloved Didi—and she still loved him. When Rafe proposed marriage to her, Didi gently turned him down. One day, Didi wrote Bo a letter, declaring her love, but couldn't bring herself to mail it.

Soon, tragedy struck when Didi, while checking out the new Section B at the Lord-Manning plant, stumbled upon illegal activity. It seemed that workers, led by her rival, Jack Simmons, were manufacturing microchips to be used in high-tech weapons being sold to foreign governments on the black market. During her investigation, Didi was blinded by an explosion in the Lord-Manning microchip room. Bo rushed to her side and, seeing her in pain, poured out his feelings. Didi, convinced that he proclaimed his love for her only because she was blind, still couldn't agree to become his wife. He wouldn't relent. With the assistance of a barber-shop quartet, Bo asked Didi to marry him. This time, she accepted!

*A*lex Crown could not accept living a life of crime. The Mob wanted Alex to replace his father, Leo Coronal, as head of the Coronal crime family. Alex had other plans, and refused. With the assistance of his son Rob and Marco Dane, Alex was going to see to it that all the Mob leaders were sent to jail. Marco infiltrated the Mob, tricking the boss, Descamedes, into thinking he was a loyal Mob lieutenant. Descamedes gave Marco a chilling test of loyalty—ordering him to kill Alex Crown! To accomplish the task, Marco "lured" Alex to a wooded area, where he assassinated him. However, as planned, Alex wore a bulletproof vest.

When Alex's letter arrived at the Crime Commission, Descamedes and his fellow mobsters were rounded up and thrown in jail. Even from the "grave," Alex Crown had reached out to betray the mobsters. But he wasn't done! When Descamedes was released on bail, he appeared on Dorian Lord's TV interview program. Knowing that the menacing Descamedes was a threat to his family, Alex took action. He lurked in the rafters of the TV studio, and in front of all of Llanview, shot and killed his enemy, then went underground.

*L*arry Wolek was finally able to put his memories of Karen in the past to enjoy a new relationship with Laurel Chapin. When Larry married Laurel, the only unhappy person in attendance was Laurel's ex-husband, Alex, who returned to Llanview incognito to try and stop the marriage. However, when he saw how happy Laurel was, Alex could not ruin the day for her. He retreated into the shadows.

Dorian Lord was the only person to discover that Alex Crown was alive. Armed with this weapon, she confronted Rob and warned him that if he didn't immediately break his engagement to Cassie, she would tell the world that Alex was alive. Rob—realizing that this meant a certain death sentence for his father—reluctantly asked Cassie for the engagement ring back. Cassie was heartbroken! Still, refusing to believe that their love had ended, Cassie simply would not let Rob walk out of her life. And Rob, heartbroken himself, could not run away from Cassie. Before long, they got back together in private, while continuing their charade in public. Eventually, Alex joined the Federal Government Witness Protection Program and shared a touching good-bye with his son, Rob. Finally free of Mob threats, Cassie and Rob were married.

Dorian's constant interference in Cassie's life finally destroyed her marriage to Herb. The Callisons divorced in 1985—and just after, made love in the courthouse elevator! Later, Dorian received a devas-

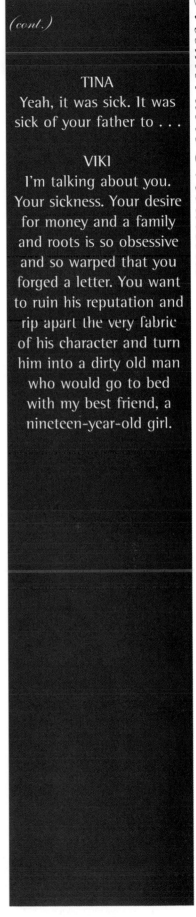

(cont.)

TINA
Yeah, it was sick. It was sick of your father to . . .

VIKI
I'm talking about you. Your sickness. Your desire for money and a family and roots is so obsessive and so warped that you forged a letter. You want to ruin his reputation and rip apart the very fabric of his character and turn him into a dirty old man who would go to bed with my best friend, a nineteen-year-old girl.

$\mathcal{N}$IKI SMITH RETURNS
1985

When Viki's long-repressed memories of seeing her father in bed with her best friend Irene Manning finally surfaced, her personality fractured— and her wild and free-spirited alter ego, Niki Smith, took possession of her body.

NIKI

You can't keep a good girl down! Hey, what's the matter with you? I mean, I didn't expect a parade, but how about a little hello for your nearest and dearest?

tating blow when her entire fortune was frozen by the IRS after Tina discovered that Victor Lord had once married Irene Clayton. Since there was no record of a divorce, Dorian's marriage to Victor was rendered invalid. Broke, Dorian was forced to go to work for an old nemesis, Asa Buchanan.

$\mathcal{D}$r. Ivan Kipling lurked back into Llanview along with a sidekick, a young, handsome man named Brody. They lived at Timberdark, which happened to be the summer rental home of Joy O'Neill, Cassie Callison, Rob Coronal, and Dan Wolek, Larry's teenage son, and his girlfriend Annie Barnes. Kipling, who was last seen being devoured by crocodiles after kidnapping Karen Wolek, now had a bionic metal hand! He simply wanted to be left in peace, and did everything in his power to scare the kids off. Kipling's stay in Llanview was short and menacing, and in rapid time, he retreated to his lair in the jungles of South America.

$\mathcal{J}$enny Renaldi was alarmed to discover that her husband David was once again secretly working as an enemy agent. Along with his old Communist comrade, Aida York, David completed a secret code to transport American military secrets behind the Iron Curtain. Now, David planned to defect to East Germany with his wife, Jenny, and their teenage ward, Michelle Boudin. At the last second, David changed his mind, telling Aida that he wanted to remain in Llanview with his family. Jenny watched in horror as the Communist agents shot David and carried him away on a plane.

For months, Jenny did not know if her beloved David was dead or alive. Just as she was getting her life back in order, David escaped from his comrades and reappeared. After explaining to Jenny that Aida had forced him to work against the U.S. government by threatening her and Cassie's lives, David came up with a plan to fake his death, then leave Llanview with Jenny. However, Brad Vernon discovered the "death" plan and asked Jenny to marry him.

This time, Brad wasn't being his usual selfish, mean-spirited self. He was doing it for Jenny, so that she could finally find happiness with David somewhere far from Llanview! After Brad married Jenny, he gave his identity and a forged passport to David. As "Brad and Jenny Vernon," David and Jenny fled Llanview forever!

After Jenny and David safely escaped, Brad, sitting in a waterfront bar, discovered something in his pocket. It was a note wrapped around a precious opal! The valuable "thank-you" gift was given to him by David to help him get a new start, too!

*T*ina Clayton's search for her real father continued with her discovery of a secret room hidden behind the bookcase in the library of Llanfair. The soft lights and music led to her realization that it was Victor Lord's love den. She also discovered eleven original paintings that had disappeared from foreign museums during World War II. When Brad saw Tina leaving the secret room, she reluctantly made him an accomplice.

Soon, Tina's adventures in the secret room yielded a startling discovery—a letter from Victor intended to be delivered to Viki. In it, Victor confessed to being the father of Irene Manning's child. Tina shuddered at the realization that she was Victor Lord's daughter!

Tina faced the problem of whether or not to bring this unsavory fact to Viki's attention. She knew that Viki would not be pleased to hear that the father whom she deified once seduced her nineteen-year-old friend!

When Tina produced the letter, Viki reacted with anger, insisting that it was a forgery, possibly created by Tina herself! Privately, Viki began having problems dealing with this new discovery. Violent headaches and the overwhelming tension of her own foggy memory

*D*ORIAN AND HERB MAKE LOVE IN THE STUCK COURTHOUSE ELEVATOR— ON THE DAY OF THEIR DIVORCE!

DORIAN
Help!!!
(Dorian bangs on the elevator with her shoes.)
(Crying) I broke the heel on my shoe. It's a new pair.

HERB
I'm sorry. I'm sorry. Honey, it's okay.

DORIAN
Oh, no! This is the absolute worst day of my entire life. Why am I crying over a pair of shoes when I'm stuck in an elevator!? I must look absolutely awful.

HERB
No, you look beautiful. I promise you, you do.
(They kiss tenderly, then sink passionately to the floor.)

VENICE, ITALY
1985

One Life to Live *went to Venice for the 1985 story in which Asa was kidnapped. Marco Dane joined the Buchanan clan in tracking him down through the canals and tiny streets of the beautiful Italian city.*

"THE SUNSETS IN VENICE WERE TRULY AWE-INSPIRING—ESPECIALLY THE WAY THE SUN GOES DOWN OVER THOSE BYZANTINE SPIRES. I'D GO BACK THERE IN A SECOND."
GERALD ANTHONY
(MARCO DANE)

of seeing Irene in bed with her father caused Viki's personality to split again. Niki Smith was back!

Wearing a red wig, Niki began frequenting one of her old hangouts, the Backstreet Bar. There she became reacquainted with an old boyfriend—Harry O'Neill! Harry was stunned to see Nicole again. He remembered how she had run away when he refused to leave his wife and kids for her. Harry found himself very much in love with Nicole, though his feelings were complicated by his new, sexual relationship with Dorian Lord.

At *The Banner*'s fiftieth anniversary gala, Viki praised her father publicly, and the guests were invited to enjoy a souvenir program commemorating the event. To Viki's horror, a photocopy of Victor's confessional letter had been placed in every program! With the news now public, a horrified Viki accused Tina, slapping her in the face, before racing away in shame.

Tina had other problems as well. Mitch Laurence, an unscrupulous scoundrel who had once been her lover, came to Llanview intent on marrying Tina for her newly found fortune. Mitch seduced Tina and continually exerted a sexual hold over her. While trapped in the secret room, Mitch discovered another document in the secret room. This letter from Victor Lord stated that if Viki should ever suffer a recurrence of her multiple-personality disorder, then his entire estate and control of the Lord Foundation would go to Tina! With Tina's reluctant assistance, Mitch began an evil drive to force Niki Smith out into the open again.

Mitch devised a secret plan to kill Clint and frame Niki/Viki for the murder! The scheme went smoothly up until the very last moment—when Tina caused Mitch's well-laid plan to backfire. Tina confronted Mitch, grabbing for the gun, and a struggle ensued. Dazed from drink, Niki watched in horror as Harry O'Neill stumbled upon the scene. Mitch, mistaking Harry for Clint, fired at him. Harry fell to the floor and died in Niki's arms. When she came out of her dual personality, Viki remembered nothing of this tragic killing. She stood by in stunned silence as Tina was arrested for the murder of Harry O'Neill. Tina's insistence that Mitch was the murderer fell on deaf ears because the unscrupulous Mr. Laurence had an airtight alibi. He claimed to be in Miami at the time of Harry's death.

During the murder trial, Tina begged Viki to testify as a witness on her behalf. Against the advice of her psychiatrist, Dr. Marcus Polk, Viki took the stand, where she was peppered with tough questions by Tina's lawyer—Harry's brother, Pete O'Neill. When the pressure proved too much, Viki turned into Niki in front of a courtroom of stunned spectators. Niki related the truth of the crime, and an APB was put out for the arrest of Mitch Laurence. Though he escaped, Mitch was eventually arrested and sent to prison.

Niki had saved the day, but Clint was terrified when Viki failed to reemerge! He was determined to get his wife back. Sending Kevin and Joey to live with their Grandpa Asa, Clint first committed Viki to a sanitarium, then took her to Llanfair. Niki managed to fool everyone into thinking Viki had returned. She perfected Viki's signature, read her diaries to learn the intimate details of her life, but was faced with one problem: How could she keep Clint out of her bed?

Meanwhile, Tina had been carrying on her own campaign to get Clint *into* bed! Her machinations reached a peak the night a drunken Clint passed out in bed. Seizing the moment, Tina climbed in next to him. Neither of them saw Niki when she opened the door. Shocked by the sight, Viki emerged. She tried to call Dr. Polk, but was chloroformed by Stick, a former cellmate of Mitch's, who had come to Llanview on behalf of his friend.

Stick was taken by surprise when Viki turned back into Niki and joined in her own kidnapping. She couldn't wait to split the million-dollar reward with him—it was Niki's one chance to be free of Clint, free of Tina, and finally free to just be herself. Stick and Niki's plot was soon discovered by a streetwise fugitive from justice, Bobby Blue. Realizing that Mrs. Buchanan was in on her own kidnapping, Bobby demanded a piece of the action.

Stick had other ideas. He planned to kill Niki and keep her share of the money. But before he could cut Niki's throat, Clint, Bo, and Rafe arrived on the scene and shot and critically injured him. In the aftermath, Tina learned from Bobby Blue that Niki was in cahoots with her kidnapper. Armed with the news, Tina approached Niki and issued an ultimatum: either she divorce Clint now, or Tina would tell all!

Niki was able to get a quick divorce, just at the time that Clint figured out that she had been pretending to be Viki. Clint shamed her into confessing, then agreed to keep the secret that the person everyone believed was Viki Buchanan was, in truth, Niki Smith.

Tina saw the divorce as the perfect time to try to snare Clint, and attempted to get him to marry her by claiming to be pregnant with his baby!

Jamaica, West Indies 1986

While their friends bundled up back home in Llanview during the autumn of 1986, Tina and Cord shared a romantic rendezvous on the Caribbean island of Devil's Claw. While frolicking under a waterfall, the newlyweds were blissfully unaware that their private island was swarming with terrorists. The island paradise of Jamaica offered up the perfect scenery for Cord and Tina's romantic romp.

"I COULDN'T BELIEVE IT WHEN OUR COSTUME DESIGNER HANDED ME THIS TINY LITTLE 'RUBBER BAND' AND SAID, 'HERE'S YOUR SWIMSUIT, JOHN.' A SPEEDO! I WAS SO EMBARRASSED PARADING AROUND IN THAT THING!"

JOHN LOPRIENO
(CORD ROBERTS)

1986

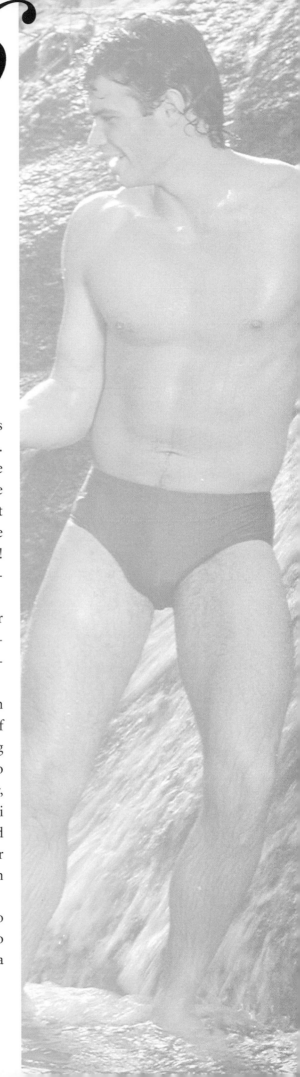

The new year began on strikingly different notes for the two Buchanan brothers, Clint and Bo. Not only did Viki/Niki divorce Clint, but he received the stunning news from Tina that she was pregnant with his baby—and would abort the child if he didn't marry her! Reeling from the shock, Clint agreed to support the baby, but marry Tina? Never! Fortunately for Clint, Dorian discovered that Tina was faking the pregnancy, and she promptly informed Clint.

For Bo, 1986 brought the answer to his prayers—despite her blindness, Didi O'Neill had agreed to become his wife. They looked forward to a romantic honeymoon after Didi underwent a corneal transplant that practically guaranteed that she would regain her eyesight.

Bo and Didi's glorious wedding appeared to end in tragedy when Bo was shot walking up the aisle! Was Bo dead? Hardly. It was all part of an elaborate scheme, engineered by Clint, to traumatize Niki into turning back to Viki. The plan worked—for a moment. Niki was aghast to see Bo shot! For a few precious seconds, Viki's personality emerged. However, Niki quickly returned, and blasted Clint for this elaborate charade. Niki refused to have anything to do with Clint, and began spending more and more time with her unwholesome friend Bobby Blue. Several weeks after the wedding, Bo and Didi, her sight now returned, left Llanview on an extended honeymoon.

As Clint continued to try to bring back Viki, Niki Smith began to panic. She decided that the only way she could survive in Llanview was to distance herself from Clint Buchanan. Wanting to be free, Niki wrote a good-bye letter to Clint, then took off!

Who Killed Mitch Laurence? 1986

Dorian made her first trip to Death Row back in 1986 when she was convicted of killing rotten Mitch Laurence, who was about to rape her daughter, Cassie. Dorian swore that she clubbed Mitch in self-defense, but with no proof, she was sent straight to the slammer. Only later, when an audio tape recording was discovered, did Dorian go free.

When Clint found Niki hiding at a country inn, he realized that it was time to take drastic measures to bring Viki back. He concocted a plan. Clint lured Tina to the inn under the pretense that he had given up on Viki and now wanted only her. He then arranged for Niki to show up at his room just as he was pretending to make passionate love to Tina. Clint's hope and dream was that the sight of him and Tina might shock Viki into reemerging.

Just as Niki walked into the room, Clint pushed Tina onto the bed. Witnessing this horrible sight, Niki stood frozen and transfixed. Everything went as Clint had hoped it would, and a healthy Viki emerged! Clint hugged Viki tightly. The woman he loved was finally back! They shared a tearful reunion.

The following day, Clint and Viki went to the Mountain View Sanitarium to have Viki evaluated by Dr. Marcus Polk. After a careful examination, Dr. Polk gave Viki a clean bill of health. However, another tragedy was about to send their lives into chaos. Right after Clint and Viki left Polk's office, the doctor was stabbed in the back with a letter opener—and Clint Buchanan's fingerprints were found on the murder weapon!

After Clint went on trial and was convicted of the murder of Dr. Marcus Polk, Viki worked with Rafe Garretson to find the real killer. They found evidence that the murder was committed by one of Polk's patients, a psychotic young woman named Tracy James.

Not only had she killed Dr. Polk, but after developing a crush on Dr. Larry Wolek, the former psychiatric-nurse-turned-patient murdered his wife, Laurel, too! Tracy tampered with the brakes on Laurel's car, sending her skidding to a tragic death. Once again, Larry Wolek was a bereaved widower. When Tracy escaped the mental hospital, she held Larry Wolek prisoner in the basement of her house, guarded by a ferocious Doberman named Illse. Finally, Tracy's reign of terror came to an end when she and her pal, escaped convict Stick, were killed in an explosion.

Viki and Clint prepared to return to a normal life at Llanfair, only to learn Tina had taken over the mansion using the clause in Victor Lord's letter that if Viki ever became Niki Smith again, Tina would get the Lord fortune. Viki had the Lord assets frozen and eventually won the Lord estate back. The path was finally clear for Clint and Viki to marry again!

On the morning of their wedding, Viki delighted Clint with the incredible news that she was pregnant! Clint, thrilled to learn that he was going to be a father, proudly told his father, Asa, how happy he was to be having his first natural child. Upon hearing Clint's statement, a cloud passed over Asa's face. It was obvious that he was hiding a secret!

*I*n faraway Vienna, a dangerous escapade unfolded for David and Jenny Renaldi, who only a year earlier had left Llanview for a safe new life in Europe. While living on the lam, they were captured by their enemies. Jenny temporarily escaped from her captors and managed to send a coded message home to Viki, Clint, Cassie, and Brad, who traveled to Austria to rescue their friends.

*W*hile Clint and Viki were in Vienna, Tina began seeing Richard Abbott, who had returned from Europe to take a job at *The Banner*. Just as things began to get serious between them, Tina intercepted a letter to Clint from a woman named Maria Vasquez Roberts. In the letter, Maria urged Clint to come to her home in El Paso, Texas. Intrigued, Tina went to investigate and met Maria, her husband Al, and their son, Cordero. She was disappointed to learn that Maria's mysterious letter was simply a request for Clint to give Cord a job as a photographer at *The Banner*. Still, Tina stuck around El Paso for one reason—Cord!

Instant chemistry sparked between Tina and Cord. Tina was charmed by the tall, handsome straight arrow. Over the course of a week, they spent every waking moment together, enjoying the pleasures of America's Southwest. Maria frowned upon Cord and Tina's budding relationship, accusing Tina of being too "trashy" for her young, naive son.

While photographing Tina in the stables, Cord confessed his love to her. Tina admitted that she wanted him as much as he wanted her. However, she told him that he was the wrong man for her. She was looking for a "Mr. Right" with money, poise, and sophistication—someone like Richard Abbott. When Richard called and asked Tina to come home, she left a note for Cord, then returned to Llanview.

Over Maria's objections, Cord followed Tina to Llanview and

*H*iding behind that saccharine smile, Maria Roberts resorted to new lows of duplicity when she set out to steal the father of her son, Clint Buchanan, away from his wife, Viki. When Viki and Clint's newborn daughter, Jessica, was kidnapped, Maria saw a way to use the tragedy to her own advantage. She coerced the kidnapper, Allison Perkins, into returning the child while she was dressed exactly like Viki's alter ego, Niki Smith. Believing that Niki was the kidnapper, and fearing for the safety of his children, Clint freaked! Just as Maria hoped, Clint broke up with Viki.

Dangerous Liaisons

got a job as a photographer at *The Banner*. He continued to woo Tina, telling her that he could give her everything she wanted. But Tina wanted money . . . lots of money. And that was something that Cord could not provide for her. Or so she believed. Unbeknownst to Tina, Cord was actually Clint's son—the product of his affair twenty years earlier with Maria. Clint and Maria had been teenage lovers, and when Maria became pregnant she never told him. Asa, disapproving of Maria and her Mexican heritage, paid off her mother to leave town with Maria. Clint was heartbroken by Maria's disappearance, and never knew that he had fathered a child, Cordero. Some twenty years later, Clint still knew nothing of his son, or of his father's involvement in Maria's disappearance.

Asa Buchanan was embroiled in a mess of his own in 1986. Tina discovered that Asa had, for years, been living another life! Posing as a sea captain named Jeb, he had married a woman named Pamela on the far-away island of Malakeva. Armed with this news, Tina decided to set Asa up. After telling an angry Pamela that "Captain Jeb" was really millionaire Asa Buchanan, Tina convinced Pamela to pretend to be on her deathbed—then get Asa to marry her for real!

Giving in to Pamela's "dying wish," Asa married her. Seconds after the ceremony, Pamela leapt out of her bed, and confronted Asa. She proclaimed herself to be the new "Mrs. Asa Buchanan" and promptly moved to Llanview and took her rightful place in the Buchanan dynasty. It was the beginning of a very stormy relationship! Asa tried everything to get Pamela out of his life. He even tried to set her up with Pete O'Neill. The more he ranted and raved, the more he fell in love. In time, Asa decided he wanted Pamela back in his life. However, it was too late! Pamela was already involved with Pete. Worse, Pamela planned to sue Asa for divorce and demand half of everything he had!

Asa worried the moment he saw Cord Roberts pop up in town. Instantly, he knew by the boy's name that he was Clint's son. He had to get Cord out of Llanview. Fearing that Clint would find out the truth, Asa arranged a job for Cord in Phoenix. Cord asked Tina to accompany him, but she said no. By now, she was engaged to Richard Abbott, yet continuing to string Cord along.

Cord was devastated when his father, Al Roberts, died suddenly of a heart attack. On his deathbed, Al wrote a letter to Cord, revealing that Clint was his actual father. Before Cord could see the letter, Asa stole it.

Returning home to El Paso for Al's funeral, Cord mourned the man who raised him and instilled a sense of morality and fair play in him. Tina flew to attend Al's funeral, and before returning to Llanview, she and Cord made passionate love. Unbeknownst to anyone, just days before his fatal heart attack, Al had confessed the twenty-year-old secret that Cord was Clint's son to, of all people, Mitch Laurence, who was pretending to be a minister.

Released from prison, Mitch Laurence returned to Llanview in the summer of 1986. More than ever, he was determined to make Tina's life miserable. Mitch adopted a wholesome new image, posing as a modern-day evangelist. In truth, he was a ruthless drug dealer and cult leader, who recruited and drugged young woman like wholesome Joy O'Neill, sensitive Allison Perkins, and teenager Mari Lynn Dennison to do his dirty work.

Mitch provided Tina with a bit of tantalizing news when he informed her of a secret he had unearthed: Cord Roberts was Clint Buchanan's son! The news stunned Tina, who was set to elope with Richard Abbott. Her head spinning, Tina kept Richard at bay as she contemplated her next move. Should she string both men along? Should she elope with respectable Richard? Or should she marry a Buchanan who didn't know he was a Buchanan? Quickly, she made a decision. Tina dumped Richard and eloped with Cord!

Using the information to her own advantage, Tina confronted Asa and blackmailed him into changing his will so that Cord would immediately receive one million dollars under the guise that the funds were left to him in Al Roberts's will. Tina had what she wanted all along—she was rich!

Reporter Cassie Callison, whose marriage to Rob Coronal ended in divorce in 1986, began investigating Mitch Laurence's operations—and nearly fell victim to his sensual charms. Learning of Cassie's tantalizing million-dollar trust fund, Mitch attempted to woo her. And Cassie, eager to get to the bottom of Mitch's dirty empire, pretended to fall under his spell.

Eventually, Mitch discovered Cassie's charade. When he attacked her, Cassie fought back desperately, striking him with a candlestick. Enraged and disoriented, Mitch knocked Cassie unconscious, then climbed on top of her. He was going to rape Cassie! However, just before he committed the dirty deed, a pair of hands picked up the weapon and hit him over the head. Mitch Laurence was dead.

Upon regaining consciousness, Cassie reacted in horror at seeing Mitch's corpse at her feet. Had she killed Mitch? Dorian rushed in, gath-

(cont.)

CLINT
Why the hell didn't I? I didn't run off, you did. You ran off! How could you do it, Maria? How could you run off pregnant with my baby and not tell me!

MARIA
Stop yelling at me!

CLINT
I've got every right to yell at you! I've got every right to snap your neck!

MARIA
My neck? What about your father's neck? He's the one who did this to us. He decided our future, Clint. I was a scared sixteen-year-old kid. What did I know? I trusted my mother and she was as scared as I was—scared that Asa would have us deported back to Mexico.

VIKI TELLS CLINT SHE'S PREGNANT (WITH JESSICA)
1986

VIKI
What happens to a person in nine months? A woman in nine months!

CLINT
You're pregnant?

VIKI
I'm pregnant. I'm going to have a baby, darling! Did you hear me? We're going to have a little Buchanan. Boy or girl. Yours and mine.

CLINT
You wouldn't tease a fellow about this, now?

VIKI
Oh, sweetheart, no, I'm going to have your baby!

CLINT
I'm speechless!

ered up any incriminating evidence of Cassie's presence, and hurried her daughter out. Despite Dorian's efforts, Mitch's chief disciple fingered Cassie as the killer. She went to trial, but the charges were dropped when Dorian confessed to killing Mitch.

Dorian stood trial and though she professed to killing Mitch in self-defense, there was no proof to back her claim. Dorian was prosecuted by newly arrived District Attorney Judith Sanders. The savvy Ms. Sanders was joined in Llanview by her husband Charles and their two children, Kate, a brainy and beautiful archaeologist, and Jamie, a troublemaking con artist who was secretly involved in drug trafficking in Llanview. Judith's dashing brother, private investigator Jonathan Russell, had recently come to Llanview and quickly became the latest in Dorian Lord's long line of lovers.

In court, Judith Sanders presented a convincing case against Dorian, who, in rapid time, was convicted of murder and remanded to Statesville Prison. Dressed in drab prison gray, Dorian encountered the wrath of an incorrigible inmate, Tiny. However, when Tiny suffered an epileptic seizure, Dorian (a former doctor) saved her life. From that day forward, the rotund Tiny and Dorian were the best of friends.

Lucky for Dorian, a hidden recorder had captured Mitch's death on audiotape. When the telltale tape (lifted and hidden by one of Mitch's robotlike disciples) eventually surfaced, Dorian was exonerated.

Viki passed out cold when she got her first look at newcomer Tom Dennison. He was in town at the behest of Cord's mother, the devious Maria Roberts, who'd noted his resemblance to Viki's late husband, Joe Riley. Maria was hoping that Joe's double could drive a wedge in Clint and Viki's marriage because Maria wanted Clint for herself!

After she found out that Tom could be Joe's long-lost brother, Viki took him to her cabin in the mountains. There, looking through Joe's old papers, they found Joe's birth certificate, which confirmed that he was born a twin. An old love letter from Joe moved and upset Viki, who found comfort in Tom's arms. The excitement of this revelatory day proved too much for the very pregnant Viki. She went into labor. In a blinding storm, Tom raced Viki to the hospital, where she gave birth to a bouncing baby daughter, Jessica.

Clint and Viki shared in the joy of

their first child together. However, soon after Jessica's birth, disaster struck. Before he died, Mitch Laurence had planted a posthypnotic suggestion in the brain of one of his faithful disciples, Allison Perkins. From the grave, Mitch instructed Allison to steal Viki's baby and make it look as if Niki Smith was the kidnapper.

Wearing a Niki-like red wig and a flashy dress, Allison ventured into Llanfair and absconded with Jessica. While the authorities, Clint, and Viki frantically combed Llanview for the missing baby, Allison took the child to her mother's house in New Jersey. Maria Roberts found out about Allison and manipulated the situation so that Clint suspected Viki had once again turned into Niki and taken Jessica. Viki was angry at Clint's suspicions, and it caused a rift between them. By the time Maria had gotten Allison to return Jessica, Clint and Viki had broken up. Their second marriage was over!

Earlier—during the kidnapping crisis—Viki felt the time was right to inform Clint of a fact that she had only recently learned. In an emotional scene, Viki told Clint that Cord was his son!

Cord was dismayed to hear that Clint Buchanan was his father, and that the million dollars that he believed had been left to him by Al Roberts actually came from Asa. Tina pretended to go along with Cord's wish to give the money back. However, while Cord was giving Asa a check for the money, Tina was buying the tiny Caribbean island of Devil's Claw, sinking every cent in their joint bank account into the real estate deal. When Tina whisked Cord away for a Devil's Claw getaway, they found the romantic paradise swarming with terrorists. The newlyweds barely made it back to Llanview alive!

When Cord learned of Tina's lies and manipulations, he broke up with her. Then, much to Tina's chagrin, he journeyed to Devil's Claw with archaeologist Kate Sanders in search of a treasure that was rumored to be hidden on the island. Though Cord and Kate maintained a businesslike approach to their journey, it was clear that an intense sexual attraction smoldered beneath the surface!

*Vienna, Austria
1986*

During the 1980s, One Life to Live had a flair for combining intriguing tales with picturesque international backdrops. Such was the case in 1986, when the soap wrapped up its long-running espionage story featuring Jenny Renaldi and her spy-husband David in exciting fashion by taping the climactic scenes in the breathtaking European city of Vienna.

$\mathcal{N}$ewspaperman Richard Abbott left Llanview after his fiancé, Tina Roberts, dumped him in favor of handsome and wealthy Cord Roberts.

1987

Nineteen eighty-seven brought the arrival of Max Holden, an irresistible charmer with big dreams. Max showed up in Llanview to ask Maria Roberts, a friend of his late mother, Patricia, for a loan to enable him to fulfill his lifelong dream of buying the Bella Vista ranch in Argentina. As soon as Maria saw Max talking with Tina, it suddenly dawned on her that this handsome newcomer could be of use to her! Maria hated Tina—she wanted her out of Cord's life once and for all—and Max Holden would provide the ways and means to make it happen.

Maria agreed to give Max a substantial loan on one condition: He must somehow find a way to lure Tina out of town. Max eagerly accepted the mission, unaware that though separated from Cord, Tina was pregnant with his baby! Cord didn't know, either. When Tina got the news of her delicate condition, she left a message on Cord's answering machine, but Maria got the message first and erased it! Thinking Cord didn't care that she was carrying his child, Tina fled town with Max. Their destination: Argentina!

In Buenos Aires, Max headed to the ranch and discovered to his horror that its owner, Don Alonzo, had been murdered. Max and Tina soon stumbled upon a drug ring operated on the premises by the evil Dante Medina and Jamie Sanders, who had fled to Buenos Aires to avoid drug charges leveled against him in Llanview. Now, Max and Tina, who was posing as his wife, found their lives in danger because he owned the Bella Vista. Dante Medina wanted the ranch—and he would do anything to get it.

NOT-SO-DEAD TINA SURPRISES CORD AND KATE MOMENTS AFTER THEIR WEDDING
1987

An unsuspecting Cord Roberts assumed his wife Tina had perished in a plunge over the Iguazu Falls. That's what made her grand entrance (with a baby in her arms) at his wedding to Kate Sanders one of One Life to Live's *most memorable events.*

TINA
Stop! Am I too late?
Cord, I've come so far.
This is your son.

Max knew Dante Medina all too well. Only a few weeks earlier, Max had romanced his impressionable daughter, Gabrielle, before leaving Argentina and heading home to the United States. At first, Gabrielle was thrilled to hear that Max was back! She hurried out to meet him, only to discover that he was married to Tina, or so she mistakenly believed. Dismayed, Gabrielle held back tears, and didn't tell Max her big news that she was pregnant with his child!

When Cord finally discovered that Tina was having his baby, he headed for Buenos Aires to try to convince her to return. Kate Sanders (who knew that her brother Jamie was hiding out there) journeyed with him. Cord and Kate grew close as they shared a sizzling tango in the streets of Buenos Aires.

Cord and Tina were reunited briefly, before Cord was knocked unconscious and Tina was taken hostage by Jamie Sanders and Dante Medina, who planned to flee with her to Brazil. As they prepared to leave, Gabrielle suddenly arrived and pleaded with her father to let Tina go free. Just then, Jamie decided to take Gabrielle hostage, too! Dante, refusing to let his daughter get involved, tried to stop Jamie. A scuffle ensued, and a horrified Gabrielle watched as Jamie Sanders shot her father dead.

In desperation, Jamie forced Tina into a small boat he had hidden in a jungle river. As he made his way down the river with Tina as hostage, a shot rang out, hitting Jamie. He fell into the rushing waters, seemingly dead. Tina, unable to free herself, could only pray as she tumbled over the ferocious Iguazu Falls and disappeared into the swirling waters.

After a fruitless search, Cord and Kate headed back to Llanview together. Max followed, selling his ranch and investing the money in Delila Garretson's new fashion design business. Max's straitlaced brother, Steve, joined him in Llanview.

Cord was devastated by Tina's "death." Despite her lies and their separation, he still loved her dearly. He also mourned the death of his unborn son, just as anguished Kate bemoaned the loss of her wayward brother. Cord and Kate comforted each other in their time of grief. Upon arriving home, Kate was doubly shocked to discover that her parents, Charles and Judith, had divorced. In rapid time, Judith was seeing Dorian's ex-husband, Herb Callison.

Clint and Viki's relationship continued to disintegrate. Headed for divorce, their broken relationship took another turn when

While undergoing delicate brain surgery, Viki had an out-of-body experience in which she visited Heaven and reunited her with her first love, Joe Riley. Joe urged Viki to return to Earth and the man she truly loved—Clint. Spurred by Joe's words, Viki recovered and reunited with her estranged husband.

Viki collapsed after witnessing a fight between Clint and Joe Riley's twin brother, Tom Dennison. When she awoke, Viki could not remember anything that had happened to her in the previous eight years. Not knowing who Clint was, Viki thought that Tom was her late husband, Joe Riley! Learning of Viki's selective amnesia, a judge refused to grant her a divorce from Clint for at least six months—which delighted Clint. He hoped that that would be enough time for Viki to regain her memory and realize that she still loved him, not Tom.

At Tom's urging, Viki went for tests that revealed she had a brain aneurysm which required immediate surgery. During the operation, Viki had an out-of-body experience in which she took a fantastic journey toward Heaven. Guided by her guardian angel, a quirky little man named Virgil, Viki joyously reunited her with many of her deceased friends and relatives, including Joe, who urged her to return to Earth and the man she truly loved—Clint.

Viki's archrival, Dorian, was busy in 1987 playing surrogate mother to Diane Bristol, a young girl she met in prison. Diane became like a second daughter to Dorian, which made Cassie jealous. Tension grew between Dorian and Cassie over Diane. Cassie's instincts that Diane was after her mother's money proved correct when Diane tried to kill Dorian. The devious girl's mission came to an abrupt end when she took a fatal tumble over the railing of Dorian's penthouse balcony.

Soon, Cassie and Dorian's stormy relationship hit a snag when Cassie became enamored with Dorian's boyfriend, private eye Jon Russell. Dorian was horrified and deeply hurt when she discovered that

ARGENTINA
1987

One Life to Live went on location to Buenos Aires, Argentina, and the surrounding environs for the 1987 story in which Tina joined Max as he fulfilled his dream of buying a ranch—only to stumble upon an international drug-dealing organization operating on the land.

her daughter was having an affair with her boyfriend! Needing to escape her pain, Dorian left Llanview to become the U.S. Ambassador to Mendorra.

Cassie and Jon moved in together, but problems immediately surfaced when Cassie came to suspect that Jon was interested in Sandra Montagne, an ex-girlfriend. When Cassie became distant from Jon, he found out that Rob Coronal was in town. He attributed Cassie's moodiness to the unexpected return of her ex-husband. As Cassie and Rob worked together to determine who killed Rob's father, Alex Crown, they grew close again, prompting Jon to ask Cassie to pack her bags and move out of his loft. Soon, Cassie and Rob reunited.

Melinda Cramer Janssen, who years earlier had been committed to a mental institution, was finally released in 1987. After years of therapy, Melinda now seemed to be a healthy, assertive, if slightly aggressive, person. With Dorian living in Mendorra, she moved in with Cassie at Dorian's penthouse.

Nineteen eighty-seven started out to be a great year for Asa Buchanan's nephew, police officer Rafe Garretson. Not only had he been promoted to Captain of Detectives, and welcomed his mentor Ed Hall back to the force, but he married Delila! However, their marriage began to suffer when Delila put her own career aspirations ahead of her family. Rafe objected to the long hours she put in as president of her own clothing company, Designs by Delila. As her designer career began to flourish, Rafe and Delila's marriage began to suffer. One day, Delila hopped into a taxicab and simply disappeared! Rafe's search for his missing wife proved fruitless. Where could she be?

As news of Tina Roberts's "death" spread through Llanview, Cord's mother, Maria, was wracked with guilt over her role in Tina's demise. She admitted to Clint that yes, she'd encouraged Max to take Tina out of town, and she'd lent him the money to buy the ranch. However, Maria claimed to have done this only because she thought Max would be good for Tina! Lying through her teeth, Maria said she never dreamed Tina was really pregnant. Her argument proved convincing— Clint believed her.

As the weeks passed, Kate and Cord grew even closer, much to the chagrin of Kate's snooty grandmother, Elizabeth Sanders. Fearing that Kate was falling in love with Cord (whom she considered beneath her), Elizabeth took action. To keep them apart, she secretly arranged for Kate to go to Egypt on an archaeological dig. Cord grew alarmed at the thought that Kate would leave town. She couldn't go. He loved her! Driven to act, Cord professed his deep feelings to Kate, who decided to stay in Llanview. Within days, Cord asked Kate to marry him.

In April, Gabrielle Medina, who heard rumors of a white woman being kept alive in the jungle, sent out a guide to investigate. He returned with a feverish and weak Tina. As her fever subsided, a bereft Tina told Gabrielle that she must have miscarried her baby in her terrifying tumble over the falls.

When Gabrielle went into labor, Tina helped in the delivery of her beautiful baby boy. Believing that Tina was married to Max—and that she could give the baby a good life—Gabrielle turned her newborn son over to Tina.

Tina hurried back to Llanview with the baby, whom she named Al after Cord's late "father." Upon her return to Llanview, Tina was aghast to discover that Cord was about to marry Kate Sanders. Hailing a cab, she raced to the church, arriving just seconds after the ceremony. The wedding guests shrieked in horror as Tina barreled through the church doors, with baby Al tucked safely in her arms, and promptly fainted!

Overwhelmed with the cataclysmic series of events, Cord was faced with a dilemma. Should he stay with Kate? With Tina's return, their marriage was now invalid. Or should he reconcile with Tina, and make a life with their baby? After careful consideration, Cord told Tina that he would do right by the child, but he wanted to begin a new life with Kate. Despondent, Tina tried trick after trick to win Cord back. Kate's anxiety grew as Cord spent more and more time with Tina and baby Al. Cord became anxious when Kate rescued her former boyfriend, mad scientist Patrick London, from a prison on the island of Zaroon.

Patrick proved even more devious than Tina in his quest to win Kate away from Cord. When he botched an attempt to kill Cord with an exploding camera, the demented Dr. London was sent to prison. Strangely, he was very quietly bailed out by Elizabeth Sanders, who arranged for Patrick to be transferred to a mental institution. Together, Patrick and Elizabeth plotted to get their revenge on Cord and the Buchanans.

When Maria Roberts learned from Gabrielle that baby Al was not Cord's and Tina's child, she threatened to expose Tina if she didn't grant Cord a divorce. Tina had no choice but to end her marriage to the man she loved. At the same time, Maria became unhinged. She wanted Clint Buchanan all for herself, and that meant she would have to murder Viki—and frame Tina for the crime! Wearing a blond wig, Maria tried to run down Viki in her car. Fortunately, Viki was saved by her gardener, Gilbert . . . who bore more than a striking resemblance to her guardian

(cont.)

"I NEARLY PANICKED BACK WHEN THE STORY CALLED FOR ME TO DO SOME FANCY HORSE-BACK RIDING IN BUENOS AIRES. HORSEBACK RIDING?? THE CLOSEST I EVER CAME TO HORS-ES WAS 'HORSING AROUND,' BUT FORTUNATELY OUR PRODUCER FIXED ME UP WITH SOME QUICK LESSONS AND BY THE TIME WE TAPED THE SCENE, I LOOKED LIKE I WAS BORN IN THE SADDLE."

JAMES DEPAIVA
(MAX HOLDEN)

Dastardly Deeds

CULT LEADER MITCH LAURENCE TRIES TO COAX MARI LYNN INTO BED

MARI LYNN
I'm sorry, Mitch.

MITCH
Well, you should be sorry. In fact, Mari Lynn, you should be ashamed. Do you realize you're the first of my disciples to reject my love?

MARI LYNN
I do love you, I do, and I believe in all of your teachings. You're angry with me?

MITCH
Oh, no, I'd like to think that the messenger above is angry. What I feel for you is pity. You know the Lord would have blessed our union. Go in peace, my little lamb. Maybe I'll bestow the honor on you at some further point.

angel, Virgil. Next, Maria applied a deadly poison to a pair of earrings that Tina planned to give Viki for her birthday. The poison, designed to kill on contact, accidently spilled on Maria during a scuffle with Tina, who watched in horror as Maria fell to the floor—dead!

Cord anxiously prepared for his second wedding to Kate. When he arrived at Maria's apartment to invite her to the wedding, Cord was horrified to discover her corpse. The wedding was postponed while Tina was arrested for murder. Max stood by her throughout the ordeal. During Tina's trial, the truth that Gabrielle and Max were really baby Al's parents came out. Tina was found guilty and sent to jail, where she encountered Jamie Sanders, who also had miraculously returned from the dead, only to be captured and incarcerated. Even more vengeful than before, Jamie wanted Tina dead!

Fearing for Tina's safety, Max and Cord busted her out of prison. During the prison break, Jamie Sanders escaped, too. Cord returned to Llanview, while Tina and Max hid out in a monastery, Monk's Hollow. Alone together, they made passionate love. When new evidence surfaced, Tina was cleared of the murder charges.

Back at home, Max tried to forget Tina by having a torrid affair with a suave and sexy older businesswoman, Lee Halpern, who was in Llanview to open a branch of her shady consulting firm, Dyna-women. In reality, Lee was actually Tom Dennison's not-so-late wife, Carol, who was believed to have died in a car accident. Tom's teenage daughter, Mari Lynn, had a bitter reconciliation with the mother she had never known. Fortunately, the girl found comfort in the arms of her compassionate boyfriend, Wade Coleman.

Asa was delighted to reunite with Lee's friend, Renee Divine. Renee, who ran a brothel in Nevada, had once had a fling with Asa. Now, years later, they picked up where they left off, and Renee was so charmed by her handsome millionaire that she gave up her "madam" business and stayed in Llanview to start a new life.

Realizing that Max could not get Tina out of his system, Lee married the newly divorced Charles Sanders—who died of a heart attack while making love to his new wife on their wedding night in Lake Tahoe. Back in Llanview, Max proposed to Tina.

*I*n Argentina, Gabrielle was shocked when she saw, while leafing through a fashion magazine, that Delila had taken credit for fashions that she had designed. Gabrielle got even angrier when she discovered that Max was Delila's partner. He'd taken advantage of her once again! Gabrielle came to Llanview to confront him.

Max's amazing discovery that he was actually baby Al's father did not deter him from pursuing Tina. Despite her lingering feelings for Cord, Tina finally agreed to become Mrs. Max Holden. Together, they searched in vain for Tina's real miracle baby, who was not dead after all! Assisted by Palupe Indians, a feverish Tina had given birth to a boy in the jungles of Argentina. Together, Max and Tina searched for the child, unaware that the baby, whom they called Milagro (Spanish for "miracle") was being held by Max's enemy, Rolo, an old associate of Gabrielle's father, Dante Medina. Rolo planned to use the baby to get revenge on his nemesis.

*O*n the run, Jamie Sanders hurried to Monk's Hollow, where he found Tina with Viki. As he was about to leave with them as hostages, Clint arrived—and Jamie shot him in the head!

Max managed to subdue Jamie (who was jailed) while an ambulance rushed Clint back to Llanview Hospital for emergency surgery. After hours on the operating table, Clint survived. However, his surgeons were unable to remove a bullet fragment, which left him blind. Worse, if the fragment shifted, it could kill him instantly!

Viki had a difficult time getting Clint to accept his blindness. Self-pitying and bitter, Clint needed help, and he found it in the person of Sarah Gordon, his tough-as-nails therapist. Sarah was a tough teacher! She refused to allow Viki or the rest of the Buchanan family to treat Clint like a helpless baby. Sarah's firm approach put her in constant conflict with her patient, who rebelled at her policy that he could live a much better life as a blind man by doing things for himself. As a result of her work with Clint, Sarah won the love and affection of the entire Buchanan family. This was especially true of Cord, who turned to Sarah after Kate finally called it quits with him and left town to pursue her scientific studies.

$\mathcal{S}$exy entrepreneur Lee Halpern decided that she could help Max, and Max felt he could help Lee. So they decided to help themselves to each other! Lee was the kind of woman Max was looking for—she offered him fun and sex, but like Max, she didn't want to get too serious.

1988

s 1988 began, Tina Lord had landed her man—Max. Now all she wanted was her miracle baby, Milagro, back! The child had been plucked away from the Palupe Indians by Max's enemy, the evil Rolo. With his female accomplice, Lita, Rolo came to Llanview demanding one million dollars for Milagro's safe return.

Max captured Rolo—but Lita had spirited away the baby to Italy. Tina and Max followed in hot pursuit. With Max posing as a monk and Tina as a nun, they entered a convent and found the miracle baby, attended by nuns. Then, with Tina rejoicing in the long overdue reunion with her tiny son, she and Max went home to Llanview, where they made plans to marry. Once at home, Tina introduced Milagro to the baby's real father, Cord. They renamed the child C.J.—Clinton James Roberts, after Cord's natural father, Clint Buchanan.

Tina seemed especially edgy on the day of her wedding to Max. Even Viki noticed Tina's uneasiness and questioned her. Was she doing the right thing marrying Max when she still had lingering feelings for her ex-husband, Cord Roberts? Tina insisted that she loved Max with all her heart, but standing at the altar, her mind began to wander back to the man who stood just inches away . . . Max's best man, Cord. During her vows, Tina absentmindedly blurted out, "I take thee, Cord" instead of "I take thee, Max." When Max heard Tina's blunder, he called off the wedding on the spot! Tina begged him, but Max refused. Tina was humiliated!

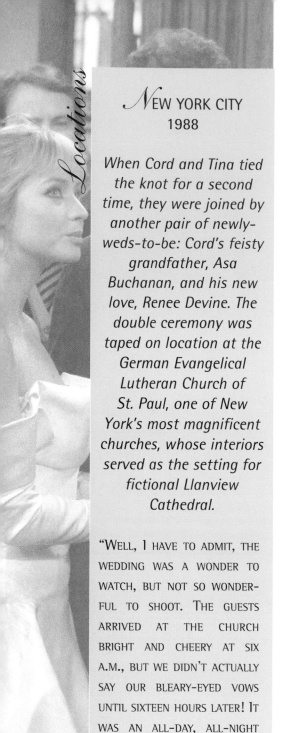

NEW YORK CITY
1988

When Cord and Tina tied the knot for a second time, they were joined by another pair of newly-weds-to-be: Cord's feisty grandfather, Asa Buchanan, and his new love, Renee Devine. The double ceremony was taped on location at the German Evangelical Lutheran Church of St. Paul, one of New York's most magnificent churches, whose interiors served as the setting for fictional Llanview Cathedral.

"WELL, I HAVE TO ADMIT, THE WEDDING WAS A WONDER TO WATCH, BUT NOT SO WONDERFUL TO SHOOT. THE GUESTS ARRIVED AT THE CHURCH BRIGHT AND CHEERY AT SIX A.M., BUT WE DIDN'T ACTUALLY SAY OUR BLEARY-EYED VOWS UNTIL SIXTEEN HOURS LATER! IT WAS AN ALL-DAY, ALL-NIGHT AFFAIR."

JOHN LOPRIENO
(CORD ROBERTS)

Tina once again set her sights on Cord. However, he was otherwise occupied—with Clint Buchanan's therapist, Sarah Gordon. Regardless, Tina made her move, using guile and her ever-present sex appeal to win him back.

Sarah was hurt, but understanding. She poured her energy into her job helping Clint, blinded by the bullet lodged in his brain, to become self-sufficient. Realizing that his days might be numbered, and wanting to live life to the fullest, Clint persuaded Viki to move with him to their Happy Horse ranch in Arizona.

No sooner had Clint unpacked his saddlebags when he decided to enter a grueling 100-mile horserace through the Arizona desert. He was determined to show everyone that he could overcome his handicap. Over Sarah's and Viki's objections, Clint saddled up his favorite horse, Oakie, and ventured out into the desert to practice. Clint was unaware that George Vasquez, the Happy Horse caretaker, had slipped asthma medication into Oakie's feed, turning the normally docile horse violent! Unbeknownst to Clint and Viki, George Vasquez was Maria's brother. Blaming Clint and Viki for her death, George was out for revenge! The drugged horse threw Clint, who hit his head on a rock and lost consciousness.

When he awoke, a groggy Clint realized that his vision had returned. He could see! But what he saw caused him to blink in amazement. He had been inexplicably transported back 100 years in time to an Old West town called Buchanan City. As he hobbled into town, Clint happened upon a showdown between two bitter rivals—the ranchers and the farmers. To Clint's amazement, the head rancher, Buck, looked remarkably like his own pa, Asa. It dawned upon Clint that he had somehow slipped back in time and landed in the home of his Wild West ancestors!

Clint was astounded by the sight of Buck Buchanan's right-hand man, Cody Vasquez; he looked exactly like Clint's own son, Cord! Equally amazing was Ginny Fletcher, the town's uptight schoolmarm, who was the spitting image of Viki! Clint realized that Ginny was Viki's own great-grandmother.

Before long, Clint learned why destiny had hurled him 100 years back in time. An old Native American clairvoyant, Clear Eyes, explained to Clint that he had been called into the past to bring Farmer McGillis's clan and Rancher Buchanan's family together to mend their fences. Clint eventually accomplished the mission and watched with deep satisfaction as the two families celebrated their newfound friendship with the marriage of Cody Vasquez to his true love, sweet May McGillis.

Clint's next mission was to reunite Ginny Fletcher with her estranged paramour, Randolph Lord. It dawned on Clint that if he did not accomplish his goal, then Viki would never be born!

*M*eanwhile, in 1988, Viki gave up hope that Clint was alive when a pair of boots and a skeleton were found in the desert. Believing he was dead, she held a memorial service to honor his memory. Bo, who had spent months searching for POWs in Vietnam, returned to the States and headed for the ranch to get to the bottom of Clint's mysterious disappearance.

*B*ack in Llanview, Steve Holden married his brother Max's former flame, Gabrielle Medina, and they honeymooned in Arizona. Steve stumbled upon George Vasquez's deception—and paid a painful price. To silence Steve, George hit him over the head with a poker and would have killed him; but Steve's life was spared by the sudden appearance of Blaize Buchanan, who had been hurled momentarily into the future to alert Viki that Clint had survived a western time warp.

Thanks to Blaize, Viki was determined to find Clint. With Clear Eyes's help, Viki made an incredible journey to Buchanan City, circa 1888. She arrived in the nick of time. Clint had become resigned to spending the rest of his life in the past. In addition, the local doctor had told Ginny (wrongly) that she was infertile. So Clint surmised that perhaps she wasn't Viki's ancestor after all. He didn't have to reunite her with Randolph Lord! He was free to marry Viki's lookalike!

Just as Clint and Ginny were about to exchange their holy wedding vows in Blaize Buchanan's saloon, Viki stumbled through the doors and locked eyes with Clint. While they shared a joyous reunion, Ginny fainted from the sight of her "twin."

Together at last, Viki and Clint worked to successfully unite Ginny and Randolph. With the future secure at last, Clint and Viki went back to Clear Eyes's cave, and—poof—they were miraculously transported back to the future!

At home in Llanview, Clint and Viki realized that their adventure in the Old West was but a distant memory. Was it real or merely an incredible shared dream?

*G*abrielle's life had turned into a nightmare! Her injured husband Steve was transported back to Llanview, where he remained in a coma. Max and Gabrielle rallied at his bedside. During the ordeal, Gabrielle and Max found comfort in each other's arms. Gabrielle's obsession with Max grew stronger than ever. She had to have him! With Steve clinging to life, Gabrielle seduced a drunken Max and they made wild passionate love. The next day, a sobered-up Max insisted that it would never happen again. But Gabrielle refused to back off. One night, in desperation, she

TUCSON, ARIZONA
1988

In a major storyline that spanned several months, Clint Buchanan traveled through time, landing in the Old West, circa 1888, and encountered Viki's great-grandmother, Ginny Fletcher. The soap spared no expense to present a story featuring authentic period clothing, stage-coaches, and gunfights. The scenes were shot on location in Old Tucson, an Arizona movie set that served as the site for several John Wayne westerns in the 1940s. Climactic desert scenes were also taped at Gates Pass, a protected natural environment in Tucson Mountain Park.

attempted to kill Steve by smothering him with a pillow, relenting just in time to spare his life. Steve survived, and thrived! He regained consciousness, and with the tender help of Nurse Brenda McGillis (a descendant of Buchanan City's May), he recovered.

In the meantime, Gabrielle lied to Max, telling him that she was pregnant with his child. Max discovered her charade, and continued to fight his lusty attraction to her. Eventually, Gabrielle felt compelled to tell Steve about what happened between her and Max. However, in her warped version of the facts, Gabrielle told Steve that Max had seduced her! Angry at his brother and fed up with Gabrielle, Steve demanded a divorce. Fortunately, Brenda was his source of strength during this difficult period. They fell in love, and once Steve was up on his feet, he married Brenda.

*I*n June, another bride, Tom Dennison's twenty-year-old daughter, Mari Lynn, married the man of her dreams, Wade Coleman. Prior to that happy occasion, 1988 had been a nightmare of a year for young Mari Lynn. After discovering that her mother, Lee Halpern, had been a prostitute, Mari Lynn accidentally shot and killed her. She was actually trying to save Lee from an attack by Donald Lamarr, Lee's former lover. Mari Lynn was indicted for murder, but when Lamarr was exposed, she was set free.

Soon after her marriage to Wade, Mari Lynn's life took an amazing turn when she was cast as one of the leads in a TV soap opera, *Fraternity Row*. The star of the show was Sarah Gordon's egomaniacal sister, Megan. A strong sibling rivalry existed between the two pretty blond Gordon sisters. When their father, environmentalist Roger Gordon, arrived in town, another side of Sarah emerged. Feeling that she never meant as much to her father as Megan, Sarah went overboard trying to please him. But despite all their problems, the Gordons loved each other a great deal.

Megan was a very career-oriented woman, afraid of relationships and rather wrapped up in her star status. She essentially shut out a personal life in order to cover up her insecurities. One man, Max Holden, was able to break through her facade. Max and Megan found themselves immediately at odds—especially when, as a practical joke, Max poured salt in her drink. Nevertheless, Max and Megan became a couple. When they finally did make love, Megan feared the new feelings of intimacy and tried to move away to California. Her producer, Randy Stone, made the move impossible by blackmailing her into signing for another year on *Fraternity Row* by bringing up a cassette of a porno film she had appeared in early in her career. Max helped Megan to counter-blackmail Randy; and before long, they were together again, much to the chagrin of Gabrielle. So she turned her attention to the newly arrived married millionaire Michael Grande.

*A*nother happy couple, Asa Buchanan and former madam Renee Divine, made plans to marry. Everyone agreed that Renee was the best thing to happen to crusty old Asa in years! The only resistance to the marriage came from Asa's newly returned son Bo. Throughout 1988, Asa and Bo were at each other's throats. Asa couldn't help but notice that Bo was acting strangely—he just wasn't himself. Asa couldn't understand why Bo was dating (of all people) Tina Lord! Bo and Tina? Never!

Asa was right on target! Bo was a faux! He was actually the demented Dr. Patrick London, who had undergone extensive cosmetic surgery to look like Bo at the behest of Asa's enemies Elizabeth Sanders and Lord Henry Leighton. Disguised as Bo, Patrick infiltrated the Buchanan empire and slowly drugged Asa, causing him to lose his mental capacities. "Faux Bo" hoped to marry Tina, then cash in on her inheritance. All the while, the real Bo was being held prisoner in a dingy dungeon, along with his wife Didi and his ex-wife Delila. They were watched over by a psychotic woman by the name of Ursula Blackwell, whom Patrick had befriended in the mental institution.

Suspicous of "Faux Bo," Cord stopped Tina from marrying him. Then, when word came that Patrick London had escaped from Langyard Clinic, everyone's worst fears were realized. Patrick was impersonating Bo!

On the run, Patrick hurried his hostage, Didi, to an amusement park, and it was there that the real Bo, having escaped, caught up with them. In the subsequent struggle, Patrick was thrown into an electrical panel. In the process, he grabbed Didi, and the two were felled by a massive bolt of electricity. Bo rushed to Didi's side, and cradled her in his arms as an ambulance arrived. Didi lived through the night, telling Bo that she loved him just before dying.

Becky Lee brought Bo's rebellious teenage son, Drew, to town to attend Didi's funeral. The other survivor, Delila, joyously reunited with her husband Rafe and their daughter, Sammi. Just as Delila returned to Llanview, Cassie prepared to leave town. She decided the time had come for her to join her mother, Dorian, in Mendorra. After her breakup from Jon Russell, Cassie reunited with her ex-husband Rob, only to learn that he was engaged to marry Englishwoman Joanna Leighton. Cassie, after

Families

Sarah and Megan Gordon were diametrically different, but equally dynamic. For sweet Sarah, honesty was always the best policy. Megan, the star of the soap opera Fraternity Row, *was afraid of intimacy and rather wrapped up in her celebrity status. What later became a close relationship between the sisters did not start out that way. Early on, Megan and Sarah had difficulty dealing with each other's ways of life. Eventually, they reconciled their differences and shared a close sisterly love. Sadly, their time together was fleeting. Both Sarah and Megan were taken from this earth while in the prime of life.*

making love with Rob one last time, bid him farewell and left for Mendorra.

Upon renewing her vows with Clint, Viki looked forward to her high school's twenty-fifth reunion. Strangely, Dr. Larry Wolek tried to convince her not to attend the affair. Still, Viki insisted, and found out that no one remembered her being at graduation. Through her own detective work, Viki learned she had left school during the senior year, had a baby girl (delivered by Larry), and had the memory erased by a hypnotist.

The discovery sent Viki reeling. Where was her child? And who was the father? Viki embarked on a long crusade to find her missing daughter. For a while, she believed that a young child photographer by the name of Christine Cromwell was her daughter—or so claimed Christine's father, Leo. As it turned out, Leo was secretly working with Michael Grande to scam Viki.

When Viki set eyes on Roger Gordon, she felt a strange sensation. Memories came flooding back to her. She soon discovered that one of Roger's daughters was her own. But was it sweet Sarah (with whom Viki had developed a strong and loving bond) or feisty Megan (who had been Viki's sworn enemy since the day they met)?

Just as Viki was trying to solve her daughter dilemma, Michael Grande began searching for the lost city of gold, Eterna, an underground mecca that had been blown up years before by its developer, Victor Lord. Michael tried to turn Viki back into Niki, who apparently knew the whereabouts of the lost city.

In November, Llanview turned out in style for a double wedding ceremony: Asa and Renee, and the second marriage of Cord and Tina. The weddings came off without a hitch. However, the same could not be said for the reception.

Two months earlier, Tina had survived the vengeful wrath of Patrick London's obsessed sanitarium friend, Ursula Blackwell. When Ursula discoverd that Tina was pregnant with Patrick's baby, she trapped her in a lighthouse with her elderly father, Cornelius. Tina's terrible trial came to an end when Cornelius ran his wheelchair into Ursula, sending her and Tina plunging through the window onto the rocks below. Cornelius died, and Ursula was remanded to a mental institution for life. Tina survived the ordeal, lost "Faux Bo's" baby, then happily married Cord in Llanview's first-ever double wedding.

Unbeknownst to anyone, Ursula had escaped from the loony bin—and was planning to blow Tina sky-high with an exploding wedding cake. However, instead of Tina, Steve Holden became Ursula's victim! During the reception, Steve noticed that the cake was rigged to explode, so he threw himself in front of his wife, Brenda. He died instantly.

Deeply saddened by his brother's death, Max refused to be consoled by Megan. She even tried to brighten his spirits by proposing marriage to him, but Max was inconsolable. Days later, Steve's widow, Brenda, received a pleasant surprise amidst the tragedy—she was pregnant with his child.

To make life even bleaker for Max, the unscrupulous Michael Grande secretly conspired with Max's mistress, Gabrielle, to wrestle away control of his hotel, the Holden Towers. Furious at her for stealing his hotel out from under him, Max grew to despise Gabrielle! Resolving to expel her from his life forever, Max pulled up stakes and moved back to Texas. But as Max Holden would discover, there was a fine line between hate . . . and love. He would return to Llanview, and cross paths with Gabrielle Medina yet again in 1989!

$\mathcal{M}$ax and Megan's on-again, off-again romance was constantly impeded by the meddling Gabrielle. Just when Megan believed she had earned Max's love, she was devastated when he testified in court that he still loved Gabrielle. Heartbroken, Megan broke up with Max for good.

1989

*V*iki's search for her long-lost daughter led her to dig through Victor Lord's private records. One day, she was perplexed to find papers documenting the existence of a mysterious place called Eterna. She read on, discovering Victor Lord's unlawful dealings with Roger Gordon's father, Danton, an architect hired by Victor Lord to design an extraordinary underground city. Designed to be the perfect utopian metropolis, the men planned to use Eterna as a fortress to store Victor Lord's secret stash of gold.

Both Roger and dirty-dealing millionaire Michael Grande had cloudy memories of growing up in a totally different world . . . a world they felt still existed somewhere near Llantano Mountain. Gabrielle, using her growing relationship with Michael Grande to do some investigating of her own, was hot on the trail of the lost city of Eterna. She was joined in the search by the money-hungry Leo Cromwell, another former resident of Eterna. He clearly remembered that the entrance to Eterna was located on Llantano Mountain—but where? Determined to find the lost gold, Leo called upon his daughter Christine to assist in his mission. She, in turn, asked Mari Lynn's husband, Wade Coleman, for guidance.

Through Michael Grande's machinations, Viki and several others, including Tina, Cord, Gabrielle, Christine, Leo, Wade, and Roger, were trapped in the underground city of Eterna! It was Gabrielle who found the entrance when she noticed a strange light coming from a hole in the ground on Llantano Mountain. She and Tina leaned in for a closer look and fell in! The others quickly followed. All the while, Michael Grande watched from afar, determined to find the cache of hidden gold. All were trapped when an avalanche sealed the entrance. There was no way out of Eterna!

Alone with Viki in the underground city, Roger Gordon finally confessed his long-buried secret. He related how he was raised in Eterna, but had found a way to escape to the outside. There he met Viki when she was in high school. They made love. One day, Viki watched in horror as the entrance to Eterna exploded. Believing that Roger was dead, she turned into Niki Smith!

Soon after, Viki/Niki gave birth to Roger's daughter—Megan! She had carried the baby as Niki, and though she had turned back to Viki during childbirth, Victor Lord immediately had his daughter hypnotized to forget the whole thing! Then he paid Roger to take the baby and leave town. Viki was amazed to learn that Megan, who had been her adversary, was actually her flesh and blood!

While in Eterna, Viki's and Roger's old feelings for each other began to resurface. Meanwhile, the demented Leo Cromwell found the gold. Michael Grande fought him for the precious cache, with Michael emerging victorious when Leo fell from a precipice to his death. The rest of the trapped group rejoiced when they made radio contact with the outside world. Led by Clint, the authorities drilled into Llantano Mountain to rescue the trapped prisoners. There was much celebrating as, one by one, the dusty survivors emerged. They watched in horror as Eterna collapsed behind them.

Home at last, Viki enjoyed an uneasy "reunion" with her reluctant daughter, Megan. In time, Viki and Megan mended their fences and came to respect, admire, and love each other.

$\mathcal{D}$uring the crisis on Llantano Mountain, Bo Buchanan found it difficult to concentrate on the strange doings at WVLE-TV, where he served as executive producer of the hit soap opera *Fraternity Row*. A behind-the-scenes stalker was terrorizing the cast and crew, and nerves were on edge.

Actress Audrey Ames, Mari Lynn's rival on the set of *Fraternity Row*, became an early victim when the stalker nearly strangled her to death. Then, on location at Llanview University, Bo and Sarah were nearly hit with a piece of falling mortar. Bo teamed up with WVLE-TV investigative journalist Melinda Cramer to unearth the identity of the guilty party: an obsessed *Fraternity Row* groupie and sometime stagehand, Neil Delaney. Before being apprehended, Neil kidnapped Sarah Gordon, and held her hostage in the University's clock tower. Bo heroically rescued her, and he comforted her in the hospital. As they grew closer, he confessed his feelings to Sarah, who remained hesitant to get involved with the recently widowed Mr. Buchanan. Bo pulled out all the stops to change Sarah's mind. Before long, he convinced her to move in with him!

$\mathcal{S}$oap star Megan Gordon wowed the audience of luminaries at 1989's delightful Daisy Awards, which honored outstanding achievements in daytime drama.

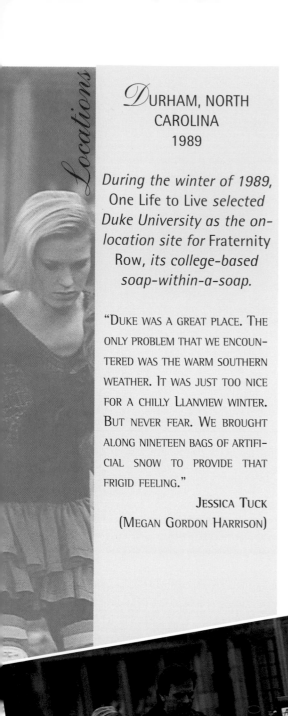

Durham, North Carolina
1989

During the winter of 1989, One Life to Live selected Duke University as the on-location site for Fraternity Row, its college-based soap-within-a-soap.

"DUKE WAS A GREAT PLACE. THE ONLY PROBLEM THAT WE ENCOUNTERED WAS THE WARM SOUTHERN WEATHER. IT WAS JUST TOO NICE FOR A CHILLY LLANVIEW WINTER. BUT NEVER FEAR. WE BROUGHT ALONG NINETEEN BAGS OF ARTIFICIAL SNOW TO PROVIDE THAT FRIGID FEELING."

JESSICA TUCK
(MEGAN GORDON HARRISON)

*B*renda McGillis, recently widowed from Steve Holden, discovered that she was pregnant with his baby. However, her new boyfriend, Dr. Larry Wolek, advised her to abort the child because of a severe case of toxemia. Brenda adamantly refused, siding with Larry's son, Dr. Dan Wolek, who had recently returned to Llanview to begin practicing medicine. Brenda's case caused enormous tension between father and son. Eventually, Larry decided to support Brenda's decision to keep the child and they reconciled. Still, Brenda could not get handsome Dan Wolek out of her head!

At the moment Brenda was about to give birth to her son Steven, Michael Grande's wife was being rushed to the hospital in critical condition. She had been a passenger in Michael's car, which Gabrielle had crashed into a ravine. Moments after the accident, Gabrielle delivered Alicia's baby, and both the critically injured mother and son were rushed to Llanview Hospital. Soon after arriving, Alicia died from her injuries. Her newborn baby, Garrick, was placed side by side with Brenda's newborn son Steven.

Gabrielle, riddled with guilt by the news of Alicia's death, sneaked into the neonatal unit to see baby Garrick. As she looked on, the baby's cardiac monitor suddenly went flat. Garrick was dead! Thinking fast, knowing that his son's death—coming on the heels of Alicia's—would destroy Michael, Gabrielle switched babies!

Over time, widower Michael Grande grew closer to Gabrielle, who still felt terrible pangs of guilt over her deception. Only her friend and confidante, Tina Lord Roberts, knew what Gabrielle had done and threatened to spill the beans. Fortunately, Gabrielle was able to convince Tina to keep her mouth shut.

*T*ina was much more concerned with her pursuit of the elusive Crown Jewels of Mendorra which eventually led her to Atlantic City. While there she was held captive by two escaped criminals she thought she would never see again: Ursula Blackwell and Jamie Sanders! Thirsting for revenge, the demented Ursula strapped Tina in an electric chair and would have fried her to death had not the police arrived to save the day! Jamie and Ursula were arrested and returned to the slammer for good!

*B*ack in Llanview, Michael Grande proposed marriage to Gabrielle just weeks after his wife Alicia's death. However, at the last moment, Gabrielle realized she could not marry a man she didn't love! Just before walking down the aisle with Michael, she fled the chapel in tears.

*B*renda refused to believe her baby was dead. And she was delighted to be proven right! When Gabrielle's baby switch was finally exposed, she was put on trial for the crime. Gabrielle's attorney, Jon Russell, set out to show that his client was mentally unstable when she committed the crime. To accomplish this, he called Max Holden (recently returned from an extended sojourn to Texas) to the witness stand and badgered him to admit that he had, over a period of years, toyed with Gabrielle's emotions, first telling her that he loved her, then telling her he loved Megan. Max, under intense pressure from Jon's hard-hitting questions, confessed to a stunned courthouse that he still loved Gabrielle! Megan, listening in horror to Max, ran from the courtroom, tears streaming down her face.

Max tried to win back Megan's love, but it was too late. Their romance was over for good. Gabrielle was found guilty by reason of insanity and remanded to a halfway house with Tina, who was sentenced to six months for helping to cover the notorious baby switch.

Reeling from her breakup with Max, Megan poured her energies into her acting career. On *Fraternity Row*, she received the acting challenge of a lifetime when she was asked to play a dual role. In addition to the straitlaced "Roxanne," Megan would now play "Ruby Bright," Roxanne's twin sister, a much more wild character. Viki immediately saw a parallel to Niki Smith, and was concerned for her daughter; but Megan was determined to take on the challenge, and even dressed up as Ruby and went to Atlantic City to do "field research." It was there that she met up with Marco Dane, who considered her his lucky charm. When Megan returned to Llanview, Marco followed her, tried to keep her from Max, and caused a series of misadventures leading up to the annual Daisy Awards ceremony, where Megan beat out her rival Spring Skye and took home a statuette as Outstanding Actress.

*A*ustin Buchanan, son of Asa's brother, Pike, had arrived in town in 1989 and became obsessed with Sarah. He set out to steal her from Bo— but how? He knew how much Sarah cared for Bo and saw the elimination of his cousin as the only solution. Austin knew that Bo and Michael Grande were mortal enemies, so he rigged the brakes on Michael's car to fail. The accident that killed Alicia Grande and her baby, and injured

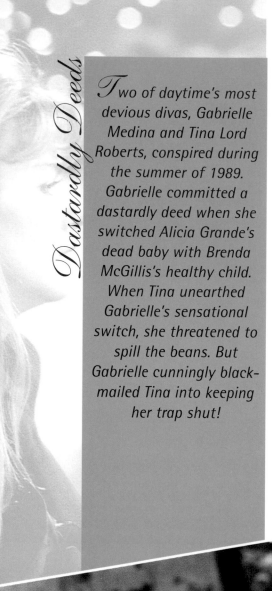
Two of daytime's most devious divas, Gabrielle Medina and Tina Lord Roberts, conspired during the summer of 1989. Gabrielle committed a dastardly deed when she switched Alicia Grande's dead baby with Brenda McGillis's healthy child. When Tina unearthed Gabrielle's sensational switch, she threatened to spill the beans. But Gabrielle cunningly black-mailed Tina into keeping her trap shut!

Gabrielle, had not been an "accident" after all! To end his plan on the perfect note, he framed Bo for the crime.

Sarah, suspecting that Austin was the real culprit, pretended to be in love with him in order to extract a confession. Austin eventually confessed to the crime, but then wanted Sarah to make love to him. She tried to put him off, but he became angry and brutally raped her.

After the rape, Sarah shot Austin. To protect her, Cord and Asa buried Austin's body. However, the evil Buchanan cousin was not dead after all! He crawled out of his shallow grave and sought revenge on Sarah. Austin's reign of terror quickly came to an end after he took Viki and Megan hostage. Clint found them and shot Austin, who plunged out a high-rise window to his death—but not before shooting Viki!

The traumatic shooting shocked Megan and caused her personality to suddenly split. Instantly, Megan believed she was her soap opera alter ego, the free-spirited Ruby Bright. "Ruby" ran off with Marco Dane. Though he loved Ruby, Marco's guilt got the best of him. Marco agreed to Clint's plan to shock Megan back to reality by arranging for him to marry Ruby. The scheme proved successful—Megan snapped out of her strange state just before tying the knot with Marco. Leaving a dejected Marco in the dust, Megan devoted her romantic attention to a new Llanview arrival, Prince Raymond Hohenstein from Mendorra, who'd lost his eyesight in a car accident. Though she loved Raymond, she realized that he stood to lose his throne by marrying a commoner like her, and she returned to Llanview to get on with her life.

*S*till smarting from his breakup with Megan, Max found himself drawn to the beguiling Gabrielle. Another fiery young woman, Andy Harrison, entered his life during the summer of 1989. One night, Max found Andy tearing up his bar, Max's Place! She turned out to be the half-sister he had never known. Andy angrily confronted Max, informing him that their mother, Patricia, had recently died—and that she blamed Max for her death. Max, who had been raised by his stepmother, despised Patricia Holden for leaving him and his brother Steve when they were kids. Patricia remarried and gave birth to Andy. Many years later, Patricia fell terminally ill and sent letters to Max begging him to come see her. Max, still pained by his mother's desertion, had ignored them; he hadn't even opened them! In time, Max and Andy reconciled. The spunky Andy Harrison settled into life in Llanview, romancing both Dan Wolek and Brenda's kid brother, Tyler McGillis.

*S*arah Gordon was anguished to learn that she was pregnant as a result of rape. Should she abort the child? Sarah was saved from the decision when she suffered a miscarriage. After months of therapy, the traumatized Sarah slowly put the painful past behind her, and became engaged to Bo. They happily planned their wedding, but the highly anticipated event turned sour when Clint and Sarah's father, Roger, could not keep from getting into jealous fights over Viki. Sarah refused to marry Bo until the fighting in the family ceased! Complicating matters, Roger revealed another secret truth that Viki had blocked out. As kids, Roger and Viki had gotten married!

At Clint's insistence, Roger and Viki's still-valid marriage was quickly annulled. Still, Roger persisted in his quest to win Viki's affections. For a time, Clint moved to the Buchanan ranch in Arizona, and gave Viki an ultimatum: either she move with him, or their marriage was over. When Viki bid Clint adieu, he turned to Gabrielle's mother, Julia Medina (the society editor of *The Banner*) for solace. Julia followed Clint to Arizona, and tried to seduce him. However, Clint pulled away, resolving to return to Llanview and give his marriage to Viki one more try.

*W*hile serving nights in the halfway house, Tina got a day job working for Ambrose and Serena Wyman who ran the Lord Love the Children Foundation, a nonprofit international adoption agency. Tina quickly discovered that the seemingly good-hearted Wymans were actually crooks. They were kidnapping children and selling them to the highest bidder!

With the help of Cord, Max, and Gabrielle, Tina confronted the Wymans in an abandoned warehouse where they were holding little Al Holden. Fearing for her son, Gabrielle charged at Ambrose, who raised his gun to her. Max, seeing that Gabrielle was about to be shot, leaped in front of her—and took a bullet meant for her! As the police apprehended the baby-sellers, Max was rushed to the hospital in critical condition, with an anguished Gabrielle holding his hand every step of the way.

𝒥ake and Megan couldn't go public with their love, because Jake was busy woo-ing Mob princess Charlotte Hesser in a quest to get the goods on her father, Carlo. So, in a symbolic show of their deep affection for each other, Jake and Megan married themselves in a simple ceremony in Viki's mountain cabin.

1990

 t Llanview Hospital, Max Holden clung to life after heroically taking a bullet meant for Gabrielle. As he hovered near death, Gabrielle waited anxiously outside the ICU and made an extraordinary pact with God. If the Almighty allowed Max to survive, then Gabrielle swore that she would devote her life to the church. Miraculously, Max rallied and recovered.

As he regained his health, Max was finally ready to love Gabrielle—but now she would have nothing to do with him! Without telling Max, Gabrielle had decided to become a nun! At the convent, Sister Amelia urged Gabrielle to carefully consider what she was about to do. The sister introduced Gabrielle to Father Tony Vallone, a former-boxer-turned-priest, who tried in vain to make Gabrielle change her mind. Her terrible nightmares, in which Max was consumed in flames, convinced Gabrielle that she must remove herself from Max's life for his own good! Gabrielle's argument proved persuasive to Father Tony, who reluctantly agreed to take her to the convent.

Max discovered Gabrielle's whereabouts and raced to the convent. When she refused to let him in her room, Max scaled the convent wall and climbed through her window. He pulled Gabrielle into a kiss, but she retreated, then ran blindly into the night. He caught up to her on the convent lawn, where he forced her to declare her love for him. The night air was thick with passion as Max kissed Gabrielle again. This time, she couldn't resist. They sank down to the ground and, by the light of the full moon, made love on the convent lawn.

IN MENDORRA, SARAH
THINKS SHE IS MARRYING
PRINCE RAYMOND—BUT
FINDS HER TRUE LOVE BO
BY HER SIDE!
1990

SARAH
What are you doing here?

BO
Shh, honey. I'm trying to
hear what this guy says.

SARAH
Where's Prince Raymond?

BO
You ask too many ques-
tions, you know that!

SARAH
I'm trying to understand
what's going on here.

BO
You said this is the kind
of wedding you
always
dreamed
of, so just
don't worry!
When the
time is right,
just say "I
do!"

Later that night, Max took Gabrielle to a country inn where he comforted her, assuring his worried lover that what they were doing was right. When he asked her to marry him, Gabrielle wrapped her arms around him and instantly agreed. After making love again, the reunited lovers drifted off to sleep in each other's arms. During the night, Gabrielle woke up screaming: the nightmare of Max, consumed in flames, had returned. Soon, her fears were realized. On the way to pick up a wedding ring, Max crashed his car into a tree. Gabrielle, waiting in her wedding dress, cried out in pain when she learned that Max's charred corpse had been pulled from the fiery wreckage! In actuality, Max Holden was alive; a hitchhiker was the unfortunate victim of the blazing wreckage. A young woman, Lily Beecham, saved Max's life, but his face was horribly burned beyond recognition. Max decided to allow his friends and family to believe he was dead rather than put them through the agony of living with his deformity.

Father Tony Vallone proved a valuable friend to Gabrielle in her time of grief. These were difficult times for Tony, because he had fallen in love with Gabrielle but was fighting his feelings to remain committed to the church. In time, Gabrielle fell in love again, too, with a newcomer, Matt Kingston. She was instantly attracted to this handsome fellow who reminded her so much of her beloved Max. Unbeknownst to anyone, Matt Kingston was Max! He had undergone extensive cosmetic surgery at the clinic of Dr. Jared St. James and returned to town to woo Gabrielle.

Eventually, Max confessed his true identity to Gabrielle; they married in a beautiful ceremony, presided over by a conflicted Father Tony Vallone—whose feelings for Gabrielle were far from resolved.

Later, Max discovered that Asa had cheated his father Wingate out of oil-rich land years earlier. Filled with rage, Max swore revenge! Gabrielle found out that Asa slept with Max's mother about the time Max was conceived. She wondered: Could Max be Asa's son? To her disappointment, the greedy Mrs. Holden discovered that Max was not Asa's son. Wanting the Buchanan money and power, she bribed an old midwife, Du Ann Demerest, to claim that Asa *had* fathered Max! Shocked by the news, Asa now wanted to do right by him, but Max rejected his "father."

Meanwhile, Gabrielle's treachery was just beginning. Father Tony Vallone caught her embezzling funds from Outlook House and, against his better judgement, helped her cover it up. In order to keep him quiet about her many financial indiscretions, Gabrielle seduced the priest. He gave in to his longing for the temptress; but later, disgusted with himself and the power Gabrielle held over him, Tony ordered her out of his life.

In 1990, Cord and Tina's second marriage was falling apart! Cord had finally had enough of Tina's lies and deceits. The final straw came when Tina became jealous of Cord's platonic friendship with Gabrielle's sweet young ballerina sister, Debra. When Cord caught his wife scheming to get

Memorable Moments

BO/SARAH/MEGAN SKI DOWN THE MOUNTAINS TO ESCAPE THE EVIL PRICE ROLAND OF MENDORRA 1990

SARAH
There's only one problem here . . . I've only been skiing once in my life!

MEGAN
Maybe I'll be able to snowplow, but I doubt it.

BO
Looks like you ladies are gonna have a crash course in downhill skiing.

SARAH
Bo, isn't there another way?

BO
Honey, I always promised you an exciting honeymoon. This is it!!

NIKI STOPS JOHNNY DEE FROM KIDNAPPING DRUGGED TINA
1990

VIKI
Freeze, bozo! Now, you are gonna do exactly what I say. You're gonna turn around real slow, and you're gonna put Tina back on the bed. Get it? And if you try any funny stuff, you are gonna have the worst case of heartburn in the history of the world. Now move!

JOHNNY
Tina and I love each other.

rid of Debra, he confronted her and demanded a divorce. Realizing that she had little hope of winning Cord back, Tina took their son, C.J., and moved to San Diego. With Tina gone, Cord embarked upon a new adventure that would soon take him halfway around the world: to the regal province of Mendorra, where a brewing feud between two princes threatened to explode into all-out war.

Early in 1990, Megan Gordon returned with her sister Sarah to Mendorra to help her former love, Prince Raymond, who was having a difficult time dealing with his blindness.

Upon their arrival, the Gordon sisters were shocked to discover that Raymond's jealous and power-hungry younger brother, Roland, wanted the crown for himself—and used them as pawns in his quest! Roland held Megan and Sarah against their will. Later, he announced to a stunned kingdom that Raymond had fallen in love with his "commoner" therapist, Sarah, and was thereby relinquishing the throne. Fearing for Sarah's and Megan's safety, Raymond had no choice but to acquiesce to his wicked brother's demands.

Prince Roland forced Sarah to send Bo a "Dear John" letter. However, Bo refused to believe that Sarah was dumping him. With Cord by his side, Bo rushed to Mendorra to rescue his ladylove. In Mendorra, Bo and Cord teamed up with Ambassador Dorian Lord, her daughter Cassie, and Debra Medina (who was appearing with the Mendorran Ballet) to infiltrate the royal palace—just as a despondent Sarah was about to reluctantly marry Prince Raymond. Sarah couldn't believe her eyes when she realized that the bearded man in full military regalia standing next to her at the altar was Bo disguised as Raymond! She joyously spoke her vows and married her "prince"!

Right after the ceremony, the bride and groom raced out of the castle! With both the Mendorran troops and Prince Roland in hot pursuit, Bo and Sarah donned skis and "schussed" their way down a mountain. They made it to freedom, but sadly, Raymond (who miraculously regained his eyesight in the nick of time) had no choice but to shoot and kill his wayward brother.

*I*n a close election, Viki Buchanan narrowly defeated Herb Callison and was elected the new mayor of Llanview. Viki vowed to stamp out drugs in Llanview—drugs that were being distributed by Michael Grande and Llanview's new crime boss, Carlo Hesser. During the campaign, Viki fingered Carlo as the drug boss, splashing his name across the front page of *The Banner*. The battle lines between Carlo and Viki had been drawn!

Soon after the election, Viki and Clint mended their relationship, and Viki gently told Roger Gordon that, while she would always love him, her place was with Clint.

The new mayor faced immediate danger when Carlo Hesser's son, Johnny Dee, ordered Llanview's corrupt Police Commissioner Harding to assassinate Viki. During a fund-raiser, Harding shot Viki. While recovering from the bullet wound, she suffered a stroke that rendered her speechless and paralyzed. With her usual poise and perseverance, Viki struggled to recover.

*I*n March, Megan Gordon encountered a man who would quickly change her life. His name was Jake Harrison—and he was a fugitive from the Florida police, searching for his double-crossing former boss, Michael Grande. Jake headed to Llanview to confront Michael, who hardly felt threatened. In fact, he warned Jake that he would call the police right away, unless Jake spied on Megan Gordon. Reluctantly, Jake agreed to pose first as a telephone repairman to bug Megan's phone and then as a magazine reporter to get information from her to discredit her mother, Viki.

Megan discovered Jake's charade, but he talked his way out of the predicament by telling her that he was actually a writer for a soap opera magazine who had been hired to get the scoop on her. Megan fell for Jake's lies . . . and Jake fell in love with his prey!

Despite his secret connection to Michael Grande, Jake managed to help Megan out of some delicate situations, and they grew closer. Who else but the tough and handsomely chiseled Jake would take the high-and-mighty Megan Gordon to a pool hall to show her how the other half lived? Before long, Megan cared as deeply for Jake as he did for her. They made the perfect pair!

*M*ichael Grande continued to act as a silent partner in Carlo Hesser's illegal drug operations. When Michael feared that Brenda McGillis was on to his drug involvement, he called on Carlo, who provided an experimental mind-altering drug that made Brenda susceptible to suggestion. Brenda, who had three men pursuing her—Michael, Larry Wolek, and Larry's son, Dan—at first refused to marry Michael when he proposed. So he increased the dosage of her drug, and gained total control of her mind.

(cont.)

VIKI
Oh, she loves Cord, and this is the end of the line for you. So you say good-bye, creep, and beat it!

JOHNNY
I'm taking her with me. You hear me? She's mine! If I have to shoot every last one of you, I will! (She shoots him—dead.)

WHO KILLED MICHAEL GRANDE? 1990

The burning question of who murdered cold-hearted Michael Grande developed in May 1990 when the body of the super-heinous scoundrel was discovered in the lounge of Llanview Hospital. Bo Buchanan, Sarah Buchanan, Clint Buchanan, Dorian Lord, Megan Gordon, Jake Harrison, Roger Gordon, and Michael's own drugged-out wife, Brenda McGillis, were among the dozens who despised him and wanted him dead.

He wined and dined Brenda but found Dan Wolek to be a constant thorn in his side. Young Dr. Wolek correctly figured out that Brenda was being drugged, but he couldn't prove it! Meanwhile, Michael appointed himself legal guardian to Brenda's son, Steven. He then left Brenda to die and prepared to leave the country with the boy.

While Dan saved the drugged-out Brenda, Michael Grande was killed at Llanview Hospital. Strangely, Roger Gordon—a patient in the hospital—was discovered in his room, comatose, moments after the murder. Could he have had something to do with the murder?

District Attorney Herb Callison launched a major investigation. When he learned that on the night of the murder, both Jake and Megan confronted Michael, he made them his prime suspects. Megan was charged with the crime, and in a quick trial filled with damaging evidence, she was convicted and sentenced to ten years in prison. When Bo arranged for a tape crew to record Megan's second Daisy Award acceptance speech from jail, Jake and his best friend, Lucky Lippman, posed as a TV crew and whisked Megan away as they searched for the final clues to solve the murder mystery. Gathering together all the suspects, Jake revealed that Roger Gordon, before lapsing into his coma, had killed Michael in self-defense. Megan was free at last!

As Megan's life settled down after the trial, she returned to *Fraternity Row*. Bo arranged to shoot Megan's new story on a deserted island called Badderly. However, when they got to the island, Bo, Megan, and Sarah found that some of the East Coast's major Mob figures were meeting there to discuss turning Llanview into a major drug manufacturing mecca.

Bo, along with Sarah, Megan, Tina, Cord, and Marco Dane, went undercover and posed as mobsters to infiltrate the underworld drug meeting. Jake swam to Badderly and joined in the dangerous game. Mob princess Charlotte Hesser took an immediate lik-

ing to Jake, and he pretended interest in her while secretly spending time with Megan.

Tina, who was on the island as a guest of Carlo's son, Johnny Dee, was stunned to see her Llanview friends—and her ex-husband, Cord. Tina kept mum, but faced a horrible dilemma when Johnny spotted her speaking to Cord. To keep Johnny from searching Cord's room, Tina stalled him . . . by seducing him. After sleeping with Johnny, Tina went to bed with Cord; after their night of lovemaking, they decided to start dating again.

In the end, the Llanview good guys managed to steal plastic explosives from the drug manufacturing lab and blew up Badderly!

They returned to Llanview, triumphant. However, there were consequences to pay. To her horror, Tina discovered she was pregnant—and she didn't know who the father was. She mistakenly believed that her child was Johnny's. Cord, in true form, agreed to raise and love the child as his own. When Johnny learned of the baby, he tried to kidnap Tina from Llanfair but was killed by the paralyzed Viki, who turned into Niki Smith, regained the use of her legs, and climbed the mansion stairs to shoot Johnny before he could drag Tina away.

Johnny's death stoked the flames of hatred for the Buchanans that burned in Carlo Hesser. He vowed to avenge his son's death. An audio cassette, secretly recorded by Johnny, and stolen from his pocket by Gabrielle just moments after the shooting, revealed that Niki shot Johnny, but that Gabrielle Holden was present at the crime scene as well. Carlo, learning that Viki/Niki killed his son, enlisted Gabrielle's aid in exacting his revenge against the Buchanans and in convincing the pregnant Tina to give up Johnny's baby to him. Gabrielle at first refused to ally herself with Carlo Hesser; but when Carlo videotaped the married Gabrielle seducing Father Tony Vallone, she had no choice but to reluctantly agree to work with Carlo.

Carlo pursued Tina as ardently as had Johnny, hounding her to yield his unborn grandson to him. Terrified for the safety of her family, Tina fled to Texas, where she went into labor during a blizzard. Cord followed Tina and announced, as he assisted in the delivery of a daughter, that medical tests had proven that *he* was the father of the child. Elated, Cord and Tina brought their newborn daughter Sarah back to Llanview and remarried yet again. Max, ashamed and disheartened to learn of his wife's indiscretions, broke up with Gabrielle. Carlo, beaten, vowed to make his enemies pay!

When the time came for Megan and Sarah to testify against the Mob leader, they were kidnapped and whisked away by their captors to Pennsylvania's Amish country. Megan was found first, and Jake devoted

(cont.)

Or could the killer have been Dr. Dan Wolek? The hotheaded young doctor despised Michael Grande for the physical and emotional pain he inflicted on Brenda, the only woman Dan ever loved.

These key suspects, along with many other Llanview residents, had compelling motives. But who hated the evil Michael Grande enough to murder him in cold blood? Everyone appeared guilty in this plot-twisting mystery, as District Attorney Herb Callison questioned all the suspects. Each seemed to be covering up something, and no one could be trusted, especially when family and friends started to become suspicious of one another!

Although Megan Gordon went on trial and was convicted of Michael's murder, the real killer was revealed to be her father, Roger, who had emerged from a coma to kill Michael in self-defense.

Murder/Mysteries

$\mathcal{M}$EGAN AND MARCO

Actress Megan Gordon was playing a dual role on her soap when she met one of Llanview's all-time smooth operators, Marco Dane. They enjoyed a friendly association until the day that Megan witnessed her mother, Viki, take a bullet. The shock of Viki's shooting caused Megan's personality to split—and she became Ruby! Seeing an opportunity to woo her away from Max Holden, mad-cap Marco convinced Megan/Ruby to run away with him. They nearly married, but Megan snapped out of her Ruby personality, ended her dangerous liaison with a heartbroken Marco, and returned to Max Holden. In 1990, Megan and Marco reteamed to play another dangerous game when they infiltrated a conference of mobsters on Badderly Island.

all his energies to helping find Sarah. Jake had a sneaking suspicion that Carlo Hesser was involved. While Bo and female agent Alex Olanov of the Federal Anticrime Bureau (FAB) continued to search for Sarah, Megan and Jake engineered a plan for Jake to get close to Charlotte Hesser in the hopes that she might have information about Sarah's whereabouts.

Megan and Jake staged a public breakup, but managed to sneak away to Viki's mountain cabin, where they shared a symbolic wedding ceremony. After spending the night together, they returned to Llanview, where Carlo quickly realized that Jake was only using his daughter. Jake agreed to marry Charlotte to protect his family from Carlo's revenge.

When Charlotte developed hysterical blindness following a car accident, Jake decided that he couldn't ask her for a divorce. Megan buried her pain by hooking up with an old boyfriend, director Hunter Guthrie, who'd come to Llanview to film a movie.

Meanwhile, agent Alex Olanov discovered that Sarah was being held in an FAB safehouse. It seemed that Bo's wife had been kidnapped by the very agency that sent Alex to find her! Bo confronted the head of the FAB, Fred Porter, and learned that he alone had made a deal with Carlo Hesser to keep Sarah from testifying against the Mob. In exchange for protection from prosecution in the Badderly affair, Carlo promised to inform the FAB on worldwide drug-trafficking activities.

While Sarah was being spirited away by her captors, her plane crashed in a severe storm. The Buchanans were convinced that Carlo Hesser was responsible for Sarah's death. As a grief-stricken Bo mourned his wife, the tension between the Buchanan and the Hesser families intensified.

*S*ALZBURG, AUSTRIA
1990

Viewers took a fairy-tale journey to the incredibly picturesque, intriguing, fictional country of Mendorra in February 1990. Thirty-five members of the New York–based crew and 1,500 pounds of costumes journeyed to Salzburg—which served as Mendorra—for six days and nights of remote taping.

"That was the biggest shoot to date, more extensive than anything we'd ever done. We chose Salzburg because of its layout, the old and new parts of the city, and because I wanted to take our viewers to places they might not have been to or seen on other shows."

Paul Rauch
(Executive Producer,
1984–1991)

*J*ason Webb arrived in Llanview just at the time Dorian Lord was feeling lonely, listless, and lusty. Her hormones slipped into high gear when she caught sight of the youthful rebel, prompting a slew of forbidden fantasies. Soon, fantasy became reality and Dorian and Jason began a sizzling affair. She bought her boy toy a motorcycle, a car, and a sleek new wardrobe, but the dangerous liaison soon came to an end—but not because of the age difference. It was Dorian's endless attempts to control the uncontrollable Young Turk that led Jason to roar out of her life.

1991

Gabrielle's painful separation from Max continued into the new year; in desperation, she tried scheme after scheme to win him back. She implored Father Tony Vallone to help her get Max to see the light. This time, Tony refused to do Gabrielle's bidding, saying that he would no longer bow to her every whim. She fell deeper into Carlo Hesser's web of crime.

When Llanview's mayor, Viki Buchanan, began interfering with Carlo's illegal operations, she became the target of his wrath. To eliminate Viki, the mobster ordered Gabrielle to slip a potent drug into her drink during a party at Llanfair. The drug was part of Carlo's diabolical scheme to turn Viki into Niki, and get her to kill her own daughter, Megan. During the party, Gabrielle could not go through with the scheme. Instead, she dropped the vial into a potted plant and prepared to testify against Carlo in court. However, when Carlo threatened her son's life, Gabrielle remained silent, refusing to finger the mobster. As a result, Carlo remained free, and Gabrielle was sentenced to fifteen years in Statesville Prison for her role in the conspiracy to get Niki to kill Megan.

Eventually, Carlo followed through with his diabolical scheme, injecting Viki with the drug himself. As he hoped, she turned into Niki, but was able to exert enough control over her alter ego to prevent Megan's murder. Niki fired Carlo's gun at Megan, and intentionally missed! Later, Bo and Alex obtained the antidote from Alex's scientist father, Nat Olanov, and Niki once again became Viki. Carlo's scheme had failed!

With Gabrielle finally out of his life, Max became fond of Lee Ann Demerest, the naive daughter of Du Ann, the midwife who birthed him. Du Ann was aware that Max was not really Asa's son—and she planned to use the information to her own advantage. By early 1991, Max and Asa had grown close. Proud of his newfound heritage, Max decided to change his name to Buchanan.

Soon after, Du Ann began blackmailing Renee Buchanan, who discovered that Max was not Asa's son—it was all a hoax perpetrated by Gabrielle! Renee tried to hide the secret from Asa by allowing herself to be blackmailed by Du Ann. When Du Ann was killed at the Buchanan Enterprises twenty-fifth anniversary party, Renee went on trial for murder. Julia Medina eventually confessed to the crime.

In the aftermath of Du Ann's murder and the revelation of his true heritage, Max returned to using Holden as his last name. Lee Ann, fed up with Asa's meddling and devastated by the death of her mother, returned to Sweetwater, but Max followed. In the dusty Texas town, Max and Lee Ann made love for the first time in the front seat of a pickup truck. However, Lee Ann was deeply disappointed when Max would not say the three words—"I love you"—that she hoped to hear. Lee Ann returned with Max to Llanview, but their romance did not last long. Eventually, Max (now divorced from Gabrielle) decided to leave Llanview and return to his roots. Leaving his son Al with Renee, Max went home to Texas to soothe his tortured soul.

Memories of his late wife Sarah continued to torture Bo Buchanan during the cold, gray winter of 1991. Though he spent much of his free time with Alex Olanov, Bo was not able to forget Sarah and this proved to

LUNA PARACHUTES INTO TINA'S TEA PARTY AT LLANFAIR
1991

MEGAN
What is that?
(They see someone parachuting onto the lawn.)

TINA
I told you! I told you this party was jinxed!

JOEY
Should I get a gun? Are we being invaded or something?

LUNA
Hey, folks! Hope you don't mind me dropping in on you like this. Thank you, I would like a cup of tea! Hope it's herbal.

be a stumbling block in their relationship. Still, Alex would not give up in her quest to get Bo into bed!

*C*assie Callison returned to town early in 1991 to attend the swearing-in ceremony for her father, Herb, who succeeded Viki as the mayor of Llanview. Bo ran into Cassie at the airport and was immediately charmed by her poise, her beauty, and her zest for life. They attended the swearing-in party together, and when Alex saw them dancing and laughing together, she fled in a rage. As Bo and Cassie began to spend more and more time together, Alex's behavior became more erratic as her unrequited love for Bo drove her to desperate measures. When Bo and Cassie fell in love, Alex flipped out! She wanted Bo—any way she could get him! But help came from an unexpected source: Cassie's mother, Dorian.

Dorian was furious at Cassie! How could her only daughter fall in love with a Buchanan? The ever-scheming Ms. Lord schemed with Alex to break up the lovers.

When Bo and Cassie decided to take a vacation at scenic Loon Lake, Alex discreetly followed them—then kidnapped Cassie! Hauling her to a nearby boat, Alex ordered Cassie to row into the middle of the lake, where she tried to drown her! Fortunately, Bo rescued Cassie; Alex, now totally unhinged, was taken away to the Mountainview Clinic. Nearly losing his latest love made Bo realize how much he wanted to be with Cassie.

Soon after the ordeal ended, Bo proposed and Cassie joyfully accepted. Dorian surprised her daughter by offering to pay for a lavish wedding. As the big day grew closer, strange things began happening. A mysterious phone call from a woman who sounded like Sarah alarmed Bo. Then Cassie received a package containing a negligee worn by Sarah on her honeymoon with Bo. Was Sarah alive—or was someone gaslighting them? The culprit turned out to be Alex, who had escaped from the sanitarium!

Bo, now convinced that Sarah was dead, was more determined than ever to make Cassie his wife. On the big day, Alex arrived at Llanfair, the site of the wedding, and lurked in the shadows. She had brought her own little gift for the bride and groom: a music box. Cassie, overwhelmed by the joyous emotions of this wonderful day, walked down the aisle and married Bo. The ceremony went off without a hitch.

Later, at the wedding reception, Llanview's police commissioner, Troy Nichols, discovered a gift box left by Alex. Bo and Troy unwrapped the box and found a poem and a music box, which played "As Time Goes By"—Bo and Sarah's song! The poem led Bo to race onto the terrace where to his astonishment, he discovered Sarah standing there!

To Cassie's devastation, Sarah threw her arms around Bo, unaware that he had just married another woman. However, when Sarah realized that she had stumbled onto Bo and Cassie's wedding, she rushed out of Llanfair in tears.

In time, Sarah recovered and explained that the plane crash that had supposedly killed her had been staged by Carlo Hesser's henchmen. She had been held for months at a deserted beach house. Alex, having discovered her whereabouts, brought her back to Llanview to spoil the most wonderful day of Cassie's life.

For weeks, Bo was torn between his new wife, Cassie, and "Paradise," his nickname for Sarah. Sarah was crushed when he decided to stay with Cassie. Alex, meanwhile, was shipped back to the mental institution, her "gift" having had the desired effect on Cassie and Bo.

$\mathcal{J}$ake Harrison celebrated the new year by getting a divorce from Charlotte Hesser. For months, the blind Mob princess preyed on Jake's sympathies. When her sight returned, Charlotte feigned blindness to hang onto her husband. But when Jake discovered her charade, he called an end to the marriage—and launched a successful quest to win back Megan's affections. Before long, they were engaged to be married!

One day, Jake sent his fiancée Megan a note to meet him. When she arrived at the designated spot, Megan was petrified! She stood before a run-down, deserted house in the middle of nowhere. She opened the creaky door and went in. Jake had lured Megan Gordon to what he called their "dream house." Megan couldn't believe her eyes! Did Jake really believe that he could turn this decrepit, broken-down rattrap into a home befitting one of America's favorite soap starlets?

At first, Megan stubbornly refused to give up her lavish apartment to move into a shack! But Jake was obsessed with providing the roof over their heads himself . . . even if it leaked. They argued mightily, but eventually Megan saw the incredible possibilities for renovating the place into the house of *both* their dreams. Together, they turned the house— with its leaky faucets and cracked windows—into a castle worthy of Llanview's storybook young lovers.

On a sunny spring day, Jake and Megan were married inside St. James Church—but not before one last attempt by Jake's former wife, Charlotte, to stop the wedding. Sneaking into the Lord Library, Charlotte stole Megan's wedding dress! Fortunately, Megan quickly tracked her down and retrieved the gown before Charlotte could burn it. The wedding was on!

Following the ceremony, the newlyweds led their loved ones out to the sprawling emerald green lawn of St. James Church, where they planted a tree as a symbol of their happiness. Then, with the guests bidding a fond adieu, a horse-drawn carriage whisked Jake and Megan away for their honeymoon.

Little did Megan's bridesmaid, Andy, know that before long, she

NEW PALTZ, NEW YORK
1991

The chilly waters of Lake Minnewaska in New Paltz, New York, provided the backdrop for the excitement and intrigue when a vengeful Alex tried to drown Cassie, her rival for Bo's affections.

"LET ME TELL YOU, THAT WAS NO STUNT DOUBLE—I ACTUALLY TOOK THE PLUNGE MYSELF—AND WHEN I HIT THE WATER, I HIT SO HARD THAT I LOST MY BREATH! I SHOULD HAVE YELLED 'CUT!' BUT I SAID TO MYSELF, 'YOU HAVE TO FINISH THE SCENE!' SO THE PANIC YOU SAW IN MY EYES WAS REAL, VERY REAL."

LAURA KOFFMAN
(CASSIE CARPENTER)

would also be tying the knot. During the summer of 1991, Andy and Megan's ex-beau, Hunter Guthrie, began to realize they had deep feelings for each other. They were happy to have time to slowly develop their relationship. However, the plans were altered when Hunter, a film director, was forced to return to Hollywood right away. In a whirlwind series of events, Hunter proposed, Andy accepted, and they were married in a beautiful ceremony presided over by Mayor Herb Callison.

Sadly, the happiness of Llanview's storybook lovers, Jake and Megan, was short-lived. Upon their return to Llanview, Jake became more obsessed than ever with being the breadwinner in his new family. To achieve this, he took an arms-trading job that required him to travel the world. Megan, sensing danger, begged her new husband to stay home, but Jake assured her that he would only be gone a short time. However, weeks, then months passed, with only an occasional phone call from Jake reassuring Megan that he was okay.

*I*n July, con artist Cain Rogan first appeared in Llanview in the disguised personality of Hudson King, an oily and charming British writer who approached Tina with a $50,000 offer to serve as his source for a book about the Buchanan family. Little did she know that this charlatan was simply digging up dirt on Asa Buchanan and selling it to Dorian Lord to publish in her sleazy tabloid, the *Intruder*. With Cord's help,

Tina exposed the phony writer, who quickly skipped town—but not for long!

Several weeks later, Heinrich Keiser, a German film director, showed up in Llanview. Once again, it was Cain Rogan in disguise! "Heinrich" tried to use Megan to gain access to Asa Buchanan's financial empire. However, before he could complete his con game, Viki and Clint saw a picture of the *real* Heinrich Kaiser and chased the impostor out of town. But he'd be back—in the person of traveling actor Humberto Calderon!

*L*ove blossomed throughout Llanview during the summer of 1991. Police Commissioner Troy Nichols met Sheila Price while she served as Viki's physical therapist after her stroke. Sheila was reluctant to become involved with Troy at first and showed no interest in a romantic relationship. Troy knew he had to win her trust and respect before he could win her heart.

Slowly, Sheila began to enjoy the attention Troy lavished upon her, but she disagreed with him in allowing her sister, Rika, to see Kerry, Troy's rap musician son. Troy, who performed in his own rap group, The K-Funk Mob, detested Rika at first. Before long, it was soon apparent to all that Kerry and Rika were in love!

*P*uppy love throve for young Kevin Buchanan and Stephanie Hobart, the niece of the Buchanan family's archenemy, Carlo Hesser. At one point, Carlo's hatred for the Buchanans caused the young lovers to steal his yacht and run away. Kevin and Stephanie tried several times to make love but were interrupted during each attempt. When their relationship grew more complicated, Kevin ran into the open arms of his friend Lee Ann Demerest. Their friendship grew into a passionate affair, and Kevin lost his virginity to the sexy Texas lass.

Still, Lee Ann cared more for Max Holden, who returned to Llanview in the fall after discovering more about the way in which Asa Buchanan had bilked Max's father, Wingate Holden, out of the deed to his land. It seems that the stress of that situation caused the senior Holden to die of a heart attack. Now, Max was back to seek the ultimate revenge on Asa—while taking time out to romance Lee Ann Demerest. Kevin repeatedly proposed to Lee Ann in the hopes that he could woo her away from the older, more worldly Max.

*A*nother May-December affair began when Dorian lured Wanda Wolek's longhaired nephew, Jason Webb, into her bed. Dorian might have seduced Jason, but she was never able to tame his wild, rebellious ways. And Jason, even while he was fulfilling Dorian's wildest fantasies, had his eye on Lee Ann as well.

*T*hroughout much of 1991, a heartbroken Viki suspected that her husband Clint was having an affair with a coworker, Sondra. Finally confronting him, Viki was stunned to hear Clint's confession that Sondra was only helping him come to grips with his impending death. Clint confessed to Viki that the bullet fragments in his head had shifted, and doctors had told him that he only had a few months to live. Viki and the children—Kevin, Joey, and Jessica—begged Clint to go through with the risky surgery that could save his life. Giving in to their heartfelt request, Clint survived the surgery and made a full recovery.

In the fall, little Jessica Buchanan accidentally set fire to Llanfair. Clint and Viki comforted each other among the ruins and set out to rebuild the family home.

*T*ina showed her stuff when she led a crusade against bigotry by having Sheila Price, a black woman, admitted to the Daughters of Llanview, an upper-crust organization of wealthy wives. During the party on the Llanfair lawn, a figure in parachute gear descended from the skies—landing smack in the middle of the terrace. The stunned guests were greeted by the sparkling smile and captivating Southern twang of Luna Moody, a New Age Goddess worshipper.

Luna took a job at Wanda's Diner and fell instantly in love with Max Holden. They shared a special connection, an extrasensory bond that few friends ever achieve. However, while Luna was falling for Max, his eyes were set on the beguiling Blair Daimler, whom he encountered during a sexy midnight dance on New Year's Eve.

Viki hired Blair to be her new assistant at *The Banner*, unaware that she was Dorian's niece. Blair was harboring more than her share of secrets. For one, she hid her crazy mother, Addie, in her loft at the local boarding house. Unbeknownst to anyone, Addie was Dorian's older sister, who had been institutionalized for years. Blair blamed her Aunt Dorian for her mother's illness, and had come to Llanview to get revenge. One of her first devious moves designed to destroy Dorian was to get her signature on a document admitting to the world that she killed her husband, Victor Lord, back in 1976. Dorian had no idea that the piece of paper she signed was a confession of her guilt!

Blair's quest to bring down her Aunt Dorian was temporarily sidetracked when she agreed to serve as Cord Roberts's interpreter during a business trip to Japan. Alone together in an exotic land, Blair tried to lure Cord into her bed. Though clearly aroused, Cord did not give in to temptation. Before heading home, Cord and Blair headed to the Middle Eastern city of Jaba to check up on Jake Harrison, who had been reported missing.

Cord and Blair found Jake, and rescued him, but later they were lured into a trap set by the evil General Gazi. Jake was recaptured and Cord was shot in the chest and fell into the Jaba River. Blair dove in after him, but his body was swept away in the rushing current. Although Blair searched all the morgues and hospitals, she could not find him. Returning to Llanview, she had no choice but to tell Tina the numbing news that her dear husband Cord was dead.

*M*egan was sad to hear of Cord's death and Jake's incarceration. To complicate matters, Megan's own health began to fail late in 1991. At first, she ignored Viki's advice to seek medical help, but finally a checkup with Dr. Larry Wolek revealed that she was suffering from a potentially fatal case of lupus, an autoimmune disease that can attack any connective tissue within the body. Without Jake to help her in her time of need, Megan turned to the kindly and wise Rev. Andrew Carpenter, the minister at St. James Church. He became her dearest friend. At the same time, Andrew's feelings grew into something more—much more. As the year came to an end, the reverend found himself facing a torturous and heartbreaking dilemma. He had fallen in love with Megan, a married woman!

$\mathcal{J}$ason Webb struggled to hide the fact that he could not read or write. In February 1992, Jason's illiteracy was discovered by the woman he secretly loved, Lee Ann Demerest Buchanan. Lee Ann taught an embarrassed and frustrated Jason how to read—and, as an added bonus, they fell in love!

1992

Megan was determined not to let lupus destroy her life. However, with Jake still being held prisoner in faraway Jaba City, Megan became deeply depressed about her worsening condition. She tried to overcome her depression by engaging in wild partying and self-destructive behavior that ultimately landed her in Llanview Hospital with kidney failure.

In the hospital, Megan befriended fellow patient Margaret (Marty) Saybrooke, a beautiful, wealthy, and very unhappy young woman of twenty-one. Marty, a sophomore at Llanview University, suffered from a serious but controllable case of systemic lupus, and an even more pronounced attitude problem. Marty's stance to the world was *Back off!* She used her considerable intelligence and wit to be sarcastic, snotty, defiant with authority, and combative with her peers. But her toughness was really just a protective covering over a very fragile shell, within which this young girl sat feeling frightened, needy, and bereft of love. As her strength waned, Megan offered Marty the friendship she so desperately coveted.

A kidney transplant proved to be Megan's only hope of survival. Viki bravely donated one of hers, but sadly, the transplant did not take. Dr. Larry Wolek broke the grim news to Viki: Megan was dying. Clint supported Viki throughout the entire ordeal, though he was still dealing with the pain of his own son, Cord's, death. Clint joined Viki in a valiant effort to keep Megan alive—at least until Jake could be located in Jaba and brought back to Llanview. Viki and Clint, along with the rest of the Buchanans and Max Holden, sat by Megan's bedside and told her glorious tales about the times of their lives.

Meanwhile, Reverend Andrew Carpenter rose above his own unrequited feelings of love for Megan and made a daring journey to Jaba to rescue Jake. In the process, the kindhearted minister was forced to shoot and kill Jake's captor, General Gazi. As the general fell to the ground, mortally wounded, he pulled out a knife and stabbed Andrew in the side. Hiding his bleeding injury, Jake and Andrew made their escape, rushing back to Llanview.

Back home, Megan's strength ebbed. As she faded in and out of a coma, she asked Viki to tell her about Jake because she wanted to die hearing her husband's name. Just then, the hospital room door opened—and Megan focused her eyes on the handsome gent who stood staring at her. It was Jake! As tears flowed freely, Jake and Megan shared several bittersweet hours together. Jake left her side only to allow Andrew and Megan to share a heartfelt and touching good-bye.

As the sun set on this sunny winter's day, Jake returned, gently telling Megan there was something outside she had to see. He carried her to the window, where she peered out onto the hospital lawn. There, with glimmering paper valentines hanging from its branches, was their transplanted wedding tree. Megan's face radiated with one last smile as she passed away in her beloved Jake's arms.

Megan's untimely death had a profound effect on her sister, Sarah, who had only recently returned to Llanview. Sarah and her husband Bo planned to divorce early in the new year, but postponed the proceedings when Sarah began to have frightening flashbacks about her kidnapping. To numb the pain, Sarah started taking tranquilizers—and got hooked! As Bo helped Sarah through this difficult period, Cassie became jealous, and for good reason. After Bo slept with Sarah, he and Cassie decided to end their relationship.

During one of her flashbacks, Sarah realized that she had witnessed Carlo Hesser killing a man during her months in captivity. But who was his victim? Sarah could only remember the dying man's last word: "Scarecrow."

By now, Carlo Hesser was a married man. Early in 1992, Carlo married the notorious Alex Olanov, who had managed to slither out of the mental institution. Mr. and Mrs. Hesser began a short and kinky marriage marked by frequent sex and lots of their favorite aphrodisiac, oysters! Soon after, Carlo Hesser was shot to death in Max Holden's attic while searching for missing diamonds that belonged to him. Sarah became the prime suspect.

When the Llanview police discovered a gun in Sarah's possession, they arrested her. But Sarah couldn't remember if she had killed Carlo; the tranquilizers had clouded her memories of the deadly night. District Attorney Hank "The Cannon" Gannon presented a strong and convincing case against Sarah, who was found guilty of murder. Bo, convinced of her innocence, eventually found the real killer: Carlo's sweet niece, Stephanie. It turned out that Stephanie had killed Carlo in a fit of rage after discovering that he had murdered her own father, FBI informant Joseph Hobart—aka "The Scarecrow."

With Carlo dead, Alex was fiercely determined to maintain control of his empire. When she found out that Carlo's rival, Moose Mulligan, wanted a piece of the action, a desperate Alex brought mild-mannered Egyptologist Mortimer Bern to town. But why? With his mop of salt-and-pepper hair and studious-looking, wire-rimmed glasses, Mortimer was hardly a threatening figure. But once Alex shaved Mortimer's head and took off his spectacles, he instantly became the spitting image of Carlo! It turned out that meek-and-mild Mortimer was Carlo's identical twin brother. Alex arranged for Mortimer to take voice lessons, dance lessons, even sex lessons, but nothing worked! Only when Mortimer met and became smitten with Carlo's former flame, Renee Buchanan, did he complete the transformation from Milquetoast to mobster.

Alex faced two other worthy adversaries in the persons of Tina Roberts and her new paramour, Cain Rogan, the shifty master of disguise who had returned to Llanview, this time as himself. Cain and Tina were hellbent on making Alex pay for allowing them to take the fall in her theft of the precious Cleopatra jewels from the Llanview Museum. With a mass of confusing evidence and finger-pointing, a bewildered DA Gannon did not know whom to prosecute—so no one ever went to jail for the crime!

Free at last after being cleared of Carlo Hesser's murder, Sarah Gordon looked forward to a long and happy future with Bo Buchanan. But sadly, she died in a car accident, with Bo at the wheel, on the day before their wedding. When Bo tried to swerve to avoid an oncoming vehicle, he lost control of his car, which plunged into the Llantano River. Sarah's death shattered Bo. Months passed before he could deal with the horrible tragedy. Like a godsend, Llanview's newest attorney, Nora Gannon, helped Bo come to grips with the overwhelming loss of his beloved Sarah.

(cont.)

Commenting on the award winners, Robert G. Lahita, MD, PhD, chairman of the board of the LFA and chief of Rheumatology and Connective Tissue Diseases, St. Luke's-Roosevelt Hospital Center, New York, said, "Their attention to detail and commitment to portraying lupus accurately demonstrates their strong sense of responsibility to the viewers and the public at large." According to Dr. Lahita, "One Life to Live has served to heighten awareness and help the LFA reach those who need help the most—the undiagnosed patients."

MEGAN'S PASSING
1992

JAKE
Can you see that?

MEGAN
Our wedding tree.

JAKE
See all the hearts I put on the branches?

MEGAN
It's so beautiful.

JAKE
All those hearts are going to become blossoms in just a few months, honey, and we're going to come back here and we're going to count these blossoms together. And maybe a soft breeze will come up, and some of the blossoms will fall off, and maybe a quiet rain will start. After it's done raining, the sun will come out like it did on our wedding day. Like on our wedding day. You said you'd never leave me. You said you'd never leave me. You'll never leave me.

When Kevin Buchanan discovered that Lee Ann was pregnant, he "did the right thing" and proposed to her—unaware that his bride-to-be secretly suspected that Max Holden was the father of her unborn child. Lee Ann and Kevin eloped. Upon returning to town, Lee Ann found herself growing closer to the rebellious Jason Webb. As Lee Ann helped an illiterate Jason to learn to read, they developed a bond that eventually evolved into love. Jason gently ended his once-sizzling affair with older woman Dorian Lord and sweetly devoted his energies to making Lee Ann happy. When Kevin caught them kissing, he angrily demanded a divorce, then fought and won custody of her newborn son, Demerest "Duke" Buchanan—who turned out to be his child after all. When the court decision was handed down, Jason and a desperate Lee Ann took Duke and fled town.

Hank Gannon's newly arrived daughter, Rachel, comforted Kevin. By the time baby Duke was safely returned, Kevin and Rachel had become intimate—much to the consternation of Rachel's disapproving daddy.

1992 would be a fortuitous year for Max Holden, who teamed up with his good-luck charm, Luna Moody, to get still more revenge on Asa Buchanan. Together with Luna, Max schemed to dupe Asa out of a small fortune by tricking him into buying a chunk of land in which they had planted fake treasure. Eventually, Max and Luna bought the land back and built their pride and joy—the Serenity Springs Spa.

Throughout their colorful adventures, Luna hid her feelings of love from Max, who insisted that he just wanted to be friends. Meanwhile, she watched with silent sorrow as Max chased Blair Daimler like a dog in

heat. However, Blair had no time for a hopeless dreamer like Max Holden. She resisted Max's advances, instead setting her romantic sights on Asa Buchanan, whose marriage to Renee had gone bust early in 1992 after Mrs. Buchanan caught her husband horsing around in the stables with Blair. Asa appeared to be the answer to Blair's prayers. Through him, she could gain financial security for her mentally ill mother, Addie, and through her new power base, get revenge on Addie's sister, Dorian Lord.

Blair blamed her aunt for putting her sister in an institution, then ignoring her for decades. In truth, Dorian was not at fault for Addie's years of misery. She had been told that Agatha (Addie) had died of pneumonia at the age of thirteen, but the disturbed girl had been committed to a mental institution by their late parents. Dorian was as stunned as anyone to learn that her sister Agatha was alive—and living with Blair!

Despite Blair's denial, Max knew in his heart that she wanted him. Alone together in Sweetwater, Texas, he seduced Blair. They made wild, passionate love in a barn. Afterward, Max's wise Native American friend, Joe Hawk, advised Max to beware of Blair—*Luna* was the woman for him! Still, Max proposed to Blair; surprisingly, she accepted. But when Asa promised to stop Dorian from having Blair's mother recommitted if she would marry him, Blair changed her mind. Max followed her back to Llanview, and was stunned to discover the woman he loved was about to marry his worst enemy. Max pleaded with Blair to change her mind. They even made love—on top of Blair's wedding dress! Nevertheless, Blair went through with her plans and became the new Mrs. Asa Buchanan.

The loveless marriage was doomed from the start. Blair did her best to stay out of Asa's bed, while still hanging onto her man. Eventually, when Asa grew disenchanted with his bride, Blair resorted to a phony pregnancy to keep him by her side. Discovering her charade, Asa tossed his wanton wife out of the family mansion—and took steps to ensure that Blair didn't get a dime of his vast fortune!

In desperation, Blair went running back to Max, only to find he was no longer available. By now, Max was beginning to see what everyone else in Llanview already knew: Luna was the only woman for him. But it wasn't until Suede Pruitt, an escaped convict who became obsessed with

HOMOPHOBIA
1992

One Life to Live furthered its legacy of smashing taboos by tackling homophobia in a central summer storyline focusing on Billy Douglas—a golden boy born into privilege, president of his class and captain of the swim team—coming out of the closet. Billy's sense of isolation and confusion in recognizing his sexuality led him to seek counseling with Rev. Andrew Carpenter. Billy soon became a victim of homophobia when Marty Saybrooke spread rumors about him and the minister. Once the story took shape, it also focused on the right to privacy as Reverend Carpenter refused to stoop to the rumormongers's level by denying the accusations.

In a rare televised opportunity, viewers saw the 20,000-panel "NAMES Project AIDS Memorial Quilt" when One Life to Live's homophobia storyline reached its climax. Filmed on location at the Church of Christ the King in New Vernon, New Jersey, the show focused on the relationship between Rev. Andrew Carpenter and his father, Sloan, who finally acknowledged that his other son, William, was gay. In the episode, Sloan joined Andrew in a moving tribute to William, who died from AIDS. More than 150 family members and friends of AIDS victims served as extras in the emotion-filled scenes.

Luna while listening to her radio show, *Loveline*, kidnapped Luna, that Max realized that he loved her.

Max set out to rescue Luna from Suede, who had been sent to jail unjustly for murdering his wife, Deborah—the spitting image of Luna! In the course of saving Luna from Suede's father-in-law, Marcus Whiteheart (who had framed Suede), and his accomplice, Jim Vern, Max gallantly faced danger head-on. Luna watched in horror as Max stepped in front of a bullet meant for her.

Rushed to the hospital, Max fought off death—literally! Inside his mind, Max was being tempted by "Death," in the form of a sexy, seductive woman. While "Death" tried to coax Max into joining her for eternity, Luna begged Max to hang on to life. As he began to slip away, Luna used her psychic energies to cross over to the other side and bring Max back to the land of the living. With the ordeal behind them, Max and Luna—now joyously in love—moved in together. They extended an offer of forgiveness to Suede, who settled in Llanview after being cleared of any wrongdoing in the long-ago death of his wife.

*S*everal other relationships were in a state of flux over the course of 1992. Sheila Price's growing attraction to handsome Hank Gannon led her to call off her engagement to Police Commissioner Troy Nichols, who left town. And Clint and Viki Buchanan's marriage ran into some serious turbulence when Viki took more than a passing interest in Rev. Andrew Carpenter's father Sloan, a retired Army general. Sloan Carpenter was writing a biographical book, entitled *Lord of The Banner*, about the late Victor Lord. When Viki and Clint tried to make love, both realized that the old passion was no longer there. Clint grew more and more jealous of the time Viki spent with Sloan.

Viki's "friendship" provided a rare respite in the tortured life of Sloan Carpenter, who during the summer of 1992 was diagnosed with Hodgkin's disease. Sensing his impending death, Sloan came to Llanview to make peace with his son, Andrew. Father and son had been estranged for years over Sloan's refusal to accept the fact that his late son, William, was gay and had died of AIDS. The reconciliation would have to wait as Sloan continued to deny the truth about William. Privately, Andrew prayed that someday his father would make peace with his late son's memory.

During his own family difficulties, Rev. Carpenter proved to be a trusted adviser to Joey Buchanan's teenage friend, Billy Douglas, who realized in 1992 that he was gay. Billy agonized over whether or not to tell his parents. He came to rely on both his friend and confidant, Joey, and Reverend Andrew Carpenter in his time of inner turmoil. One day in the rectory of St. James Church, Billy, distraught, came to Andrew once again for help. The trusting minister placed a comforting hand on the boy's shoulder. Just then, troubled Marty Saybrooke peered in the door. For weeks, Marty had been trying to seduce Andrew, but he had gently spurned her overt advances. Jealous and angry to see Andrew expressing warmth and care for someone other than her, Marty went to Billy's parents and proceeded to tell the vindictive lie that the pastor was trying to seduce their son!

The charges against Reverend Carpenter spread through Llanview like wildfire! Andrew, claiming a basic right to privacy, refused to publicly reveal his sexual preference. Massive homophobia ensued, and a vicious war of hate divided the citizens of Llanview. Through it all, Andrew held his head high, even sustaining a brutal beating from a homophobic bigot, all the while proudly refusing to quit his post. Cassie, who was now dating Andrew, began receiving hate letters during this difficult period of anger, derisiveness, and misunderstanding in Llanview.

In the fall, Andrew earned his father's anger when he announced that his own brother, William, was a gay man who'd died of AIDS. Sloan was further enraged when Andrew declared that he had arranged for the NAMES Project AIDS Memorial Quilt to come to Llanview and planned to add a special square honoring his brother to the tapestry. Sloan refused to allow the Carpenter name to be soiled in such a way! He was joined in his anger by Billy Douglas's father, who urged his fellow citizens to join him in boycotting the ceremony.

In a touching scene at St. James Church, Andrew delivered an impassioned speech about the destructive danger of hate and the divine power of love. Then he dared the emotionally drained procession to join him as he took the newly fashioned panel honoring his brother to the church lawn, where he proceeded to add it to the sprawling quilt. Suddenly, Andrew felt a hand gently touching his shoulder. Looking up, he saw the tearstained face of his father, who offered to help lay the panel. Over the past months, his love for Viki had enabled Sloan Carpenter to grow significantly as a human being. Now, he was finally ready to come to terms with his son William's death. After the quilt ceremony, Sloan and Andrew embraced tightly— and Llanview began the slow and rewarding process of healing.

(cont.)

"THE QUILT WAS A HEALING INSTRUMENT BY WHICH THE THREE-MONTH STORY WAS RESOLVED. WE FELT IT WOULD BE A PERFECT CLIMAX TO OUR STORY TO TAP INTO THE REAL-LIFE DRAMA OF LOVE THAT CREATED IT."

LINDA GOTTLIEB
(EXECUTIVE PRODUCE,
1991–1995)

Was it a Christmas miracle? Cassie was overjoyed when she discovered a newborn boy in the church manger. However, just a few short weeks later, she was put through the emotional wringer when the baby was returned to his natural mother, Beth Garvey. The heartbreaking loss, combined with the residual pain of her own earlier miscarriage, caused Cassie to suffer a mental breakdown.

1993

*D*orian Lord bit her lip as she reluctantly watched her daughter Cassie marry Rev. Andrew Carpenter, the son of Sloan, who was writing a tell-all book about her long-ago marriage to Victor Lord. Despite her reservations, Dorian was resigned to accepting Cassie's marriage to Andrew. But Marty Saybrooke wasn't. The troubled girl, still smarting from Andrew's rejection, showed up at the church drunk, determined to stop the wedding, only to be hustled away by Viki. After the wedding, Dorian left town for several months on a whirlwind tour of America's most luxurious heath spas.

*V*iki and Clint, now tenuously reconciled, hoped to bring the magic back to their marriage. But early in the new year it became apparent that the joy they had shared for so long was gone. Eventually, the Buchanans moved into separate rooms at Llanfair . . . though for the sake of their children, Clint refused to move out of the family home. His heart aching, Clint found a friend in beautiful Lindsey Butler, a *Banner* reporter.

As Clint and Viki grew more distant, Viki found herself burning with sexual curiosity about Sloan Carpenter. Viki, always the paradigm of proper behavior, spent her idle time fantasizing about the general. When Sloan asked Viki to go away with him to the Winwood Hills Spa in Vermont, she agreed—unaware that, by sheer coincidence, Dorian was luxuriating at the same spa. When Dorian saw Sloan and Viki together, she smiled with devilish delight. Disguising her voice, she placed a call to Clint telling him that Viki had broken her leg and needed his help.

TRAPPED TOGETHER IN LLANFAIR'S SECRET ROOM, DORIAN AND VIKI CONFRONT THEIR PAST
1993

They have been bitter enemies throughout their adult lives, but the gloves finally came off when Viki and Dorian confronted each other about the events that had transpired over the past twenty years. Trapped in a secret, almost airless room, the two women rehashed their bitter rivalry—with Dorian striking the first verbal blow. . . .

Clint raced to Vermont—only to walk in on Sloan and Viki in bed! Outraged by his wife's inappropriate behavior, Clint filed for divorce. To clear his head, Clint went to his ranch in Arizona, where he was seriously injured in a plane crash.

Clint's younger brother Bo fared much better in the romance department. On New Year's Eve, he shared his first kiss with attorney Nora Gannon. For several weeks, Nora hid from Bo her fear that she had been the driver of the car that ran Bo and Sarah off the road. Much to their relief, it turned out that Nora, who was plagued by blinding headaches and blackouts, was not to blame. As their love blossomed throughout the year, Bo realized that this feisty attorney was the woman with whom he wanted to spend the rest of his life. Nora exuberantly accepted his proposal of marriage.

After being rejected by Max on New Year's Eve, a bitter Blair Buchanan forced her way back into Asa's mansion and staked her claim to his vast fortune. Blair fought tooth and nail to stop Asa from throwing her out again. Eventually, they took their battle to court, where the judge ruled in Asa's favor. Blair was left penniless! With her tail between her legs, she scurried out of Llanview, but not before stealing $100,000 of Dorian's money!

At Llanfair, the Buchanans were astonished by the return of the not-so-late Cord Roberts! Months earlier, Cord's bullet-ridden body had been carried away by the rushing waters of the Jaba River. Everyone believed he was dead—even Tina, who had put Cord's "death" behind her and became romantically entwined with Cain Rogan. But now Cord, who had been held in a Middle Eastern prison camp, had returned to Llanview.

Tina, stunned by Cord's return, secured a promise from friends and family not to tell him about her new relationship with Cain. Her game of musical men only lasted until the day Cord stumbled upon Tina and Cain in the throes of passion. Cord found Tina's infidelity very difficult to accept. Suffering from post-traumatic stress disorder, the now bitter and edgy Cord channeled his energies into breaking up his wife and her new lover. He headed for Texas to find one of Cain's old grifting partners.

While in Texas, Cord met up with Angela Holliday, Cain's old grifting partner, who was now a traveling faith healer. After discovering that Angela and Cain were once married—and had never divorced—Cord returned to Llanview and burst in on Tina and Cain's wedding. As Cord had hoped, the ceremony came to a grinding halt! In the following weeks, Angela came to Llanview, along with her loyal follower, Rebecca Lewis, to set up her ministry, the Tabernacle of Joy. Unbeknownst to Rebecca, the ministry was a sham! Angela was a con artist, intent on fleecing the pocketbooks of her flock of Llanview followers. Even her tidy bun of blond hair was a fake.

A con man at heart, Cain could not resist teaming up with Angela to bilk Dorian Lord out of $50,000. Sometime later, the truth about Angela's scam came out, and her loyal followers turned against the phony evangelist. Caught red-handed, Angela evaded the law and hustled out of town. When Cain and Tina married quietly in the Lord Library at Llanfair on the following Valentine's Day, neither had a clue that the minister performing the ceremony was actually an actor hired by Angela Holliday!

𝒦evin Buchanan, now involved in an interracial relationship with Rachel Gannon, decided to allow Lee Ann to have partial custody of Duke—but only if she dumped Jason Webb. Before Lee Ann could make a decision, Jason made it for her by arranging with Marty Saybrooke to have Lee Ann "accidentally" walk in on them. Her heart sank as she watched Jason and Marty locked in a passionate kiss. With his own heart breaking, Jason lied to a stunned Lee Ann that he and Marty were having an affair! Jason hid his pain as he watched Lee Ann get partial custody of Duke and take leave of Llanview forever. Jason eased his grief by resuming his May-December affair with a very willing, very enticing Dorian Lord.

𝒲ith Blair out of his life, Max Holden tried to no avail to get Luna Moody into his bed. Though Luna desired Max, she wouldn't sleep with him because of a premonition telling her that if they consummated their relationship, Max would die! To Max's relief, her psychic abilities eventually told her that they could make love on Valentine's Day at a lodge on Lake Serene. However, the plan went awry when Luna encountered a blinding snowstorm and was forced to take refuge in a shack. With the help of a trusty St. Bernard (whom they later named "Valentine"), Max rescued Luna—and they shared a gloriously passionate first night together at the Mountain Sunset Lodge.

Max and Luna's romance hit a temporary roadblock when they discovered that their spa, Serenity Springs, sat atop a huge oil reserve. Always looking to make a quick and easy fortune, Max wanted to drill

(cont.)

DORIAN
Don't you dare try to blame me for the unhappiness in your life! Look around you, sweetheart. Put the blame where it really belongs. On the man who built this secret room, for his secret pleasures. The man who didn't even tell you that you'd given birth to a little baby daughter named Megan. The man who seduced your college roommate Irene Manning and fathered Tina. The man who tried to stop you from marrying Joe Riley. But no! Not even now, when you finally know all the sordid details of Victor Lord's past, can you find fault with dear darling Daddy!

VIKI
Enough. He was my father!

LONG ISLAND, NEW YORK 1993

Classic movies like Wait Until Dark *and* Cape Fear *served as the inspiration for* One Life to Live*'s story in which convicted rapist Todd Manning stalked his former attorney, Nora Gannon, at a beachhouse in episodes that aired in December 1993. Scenes for this climactic, chilling storyline were taped on location at a beach on Long Island, New York.*

immediately. But Luna objected, feeling that it would destroy the "serenity," not to mention the ecological balance of the land.

Dollar signs lit up in Asa Buchanan's eyes when he heard that oil had been found on the very land that he had lost to Max Holden two years earlier. Aiding Asa in his quest to get the land back was—of all people—his new paramour, Alex Olanov. When Carlo Hesser's lookalike twin Mortimer Bern left town, Alex desperately needed a new power base. She yearned to meet a prominent man of wealth, position, and power. Someone like Asa Buchanan. Or better yet, Asa Buchanan himself! Alex kept a "boy toy"—Luna's kid brother, Ty—on the side while she wooed Llanview's crotchety millionaire oil baron. Asa enjoyed Alex's sexy come-ons, and quickly enlisted her help in getting Max and Luna to sell the oil-rich land.

Eventually, Max agreed to Luna's wishes and decided not to drill on the land. Max and Luna forged ahead with plans for a wedding to end all weddings. However, Max was afraid that Luna was getting cold feet when she started seeing the ghost of her dead husband, Bobby Ever. The "ghost" urged Luna not to marry Max or he would end up like Bobby—dead. Luna nervously agreed to a December wedding; but at the prompting of Bobby, she ran off before the big day. Max followed her and vanquished the ghost. After some convincing, Luna agreed to return to Llanview, where she become the new Mrs. Max Holden in a unique, spiritual wedding.

*D*orian Lord wasn't feeling very spiritual when she read an advance edition of Sloan Carpenter's comprehensive biography of her late husband, Victor Lord. In the book Sloan alluded to the fact that Dorian may have been responsible for Victor's untimely passing back in 1976.

Sloan's insinuations only made what was shaping up to be a bad year even worse. While in bed, Jason Webb found a lump in Dorian's breast. At first, Dorian, deeply in denial, ignored the lump. However, when tests revealed that the lump was cancerous, Dorian (with her pregnant daughter Cassie by her side) sought the necessary treatment.

Now, only months later, Sloan's scandalous book turned Dorian's life upside down—and she wasted no time in getting revenge. Dorian fired back by skillfully persuading a young and impressionable coed, Emily Haynes, to file sexual harassment charges against Sloan, the new dean of Llanview University. Sloan was astounded by the trumped-up accusations—he had never even considered making a pass at this girl! It was not long before Dorian's scheme was exposed and Sloan was exonerated.

Once again, Dorian had become the most-hated woman in Llanview. Even Cassie, one of her mother's most ardent supporters, threw up her hands and gave up. In a mother-daughter confrontation at Llanfair, Cassie ordered Dorian out of her life for good. The heated exchange, in combination with Cassie's already high blood pressure and an accidental tumble down the stairs, caused her to go into premature labor. Little William Carpenter lived only a few hours before dying. The terrible loss drove Cassie's normally placid husband Andrew to lash out at Dorian and nearly strangle her to death!

Desperate to salvage her reputation, Dorian lured Viki into Victor Lord's secret room at Llanfair. Once inside, Dorian bolted the door behind them, vowing to keep Viki prisoner until she promised to stop Sloan from publishing the book. However, the scheme went awry when, in a struggle with Viki, the key fell down an air vent. In a night to end all nights, tempers flared over past jealousies, betrayals, and deceptions. With time and oxygen running out, Viki dared to get to the source of their conflict, challenging Dorian to the truth: Did she marry Victor Lord only for his money? Did she kill him? Dorian denied the accusations and upon securing their freedom, the two enemies resolved only to go on with their lives with more animosity than ever!

*T*he most sensational story to hit Llanview in years had its beginnings when troubled party girl Marty Saybrooke had a one-night stand with Llanview University's star football player, Todd Manning. She hadn't slept with him since then, but reluctantly agreed to tutor Todd so he wouldn't be kicked off the team. But even with Marty's help, Todd failed miserably—and blamed her!

Lashing out, Todd lied to Marty's new songwriting partner and budding boyfriend, Suede Pruitt, by claiming that she'd seduced him.

After a vicious fight with Suede, Marty started drinking . . . then noticed an invitation to the Kappa Alpha Delta fraternity's Spring Fling. She decided to go, and before long was totally out of control—dancing on tables and swigging gin—much to the delight of the rowdy frat boys.

KAD brother Kevin Buchanan, concerned for Marty, offered to give her a ride home, but Marty waved him off. Later, when she could hardly stand, Kevin carried Marty up the stairs to his room to sleep off her drunken binge. Meanwhile, down at the party, Todd Manning motioned to his pals Powell Lord III and Zach Rosen to follow him upstairs.

The crowd's loud and raucous noise prevented anyone from hearing Marty's screams as she was brutally gang-raped by Todd, then Zach, then a reluctant Powell. Kevin sat on the porch of the frat house, oblivious to the barbarous act taking place in his own bed. Later, he found Marty in a state of shock. She recoiled in horror, wrongly believing that Kevin was one of her attackers.

Marty filed rape charges against Todd, Powell, Zach—and Kevin, too! In her confusion, Marty wrongly believed that Kevin was among the men who gang-raped her! Only later did Marty realize the error of her ways and exonerate a relieved Kevin. Attorney Nora Buchanan, believing Todd's assertion that Marty wanted to have sex with them, agreed to represent the boys. The trial went well for the defendants and Todd had hopes for an acquittal after Nora's brutal cross-examination of Marty. However, when Nora discovered to her horror that Todd had raped another coed, Carol Swift, she realized he was guilty. What to do? Nora, sick with the knowledge of the boys' culpability, delivered an intense summation, during which she made it evident to all that her three clients were guilty as sin. Because of Nora's sudden turn against Todd, Zach, and Powell, a mistrial was declared.

Todd once again swore revenge on Marty. After she spoke out on Luna's radio show about her experience, Todd waited for her in the alley outside the radio station. He pinned her against the wall and threatened to rape her again. Seeing this, Luna raced into the alley, grabbed a metal pipe, and hit Todd across the face with it. The attack left him deaf in one ear, and his face was scarred. When Todd's father Peter visited him in the hospital, he called him a pathetic excuse for a son and abandoned him.

Later, Marty confronted Todd in the hospital, where he arrogantly confessed to raping her. Unbeknownst to Todd, Marty got his confession on tape! Sentenced to eight years in jail, Todd seethed with anger. More than ever, he burned for revenge on the two women who ruined his life: Marty and Nora.

Nora Gannon faced a life-threatening crisis of her own when she was diagnosed with a malignant brain tumor that required immediate surgery. She reluctantly opted to go under the knife—without informing Bo! Just after the operation, Bo found out the truth and raced to her side, where he stayed throughout the ordeal. Afterward, Bo took Nora to a beach house to recuperate, then left for New York on business. While he was gone, Nora temporarily lost her eyesight, then found herself trapped in the house by a knife-bearing Todd Manning—who had escaped from prison! As Todd held his knife to Nora's throat, he wickedly declared that now *she* was on trial—and he was the judge and the jury. Todd viciously tried to rape Nora, but she thwarted his attempt by bashing him over the head with a lamp. In the nick of time, Bo, who'd heard about Todd's escape on the radio, came back to the beach house and rescued Nora. Unfortunately Todd Manning slithered into the night!

A "miracle" brought renewed happiness to Cassie Carpenter during the year-end holidays. Just weeks after losing her baby, Cassie discovered a newborn in the manger outside St. James Church. Cassie and Andrew led a search for the baby's mother. As she cuddled the precious boy in her arms, Cassie privately hoped that the mother would never turn up—because she yearned to raise the child as her own!

*A*cting on an anonymous tip delivered by Dorian, Clint went to a Vermont inn—and walked in on Sloan and Viki in bed! Outraged by his wife's behavior, Clint filed for divorce.

$\mathcal{M}$arty Saybrooke and Dylan Moody proved to be each other's best friend in 1994 . . . and before long they fell in love. Laid-back and easygoing, Dylan offered Marty a shoulder to lean on in the aftermath of the rape trial, while Marty helped Dylan (whose wife cheated on him) to trust women again.

1994

*E*arly in 1994, Alex Olanov and Asa Buchanan teamed up to open Llanview's hot new casino, the Wild Rose Club. Among the opening-night guests were Max Holden and Luna Moody. Max had a great time—and secretly began coming back for more. Blair Daimler, spotting an opportunity to be reunited with him, often appeared at his side to encourage him. As Max's gambling addiction grew, so did Blair's longing to sleep with him. She secretly tried to sabotage Cord's and Luna's plans to help Max get over his gambling habit. One night, after catching Max in a serious lie, Luna packed his bags and asked him to leave.

Luna's rejection only served to fuel Max's uncontrollable addiction. He grabbed Blair and headed for Atlantic City, where, using money secured from a loan shark, Jimmy Glover, they shared an evening of wild gambling—followed by a night of even wilder sex! Their naughty escapade was interrupted by Luna's arrival. She'd come to Atlantic City to patch up her marriage, only to see evidence of Max's infidelity. In the aftermath, Luna returned to Llanview, and Max took his son Al to his ranch in Sweetwater. Blair came along for the ride.

Before long, a forgiving Luna arrived in Sweetwater, looking to convince Max to come home to Llanview. Cord, in an effort to help Luna get back together with Max, kidnapped Blair and took her to Asa's near-by ranch. With Blair out of the picture, Max, Luna, and Al went to the county fair. But Blair refused to stay put! When Cord turned his back, she hit him over the head with a vase, hopped in his truck, and raced back to Max—straight into disaster! As she arrived at the fair, Al ran out into the

In the fall of 1994, the citizens of Llanview pondered the question: Who was the masked serial rapist lurking in the hospital parking lot? Three women were attacked and all the clues pointed to Todd Manning. But Todd insisted he was innocent—someone was setting him up!

road, with Luna chasing him. Blair hit the brakes—too late! She ran down Luna, who became paralyzed.

The accident shocked Max back into reality. Realizing he loved Luna and was addicted to gambling, Max told Blair that whatever they had was over. Back home in Llanview, a dejected Blair tried to commit suicide by turning up the gas on her stove. Thankfully, Cord found her, facedown on the floor, and saved her life. As she recovered, Cord tenderly helped Blair through the troubled times. Ready to gain control over her life, Blair pleaded for Cord to help her get over Max. Soon enough, they were making love!

*T*odd Manning, injured from his botched attack on Nora Gannon at the beach house, found his way to the Tabernacle of Joy. There, he managed to con sweet Rebecca Lewis into helping him. Todd regained his strength, then set out to make Marty pay! Luring her to the abandoned Tabernacle, Todd leaped from the shadows and attacked her. From outside, Marty's boyfriend, Suede Pruitt, heard her urgent screams. He raced to her rescue and a ferocious fight ensued. In the struggle, Todd pushed Suede, who stumbled back and hit his head on a metal wrench on the floor. Marty screamed for an ambulance, but to no avail. Within minutes, Suede was dead.

Todd took Rebecca hostage and fled the scene of the accidental killing. His flight from the law seemingly came to an end when Bo Buchanan and Rebecca's closest friend, Powell Lord, tracked the fugitive down in the woods. In a fight on a footbridge, Bo and Todd wrestled for a gun. Suddenly, the weapon went off—and Todd fell into the icy river.

Back in Llanview, Marty and her friends mourned Suede's untimely passing. The song that Marty and Suede had composed, "Teach Me How to Dream," wafted through the church during the deeply emotional memorial service.

With Todd presumably dead, Rebecca found love with her best friend Powell Lord. Unbeknownst to everyone, however, Todd had survived his icy ordeal, and made his way back to Llanview. Hiding in a shed on the grounds of Llanfair, he befriended Cord and Tina's children, Sarah and C.J., who believed their new pal was a genie! In time, Todd's run from the law came to an end. On the night of the annual Costume Ball at Serenity Springs, Todd was cornered and forced to surrender.

With Todd Manning's reign of terror finally over, Marty, Rebecca, Nora, and countless others who had been traumatized by him, breathed a collective sigh of relief. But, in a remarkable twist, Todd would soon become a free man: The police cruiser taking him to Statesville Prison suddenly blew a tire and spun out of control, nearly colliding with a car driven by Marty, with C.J. and Jessica in the backseat.

As Marty's car teetered on the edge of an abyss, Todd bravely saved her life. For his courageous deed, Todd was granted a pardon!

As the winter turned to spring in Llanview, Cassie Carpenter was feeling a sense of unmitigated joy and completeness. She had everything she wanted—especially after finding her angelic baby in the manger at St. James Church on the previous Christmas Eve. Cassie's fragile world quickly fell apart, though, when the baby's natural mother, teenager Beth Garvey, whom Jason Webb had rescued from a suicidal dive into the Llantano River, reclaimed the child. Cassie desperately offered Beth money for the baby, whom she had named "River." When Beth refused, Cassie stole the baby, but was eventually caught. Devastated by the turn of events, Cassie suffered a near-complete breakdown.

Andrew, forced to commit his wife to a mental institution, turned to Marty Saybrooke for comfort. Soon, Andrew could not stop fantasizing about Marty. Cassie got well, and eventually returned home. During the summer, a killer flu took Beth's life. Her last request was to have Cassie and Andrew adopt River, knowing that they could provide a loving home for her son.

Meanwhile, a troubled Andrew's erotic fantasies about Marty grew more powerful than ever! Andrew prayed to God to help him overcome his yearnings. As for Marty, though she shared a few dates with Luna's handsome brother, Dylan Moody, her sexual feelings for Andrew also began to resurface. One night, the inevitable happened. Andrew grabbed Marty and kissed her passionately. Horrified, they pulled apart. Over the next few weeks, they shared a few more clandestine kisses, but Marty realized that Andrew didn't feel as strongly about her as she did about him, they called a halt to the sizzling situation—but too late. Blair Daimler had witnessed one of their scandalous meetings and threatened to relate the dirty details to her cousin Cassie.

Could Dorian Lord have killed her husband, Victor Lord, in 1976? That was the question the concerned citizens of Llanview were asking in the wake of new evidence connecting her to the crime. The decision lay with a jury, as the long-awaited trial of The Commonwealth of Pennsylvania vs. Dorian Lord began in 1994.

One person whose testimony Dorian feared was Victor's former nurse, Ethel Crawford. Sloan and Viki secretly followed Dorian to Ethel's

(cont.)

Not for a second did anyone in town dream that the maniac stalking female hospital employees was Powell Lord III! Yes, he had been one of the three fraternity brothers who gang-raped Marty Saybrooke, but ever since, he had apparently been living an exemplary life. Only recently, Powell had asked one of his victims, sweet Rebecca Lewis, to marry him. It came as quite a shock to learn that Powell's mind had snapped and he was responsible for the rash of rapes in Llanview. Upon his capture, the sick young man was committed to a mental institution.

At Rodi's Bar, Todd Manning shared a drink, and later a night of passion, with the conniving Blair Daimler. When she discovered—before he did—that Todd was Victor Lord's son and heir, Blair schemed to marry the future millionaire by telling him she was pregnant with his child.

apartment. When she left, they found Nurse Crawford lying inert on the floor—comatose from an overdose of insulin. Could Dorian have tried to murder this key witness? In rapid time, Dorian was arrested and released on bail.

Defended by Nora Gannon, Dorian's case looked bad when a new autopsy on Victor Lord's body revealed tiny pillow fibers in his lungs, indicating that his life had been snuffed out. The finger of guilt once again pointed straight at Victor's "black widow," Dorian.

During the sensational trial, District Attorney Hank Gannon called upon an arsenal of witnesses, including Ethel Crawford, who delivered damning evidence. A hush fell over the courtroom as Ethel revealed that she saw Dorian Lord smother Victor—killing him in cold blood. Upon hearing this sensational testimony, Dorian screamed out, accusing Ethel of telling lies! Nora intently cross-examined the retired nurse, painting her as a blackmailer, a liar, and a woman bent on revenge. Her efforts were in vain. Even Dorian's last-ditch effort to take the stand in her own defense failed miserably. Hank Gannon tore her apart! In short order, the jury returned a verdict of guilty. Dorian was sentenced to death.

Dorian's future looked bleak, until an eleventh-hour witness stepped forward bearing evidence he claimed could exonerate her. The young man, David Vickers, went to Viki claiming to be Victor Lord's son by Irene Clayton. To support his sensational claim, he handed her Irene's diary, in which she admitted killing Victor herself! When the diary was authenticated, the DA had no choice but to drop the case. Dorian was free!

Unbeknownst to anyone but Dorian, David was a fraud. The diary verified by the experts was little more than a brilliant forgery. In exchange for saving her hide, Dorian gave David $50,000. Together, they had pulled off the scam of the century!

$\mathcal{D}$uring the summer of 1994, Tina returned to Llanview, having ditched Cain, and met David. Immediately, sparks flew! Tina was enchanted by the muscular, handsome man who shared her passion for life. But he was her brother! Tina fought to break the bond while a sexed-up David did everything to win her affection! The attraction between them was not to be denied. One night, while alone together at Viki's cabin in the mountains, "brother" and "sister" gave in to their passion and slept with each other. Later, to alleviate Tina's revulsion at this apparently incestuous act, David confessed to Tina that he wasn't her brother after all. She was understandably furious at first, but in time Tina forgave David—and even married him in a secret ceremony in Las Vegas, with an Elvis impersonator performing the ceremony.

$\mathcal{I}$n the aftermath of Dorian's release, Viki received several traumatic shocks. The first came when she discovered that her younger son, Joey, was having a sizzling affair with Dorian! Seeking the ultimate revenge against Viki, Dorian had artfully seduced Joey, whom she had hired as a summer handyman. However, Dorian never expected that she would actually fall in love with "her Joe."

Viki's second shock came when her lover, Sloan, stoically broke their engagement, claiming that he was still in love with an old flame, Beverly Crane. Viki was heartbroken. Clint, of all people, discovered the truth: Sloan's Hodgkin's disease was out of remission and he was dying. If there was ever a time he needed Viki's love, this was it. With his cancer spreading rapidly, Sloan reconciled with Viki and they married in a touching hospital-room ceremony—with a teary Clint (still carrying a torch for Viki) watching from afar.

$\mathcal{C}$lint's daddy, Asa, stunned the people of Llanview when he tied the knot with Alex Olanov in an outrageously decadent ceremony held in New York's Central Park. Alex, dressed as her heroine, Cleopatra, arrived on a barge, only to be kidnapped by Asa's enemies, Buck Miller and Bulge Hackman. On horseback, the Buchanan boys rescued the damsel in distress—and the wild wedding proceeded without a hitch.

A hitch did develop in Hank Gannon's carefree life when, out of the blue, his no-good brother RJ showed up in Llanview. Max Holden recognized RJ Gannon instantly: he was the very same loan shark who'd called himself Jimmy Glover and made Max's life miserable when he was slow in paying back money in Atlantic City. Upon his arrival, RJ hid from Hank and Nora, while befriending their daughter—his niece—Rachel, who had broken up with Kevin Buchanan and moved in with her new beau, Dr. Ben Price.

Randall James Gannon, the younger brother of Llantano County's District Attorney Hank Gannon, served nine years in Joliet State Prison for aggravated assault and armed robbery. His brother's wife, Nora, represented him and lost the case, and RJ held a grudge against both Nora and his goody-goody brother ever since. Now, it was payback time!

RJ tried to destroy Hank's career and reputation by producing a tampered videotape from Hank's college days, showing him standing by as a murder was committed. First he attempted to blackmail Hank with the doctored video, then tried to seduce Hank's fiancée, Sheila Price, in exchange for the tape. To preserve Hank's pristine reputation, Sheila nearly gave in to RJ's demands, but she was saved when he was arrested and detained on minor misdemeanor charges. RJ's vengeful mission was eventually foiled when Bo Buchanan found the real video, exonerating Hank.

Todd Manning, a free man after receiving his unexpected pardon, proposed to Rebecca, who tenderly turned him down because she had already accepted Powell's proposal. Todd's return to society hit another snag when he became the central suspect in a series of rapes. While Marty viciously convinced nearly everyone in town that he was the culprit, Todd desperately set out to prove his innocence by finding the guilty party himself. His private detective work paid off in spades! Todd was shaken to the core upon discovering that Llanview's masked rapist was none other than his old fraternity brother, Powell Lord III!

Powell, in the midst of a nervous breakdown, had snapped. Eventually, he took Todd hostage, forcing him to beg for his life. But Todd overpowered Powell, who was shipped to a mental asylum. After this incident, Todd and Marty called a tentative truce when he told her that he understood the horror he had put her through. Sadly, Rebecca had been through too much herself. At the conclusion of the serial rape mystery, she said a tearful good-bye to Todd, then returned to her native Texas.

Todd received a shock when his father died suddenly in December. Strangely, the wealthy Peter Manning left Todd nothing—except for a chain bearing a locket and a key. In letters from his mother,

Devious David Vickers came to Llanview aiming to get his hands on the late Victor Lord's vast fortune. Before long, those same hands were aching to explore Tina's curvaceous figure. Problem was, David had already scammed Tina into believing they were brother and sister! How could he bed the blond beauty without blowing his cover? Though she fought her dangerous attraction to him, Tina eventually let lust lead the way. Only after they enjoyed a night of forbidden passion did the voracious Mr. Vickers confess his dirty-dealing scam—then he whisked Tina away to Las Vegas for a wacky wedding.

Todd discovered that he was adopted and there was a large sum of money for him somewhere. But where? And who were Todd Manning's real parents? Dorian and David decided to find out the truth—and they were aghast to track down the clues and make the incredible discovery that Todd Manning was the Lord heir, worth nearly $30 million!

After his father's death, Todd retreated to Rodi's Bar to drink away the pain and confusion. There he met up with Blair Daimler, who was going through problems of her own in her shaky relationship with Cord Roberts. Over drink after drink, Todd and Blair bonded. At first, they were simply misery-loves-company companions. Before long, they were making love!

$\mathcal{B}$lair blamed Marty for Todd's "death," and vowed revenge. During a screaming match with her bitter rival, Blair hacked off all her Marty-like hair, then collapsed! Rushed to the hospital, the newly shorn Blair gave birth to a baby girl, Starr.

1995

*S*loan Carpenter's death capped a painful period of personal trauma for Viki. He had been the one light in her life as she endured the pain of Dorian's sensational murder trial and her subsequent acquittal. Later, Viki struggled to contain her worry and anxiety upon discovering that her son Joey had landed in Dorian's bed!

With Sloan's passing, Viki was heartbroken. Soon after she began her mourning period, Dorian arrived at Viki's door with incredible news: David Vickers was not Viki's brother as he had claimed. According to Dorian, David and Tina had been plotting to get their greedy hands on the $27.8 million intended for the Lord heir. Viki was stunned to hear from Dorian that her sister had eloped to Las Vegas with the devious David Vickers!

Barely controlling her fury, Viki hurried to confront David with the horrible truth. David was forced to confess his evildoing, but he swore that Dorian was behind the entire scam. Then it dawned on Viki—if David had lied about Irene Manning killing her father, Dorian must be the murderer after all! Meanwhile, with the walls closing in around her, Dorian booked a flight to Geneva. In near-hysterics, Viki rushed to confront Dorian. Knowing the police would soon arrest them, David hurriedly left for Spain, with Tina agreeing to meet him as soon as she could.

In her haste to get to Dorian, Viki's car skidded off the road. Shaken and bewildered, she showed up just in time to prevent Dorian from fleeing. In a bitter exchange, Dorian warned Viki that if she reopened the Victor Lord murder case, then Dorian would be forced to reveal "Viki's secret." What could she mean? When Viki threatened to call

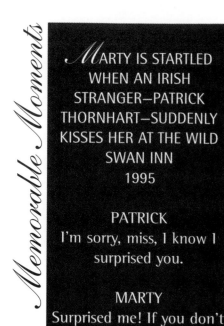

the police, Dorian launched into a vicious diatribe about her late husband, revealing that he had seduced Viki—his own daughter—when she was a little girl.

Unable to bear another word, Viki snapped. She attacked Dorian at the top of the staircase and with a powerful shove, threw Dorian down the steps! After Dorian tumbled down the steps, Viki calmly collected her crumpled body, heaved it into the trunk of her car, and took off. For weeks, Dorian remained a prisoner—first in Viki's cabin on Llantano Mountain, and then in the Plexiglass enclosed secret room at Llanfair. Dorian quickly discovered that her vengeful captor wasn't really Viki after all. The strain of the traumatic events had caused Viki to take on several new personalities, among them the cool and calculating Jean Randolph, who locked Dorian in the secret room, then told the world that Dorian had confessed to Victor Lord's murder before skipping the country. All the while, Dorian languished in her dank and dark makeshift prison, wondering if she would ever see the light of day again.

*B*lair's eyes lit up like Christmas trees when she made the amazing discovery that Todd Manning was the *real* Lord heir. Blair plotted to use the information to her own advantage. Ever the manipulator, Blair set out to marry Todd so that she would have the money to pay for Addie's care. Blair lied to Todd, telling him that she was carrying his baby. Determined to do the right thing, Todd proposed—just as Blair had hoped he would. Together, they flew to Key West, Florida, and tied the knot on the beach. Blair's gambit had paid off; she was Mrs. Todd Manning, and soon she'd be rich!

Just weeks after marrying Blair, Todd learned the truth when Tina divulged that he was her brother. The news flabbergasted Todd—but it all made sense to him. His father was scum, just like him! What kind of a man would have an affair with his daughter's best friend?

As he regained his bearings and got his hot hands on his $27.8 million, Todd set out to become an even bigger publishing tycoon than his father ever was. He bought the *Intruder* tabloid newspaper from Dorian, renamed it *The Sun*, and began hiring the best and brightest staff members away from *The Banner*. Todd and Blair were pleased with their first edition, with its bold headline declaring that cops were selling guns to kids in Llanview's Angel Square. At *The Banner*, Kevin and Clint were left wondering how Todd got this big story before they did. They had no idea that Todd's inside source, his "Deep Throat," was none other than Viki—whose Jean Randolph personality was leaking information to the enemy camp.

Todd, heeding Tina's warning that Blair was a lying gold digger, forced her to take a pregnancy test—while he watched. To her incredible surprise and relief, she really *was* going to have a baby! However, just weeks later, she was terrorized and mugged on the docks of East Llanview by Javier and Luis, two members of the Arrows gang. Sadly, she lost the baby. Young Cristian Vega, an artistic and bright teenager, happened upon Blair on the docks—and he was unjustly charged, and later cleared of the crime. In time, the youngster from the wrong side of the tracks grew close to his schoolmate, blue-blooded Jessica Buchanan.

*M*ax confronted Todd with startling news. Having learned from Addie that Blair was not really pregnant when she married Todd, Max spilled the beans about her deceit to Todd. An enraged Todd went wild, nearly raping Blair, until she reminded him of what he had done to Marty. Todd came to his senses and stopped. Nevertheless, the Manning marriage was over. Todd filed for divorce, and Blair worked tooth and nail to get ultimate control of her thriving cosmetics company, Melador. Much to her surprise, Blair soon learned that she was pregnant with Todd's child—again. This time, she vowed not to tell him about the baby. Blair Manning was determined to make it on her own!

*B*lair's aunt, Dorian Lord, was equally determined to get out of the secret room in which she'd been confined by Viki's alter ego, Jean Randolph. During her confinement, Dorian saw Viki's personality splinter into several other alters: vengeful Tori, violent Tommy, and Princess, the little girl who was molested by her father. Most of the time, Jean—the gatekeeper—remained in control of Viki's psyche.

Dorian pleaded with Jean to set her free, promising never to reveal a word of Victor's sexual abuse of young Viki. Finally, Jean agreed to let Dorian free on two conditions. One, she must not tell anyone about Viki's alternate personalities. Two, she must marry David Vickers! This way, Jean could keep David away from Tina, and Dorian away from Joey. Dorian had no choice but to agree to Jean's terms—especially after Jean craftily broke into the police evidence room and stole David's phony diary. Now, Jean had the evidence to destroy Dorian and David in her own hot little hands!

Upon her release, Dorian hid her pain and broke up with Joey. Jean paid a surprise visit to David (who had returned from Spain and was promptly arrested) in jail, telling him to divorce Tina or she would be forced to press charges against him. Reluctantly, David agreed, lying to a stunned Tina that he never loved her.

Dorian married David, and her stomach sickened every time this man she despised referred to her as his "little potato." Now, as man and wife, Dorian and David would not have to testify against each other. That was an added bonus, but it did not make life any more pleasurable for the miserable newlyweds.

Complicating matters for Dorian and David was the arrival of Dorian's niece, Kelly. A free spirit, with a larger-than-life imagination and a deep-rooted need to be the center of attention, Kelly Cramer developed a wild crush on David. Though she claimed otherwise, Kelly was a virgin. But even through one failed seduction attempt after another, she was determined to make David her "first." At the same time, Kelly was being tutored by her schoolmate, Joey Buchanan, who couldn't help but notice this pretty, perky blond beauty!

Early in 1995, Hank Gannon married his longtime love, Sheila Price. Their memorable day was nearly spoiled by Hank's still-vengeful brother, RJ, who picked the wedding reception to break the news to the humiliated groom that he had slept with his ex-wife Nora while they were still married. RJ Gannon earned Hank's wrath, but gained the trust of Hank's daughter, Rachel, who was now engaged to Sheila's brother, Dr. Ben Price.

Rachel, a struggling law student, turned to drugs to keep her alert and able to face the long hours of study. Her problems were compounded by a sense of inferiority to her high-achieving parents, Hank and Nora. As her problem worsened, Rachel's life began to spiral out of control. She broke up with Ben (who left to practice in England), then got involved in a sexual relationship with Javier Perez, her drug supplier. Concerned for Rachel, Javier informed his boss, Rachel's uncle RJ, who came down hard on his niece, urging her in vain to stop using drugs. When Rachel nearly overdosed on heroin, RJ joined Hank and Nora for an intervention. Against her will, Rachel was sent off to a rehab clinic to kick her habit.

In late spring, Max and Luna welcomed twins—Frankie and Leslie—into the world. The couple, still very much in love, doted on their two new additions.

The summer of 1995 brought the much-anticipated wedding of Nora Gannon and Bo Buchanan. To the surprise of the reluctant bride and groom, legendary rock-and-roll star Little Richard pronounced them man and wife. After the ceremony, the guests danced in the aisles, then headed for a 50s-style sock hop reception.

Also during the summer, Viki's alter, Tori, set out to destroy everything that Victor Lord built in his lifetime—including his home, Llanfair, and his newspaper, *The Banner*. On the night of Bo and Nora's wedding, she torched Llanfair, only to discover to her horror that Viki and Clint's daughter, Jessica, was inside! Momentarily turning back to Viki, she saved Jessica—but Llanfair went up in flames . . . again.

By now, Viki's fragile psyche was splintering on a daily basis. Over a period of days, each of her alternative personalities emerged. Tori surfaced, and traded the phony diary with Dorian. David witnessed their exchange and promptly stole it away. Now, with this crucial article in his possession, he hoped to win Tina back.

Kevin Buchanan was the first to realize the extent of his mother's sickness—but before he could do anything, she smashed a vase over his head and ran to *The Banner* and threatened to burn down the building. Tori took Clint hostage at gunpoint, brought him to the Lord mausoleum, and nearly murdered him. Only when Dorian injected her with a tranquilizer did she stop. As Tommy, she went on the run again, and was subsequently captured.

Under the guidance of Nora's psychiatrist sister Susannah Hanen, it came to light that Viki had one more alternative personality buried deep in her psyche: her father, Victor Lord. During therapy, Viki discovered the dreadful truth that her alter, Tori, was the one who had pressed a pillow onto her abusive father's face, smothering him to death. Because of the extenuating circumstances surrounding the long-ago murder, Viki was not put on trial. Instead, she was called to a hearing before Judge Barbara Fitzwater, who allowed a relieved Viki to return home for further healing.

With the telltale diary now in his hands, David Vickers hoped to divorce Dorian and reunite with Tina. However, his cold heart sank when Tina told him to take a hike! Smarting, David changed his tack, choosing to make Dorian suffer by remaining married to her! Meanwhile, Kelly finally wore down David's resistance and got him into bed. Just as they were about to make love, Dorian and a photographer burst in the room! Dorian was stunned to see that David's paramour was her own niece! In the aftermath, Dorian offered David three-fourths of her fortune and a divorce. He greedily accepted. Needing a hug, Kelly ran straight into Joey's comforting arms.

Coming to her senses, Dorian was not about to give away her fortune. With Blair's help, Dorian donned a blond wig and became Madame Helmore. Then she seduced a drunk, amorous, and blindfolded David. Later, when David saw photos of his scandalous affair with "Madame Helmore" in *The Sun*, he realized he'd been duped. Dorian triumphantly

(cont.)

HANK
You're a liar! He's a liar, isn't he, Nora?

RJ
There was a time when we wallowed together.

NORA
Shut up!

RJ
What? I'm sorry, I didn't realize we were keeping this our little secret.

declared that now she could get a divorce from David without paying him a penny! Because of his adultery, David would have to forfeit his million-dollar divorce settlement! After David signed the divorce papers, Dorian finally divulged that she had been Madame Helmore, his adulterous partner. David's fury turned to passion—and the divorced couple shared one last round of wild sex!

*I*n the fall, Llanview elected a new mayor—Alex Olanov—whose platform was the growing crime problem in Llanview's Angel Square. Throughout the year, the east side of Llanview had been rife with gang violence. Luna's good-hearted brother, Dylan Moody, along with his new girlfriend, Marty Saybrooke, committed countless hours to renovating the Angel Square Community Center—which they hoped would serve as a centerpiece of harmony in the district. However, even the new Community Center became the scene of several bloody skirmishes between rival gangs, the Arrows and the Prides. Marty began worrying about Dylan's safety, and their relationship suffered as a consequence of the ever-present danger.

The increasing violence prompted Dorian's maid, Carlotta Vega, a longtime resident of Angel Square, to make her impressionable son, Cristian, promise never to join a gang. Her elder son, Antonio, the former leader of the Prides, was serving time in Statesville Prison on a murder rap. Now, a war was being waged between the "good" gang, the Prides, and the "bad" gang, the Arrows, and young Cristian was caught in the middle. Would he give in to peer pressure and join his friends in defending Angel Square from the assault of the Arrows? If he chose to fight, Cris might just end up like his older brother—in jail.

*A*fter his GED and a college degree in prison, Antonio was given an incredible opportunity to turn his life around. Llanview's police commissioner, Bo Buchanan, needed someone to go undercover to find out who was selling guns to the gangs in Angel Square. In August, Bo arranged for Antonio's release and teamed him up with a young, idealistic female police officer—Max's sister, Andy Harrison. At first, Andy and Antonio were wary of each other. Andy's romance with Kevin Buchanan had recently gone bust and she was reluctant to share her innermost feelings with another man. But eventually, their distrust grew into love.

Antonio tried hard to turn things around. But violence continued to be an integral part of his life. When Arrow gang member Luis plotted to "take out" Dylan Moody at Llanview's Community Center, he shot and killed Dylan's sister, Luna, by mistake. Max sank into an all-consuming depression when his true love passed away, leaving him with a lasting legacy—their twins, Frankie and Leslie.

After Luis shot Luna, Antonio burst into the center and ordered him to drop the weapon. When Luis made no move to do so, Antonio fired and killed him. An all-out gang war erupted in Llanview's Angel Square. When Andy shot another gang member, Ice Dixon, in self-defense, she was accused of murder. With no witness to corroborate her story, Andy was fingered as Llanview's dirty cop and found guilty while the real culprit, Det. Nick Manzo, remained free. To make matters worse, Antonio was fingered as her accomplice, and his parole was revoked. Eventually, Bo coerced Manzo into confessing that he was the cop selling guns to kids. Andy and Antonio were set free, though she told him she didn't trust him enough to make a commitment.

Teens Cristian Vega and Jessica Buchanan shared the joy and wonder of first love, while her father, Clint, and his mother, Carlotta, shared a tender kiss. Best of all, Angel Square had begun the process of

VIKI CONFESSES TO HER FAMILY THAT SHE KILLED VICTOR LORD
1995

VIKI
I will never ever forgive myself.

JOEY
Your father was abusing you!

VIKI
Did that give me the right to kill him?

JESSICA
What do we do now?

VIKI
I don't know, Jessie. I wish I did. All I know for sure is I have to somehow make things right for you. For all of you. For my family. This illness in itself is bad enough, but when I see all the pain and the hurt it has caused you, it's got to stop. And somehow I have to find a way not to leave you again.

repairing the inner strife that had threatened to tear apart the neighborhood. Peace was finally at hand.

At St. James Church, romance was at hand! Todd and Blair, who'd reconciled in the fall, became man and wife. Afterward, they held a private reception at the Palace Hotel, where they vowed their everlasting love. Golden balloons fell from the heavens to herald their renewed commitment.

Medical student Marty Saybrooke's autumn journey to Ireland was never intended to be a pleasure trip. She had traveled to the remote Irish isle of Inishcrag to successfully confront her Aunt Kiki, who had been squandering Marty's inheritance in a wild spending spree throughout Europe. At the end of a satisfying day, Marty didn't notice the rough-hewn and handsome stranger finishing his glass of Irish whiskey and starting out the door. Just then, the stranger froze in his tracks, a look of panic in his eyes. Two burly men walked in the pub, and the stranger knew instantly that they were looking for him. He quickly turned his back, his eyes rapidly scanning the room. They came to rest on the girl with the long, flowing hair, contentedly sitting on a nearby bench. He hurried to her side and kissed her!

Without a second to ponder what was happening, Marty played along—pretending to be his lover. When the two thugs left, the stranger breathed a sigh of relief, and thanked his "wife" for taking part in this hastily arranged charade. By acting casually and posing as his wife, she had helped him elude his hunters. She had saved his life!

So began the romance of Margaret "Marty" Saybrooke and Irish poet Patrick Thornhart. Patrick was being followed by members of the Men of 21, who suspected that he had the coded sheet music that could reveal their terrorist plans. Marty believed Patrick's story that he was innocent of any wrongdoing. He lied to her, saying that he was merely a physicist on a government mission. But when she found a piece of bloodied sheet music in his possession, doubt crept into her mind. This stranger had placed her life in danger. After they were kidnapped and interrogated at gunpoint by Inspector Quilligan of the Irish Special Branch, Marty had had enough of her dangerous new friend. She was going home to her estranged boyfriend, Dylan.

However, Marty was unable to leave Inishcrag because of a fierce storm. During her enforced captivity, she and Patrick bonded. When the stormy weather abated a bit, they went on bike rides through the countryside, and long walks over the rolling hills. A strong but unspoken attraction grew stronger. Agreeing to make time stop for just one night, Patrick and Marty made love.

Back in Llanview, newlyweds Todd and Blair made final preparations for their honeymoon. But just before leaving, Todd undertook a mission to locate Marty Saybrooke. Hoping to finally make things right with the woman he raped, Todd went to Ireland, sent Marty back home to her dying young friend Paloma, then remained on the isle of Inishcrag to help her new friend Patrick Thornhart out of a jam. However, Todd (wearing Patrick's coat) was mistaken for the Irishman and shot, thrown in the trunk of a car, and driven off a cliff. He was last seen lying on an Irish beach, his eyes wide open. Was Todd alive or dead?

At home, Todd's widow Blair bitterly absorbed the news of her husband's death. She blamed Marty for Todd's untimely demise and became hell-bent on revenge. Meanwhile, Marty's world became even more complicated when Patrick grabbed Todd's ID and boarded the next flight to the States. He had to find Marty! Soon after arriving in Llanview, Patrick was stunned to discover the woman he made passionate love to was engaged to marry another man, Dylan Moody!

(cont.)

In 1995, several formerly invisible personalities emerged as a means to cope with her various needs and emotions. Over a period of months, the many faces of Viki were revealed to the audience. She expressed rage through the angry young boy Tommy, who pushed Dorian down a flight of stairs. Viki found fun through the free-spirited Niki Smith; control through the cool and calculating gatekeeper, Jean Randolph; fear through Princess (pictured here), the terrified seven year-old girl who suffered Victor Lord's abuse. Another fragment of Viki's personality— nineteen-year-old Tori— wanted desperately to reveal the extreme violation perpetuated upon Viki by her father. Lastly, Victor Lord's personality appeared, threatening to punish Viki if the code of silence was ever broken.

$\mathcal{B}$LAIR AND PATRICK

In the wake of Marty's marriage to Dylan, Patrick fled the church with the dangerously sexy Blair Manning. Blaming Marty for her husband Todd's apparent death, a vengeful Blair wanted nothing more than to seduce Patrick, then flaunt the fact in Marty's face. Patrick resisted Blair's seductive efforts at first, but finally gave in and shared two nights of passion with her. The repercussions ran deep. Unbeknownst to the couple, Blair's "late" husband had returned to Llanview in time to see his wife in the Irishman's arms.

1996

*M*arty Saybrooke went to Inishcrag looking for peace and strength. She found far more than she ever could have imagined, thanks to her Irish poet, Patrick Thornhart. Nothing could ever live up to the time she spent with Patrick on that magical isle. But her association with Patrick came with a price—a dangerous one. Fearing for her own life and doubting Patrick's sincerity, Marty went home to the safety and security offered by gentle Dylan Moody. Following her across the Atlantic, Patrick pleaded with Marty to believe in him; he was not a "cold-blooded killer," as the Irish newspapers claimed. Still, Patrick understood that he could not allow his Margaret to get too close to him, for it would only endanger her life. Though he wanted her dearly, Patrick knew he had to drive Margaret away from him. Meanwhile, he moved forward with a plan to undermine the Men of 21 and elude Inspector Bass of the Irish Special Branch, who arrived in Llanview in hot pursuit of him. Patrick managed to convince Llanview's police commissioner of his innocence, despite Bass's claims that Thornhart was guilty of multiple murders, including that of Todd Manning.

While the corrupt Irish cop, Bass, pressed the Llanview police to extradite Patrick back to Ireland, Commissioner Bo Buchanan tried to stall him. Bo moved Patrick and Marty to Viki's cabin in the mountains to decipher a coded piece of sheet music—a lilting piece that Patrick's former lover, the Irish Special Forces agent Siobhan Connelly, had entrusted him with as she lay dying from terrorists' bullets. Working side by side, Patrick could not hide his feelings any longer. He tried to convince Marty that he loved her dearly. Marty shunned his declaration of love. Unable to confront her own tender feelings, she fled the cabin in

GANG WARFARE
1996

East Llanview's neighbor-hood of Angel Square was torn in two in early 1996 by rival gangs, the Arrows and the Prides. Cristian Vega, a talented young artist, resisted pressure to join the Prides, the gang once led by his imprisoned older brother, Antonio. Local citizens, determined to find a way to take back Angel Square from the gangs, founded the Community Center to get kids involved in more con-structive activities. Despite these measures, East Llanview's young people, exemplified by Cristian, were often drawn to the violence that threatened Angel Square.

tears. Later, in a tense confrontation with Patrick, Marty defiantly declared she was going to go ahead with her plans to marry Dylan Moody.

For solace and assistance, Patrick found a trusting friend in a fellow Llanview newcomer, Maggie Carpenter. Staying at the rectory with her cousin Andrew and his wife Cassie, Maggie met their friend Max Holden. Max was having trouble dealing with the news of his small son Frankie's deafness. Maggie's heart went out to the motherless baby, to his sister, and their older brother Al, whose sensitivity and courage reminded her of her own brother Mark, whose deafness and troubled relationship with their father had driven him to suicide. When it came to their own interaction, Max and Maggie were instantly combative. Though months had passed, Max was still bitter and depressed over his wife Luna's murder, and he found Maggie's intrusion into his family off-putting. Despite his initial contempt for her, Max gradually began to see Maggie in a new light—and showed her how he felt by kissing her. It was then that Maggie hit Max with an eye-opening announcement. She was planning on becoming a nun! Over Max's protests, Maggie took her final vows in Boston.

Blair, very pregnant with Todd's baby, seethed with anger at Marty Saybrooke. Convinced that Marty was directly responsible for Todd's death, Blair made ruining Marty's life her pet project. In one particularly bitter encounter at The Sun, Blair hacked off all her Marty-like hair, then doubled over in pain. Rushed to the hospital, Blair gave birth to a baby girl, Starr. In the weeks after the birth, Blair continued to seek vengeance on Marty by trying to seduce Patrick.

While Marty, Patrick, and Bo feverishly worked to solve the mystery of the Men of 21 case, Asa began sending cryptic E-mail letters to a foreign businessman who identified himself only as "Poseidon." Alex, suspecting that her husband was up to something, secretly began corresponding with Poseidon herself. Alex, the newly elected mayor of Llanview, eventual-ly discovered that Poseidon, himself a member of the Men of 21, was none other than her not-so-late husband, Carlo Hesser. Alex fainted . . . but then upon recovering, enjoyed an orgy of sex with her hot-to-trot hubby!

While romancing Alex, Carlo "Poseidon" Hesser made a $30 million business deal with Asa, who continued to correspond with his unknown partner via the Internet. With the plans finalized, Asa planned to meet Poseidon and another secret partner, Lord Cove, at the Palace Hotel to hand over the money. Unbeknownst to Asa, he was about to become a victim of the Men of 21. Arriving at the hotel with a steel case stuffed with bills, Asa was hit over the head; when he awoke, the money was gone.

*D*isguised as Major Austin, a munitions expert, Bo Buchanan infiltrated the organization and was nearly killed by a bomb set to go off by his double-crossing boss, Bass. Patrick overheard Poseidon, but before he could warn Bo that he was going to be killed, Bass shot him. Seriously wounded, Patrick staggered to Marty's door, then collapsed! Marty stashed Patrick in her attic. Heartsick over hiding Patrick and lying about it, Marty nursed him back to health, then went ahead with the wedding to Dylan.

A dejected Patrick rose from his sickbed and arrived at the Palace Hotel in time to save Bo and help defuse the bomb. Bass was arrested and subsequently poisoned. Though Patrick tried to stop her, Marty married Dylan Moody. Heartbroken, Patrick grabbed Blair and dashed away to the stables where Blair played upon his anguish, luring him into an embrace. However, her well-timed seduction attempt failed as Patrick flashed upon memories of making love to Marty in Inishcrag. He broke free of her grasp.

*C*arlo Hesser shocked the residents of Llanview when he made his appearance at the first annual "Friends of Llanview" dinner. Seeing his nemesis alive caused Asa to suffer a heart attack. Upon his recovery, Asa sent Alex for a divorce from Carlo, then remarried her. But all the while, she engaged in a sizzling affair with her bald-headed ex-husband. To test her loyalty *and* get his $30 million back from Carlo, Asa sneakily convinced everyone he had gone insane!

Patrick was equally jolted when he heard Carlo's voice—and realized he was Poseidon. With fierce determination, he set out to prove that Carlo and Poseidon were the same person. Boarding a rented fishing boat, Patrick was unaware that Marty had followed him. When the vessel, sabotaged by Carlo, sank at sea, Marty and Patrick jumped overboard and swam to a deserted island. Alone together, Patrick listened in wonderment as Marty finally confessed her love to him. Back home, she resolved to tell Dylan. Afterward, she promised to meet Patrick on Llantano Mountain. Patrick waited . . . and waited. However, Marty never came—because just before she was to tell Dylan, he suffered a serious back injury. Torn between her love of Patrick and her commitment to Dylan, Marty decided she couldn't leave her husband now. In agony, she told Patrick they were through.

Hurting, though respecting Marty's decision, Patrick finally gave in to Blair's seductive efforts. After one particularly romantic dinner, they made love. Afterward, Blair insisted to her lover that nothing was wrong, went home, took out her wedding dress, and cried her eyes out. In the weeks after they made love, Blair and Patrick (both hurting from the pain of their lost loves) grew closer.

One hot summer night, Patrick and Blair were about to make love on the floor of her penthouse apartment as a mysterious man stood in the

WHO KILLED CARLO HESSER? 1996

If Carlo Hesser was indeed the international crime lord Poseidon, then it was a fitting metaphor that his life came to an end in the water during the fall of 1996. What started out as a charity fund-raiser aboard the ocean liner S.S. Orion, ended in terror when the lights suddenly went out aboard the ship. When they came back on, Carlo Hesser's body was discovered floating in the salty waters with a bullet through the forehead.

shadows. In stunned silence, he absorbed the shocking sight of the two souls in the heat of passion. It was Todd Manning!

Harnessing his rage, Todd ran off into the night. Keeping his astonishing return secret from everyone except his sister, Viki, Todd was overjoyed to hold his daughter Starr in his arms. Determined to make Blair pay, Todd kidnapped Starr. He finally returned her and revealed his miraculous "return from the dead" to his unfaithful wife. Blair's prayers had been answered—Todd was home!

However, having seen Blair in Patrick's arms, Todd was not nearly so delighted. Resuming his position as publisher of *The Sun*, Todd set out to make her life miserable. Still, he was torn by lingering feelings for the mother of his child. Should he end their union or give Blair a second chance at proving her love? Just when it seemed that they might reconcile, Todd was stunned to discover that Blair was pregnant again—with Patrick Thornhart's child!

Alive and well, Carlo Hesser secretly undertook a second reign of terror. Joining forces with RJ Gannon, he schemed to get rid of Asa and settle a long-standing score by getting revenge on Viki Buchanan, who had killed his son, Johnny Dee, in 1990. To accomplish that sinister goal, Carlo coerced famed psychiatrist Elliot Durbin into hypnotizing Viki into killing her own son, Kevin. It was to be the evil man's final act in a cruel revenge plot. Despite a nearly overpowering posthypnotic suggestion, Viki could not bring herself to murder Kevin, who breathed a sigh of relief after talking his mother out of killing him. Having botched his job, Dr. Durbin was unceremoniously murdered by an angry Carlo!

At the same time, Carlo sought to find a worthy male heir to someday assume his "throne." He liked what he saw in one young man who crossed his path. The kid had style, smarts, and spunk—not to mention a girlfriend who was a cop. Carlo chose Antonio Vega to fill his shoes! Though trying to follow a straight and narrow path, Antonio could not escape Carlo's clutches. He desperately needed money to buy back the family diner for his mother. However, because of his prison record, no one would give him a loan . . . no one but Carlo Hesser. Now, Antonio owed Carlo, who dug his claws deeper into his prey by arranging for Antonio's kid brother, Cristian, to receive the scholarship money he desperately needed to attend Llanview University.

Antonio hated working for Carlo Hesser. More than that, he hated lying to Andy. Andy, now a detective, swore to Bo that her boyfriend was leading an honest life. After making love on Valentine's Day, they were indeed a couple, united in love. But to her horror, Andy stumbled upon evidence that Antonio was in cahoots with the crime kingpin and now found herself in a perplexing dilemma—trapped between her love for Antonio and her allegiance to the police force.

Eventually, a bitter Antonio wanted out. Commissioner Bo Buchanan, now aware of Antonio's misdeeds, convinced him to go undercover to get the goods on Carlo. There was one critical drawback: No one, not even Andy, could know of their secret plan. This sticky situation put a severe strain on Andy and Antonio's already tenuous relationship.

*A*sa, while faking insanity, enlisted the aid of his longtime rival, Max Holden, to get back at Carlo for stealing both the Buchanan money and Alex's affections. Together, Asa and Max cooked up a scam to get Carlo by unpatriotically poisoning his hot dog on the Fourth of July, then making him believe he was dying of a dreaded disease. Only Serenity Springs's curative waters, Carlo believed, could keep him alive. Fearing death, he fell for the scam and told Max he was willing to pay millions for the water. Soon, Maggie realized Max and Asa were in cahoots, and joined in the mission to bilk the Mob boss. Simultaneously, the "dying" Hesser asked Alex to give him a male heir. But Alex was barren! Desperate to give Carlo what he wanted, she committed her "crazy" husband Asa to a sanitarium, divorced him, then told Carlo she was carrying his baby. The pregnancy was, of course, fake! Strapping a fluffy pillow to her stomach, Alex secretly plotted to adopt a baby and pass it off as hers.

Eventually, Carlo discovered that Max had duped him—he wasn't going to die after all! To get back at Max and Maggie, he trapped them in a cave in North Carolina. Convinced that they were about to die in the sealed-off cavern, Max tenderly told Maggie that he loved her. They came together in a sizzling embrace.

Max and Maggie survived their ordeal after being rescued by Antonio, who returned to Llanview to face the wrath of his enraged employer, Carlo Hesser. Refusing to be intimidated, Antonio called Carlo's bluff and talked his way out of his predicament.

With his criminal world collapsing around him, Carlo went ahead with his plans to wed his "pregnant" Alex. On the big day, Asa showed up, tickled pink to be able to reveal to the mobster and the blonde that he was completely sane! Carlo watched in horror as Asa tore Alex's wedding gown, exposing the pillow underneath! Carlo, in a fury, ordered Alex out of his life.

*B*y late autumn, Bo, Marty, and Patrick discovered the truth about the Men of 21 conspiracy from a microchip hidden in a book of Irish airs. To their horror, they learned that the beloved Mr. Kenneally, who had come to Llanview during the summer, was the brains behind the terrorist organization.

*T*o everyone's delight, Dylan regained the use of his legs and walked again. His exuberance at being able to be a real husband to Marty again was short-lived. Luna's ghost warned him that Marty's love for Patrick was an obstacle too great for him to overcome. After careful considera-

(cont.)

Nearly everyone in Llanview wanted to snuff out Hesser's life. Was it Blair Manning? She knew he was responsible for Todd's near-death in Ireland. Or was Todd the killer? He was unaccounted for when the lights went out. Or how about Antonio Vega? He was charged with the murder after having been seen coming off the boat on the night of the murder. Or was it Kevin, Max, RJ, Asa, Patrick, or Viki? Each had a compelling motive in this plot-twisting whodunnit.

It came as a surprise to the citizens of Llanview when Carlo's twin brother Mortimer Bern took the stand and revealed that the killer was none other than Carlo's jilted ex-wife, Alex! But questions remained: Did she really kill Carlo—or was Mortimer the unintended victim?

tion, Dylan did the gentlemanly thing and bowed out of Marty's life, returning to North Carolina.

*B*y now, nearly everyone in Llanview had reason to despise Carlo Hesser. On the night of the Manning Charity Ball aboard the S.S. *Orion*, which was docked in Llanview Harbor, Carlo's reign of terror ended. While leaning over the boat's railing the next morning, Blair was stunned to see Carlo Hesser's body, a bullet hole in the center of his forehead. Todd Manning tried in vain to implicate his enemy, Patrick Thornhart, in Carlo's death. However, within weeks, a suspect—Antonio—was fingered. But someone was setting him up. In December, Llanview's District Attorney Hank Gannon formally charged Antonio Vega with murder.

*N*ineteen ninety-six would be an eventful year for the Gannon clan. Hank's year-old marriage to Sheila Price ended after Sheila told Hank she was pregnant. Hank responded negatively to his wife's condition, causing Sheila to miscarry the baby. She then moved to London.

After fleeing the rehab center where she was sent to overcome her drug addiction, Hank and Nora's daughter Rachel hid in New York City, where her world spiraled out of control. She found work with a shady "dating service." Thanks to the assistance of her stepbrother, Drew Buchanan, Rachel returned to Llanview to confront her problems and overcome her addiction.

*A*fter telling Bo that his mother, Becky Lee, was dead, Drew was mortified when she turned up in Llanview. Trying to keep his "momma's" return under wraps, Drew hid Becky Lee in a cheap motel. She demanded that he get some fast cash from his deadbeat dad to finance the resurrection of her singing career. Eventually, a stunned Bo discovered Becky's "return from the dead." Though he was disturbed by Drew's elaborate lie, Bo eventually forgave his son. To everyone's relief, the greedy Becky left town in the fall after Nora paid her off.

*K*evin Buchanan returned to Llanview in 1996 and became an investigative reporter for *The Banner*, where he engaged in a playful, prank-filled, and always flirtatious battle for scoops with rival reporter Cassie Carpenter. Though she was a married woman, Kevin doggedly pursued a forbidden romance with a reluctant but sexually intrigued Cassie.

*K*elly and David's steamy game of cat and mouse continued in 1996 as he tried to get a large divorce settlement from his wife, Dorian. It appeared that Kelly's obsession with David was over when she found herself falling deeper in love with Joey. She confessed to Joey that she was still a virgin, and pleaded with him to make love with her; when Joey refused—he was not about to be used!—Kelly was convinced that he still loved Dorian. When Kelly caught Joey and Dorian having sex, she fell back into David's trap. Using David to make Joey jealous, Kelly went to a tacky motel with him, hoping Joey would show up and "save" her. When David aggressively tried to seduce her, Kelly hit him over the head with a lamp and killed him. Or so she thought!

David returned and kidnapped Kelly, holding her for ransom aboard a yacht. When a fire broke out, Joey raced aboard the yacht and saved the day! With a "gift" of $50,000 of Dorian's money in his pocket, David Vickers finally left Llanview for good—without an ounce of remorse for his dastardly deeds!

With love overflowing, Joey whisked Kelly away to Paris, where they shared their first night of passion. Upon returning home, Kelly moved into the carriage house on the grounds of Llanfair with the young man she loved and trusted.

That trust was put to the test in the summer of 1996, when Joey, while on a run through the woods, encountered an enchanting "nymph" bathing in the nude. Entranced by her beauty, he returned time and again, finally learning that her name was Olivia and she lived in a nearby cottage. Eventually, Kelly witnessed a shocking sight when she saw Joey kissing Olivia! Tearfully, she broke up with him. After weeks of heartache, Joey managed to woo Kelly back.

*C*assie's mother, Dorian, revived her longtime battle to destroy the Buchanans when she hired an attractive young woman, Cameron Wallace, to infiltrate Buchanan Enterprises. Unbeknownst to anyone, Cameron was leading a dangerous double life—as Joey's Olivia! It was Dorian's hope that Cameron, by engaging in some clever corporate espionage, could topple the company from within. Once again, she was thwarted when Cord exposed Cameron's scam.

*I*n December, Sister Maggie Carpenter made a difficult decision—but one that delighted Max— when she decided to leave the convent. Max praised her brave decision, and proposed that they make a fresh start. Together, they went out on their "first date!"

At the year's end, Antonio Vega faced his date with destiny. With Nora Buchanan as his attorney and his lover, Andy, at his side, Antonio anxiously prepared to go on trial for the murder of Carlo Hesser.

Dastardly Deeds

*W*hy would Viki attempt to shoot her own son, Kevin? Blame Carlo Hesser for the near-tragedy. In the final stage of his plan to exact revenge on Viki, Hesser ordered psychiatrist Elliot Durbin to hypnotize her into shooting Kevin. Though a shot was fired, no one was hurt, and Kevin gently convinced his hypnotized mother to put the gun down. Naturally, while this was taking place, the real villain— slippery Carlo Hesser—was nowhere to be found.

*E*veryone believed that Patrick Thornhart died when he was shot by terrorists soon after his marriage to Marty. Miraculously, the Irishman survived, and slipped out of town to lead a life on the run with his ladylove.

1997

s 1997 began, Antonio was about to go on trial for Carlo's murder. Carlo, prior to his death, had rigged all the evidence to point overwhelmingly to Antonio's guilt. After finding a bloody shirt planted by Carlo in his home, Antonio fled to New York City, where he was hunted down by Bo. Andy was given the chore of arresting Antonio.

Beautiful lawyer Tea Delgado, a Vega family friend newly returned to town, helped Nora defend Antonio. Andy reluctantly testified against Antonio. Just after Nora closed her hopeless case, Bo rushed in with a surprise witness, Mortimer Bern, Carlo's twin brother. Mortimer testified that he had been present the night Carlo was killed on the yacht—and that he had witnessed Alex murder Carlo. Asa had known the truth all along: he, too, had been a witness but hadn't come forward since he thought that disclosure might have a negative impact on his chances of recovering the $30 million Carlo had swindled from him. Now he verified Mortimer's account, but was later arrested and jailed for perjury for his earlier false testimony.

While these sensational revelations were being heard in the courtroom, a desperate Alex went off the deep end, taking Andy hostage and holding her in an abandoned building. His name cleared at long last, Antonio rushed in and saved Andy.

Alex had confessed to Andy that she had murdered Carlo. After she was taken into custody, though, she contacted Todd and offered an exclusive story to *The Sun* if he would pay her legal fees. To defend Alex, Todd hired crafty attorney Tea Delgado, who cleverly spotted several

KELLY TELLS BLAIR SHE
WAS THE HIT-AND-RUN
DRIVER
1997

BLAIR
You killed my son. You
put me in that bed. You
put me in this place.
You've kept me apart
from my daughter
through the worst crisis of
her life. And you think I
can forgive you?

KELLY
I am so sorry, Blair. I
never thought anything
like this would . . .

loopholes in the supposedly "airtight" case. Thanks to Tea, the charges against Alex were dropped. She literally got away with murder. Freed from jail, Alex gleefully left town with Mortimer—or was it his twin brother Carlo, pulling the ultimate scam?

In the summer of 1997, Andy and Antonio were married in a glorious Angel Square ceremony. They immediately moved to Berkeley, California, where Antonio had been accepted to law school.

*A*fter disguising themselves as siblings and successfully shaking down Cameron Wallace (Olivia) to get her to confess that she had been working for Dorian, Max and Maggie (who was no longer a nun) went to St. Martin, and finally made love, but then Maggie was summoned by another guest at the hotel—her father, Rev. John Carpenter. Maggie secretly helped John smuggle the body of his newly deceased lover out of the room. (Maggie later learned that the dead woman was Eleanor Armitage, the wife of media mogul Guy Armitage.) Later, Guy's handsome son Ian came to Llanview in search of his mother's missing locket and flirted with Maggie. Maggie felt a psychic, mysterious connection to Ian that was almost physical. When, after much pressure, Reverend Carpenter was finally ready to confess what he knew about this situation, he suddenly died of a heart attack. The locket led Max, Maggie, and Ian to New Orleans, where they learned from an old servant named Hannah—and a buried letter from Eleanor—that Maggie and Ian were the twin children of Eleanor and John. Eleanor had kept Ian at birth and passed him off as Guy Armitage's son but gave Maggie to John to raise. Maggie and Ian were delighted to learn they were siblings. Max felt relieved that Ian was no longer competition for his girlfriend.

*I*n Rio de Janiero, where reporters Kevin and Cassie had gone to follow a lead on Carlo's death, Cassie swore to Kevin she would not be unfaithful to her husband Andrew no matter how physically attracted she was to Kevin. But Cassie grew jealous on their return to Llanview when Kevin took up with Tea Delgado. Finally, Andrew gave Cassie an ultimatum: She had to choose between him and Kevin. Cassie ran to Kevin's home, where the two made love for the first time. Cassie and Andrew separated, and a bitterly hurt Andrew took custody of their son River.

*A*s the year began, Blair, who was still married to Todd but pregnant by Patrick, was debating terminating her pregnancy. Patrick talked her into

$\mathcal{K}$nowing that he was being framed for a crime he did not commit, Patrick Thornhart unleashed his anger upon Todd Manning. Fortunately, Mel Hayes intervened to stop Patrick from killing his bitter enemy.

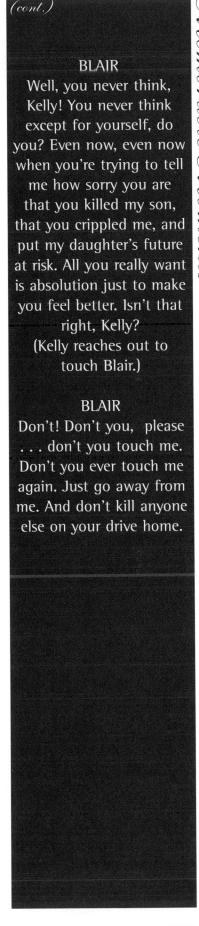

(*cont.*)

BLAIR
Well, you never think, Kelly! You never think except for yourself, do you? Even now, even now when you're trying to tell me how sorry you are that you killed my son, that you crippled me, and put my daughter's future at risk. All you really want is absolution just to make you feel better. Isn't that right, Kelly?
(Kelly reaches out to touch Blair.)

BLAIR
Don't! Don't you, please . . . don't you touch me. Don't you ever touch me again. Just go away from me. And don't kill anyone else on your drive home.

keeping the baby and said he would stand by her. He told a troubled Marty, however, that the baby would not stand between *their* committed love. Later, Patrick proposed to Marty and she accepted. Todd, meanwhile, went to court in an attempt to obtain custody of his and Blair's daughter, Starr. The judge awarded temporary custody to Blair but put off a permanent decision until a social worker could make a detailed report on her observations of both parents. A competition between Blair and Todd to impress the social worker ensued.

Todd took Starr for an approved visit and did not return at the appointed time. Blair freaked, thinking Todd had again kidnapped Starr; actually, he had taken her to the hospital after the little girl developed a

HARLEM, NEW YORK
1997

Detective Alex Masters from the ABC soap The City *joined Llanview's Police Commisioner Bo Buchanan in a search for fugitive Antonio Vega. Cast and crew went uptown and took to the streets. Under an elevated highway surrounded by a meat plant and several auto repair shops, the crew filmed the action-packed sequences as astonished local citizens—"real people"—went about their normal workday.*

high fever. Starr was diagnosed with aplastic anemia. Viki and Dorian joined the distraught parents in an effort to organize a search for a bone marrow donor to save Starr. Doctors felt, however, that the best chance for a match was from Blair's unborn son. This talk made Patrick very uneasy.

When Todd and Blair continued to carp at each other, Viki read them the riot act and told them they had to cooperate if they wanted to save Starr. Todd suggested to Blair that they "reconcile" while they searched for a donor and that she and Starr move back in with him—as a public relations gesture. Blair agreed. Marty was pleased with Blair and Todd's apparent reconciliation, but Patrick, who hated the idea of Todd as his son's stepfather, was very unhappy. Todd and Blair, with help from Dorian, Viki, and Kelly, organized a donor drive. But before lab work could be completed on potential donors, Starr's condition deteriorated. Patrick, with serious misgivings, agreed to allow Blair's fetus to be tested for compatibility. When the fetus proved to be a perfect match, Patrick pleaded that they delay the marrow transplant as long as possible. Blair told him they had already run out of time. When Patrick tried to continue the argument, Marty exploded: His precious son would be fine—it was Starr who could die. An upset Blair left the hospital. Patrick went after her, muttering something about taking care of things. He caught up with Blair before she got into her car and said he would drive.

Meanwhile, Kelly's boyfriend Joey had moved to Paris and asked her to move there, too. Dorian, who hoped Joey and Kelly would break up, persuaded Kelly to stay in Llanview and help with the bone marrow drive for Starr. When Joey sent Kelly a Dear Jane letter, a distraught Kelly jumped into her car and drove aimlessly into the night. Her car began to weave. Patrick and Blair, in an opposite lane, went into a ditch to avoid Kelly's swerving car and slammed into a tree. A panicked Kelly fled the scene of the accident. Blair, gravely injured, was taken to the hospital. Her unborn son by Patrick—the donor needed to save Starr—died as a result of the accident. Blair was so severely injured she had to leave Llanview for surgery and further treatment. Starr's custody reverted to Todd. (Later, Alex was found to be the perfect bone marrow match for Starr, and the little girl was cured.)

Todd, recalling Patrick's words about "taking care of things," assuming Patrick had deliberately caused the accident because Marty was becoming unstrung over Blair's unborn baby. He swore vengeance on

Patrick. He used his ready cash flow to investigate Patrick's past. Through barkeep/terrorist Kenneally (now in jail), he learned that several years earlier Patrick had played a minor role in bombing the yacht of a Lord Whiting. Later, Todd planted a bomb in Guy Armitage's ship gussied up in a Patrick-type wig. Armitage unexpectedly returned to the yacht before the explosion, ignored Todd's cries to get off, and was caught in the blast. Alex, who had been Guy's dinner date, fingered Patrick as the killer. Guy died of his wounds, and no one witnessed his dying accusation that Todd was responsible.

*O*n a business trip to Washington, D.C., Dorian met and immediately slept with Mel Hayes, a charming (if alcoholic) Pulitzer Prize–winning reporter. Dorian helped Mel get a job at *The Banner*, and he moved to Llanview. Mel built a good working relationship with his bosses, Viki and Clint. Viki encouraged Clint to finally vent his long-hidden feelings about their divorce and her subsequent marriage to the now deceased Sloan. Viki was later shocked when she had a romantic dream about Clint. Viki lovingly affirmed Jessica's decision not to sleep with her boyfriend, Carlotta's younger son Cristian.

*M*el, an investigative reporter, discovered that Kelly was responsible for Blair and Patrick's accident and after arguing with Kelly's aunt Dorian, persuaded Kelly to confess the truth to all. Prior to this, Kelly had told the truth only to Bo's scheming son Drew, who tried to blackmail Dorian with the information, but later left town after being exposed. Meanwhile, Patrick, who had stood wrongly accused in the Armitage bombing, confessed to Marty that he had participated in a bombing in Ireland to get back at Lord Whiting, who had impregnated and then abandoned his sister, who later died of a botched abortion. But Patrick maintained his innocence in the Armitage bombing, and he and Marty decided to go ahead with their planned wedding. Todd, meanwhile, stepped up a smear campaign against Patrick in his newspaper and other media outlets, and Patrick and Todd came to blows.

*W*hen the police discovered that Alex Olanov killed Carlo Hesser, they tracked the diabolical murderess down at an abandoned beauty salon where she was holding Andy Harrison at gunpoint. After the building was surrounded, Antonio Vega slipped in through a back entrance and captured Alex. Amazingly, the cunning Alex used her quile and sexual wiles to her advantage—and walked away from her spree of crimes with little more than a slap on the wrist!

Dastardly Deeds

In May, Todd Manning hoped to frame his arch-enemy, Patrick Thornhart, for the bombing of Guy Armitage's yacht. According to his well-crafted plan, no one would be hurt except Patrick. However, everything went horribly awry when Guy unexpectedly returned to the yacht—and died when the ship exploded.

$\mathcal{A}$ recovering Blair was devastated by Kelly's confession that she was responsible for the accident. Later, she learned that Todd might have been responsible for Guy Armitage's death and suffered a stroke. Meanwhile, Todd, determined to have permanent custody of Starr, divorced Blair and paid his attorney, Tea, $5 million to marry him so Starr would have a solid stepmother and he could gain custody. Tea had a hard time getting along with Todd's best friend, a parrot named Charlie Parker, whom Todd had been confiding in since the bird had flown into Todd's window in the spring. Later, the bird was renamed Moose.

$\mathcal{C}$arlotta, happy to see her son Antonio's name cleared in Carlo's murder, started having vivid sexual fantasies about the men of Llanview. Fantasy met reality when she and Hank made love, starting a new romance. A newcomer in town, a record producer named Jacara Principal, developed a crush on Hank; her interest was shot down by Carlotta. Hank also had to adjust when Carlotta decided to adopt Eli, a teenager with AIDS, whom Andrew had befriended. Carlotta's son Cris also had trouble accepting this troubled teen into his family home.

$\mathcal{H}$ank's brother, RJ, opened a jazz club called Club Indigo in partnership with Jacara. Several live acts performed in a jazz festival. Later, RJ and Jacara became romantically attracted to each other, and he confessed part of his criminal past to her. Unfortunately, he was still involved in shady dealings with a record artist's manager, and Jacara pulled out of her Club Indigo partnership with him when she found out about it. RJ's criminal connections in New York City continued to press him for money.

$\mathcal{F}$or several months, Bo's wife Nora had been suffering symptoms she thought meant pregnancy. After tests, Dr. Larry Wolek told Nora she had entered into perimenopause, a condition leading up to menopause. Bo was loving and reassuring to Nora, who freaked out nonetheless. Rachel, who was working at her uncle RJ's club as a talent booker, also reassured her mother. Later, young Georgie Phillips arrived in town to take a job as Nora's assistant. Georgie provied too good to be true. Secretly, she envied Nora's life and was determined to get it for herself. Slowly and carefully, she insinuated herself into Nora's life, and worked to ingratiate herself to Bo.

*T*wo Irish terrorists, tipped off by a double-dealing Kenneally, came to town with assassination in mind. Their mission was to kill Patrick, his bride-to-be Marty, and Todd (who knew too much about the Whiting bombing from his dealings with Kenneally). Just after Patrick and an already pregnant Marty were wed on Llantano Moutain, the terrorists struck. Mel was shot. One terrorist was shot by Bo, the other went after Todd. Patrick arrived just in time to save Todd's life, but was shot in the struggle and appeared to die. In the ambulance, though, Marty discovered that he was still alive. To keep themselves safe from avenging terrorists forever, Patrick and Marty decided to secretly move to Ireland together and let the world continue to believe Patrick was dead.

Mel was rushed to Llanview Hospital, where his life was saved. His semi-estranged daughter, a New York City social worker named Dorothy, rushed to her father's bedside bringing with her Mel's mother, Mary. Dorothy, who had been mad at her father because he wouldn't stop drinking, later decided to move to Llanview. She and Dorian did not hit it off. Mel's mother Mary turned out to be celebrity sex therapist Dr. M. Maude Boylan, whose books Viki and the women of Llanview had been reading. After

Viki experienced trouble having sex

CASSIE AND KEVIN

For months, Cassie's encounters with Kevin were simply too hot to handle. After all, Cassie was not only married, she was married to a minister, Andrew Carpenter. Still, Cassie could not get Kevin out of her mind—especially after their jobs as competing reporters kept bringing them together. During an investigative trip to New Orleans, they crossed the line! Though plagued by guilt over her feelings, Cassie gave in to her raging libido and made wild, passionate love with Kevin.

with Clint—she was still conflicted with feelings about her dead father Victor—she went to see Mary for therapy.

*W*hen Dorian drastically overreacted to Blair's ex-husband Todd's ongoing custody of Starr, Mel became curious about Dorian's childhood and the background of all the Cramer sisters. Cassie went to Austria to get information on Dorian from employees of her father David. Kelly went to see her mother Melinda, Dorian's sister, in a mental hospital in California. The two had not seen each other since Kelly was eight. Kelly took a medicated Melinda back to Llanview with her. Kelly and Ian grew close when he helped Kelly visit Melinda. Kelly was conflicted when her ex-boyfriend Joey moved back to Llanview and was instantly attracted to Dorothy.

*M*aggie decided to open a circus school and bought a warehouse building on the waterfront in Llanview to house it. Max, who had his own waterfront plans and wanted to lease the building from Maggie, planned an accident that would convince Maggie that the building was more trouble than it was worth. The plan backfired when turning up the boiler caused a fire rather than a flood. The building was destroyed, and Maggie was almost killed. When Maggie, who was engaged to Max, discovered his role in ruining the building, she broke up with him and left Llanview.

*T*ea, who was in a marriage of convenience to Todd, told Todd she was warming to him. Todd's inner demons prevented him from outwardly showing affection toward his new wife. Todd's ex-wife, Blair, set her sights on Ian Armitage. She wanted his wallet, not his body! Max, out for revenge, promised to help her in the quest. While working together to snag Ian, the flames of passion ignited again between Max and Blair. However, Max's world came crashing down when his twins, Frankie and Leslie, were kidnapped for a $5 million ransom. With Max in hot pursuit, the kidnapper's car skidded off the road and plunged into a river—with the children apparently inside. Max, inconsolable over the loss of his beloved children, blamed RJ Gannon, who denied any involvement in the kidnapping.

*J*oey Buchanan returned from Paris, and tried in vain to win back Kelly's affections. Though she cared deeply for Joey, she enjoyed being wooed by wealthy Ian Armitage. Ian fell in love with Kelly, and vowed to make her feel the same way about him.

$\mathcal{R}$ev. Andrew Carpenter showed his endless compassion when he befriended and counseled Eli Trager, an HIV-positive teenager whose mother had just died of AIDS.

$\mathcal{C}$assie sought more custody time with her son River, and to Kevin's dismay, spent a night at Andrew's home when she was distraught over finding out about her mother's family background. As Mel recovered from his gunshot wounds, he was determined to remain sober. However, staying on the wagon proved difficult for the alcoholic writer.

$\mathcal{D}$orian was both furious and distraught as more and more information about the tragic childhoods of the dysfunctional Cramer sisters—Addie, Melinda, and Dorian—came to light. She secretly replaced Melinda's medication with sugar to ensure that her disturbed sister never revealed their long-buried family secrets.

Part Two

Victoria Lord
Llanview's First Lady

Through widowhood and divorce, split personality, and stroke, Victoria Lord Riley Burke Riley Buchanan Buchanan Carpenter has maintained a remarkable inner strength. Her unwavering priorities involve putting her children and family first, even as she struggles with her own perpetual problems. Viki's greatest joy is the happiness of others.

Over thirty years, Viki has taken a round trip to heaven, traveled back in time, coped with multiple personalities, won a mayoral election, and recovered from a stroke, several shootings, surgeries, and countless near-fatal accidents. Behind the kind, thoughtful, and understanding exterior there is strength, toughness, and a resiliency that has allowed Llanview's undisputed First Lady to take each traumatic turn in stride.

Viki reflects in 1991:

VIKI
I have my husband, my children, and one precious, irreplaceable
life to live.

1971

1975

1976

1976

1991

The complicated relationship between Victor Lord and his eldest daughter, Victoria, has taken center stage since *One Life to Live's* debut in 1968. Widower Victor Lord demanded perfection from Victoria. In the process of molding her into the son he never had, the publishing tycoon heaped mental and physical abuse upon Viki. Unable to live up to her father's impossible demands, Viki endangered her own emotional well-being.

Viki fell in love with Joseph Francis Riley. Against her father's wishes, she married him, only to have her first love die in a car accident. Two years later, Joe miraculously returned only to discover that Viki was engaged to another man, Steve Burke.

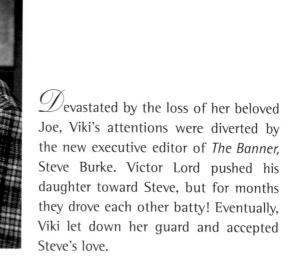

Devastated by the loss of her beloved Joe, Viki's attentions were diverted by the new executive editor of *The Banner,* Steve Burke. Victor Lord pushed his daughter toward Steve, but for months they drove each other batty! Eventually, Viki let down her guard and accepted Steve's love.

In 1974, Viki's godfather, Laszlo Braedecker, arrived in town to help her make a difficult choice between her two husbands, Steve and Joe. The kindly man urged Viki to follow her heart's desire, thus swaying her in the direction of her first love, Joe. The role of Lazlo was played by celebrated screen star Walter Slezak, the real-life father of actress Erika Slezak, who portrays Viki.

"UNBEKNOWNST TO ME, MY FATHER RECEIVED PERMISSION TO MAKE A SMALL CHANGE IN THE SCRIPT. INSTEAD OF SAYING, 'VICTORIA, YOU ARE AS BEAUTIFUL AS I REMEMBER YOU,' HE SAID 'VICTORIA, YOU ARE SO BEAUTIFUL. YOU COULD BE MY OWN DAUGHTER.' IN THOSE DAYS, WE DIDN'T STOP THE TAPE, SO I PLAYED THE REST OF THE SCENE IN TEARS. IT WAS A MOMENT I'LL NEVER FORGET."

— ERIKA SLEZAK (VIKI CARPENTER)

At first, Viki was relieved when Tina's long-lost father, Ted Clayton, showed up in town to tame his rebellious daughter. To her horror, Ted turned out to be both a phony and a con artist who drugged Viki in an attempt to gain control of her money and emotions.

After Joe's passing and the birth of their son Joey, Viki returned to work at *The Banner*, where she worked side by side with her late husband's hand-picked replacement, Clint Buchanan. While running the newspaper, Viki and Clint engaged in an all-out war, until they finally wound up in a passionate embrace!

Viki discovered to her amazement that, as a young girl, she had married Roger Gordon and given birth to his daughter Megan. In 1990, Viki's feelings for Roger rekindled, and their newfound closeness nearly came between her and Clint.

"GOOD-BYE, MY DARLING."

Only death could finally separate Viki and her greatest love, Joe. In 1979, Joe developed a brain tumor and died shortly before the birth of his second child, Joey.

In 1987, Viki underwent surgery for a brain aneurysm, slipped into a coma, and had an amazing out-of-body experience. While en route to the great beyond, she encountered many of her late loved ones, who helped her make a difficult choice: remain in heaven, or return to the land of the living. She chose Earth, and recovered from surgery with renewed strength and conviction.

*I*n 1988, viewers journeyed 100 years into the Old West to meet Virginia Fletcher, a St. Louis schoolmarm with a yen for adventure. Miss Ginny, who turned out to be Viki's great-grandmother, nearly tied the knot with a visitor from the future—Viki's husband, Clint.

*I*n 1989, Viki landed in Eterna, a ruined city deep inside Llantano Mountain. While trapped in the underground fortress, Viki encountered the dangerous Leo Cromwell, who was willing to kill to get his hands on a hidden stockpile of gold.

*I*n 1990, Viki ran for mayor of Llanview and waged war on the city's underworld elements and crooked politicians. After falling victim to an assassin's bullet, she suffered a debilitating stroke. Confined to a wheelchair, Viki demonstrated remarkable resiliency as she struggled to walk and talk again. After months of painstaking therapy, she made a full recovery, much to the relief of her daughter Jessica.

$\mathcal{N}$iki Smith, the most prominent of Viki's multiple personalities, has emerged many times over the past three decades—always bringing trouble with her. The fun-loving floozy has proven to be the most outrageous of Viki's alter egos.

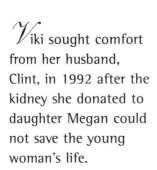

$\mathcal{V}$iki sought comfort from her husband, Clint, in 1992 after the kidney she donated to daughter Megan could not save the young woman's life.

$\mathcal{F}$ive alter egos took over Viki's life in 1995 to protect her from the awful truth that her father had sexually abused her as a child. The cool and calculating Jean Randolph served as the gatekeeper, controlling the emergence of each of the multiple personalities.

$\mathcal{I}$n Viki's incredible world, discovering a long-lost sibling is as common as returning from the dead! In the mid-1990s, she encountered both phenomena in the form of Todd Manning, the brother she never knew she had. After being presumed dead for over a year, Todd returned to life, stunning Viki by popping up in a graveyard. Brother and sister established a connection due to the terrible legacy they both share: their abusive father, Victor Lord.

$\mathcal{J}$OE AND VIKI RILEY, ON THEIR WEDDING DAY
1974

Victoria Lord 225

Llove, Llanview Style

Love rarely conquers all. But however fleeting, nowhere does love triumph like it does in Llanview. Whether relationships survive for the long haul or not, these timeless twosomes gave us many unforgettable memories on the road to romance!

MARTY SAYBROOKE AND PATRICK THORNHART

An old Celtic fairy tale brought these eternal lovers together under a full Irish moon. Patrick and Marty shared more than a bed on the night they made love on the isle of Inishcrag. When their bodies touched, so did their souls.

ANDY HARRISON AND ANTONIO VEGA

The courtship of the cop and the ex-con was filled with detours and potholes. First, Andy stood trial for a shooting she didn't commit. Then, just as their path to happiness seemed clear, Antonio was accused of killing his boss, Carlo Hesser. Somehow their electrifying love survived—and thrived.

JESSICA BUCHANAN AND CRISTIAN VEGA

Lovelorn teen Jessica endured a classic coming-of-age trauma, loving a boy of whom her parents didn't approve. She was a rich girl from the right side of the tracks, while boyfriend Cris, a Latino, struggled to free himself from Llanview's gang life— a situation that put Jessie in harm's way far too often. Time and maturity have brought these star-crossed kids close together. No matter where their lives take them, neither Jessica nor Cristian will ever forget the joys of their sweet and innocent first love.

KELLY CRAMER AND JOEY BUCHANAN

Kelly Cramer, a rebellious yet hopelessly romantic teen searching for love, thought life was over when she was dumped by erratic older man David Vickers. Then along came down-to-earth Joey Buchanan, a kind and generous friend who made Kelly smile! Eventually, their offbeat relationship reached a new plateau when Joey whisked Kelly away to Paris, the glittering City of Lights, for a weekend of romance and pure unadulterated fun.

TINA LORD AND CORD ROBERTS

In 1986, Tina whisked her new husband Cord off to her own private Caribbean island where they shared a romantic beachfront romp. Cord and Tina maintained a cosmic connection and an erotic energy that guided them through three marriages and three divorces.

VICTORIA LORD AND JOE RILEY

Is love better the second time around? For Viki and Joe it proved to be the charm. Fate threw an endless series of obstacles in their way before they were finally able to find marital bliss in 1974. The newlyweds shared a quiet spring wedding in New York City, then celebrated with a private reception for two in Central Park.

MEREDITH LORD AND LARRY WOLEK

The heartbreakingly romantic saga of sweet Meredith and starry-eyed Larry proved to be one of the most popular in *One Life to Live's* first three decades on the air. In the beginning, their devotion was tested sorely and often by Meredith's stuffy father Victor Lord, who was determined to keep his blue-blooded daughter apart from "riffraff" like Larry. Eventually, they overcame life's obstacles and, with their son Danny, Larry and Meredith found happiness—though it all ended much too soon when Meredith died tragically in 1973.

SAMANTHA VERNON AND RAFE GARRETSON

After a miserable marriage to Asa Buchanan, Sam found momentary contentment with his kind-hearted nephew, Rafe. In a tragic twist of fate, Samantha drowned in a hot tub. She was pregnant at the time, and her legacy lived on when the embryo was transplanted to her best friend, Delila Ralston. Heartbroken by his wife's tragic passing, Rafe eventually fell in love again—with none other than Delila!

Llove, Llanview Style 229

ℳEGAN GORDON AND JAKE HARRISON

The magnetic attraction of polar opposites isn't just a convention of romance, it's a force of nature; and nowhere was its power more apparent than in the love affair between Megan and Jake. She was a spitfire in silk stockings. He was trouble in a tight T-shirt. How could they help but fall hopelessly in love?

$\mathcal{P}$AT ASHLEY AND TONY LORD

As kids, they shared a torrid romance in Rio. The lovers went their separate ways, and unbeknownst to Tony, Pat gave birth to his son. Ten years later, fate brought them together again in Llanview, where their tortured love story culminated in marriage. Sadly, after only a short time as man and wife, Tony died while on a dangerous reporting assignment in Beirut.

$\mathcal{D}$ORIAN LORD AND MEL HAYES

Dorian Lord found a unique way to express her desire for new lover Mel Hayes when she performed a sexy fan dance during the summer of 1997. The naughty newsman and his mischievous mate proved that middle-aged couples can be sexy, passionate, funny, and dramatic—often at the same time!

CARLA GRAY AND ED HALL

Carla Gray thought she loved top cop Ed Hall with all her heart. Everyone thought these two simpatico souls would be together forever, but the relationship came to an end when Carla found herself overwhelmingly attracted to devil-may-care doctor, Jack Scott. It didn't take long for Carla to realize that Dr. Scott was a scoundrel, but alas, she arrived at the revelation too late to recapture the magic with Ed.

JENNY VERNON AND PETER JANSSEN

No two people deserved happiness more than Dr. Peter Janssen and nurse Jenny Vernon—and none had less of it! Peter patiently waited for years for Jenny to extricate herself from a bad marriage to Brad, only to share but a precious few months with his beloved new wife. Their tender romance came to a tragic end when Peter's car skidded out of control and he was killed.

CASSIE CARPENTER AND KEVIN BUCHANAN

In an effort to deny her underlying attraction to Kevin, Cassie fought with her fellow reporter like a kitten with a puppy. Cassie knew that if she gave in to her guilt-filled flirtation with Kevin, the resulting scandal would be even muddier than the Serenity Springs mud hole they shared in 1996. Eventually, Kevin and Cassie's love proved too powerful to resist. The preacher's wife shocked everyone when she acted on her feelings for Kevin, breaking up her marriage-to-be with the man she loved.

Loving to the "Max"

The many loves of Max Holden

MAX HOLDEN

Max Holden loves to fall in love! The tall Texan thrives on that certain intoxication that one feels when holding a special someone. For more than a decade, this adventurous dreamer has loved, lost, and loved again. When it comes to romance, you can always count on Mr. Holden to love 'em to the max!

$\mathscr{I}$t was love at first sight when Max laid eyes on Megan Gordon, but the feisty actress presented a challenge because she couldn't stand him! Her resistance just spurred him on—he wanted nothing more than what he couldn't have. Eventually, Max charmed his prey, and together they proved that oil and water *can* mix.

Gabrielle was a nice, sweet girl next door, and Max saw her as good for a fling while he was in Argentina. She came after him with a vengeance, tracked him down, and then basically ruined his relationship with every other woman in his life. There was never a boring moment in Max and Gabrielle's fiery relationship. Over their many years together, they had wild, violent fights and made wild, passionate love!

When Gabrielle was sent to jail, Max poured his passionate energies into a relationship with Lee Ann Demerest, the sweet but naive daughter of the midwife who'd delivered him back home in Sweetwater, Texas. When Lee Ann asked Max to marry her, he politely declined. What he didn't know was that Lee Ann was pregnant and the baby could have been his. (It wasn't!)

Blair Daimler had no time for a hopeless dreamer like Max Holden. Though she desired him in bed, Blair bypassed Max and became engaged to rich Asa Buchanan. As their wedding approached, Max pleaded in vain for Blair to change her mind. Later, they even made love—on top of her wedding dress!

*O*n a mission to destroy her marriage to Cord Roberts, Max invited Tina to Buenos Aires. Over time, he lusted after Tina, then he loved her, then he made a lot of money off her. But their tentative pairing fell apart when, at their wedding, Tina uttered her ex-husband's name instead of his. That was more than one man could take!

MAX
You felt something for me. You can't deny that!

TINA
You let me go! I still love Cord and I've always been honest with you!

MAX
But damn it! You can't deny you felt something for me. Something that has nothing to do with money or name. Something you never had with Cord!

TINA
You leave me alone! I love Cord and I always will and I'll never forget it! Let me go! Just let me go!

MAX
We love each other.

GABRIELLE
A love that's just given you pain. You'd be so much better off without me. How much pain do you have to go through before you realize that? Please, let go of me.

MAX
No. It's a noble thing to want to go into a convent. But not for the wrong reasons. I'm not going to let you go. You hear me? Never.
(They kiss.)

GABRIELLE
Oh, Max.

MAX
It's what you want. It's what you need. It's what we both need.

*M*ax was attracted to Maggie Carpenter, but common sense told him that they could never share a future because Maggie was a nun! Fighting to keep his feelings in check, Max was unaware that Maggie was struggling with her own dilemma. How could she keep her commitment to God without keeping her distance from Max? Praying for guidance, Maggie went ahead and took her final vows, but eventually left the order for a disorderly life with maddening Max.

*M*ax climbed a convent wall to stop Gabrielle from becoming a nun. Under the moonlight, he pledged his love on the convent lawn. . . .

When Luna Moody blew into town, Max didn't know what hit him! She had to be the strangest, most unique character who had ever come into his life—and at first he didn't even notice her! Then one day it finally hit him that she was "the one." Rarely have a man and woman been so in tune with each other. Max and Luna read each other's thoughts, finished each other's sentences, and were able to communicate without words in ways that neither had experienced before.

Magnificent Men

Meet the magnificent men of Llanview! While these nine honorable gents share the same zip code and inherent sense of decency, they are all as different as night and day.

Cordero Roberts

Over his eleven years in Llanview, Cord established himself as a lover, not a fighter. Still, this tall, dark, and moral man proved to be a strong believer in the age-old philosophy that a man should come to the aid of the woman he loves.

Kevin Buchanan

A cocky charmer with a keen sense of humor, this ace reporter's underlying earnestness and compassion have proven irresistible to the women of Llanview—especially another man's wife, Cassie Carpenter.

Antonio Vega

Growing up on the tough streets of East Llanview, Antonio learned to use his wits and his fists to survive. A modern-day cross between Robin Hood and James Dean, this smoldering Latino never trusted the system, so he did things his way. Proud and passionate, his love for his family and his heritage are the most integral parts of his multifaceted life.

Reverend Andrew Carpenter

Andrew's not holier-than-thou, and he doesn't profess to be perfect, either. But when the chips are down, you can always count on Andrew to battle injustice with a message of tolerance. As a dear friend or a faithful lover, Andrew is a man of pure passion.

Patrick Thornhart

Over the course of his tempestuous two years in Llanview, Patrick Thornhart proved himself to be the ultimate romantic hero—passionate, wounded, and sincere. A latter-day Heathcliff, this brooding Irish poet cherished midnight picnics under the stars with the woman he loved, and restful evenings curled up before a fire of smoldering peat with his beloved Margaret nestled safely in his arms.

Dr. Larry Wolek

Since 1968, Larry has been Llanview Hospital's quintessential "good doctor." In the romance department, each of his four marriages has ended in abandonment of one kind or another, but Larry's outlook on life remains forever optimistic. As a doctor, he's kind, gentle, and maintains a smooth bedside manner guaranteed to assuage the fears of even the most impatient patient.

Joey Buchanan

Can this guy cook! Llanview's ladies licked their lips in anticipation of one of Joey's gourmet Italian dinners. When he wasn't serving up epicurean delights, this romantic soul was known to whisk his lover off to the world's most romantic cities at the drop of a hat.

Hank Gannon

Hank is an extremely smart and ambitious workaholic, obsessed with the enforcement of the law. This maverick district attorney will do anything to win a case—except compromise his ethics. In his style, DA Gannon is contemporary and urban. He prefers elegant, modern Italian suits by day, and leather by night.

Dylan Moody

Dylan was a rare breed—a soft-spoken, sensitive guy who placed manners and courtesy above all else. When it came to wooing the woman he loved, this charming Southerner always exhibited a fascinating flair for the unexpected.

In Memoriam. . . .

Though these six souls left us much too soon, we continue to celebrate their warmth and understanding, their wisdom and counsel, their kindness and generosity, their patience and forbearance, and their enduring strength of character. These timeless characters are gone, but not forgotten. . . .

Meredith Lord

You would never know from her easygoing personality and generous soul that Meredith Lord was born to great wealth. When she wasn't volunteering at Llanview Hospital, sweet "Merrie" was providing a simple and loving home for her husband Larry and son Danny. She overcame a near-fatal blood disease to marry the man she loved, only to die tragically.

Joe Riley

One Life To Live's original heartthrob, fun-loving Joe Riley brought a zest for life to his job as investigative journalist for *The Banner.* Joe's dashing good looks and glinting Irish eyes caught the attention of Victoria Lord, who couldn't help but fall in love with him.

Luna Moody

Luna was a New Age heroine to be reckoned with! She parachuted into Llanview in 1991 with an armful of healing crystals—and immediately charmed the people of Llanview with her tender, homespun wisdom. Though Luna's head was often in the clouds, her feet were planted firmly on the ground, and her heart was always in the right place.

Didi O'Neill

With her positive outlook and ever-cheery disposition, Didi enriched the lives of everyone she touched. Bo Buchanan, disillusioned with his greedy family, had his faith in humanity restored the moment he met this warmhearted soul, who was tragically taken from him after just four years of bliss.

Megan Gordon　　　　　　　　　　　　　*Sarah Gordon*

Sarah was a most honorable and decent young woman. She believed in doing what was right, and that honesty was always the best policy. Sarah was so nice that sometimes it was easy to take advantage of her kindness.

Though she was only on this Earth for a scant few years, Megan lived life to the fullest. In her first year in Llanview alone, she ventured into an underground city, gained a new mother, developed a tacky split personality, was falsely arrested for prostitution, got locked in a meat freezer, and won a prestigious Daisy Award!

Hard-luck Heroines

These Llanview ladies took extensive classes at the school of hard knocks. To a person, they triumphed over tragedy, sharing their special charms with those they loved for the past three decades.

Pat Ashley

Pat was excited when her sister Maggie wrote to say she was coming from England to visit. Little did she know that Maggie Ashley would become the twisted sister from hell. Maggie's demented jealousy led her to lock Pat in the basement and steal her identity *and* her boyfriend!

Jenny Wolek

Jenny sacrificed her lifelong ambition to become a nun to marry Tim, the young man she loved. In a tragic twist of fate, Tim was critically injured just days before their wedding when he fell down a flight of stairs. Just hours after their hospital room wedding, Tim passed away.

Wanda Webb

Poor Wanda! This wisecracking waitress fell instantly in love with Joe Riley when he walked into her diner in 1972. She fantazised about settling down with Joe, but he only had eyes for Viki. Wanda finally found the man of her dreams in Joe's best buddy, Vince Wolek. As (bad) luck would have it, Vince was murdered just a few short years later.

Nora Gannon

An impassioned lawyer, Nora will battle the most powerful opponent to win freedom for her clients. But her verbal sparring with husband Bo is what really makes her feel alive. Nora's a queen in the courtroom but a washout in the kitchen. Bo knows, better than anyone, that his wife simply cannot cook! Nora has always maintained her biting wit and zest for life—through blindness, brain tumors, and blackouts.

Margaret "Marty" Saybrooke

Her habit for hitting the bottle and telling tall tales were turn-offs to the townsfolk of Llanview, serving to further isolate this full-time wild child. A series of personal horrors and tragedies led Marty to grow as an individual. Once she learned to confront her fears and love herself, Marty was finally able to shower affection on those dear to her. No one came to appreciate Margaret's magic more than her only true love, Patrick.

Carlotta Vega

A woman of unquestionable integrity, Carlotta has endured more than her share of heartache. In rapid succession, her son was charged with murder, her husband dropped dead, and her family diner was taken away. Still, Carlotta refused to give in to despair. She took the hits with nary a flinch, and proudly moved on with her life.

Sinners

Bad Girls

Life in Llanview would be duller than dishwater without sexy troublemakers stirring things up. Whether they are clawing their way up the social ladder or parading through men at a lightning-quick pace, there's a certain breed of Llanview lady who knows exactly what she wants—and knows how to lie through her teeth to get it!

Karen Wolek

Bored by her marriage to workaholic Dr. Larry Wolek, Karen (no relation to Larry's first wife, Karen) began secretly spending her afternoons entertaining local businessmen who lavished extravagant presents upon her—things she could never buy for herself on the tiny allowance provided her by her budget-minded husband. Karen soon discovered that the men expected a "gift" from her in return. So she became a "freelance" prostitute, working for jewelry and expensive clothing. Before long, Karen was working full-time for pimp and pornographer, Marco Dane.

Blair Manning

Blair salivated upon discovering that Todd Manning was Victor Lord's son—and worth $27.8 million! Intent on getting her greedy hands on the fortune, Blair lied to Todd that she was pregnant with his child. Todd married her, posthaste; but after getting an earful from Blair's ex-husband, Asa, about her history of deception, he ordered his new wife to take a pregnancy test. To Blair's amazement and relief, she really was pregnant! Years later, this she-devil continues to do bad things for good reasons as she searches for the love and security she can never find.

Ursula Blackwell

This fiery redhead sent soap opera psychosis soaring to new heights when she went on a mad rampage in the late 1980s. In a bid to rid the world of Tina Roberts, Ursula rigged her wedding cake to explode! Instead of Tina, the innocent Steve Holden was blown to bits by the mad bomber's power-packed pastry.

Kelly Cramer

Filled with larger-than-life romantic dreams, teenage whirlwind Kelly Cramer strutted into town in 1995 after being kicked out of a convent school. She immediately scoped out the handsome crop of Llanview men before falling head over heels in *lust* with her aunt Dorian's sexy husband, David Vickers. Wild-child Kelly had seemingly reformed her wayward ways, until she caused an accident that injured her cousin Blair Manning and killed Blair's unborn baby. Poor Kelly! She didn't exactly have the best role model growing up: her mother, Melinda, has had several stints in mental institutions because of her own maniacal man troubles.

Tracy James

When Dr. Larry Wolek treated sweet Tracy James after a fall, he thought she was just a dedicated art student at Llanview University. Only after she developed a "fatal attraction" for him did Larry learn that Tracy was a psychiatric nurse who should have been committed herself! When Larry rejected her, Tracy lured him to her house, then locked him in the basement study with her ferocious dog, Ilse, as his guard.

Maria Roberts

Maria showed warmth with but one man— her son, Cordero. This hot-blooded Latin lady was the incarnation of pure ice when she schemed to get her teenage sweetheart, Clint Buchanan, back at any cost. Hell-bent on murdering Clint's wife, Viki, Maria got her hands on a powerful poison—but during a confrontation with Viki's sister, Tina, she accidentally spilled the deadly fluid on herself!

Olivia DeWitt

Scam-artist Olivia DeWitt should have known better than to owe something to Dorian Lord. Olivia, a grifter whose neck Dorian once saved, paid her benefactor back by posing as businesswoman Cameron Wallace to infiltrate Buchanan Enterprises. At the same time, Olivia, who lived in the woods, aroused Joey Buchanan by taking naked dips in a pond while he watched. Joey's infatuations with this sexy nymph nearly destroyed his romance with Kelly Cramer.

Alex Olanov

Was Alex Olanov truly evil or simply misunderstood? This blond minx made a career out of doing something truly despicable, then pinning the dirty deed on an innocent party. Once, she nearly cracked open Asa's skull with a sculpture and framed Tina for the crime. On another occasion, she tried to frame Renee Buchanan for a jewelry heist at her own hotel. When it came to the opposite sex, her jealousy often boiled over into a black rage. Remember when she tried to drown Bo's lover, Cassie? Alex seemed most content with Carlo Hesser, relishing their kinky, borderline dangerous liaisons!

Edwina Lewis

Dorian Lord proudly hired ace reporter Edwina Lewis to work for the *Lord Press* in 1978. Snobby Edwina set her sights on fellow reporter Richard Abbott, and nearly went ballistic when he preferred "that country hick," Becky Lee Hunt, to her. So she schemed, conned, and connived—unsuccessfully—to break them up. Naughty Edwina's whole life was a lie. While she professed to be a blue-blooded former debutante, Edwina was actually a poor, adopted girl from the wrong side of the tracks. It soon became clear where she got her "bad" genes: Edwina's natural father was the super-evil Dr. Ivan Kipling.

Angela Holiday

Cord was suckered by this con artist masquerading as an evangelical minister. Angela's former husband, Cain Rogan, himself a classic con man, taught her everything she knew about grifting. In 1993, she arrived in Llanview and set up her Tabernacle of Joy, telling everyone she had seen the light and been saved. Actually, Angela was stealing money from her congregation.

Rachel Gannon

A strong-willed daughter of divorced, overachieving parents, Rachel hoped to follow in their footsteps and become a high-powered lawyer. But when she couldn't keep up with her studies, Rachel turned her back on her family and became addicted to drugs. She ran from rehab, settled into the seamier side of New York City, and went to work for a call girl agency!

Marcy Wade

While working as an executive secretary at *The Banner* back in 1971, Marcy Wade possessed an uncanny ability to lie and deceive without ever letting on that she had an agenda. Marcy wanted her boss, Steve Burke, even though he was in love with Viki Riley. But that didn't stop Marcy! She tried to drive Viki over the edge of madness by making her believe that her alter ego, Niki, had come back. While dressed as Niki, Marcy's scheme backfired, and she paid for it with her life.

Gabrielle Medina

When viewers first laid eyes on Gabrielle Medina, she was pregnant and manless in Argentina, left in the lurch after a brief fling with Max Holden. Tired of being stepped on, Gabrielle evolved from a victim into a vindictive vamp who committed countless crimes of the heart in her tenacious pursuit of Max, the only man who fulfilled her burning desire.

Tina Lord

Part vixen, part victim, and only partly sincere, Tina Lord has had men falling at her feet ever since she was a teenager. While perfecting the art of the vamp, Tina has also been one of Llanview's most hapless heroines, spending her days and nights fending off psychos, attackers, and one disaster after the next!

Who else but this pampered, petulant prima donna can claim to have tumbled over a waterfall, given birth without knowing it, been seduced by a faux Bo, slept with a mobster to protect her husband, and fallen in love with a man she thought was her brother?

1978

Greg Huddleston was teenage Tina's very first boyfriend. Good guy Greg couldn't help but notice that his sweet and virtuous girl was becoming attracted to slimy Marco Dane.

In 1980, Tina enjoyed her first grown-up romance with handsome country-and-western singer, Johnny Drummond. The following year, Johnny gave Tina her first broken heart when he left her in the dust and jumped into a romance with his singing partner, Becky Lee Abbott.

Tina's acute self-absorption and near-pathological gullibility made her an easy target for notorious boyfriend Mitch Laurence, whose phony devotion to Tina grew after he learned she was an heir to the Lord family fortune.

When Tina returned to town in 1985, she strove to win her sister Viki's love. But Tina kept losing her trust with one bumbling lie and deception after another. Over the years, Viki has seen Tina at her manipulative worst and her lovable best, and has come to accept her sister for what she is—one of a kind!

*1*992

*1*996

Tina had never met a man like kindhearted Cord Roberts. Though smitten with the tall Texan, she resisted his advances—until she discovered he was worth one million dollars!

TINA
She hates me so much, Cord! Your mother's not going to stop until she turns you completely against me.

CORD
Honey, that is never going to happen.

TINA
Yeah, not if we elope right now, then she won't be able to do or say anything to stop us.

CORD
Girl, it's not that I'm not tempted because I am. But what about the plans we've made? Now, I've already asked Clint to be my best man.

TINA
Who cares about Clint, he hates me almost as much as your mother does and besides, we don't need anybody's permission.

When a pregnant Tina fled turbulent Llanview for the peace and tranquility of Max Holden's Argentinean ranch, she never expected to be taken hostage by the notorious Jamie Sanders. The wounded Jamie bailed out of their boat, leaving Tina to pray for her life as she took a terrifying tumble over the Iguaza Waterfall.

After being rescued by Palupe Indians, Tina believed she had suffered a miscarriage. Only much later did she learn that she had actually given birth to a boy deep in the jungles of Argentina.

*T*ina's active fantasy life slipped into overdrive in 1991 when she imagined herself as La Perdita, a seventeenth-century Spanish pirate queen who had been captured by the famed British admiral Lord Nelson Cartwright. Naturally, the stuffy admiral bore a striking resemblance to Cord Roberts, Tina's modern-day husband.

*W*hy is it that, over the years, Tina seemed to fall prey to one unethical opportunist after another? In 1993—after Cord was presumed dead—Tina allowed herself to be duped by con man Cain Rogan, who broke her heart with his dishonest ways. Still, Tina stuck by Cain's side, which caused quite a dilemma months later when Cord returned from the dead!

*C*ord Roberts was Tina's ticket to the wholesome life until her compulsive lies drove him away. However, their love proved so strong that Cord came back for more, marrying Tina three times!

TINA
You good-for-nothing *philanthropist!*

DAVID
That's *philanderer.*

****

TINA
I came here to give you a piece of my mind!

BLAIR
Think you can spare any?

Dorian Lord

Deceitful, duplicitous, determined. Dorian is all that . . . and much more! This high-and-mighty mogul does everything with conviction—and when she sets her mind to something, don't dare stand in her way!

On occasion, Llanview's manipulative vampiress has shown a tender heart toward those she loves. Still, while her intentions are good, her underhanded methods always get her in hot water. After twenty-five years, <u>One Life to Live</u>'s "Queen of Mean" remains as vital and vitriolic as ever!

$\mathscr{D}r.$ DORIAN CRAMER

In 1975, Dr. Dorian Cramer became physician-in-residence for the wealthy Victor Lord, who had no clue that the town pariah had more than his health on her mind. Desperate for money to pay for the care of her mentally ill sister, Melinda, Dorian saw the rich Mr. Lord as the answer to her prayers. Dorian's first goal: make Victor dependent on her. Her second goal: marry the rich publishing tycoon!

$\mathscr{D}$orian proved that she was as conniving as ever when, after years in a mental institution, her sister Melinda returned to town and fell in love with Dr. Peter Janssen. Dorian comforted Melinda, while secretly undermining her sister because she wanted Peter all for herself!

$\mathscr{I}$n 1980, Dorian had an affair with Clint Buchanan, the new editor of *The Banner*. But before long, Clint was beginning to notice another formidable woman—Viki! Tired of Dorian's incessant meddling, Clint called it quits with her.

Dorian and Clint's first time. . . .

DORIAN
What do you want for breakfast?

CLINT
Breakfast?

DORIAN
You are going to stay the night, aren't you?

CLINT
No, no, I'm not!

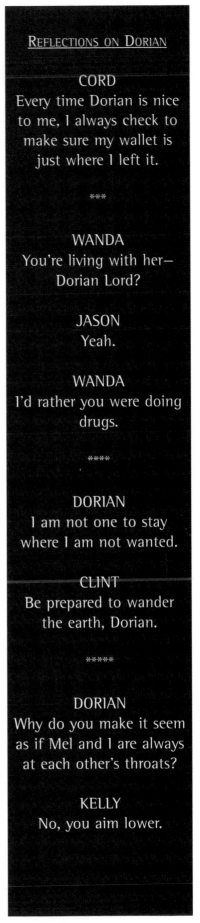

*I*n 1980, upwardly mobile Dorian saw an opportunity to become Pennsylvania's First Lady—and grabbed it! To insure her fiancé Herb Callison's victory, dirty-dealing Dorian bought him the election. Soon after Dorian and Herb moved into the Governor's Mansion, the scandal broke. Dorian's dream to be the First Lady of the State of Pennsylvania collapsed when Herb resigned in disgrace.

DORIAN
(at her surprise birthday party)
I'm a bit overwhelmed. Lately, people have been gathering to bury me rather than to praise me.

TODD
Maybe we can do that later.

****

DORIAN
How is it going to look if you walk out on me?

NORA
Like I have a brain in my head.

****

DORIAN
Is it expecting too much to get some loyalty from my daughter?

CASSIE
I *am* loyal. I'm just not brain-dead.

***

DORIAN
I really don't want the pity of any of my friends.

VIKI
That's okay—you don't have any friends.

*C*assie, Dorian's teenage daughter by her medical school lover, David Renaldi, came to Llanview in 1981, but mother and daughter did not exactly share a tearful reunion. At first, Dorian denied she even had a daughter! For nearly two decades, mother and daughter have enjoyed a volatile relationship.

*W*hen Dorian failed to steal ex-lover David Renaldi away from his new fiancée, Jenny Vernon, she sabotaged their wedding by bringing David's secret wife, Liat, to town in time to stop the ceremony from taking place.

$\mathcal{D}$orian and her lawyer-lover Jon Russell teamed up with Cord and Tina for a 1986 jaunt to Tina's private island, Devil's Claw. The pleasure trip turned terrifying when they discovered the island was swarming with bomb-bearing terrorists!

*R*evenge, not love, brought Dorian and David Vickers together in a twisted marriage. Dorian, desperate to rid herself of David, but not to give him her fortune, came up with a kinky scheme to dupe him into committing adultery. Disguised as "Madame Helmore," she seduced a drunken, frisky, and blindfolded David. Later, when David saw photos of his scandalous affair with Madame Helmore in *The Sun,* he realized he'd been duped into adultery—and would have to forfeit his million-dollar divorce settlement. Only later did he learn that his lover was his very own wife!

DORIAN
Well, Viki. I get accused of
murder and they sell tick-
ets to my execution. You
confess to it and they
make you prom queen!

DORIAN
(to Viki)
When you were in therapy
integrating your many personalities, why didn't you
tell the small-minded suspicious one to take a hike?

Seeking revenge on Viki, Dorian set out to
seduce her son Joey in 1995 with a very
sexy dance lesson. . . .

DORIAN
Forget the steps. Just put your hands
on mine. Now make eye contact.
We're not dancing, we're communicating with our bodies, our eyes, our
hands. You see, this hand here on my
back talks to me. The energy flows
across your arms, your shoulders. In
ballroom dancing, the man is the
leader. You lead me through your
hands, your legs, your thighs, your
hips. Now, let's just move.

Dorian and Viki's Twenty-Five-Year Rivalry

DORIAN
(to Viki)
I can't wait until you write your autobiography—*I Led 13 Lives!*

***

DORIAN
(to Viki)
Why don't you take off that halo and show us those tasteful little horns that you hide so well!

***

DORIAN
You know, they really should have named you after a different queen, Viki. Not Victoria, but Queen Marie Antoinette, because you keep losing your head.

***

DORIAN
How does that woman do it? Viki can shoot and smother and burn her way across this town and still come off as the patron saint of psychopaths.

*I*n Washington, D.C., a drunken Mel Hayes bumped into Dorian in the hotel bar, and the two ended up in her suite for a night of heated passion. Afterward, the newly acquainted lovers dined on room service caviar and a couple of BLTs, then sank to their knees for round two!

Sinners

Bad Boys

Your mother warned you to stay away from these guys!

Over the years, Llanview has had its share of bona fide instigators who love to stir the pot of intrigue. These selfish demons are known to let their private agendas take precedence over everyone else's wishes. No scheme is too devious, no plot too profane for these devils who delight in other people's despair. When they need to express themselves, they do so in creative ways: blackmail, seduction, forgery—and an occasional murder attempt!

Dr. Mark Toland

Mark Toland's promising medical career crumbled on the day he encountered Dorian Cramer. When Dorian sent out seductive signals, Mark couldn't help but yield to lust. After completing his hospital rounds, Mark shared assignations with Dorian at their secret love nest—while his faithful wife Julie patiently waited at home.

Carlo Hesser

Like a cat with nine lives, heinous Hesser keeps coming back to life. All of Llanview thought Carlo died in 1992, so imagine their surprise when he snuck into town in 1996 under the assumed name Poseidon and swindled Asa Buchanan out of $30 million. For good measure, cunning Carlo seduced his onetime wife, Alex, who had married Asa while Carlo was presumed dead. A bullet to the brain ended Carlo's life—or did it?

Marco Dane

A man of many faces, Marco was a smooth operator whose dreams of glory usually led to trouble, not triumph. His rather unorthodox job résumé includes such exploits as pimping, pornography, and masquerading as his own twin brother.

Cain Rogan

This capable con artist led three lives before revealing his true identity in 1992. Employing a variety of accents, mannerisms, and sartorial styles, he conned Llanviewites as sleazy British journalist Hudson King, German film director Heinrich Kaiser (pictured here), and professional gambler Humberto Calderon. As himself—Cain Rogan—this pathological liar continued his con game before skipping town with his new wife, Tina.

Michael Grande

No fiendish feat was too much for suave and slick Michael Grande. He tried to arrange the murder of Roger Gordon, and attempted to drug and poison Brenda McGillis to get his hands on her baby. By the time his reign of terror came to an end, nearly everyone in Llanview had a motive for murder—but it was Roger who did the deed.

David Vickers

Posing as Victor Lord's long-lost son, David showed up in Llanview to stake his claim to a multimillion-dollar inheritance. Over the next two years, this randy fellow wormed his way into his "sister" Tina's bed and infuriated his wife Dorian by trying to bed her impressionable niece, Kelly. Without an ounce of remorse, David finally slithered out of town—with $50,000 of Dorian's money burning a hole in his pocket.

Johnny Dee

Cool, clever, and extremely ambitious, Johnny's number-one goal was to make his father, Carlo Hesser, proud. Johnny was delighted when Carlo ordered him to marry the beautiful Tina Lord Roberts in order to get closer to Tina's influential sister, Victoria Buchanan, the mayor of Llanview. Ultimately, Johnny's obsession with Tina did him in. When he tried to kidnap her, Viki/Niki shot him dead!

Jamie Sanders

This bad seed sprouted every few months to wreak havoc. The son of prominent parents, Jamie preferred drug trafficking to politics. Viki nearly lost her life to Jamie when he chloroformed her, then squeezed her into a coffin en route to a crematorium! Fortunately she was saved in the nick of time. Clint wasn't so lucky—Sanders sadistically shot him in the head.

Talbot Huddleston

One of Llanview's leading citizens, Talbot had a secret penchant for hookers and violence. The townspeople were stunned to discover that this prominent socialite slept with Karen Wolek, savagely beat Katrina Karr into a coma, and murdered Marco Dane.

RJ Gannon

Viewers were introduced to the charismatic yet menacing RJ while he was operating a lucrative loan-sharking business in Atlantic City. Relocating to Llanview, RJ worked side by side with the notorious Mob kingpin Carlo Hesser. His shady dealings constantly kept RJ at his good-guy brother Hank's throat—and vice versa.

Ivan Kipling

No idea was too devious, no plot too wicked for the demented Dr. Ivan Kipling. Posing as Dr. Hugo Wilde, Ivan returned to Llanview in 1982 and implanted a device in the brain of his enemy, Dr. Larry Wolek. Then he kidnapped Karen and whisked her away to his South American hideaway. After undergoing emergency surgery to remove the implant, Larry hurried to South America and saved his wife's life.

Brad Vernon

When a bum knee ended Brad's dream to become a tennis pro, he spent the next decade serving up one scheme after another. His vices—sex, gambling, and more—always caught up with him. The handsome devil spent two memorable stints in Statesville Prison.

Todd Manning

Todd Manning is one of the most complex and unforgettable characters ever to wreak havoc in Llanview. Years after his cruel and brutal rape of Marty Saybrooke, Todd remains a tortured soul, always skirting the line between good and evil. He's an enigma—complex and ambiguous—an absolutely vicious and self-destructive individual.

Anyone who has ever encountered the wrath of Llanview's demon-driven Prince of Darkness knows just how dastardly he can be. Under his tough-as-nails veneer lurks a loving father who is determined to break the cycle of abuse in his family by showering love and affection on the true love of his life—his precious daughter, Starr. Still, whenever he gets slammed, Todd Manning inevitably reverts to his old ways, and that can only mean one thing for the citizens of Llanview: danger!

When Todd Manning first skulked into Llanview, he was just another arrogant fraternity brother at the local university. However, when Todd led the vicious gang rape of Marty Saybrooke, he transformed from a contemptuous cad into a heinous criminal right before our eyes. Todd and his fellow frat boys, Zach, Powell, and the innocent Kevin, stood trial for that monstrous act.

Sentenced to Statesville Prison, Todd was befriended by Rebecca Lewis, a devout religious disciple who set out to save his soul. When he escaped from prison, Todd convinced sweet Rebecca to hide him. Alone with the innocent girl, Todd fell in love for the first time. When he proposed to her, Todd was enraged to hear that she had already agreed to marry his fellow frat brother, Powell.

$\mathcal{A}$fter their first divorce, Todd and Blair discovered, to their mutual wonderment, that they were still very much in love. So they decided to try marriage again. Blair jubilantly accepted Todd's proposal, then revealed an amazing secret—she was pregnant with his child! After their November 1995 wedding, the bride and groom shared a private dance amidst a shower of golden balloons.

As much as she tried, Marty Saybrooke could never seem to get Todd out of her life. Following the rape, an ironic twist of fate brought Todd and Marty together again when the prison van transferring him to a maximum security prison crashed, and Todd escaped yet again. Incredibly, the van hit a car driven by Marty Saybrooke, and carrying little C.J. Roberts and Jessica Buchanan. Instead of running to freedom, Todd saved their lives. His act of heroism warranted a full pardon from the governor.

Todd paid a terrible price for helping out Patrick Thornhart on the Irish isle of Inishcrag. Disguised as Patrick, Todd was shot by terrorists who were gunning for Thornhart, then thrown in the trunk of a car and dumped over a cliff into the ocean. He was presumed dead, but in actuality, a barely alive Todd washed up on shore and was nursed back to health by a kindly Irish fisherman.

$\mathcal{G}$rowing up, Todd was often neglected and verbally abused by his adoptive father, Peter Manning. In real life, abused children sometimes treat their own offspring in kind. But Todd vowed to break the vicious cycle of abuse with his own daughter, Starr. The little girl is the one shining star in his self-described "screwed-up life."

TODD
(to baby Starr)
I would never make you feel stupid or worthless or bad. I will never betray you in any
way—I swear.

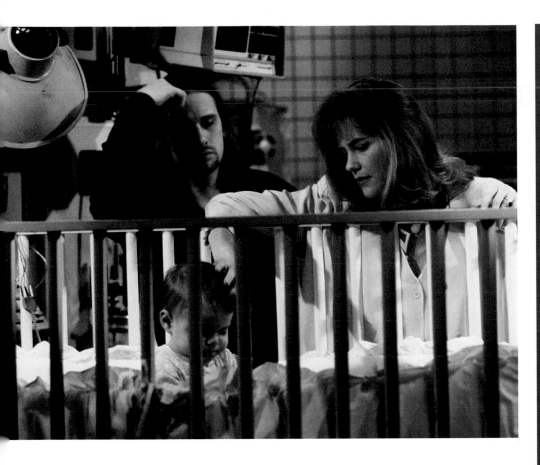

Out of the blue, a perky parrot dropped into Todd's office at *The Sun*—and made himself right at home! Before long, lonely, vengeful Todd had made a new friend. The jabbering, cynical bird quickly became Todd's most trusted confidant. Who else could understand and accept the dark corners of his twisted psyche?

VIKI
How did you survive?

TODD
What can I say? I guess someone down there likes me.

****

MARTY
You're alive!

TODD
Well, I guess when really bad people die, they go to Llanview. I figured if I was going to come back, I would be like a cockroach or a gopher. But God really has a sense of humor. So I came back as me.

****

BLAIR
You died!

TODD
What can I say? I can't do anything right.

****

TINA
(sees Todd)
Oh God!!

TODD
No, just me.

TODD
(to Viki)
Risk? Risk for you is
wearing white after Labor
Day!

****

TODD
(to Viki)
Why do you think every-
thing you say is gospel? Is
it because your name is
Lord?

*T*odd would do anything for his daughter, Starr, even marry a woman he doesn't
love. During his custody battle with Blair
during the summer of 1997, Todd con-
tracted to marry his lawyer, Tea Delgado,
as a means to show the courts he had a
stable family life. The ploy worked; Todd
won custody of his daughter, and Tea got
herself a devil of a hubby!

Weddings to Remember

For better or worse, <u>One Life to Live</u> throws a heck of a wedding. "Dead" spouses suddenly reappear; couples marry for power, not love; and bombs threaten to burst newly-weds' bubbles. Take a fond look back at some memorable <u>One Life to Live</u> nuptials.

"MARRIAGE IS A WONDERFUL INSTITUTION—AND I'M MORE THAN READY TO BE INSTITUTIONALIZED."

—NORA GANNON, 1995

Asa's eighth wedding was wilder than the previous seven put together! The bride wore a golden dress à la her idol, Cleopatra, and arrived via a bejeweled barge with bare-chested, palm-toting attendants at her side.

MARK TOLAND AND JULIE SIEGEL

Julie Siegel's marriage to handsome Dr. Mark Toland got off to a rough start. Her continued frigidity in the bedroom left Mark unsatisfied, and eventually his frustration led the virile young man into an affair with a fellow doctor, Dorian Cramer.

APRIL 1990

It's hard to picture Romeo without Juliet, Rhett without Scarlett, or *One Life to Live's* young hero, Cord Roberts, without a certain fiery gal at his side. Despite the divorced couple's stormy history, viewers always sensed that Cord and Tina truly belonged together; and in 1990 they renewed their wedding vows for the third time.

APRIL 1974

With their loved ones (including adopted-son-to-be Josh) at their side, Ed Hall and Carla Gray joyously entered into the holy state of matrimony.

JANUARY 1981
Dorian Lord finally had the power base she dreamed of when she married the newly elected governor, Herb Callison.

APRIL 1985
Dr. Larry Wolek and Laurel Chapin's wedding almost didn't happen when Laurel's ex-husband Alex secretly showed up; but he couldn't bring himself to stop the ceremony.

NOVEMBER 1982
Clint Buchanan and Viki Riley's first wedding day had a near-tragic end when a Mob hit man planted a bomb in their car. The device detonated, but thankfully neither newlywed was in the car at the time.

AUGUST 1986

Rafe Garretson kept marriage all in the family when he became the third Buchanan man to wed Delila Ralston.

MAY 1888/1988

Trapped in a Wild West time warp, Clint nearly married schoolmarm Ginny Fletcher, who was the spitting image of his modern-day wife Viki. Just as they were about to exchange vows, Viki traveled back to 1888 and burst into the saloon to stop the ceremony.

FEBRUARY 1996

Marty Saybrooke was not certain how she would answer when the priest asked, "Margaret, do you take this man to be your husband?" Though she stood at the altar with Dylan Moody, Marty had grown to share a passionate, once-in-a-lifetime bond with her true soulmate, Patrick Thornhart. At the moment of truth, Marty suppressed her inner turmoil and uttered those two fateful words—"I do."

February 1988

While marrying Max Holden, Tina absentmindedly uttered the wrong groom's name at the altar.

TINA
I take thee, Cord . . .
(Gasps)

TINA
Oh, what I meant, look, what I meant to say was that I take thee Max.

MAX
No, no, Tina.

TINA
No, Max, please take my hand. You know what I meant to say.

MAX
You said it. I heard it. We all heard it. I can't go through with this marriage.

MAY 1995

For months, Bo Buchanan and Nora Gannon both avoided making wedding plans. Whenever they took the time to get serious about their big day, something would come along to distract them. Fortunately, their closest friends appointed themselves "wedding police," taking matters into their own hands to throw a rock-and-roll wedding, complete with a sock hop reception!

Bo's impromptu wedding vow

BO
Since the first time I ever saw you, when you spilled that club soda all over the front of my suit, you wound up in my heart and in my life like nobody else. You know, we've had a problem or two . . .

NORA
. . . or three . . .

BO
Yeah, it's been some dance though, hasn't it? My life's never felt so full. I've never felt so alive. I hope the music keeps playing for us as long as it possibly can, because as long as I've got you, that dance can just go on forever.

SEPTEMBER 1985

Dorian desperately tried to stop her daughter, Cassie Callison, from marrying Rob Coronal. Despite Dorian's interference, the teenage sweethearts tied the knot in September 1985. After a divorce, they married again four years later.

MARCH 1988

Cord Roberts and Kate Sanders had only just tied the knot when Cord's "late" wife, Tina, burst into the church carrying a child she claimed was Cord's baby!

JANUARY 1988

When she couldn't have Max Holden, a forlorn Gabrielle Medina did the next best thing—she married his brother, Steve!

*H*er love tamed his wild heart. His devotion rescued her from a self-loathing abyss. Todd Manning's and Blair Daimler's parallel journeys to humanity served as one of *One Life to Live*'s most touching love stories. Barely a week after Blair walked down the aisle with the man of her dreams, Todd flew to Ireland where he was shot and presumed dead.

*A*UGUST 1997

The cop easily captured her man when Detective Andy Harrison took the plunge with her true love, Antonio Vega. After the wedding, the guests celebrated by dancing in the streets, then bid the bride and groom *adios* as they headed for an exciting new life in California.

When the ghost of Luna Moody's late husband came back from the dead to tell her to call off her wedding to Max Holden, the bride-to-be freaked, then skipped town. Max retrieved her, and the giddy couple married in a sunset ceremony at their own Serenity Springs spa.

$\mathcal{I}$rish poet Patrick Thornhart and his ladylove, Margaret "Marty" Saybrooke chose their favorite place, the top of Llantano Mountain, to be joined in holy matrimony. But after the ceremony, their happiness was shattered by terrorists' bullets!

JANUARY 1993

Cassie Callison stood by her man, Andrew Carpenter, through the toughest of times—and in an unusual reversal, *she* was the one who proposed marriage! On their wedding day, a vengeful Marty Saybrooke tried to stop the marriage, but by the grace of God, the ceremony and reception came off without a hitch.

Jake and Megan's Wedding

MAY 20, 1991

Like most soap opera couples, the road to Jake and Megan's wedding was a long and rocky one. First, Jake's soon-to-be ex-wife, Charlotte, caused trouble, pretending to be blind and needing Jake's help. Then, Hunter Guthrie, an old flame of Megan's, turned up in Llanview, ready to catch her on the rebound when Jake let her down. But he didn't! True, Jake put a scare in his nervous bride's mind when he showed up on the back of his best man Lucky's motorcycle because his car ran out of gas, but he made it to the altar nonetheless!

After the teary-eyed ceremony, the bride and groom planted a tree on the lawn of the church as a symbol of their everlasting love, then capped the unforgettable day by leaving in a horse-drawn buggy.

Daytime Dynasties

Upon its premiere in 1968, _One Life to Live_ became the first daytime serial to present an array of ethnic, social, and class types, in addition to bringing African-American characters to the forefront of major storylines. The original story centered on the Woleks, a blue-collar Polish family; the blue-blooded Lords, and the Irish Catholic Rileys, who married into the Jewish Siegels.

Since the beginning, Llanview has come closer to resembling our nation's melting pot than any other fictional soap opera city. In the late 70s, the Buchanans, a close-knit clan from Texas, galloped into town. In the 1990s, the soap returned to its multicultural roots by introducing the Vegas, a working-class clan from the poorer section of East Llanview. Today, after thirty years and nearly 8,000 episodes, _One Life to Live_ remains a family affair!

THE SIEGELS
Widow Eileen Siegel held high hopes that son Tim would follow in the footsteps of his late father, Dave, and become a lawyer. In 1975, Eileen was distressed when Tim came home to Llanview to announce that he had dropped out of law school.

THE LORDS

As the ruthless head of Llanview's most prominent family, Victor Lord founded *The Banner* newspaper, raised two daughters, and fathered three illegitimate children. Years after his 1976 death, the clan learned the true depth of their patriarch's depravity when it was revealed that he had sexually abused his daughter, Victoria.

THE WOLEKS

The struggling but proud Wolek clan grew up in South Philadelphia. Older siblings Anna and Vince worked two jobs apiece to put their kid brother Larry through medical school. In 1975, the trio of siblings welcomed cousin Jenny, a novice nun, into the tight-knit family fold.

THE CRAIGS

Widower Jim Craig had his hands full raising his only daughter, Cathy. As a teenager during the turbulent 1960s, Cathy rebelled against her father and his new bride, Anna Wolek, by turning to drugs. Years later, Cathy brought more angst to the Craig clan when she kidnapped Viki Riley's newborn son, Kevin.

THE WOLEK SISTERS

There is something special about the bond between sisters. Siblings Karen and Jenny Wolek were as different as night and day. Karen was flashy and upwardly mobile. Raised by a family of modest means, Karen yearned for the high life, while ex-nun Jenny was content with the simple joys. Despite their differences, they were as close as two sisters could be.

THE VEGAS

As matriarch of the Vega family, Carlotta is a beautiful, strong, hardworking woman who maintains great pride in her Latino heritage, and great love for the American dream. Raising two sons, Antonio (pictured here) and Cristian, while running the family diner, Carlotta has always placed the interests of her children above her own.

THE GANNONS

Llanview's District Attorney Hank Gannon has enjoyed more success in the courtroom than he has as a daddy. But he and his ex-wife Nora presented a united front when they confronted daughter Rachel after her addiction to cocaine spiraled out of control in 1996.

THE HESSERS

In 1990, cold-blooded Carlo Hesser ruled his Mob family with an iron hand. At the same time, the syndicate head always kept a warm spot in his heart for his two children—daughter Charlotte and adopted son Johnny Dee.

THE LORDS—THE NEXT GENERATION

In the mid-1990s, Blair Daimler married Todd Manning after discovering a sizzling secret: he was the true heir to Victor Lord's $27.8 million fortune. Blair and Todd's daughter, Starr, carried on the long bloodline of Llanview's most prominent family, the Lords.

The Buchanans

Deep in the heart of Llanview resides a tribe of transplanted Texans by the name of Buchanan. The original trio of cowboys—crusty codger Asa and his sons Bo and Clint—made their fortune as miners of black gold, but now the clansmen trade in the high-power publishing and business worlds. Though they all have their own distinctive lifestyles and personalities, they share one common bond: togetherness. They are Buchanans—do or die!

Asa Buchanan

Born and raised in Texas as the son of a poor rancher, Asa is the cantankerous, bourbon-swigging patriarch of the Buchanan clan. The much-married and often-overbearing Asa may spend most of his time manipulating the people in his life, but they know that when the chips are down, family comes first. The Buchanans can always count on ol' Asa to scheme away—and save the day!

Asa arrived in Llanview in 1979 and set his sights on twenty-year-old Samantha Vernon. During their wedding ceremony, Asa's first wife Olympia (whom he had held prisoner) showed up at the church, but was subdued before she could interrupt the ceremony. When Samantha learned the truth about Asa's bigamy, she dumped him.

$\mathcal{D}$elila's beauty and youthful sex appeal often drove Asa crazy with jealousy. Soon after making her wife #3, Asa went on a fishing trip where he faked his own death to see if his "widow" and "grieving" son Bo were having an affair.

$\mathcal{A}$sa came to Becky Lee Abbott's rescue in 1983. After Becky had an affair with Asa's son, Bo, she found herself pregnant. But Bo had married Delila! So Asa offered to marry her so that he could be a father to his own grandson. Asa's ill-fated coupling with wife #4 lasted little more than a year.

When Asa went to the island of Malakeva on business, viewers discovered that he had been secretly married to yet another wife, Pamela Stuart, for more than a decade! Between his Olympia and Sam marriages, Asa masqueraded as old sea captain Jeb Stuart and took Pam as his bride. When she discovered his charade, Pamela shrewdly faked a terminal illness to trick Asa into a deathbed marriage—then surprised the shameless "trigamist" by springing back to life!

PAMELA LEARNS THAT HER LYING HUSBAND HAS BEEN LIVING A DOUBLE LIFE
1985

PAM
You married me ten years ago when you were already married to someone else. You claimed you loved me and yet you married over and over and over again.

ASA
That was my other life.

PAM
Why couldn't I be a part of that other life?

Asa's thirst for the opposite sex was temporarily satiated upon meeting up with an old friend, ex-madam Renee Divine. While living in Reno, Nevada, Renee found herself on the wrong side of the tracks, and decided to make something of it. While toiling in the world's oldest profession, she met Asa. Years later, the feisty Ms. Divine reconnected with the curmudgeonly cowboy, and promptly became wife #6.

Renee CATCHES ASA WITH BLAIR IN THE STABLES
1992

BLAIR
Renee, this is all my fault. I turned to Asa in a moment of weakness and he was kind enough.

RENEE
Darling, we know why you're here and what you're doing. The surroundings are appropriate; however, horses have a little more discretion. But then again maybe that's because they're Thoroughbreds. When they go to stud, they do it selectively.

ASA
Renee, nothing, nothing happened here.

RENEE
Lying has become like breathing for you, hasn't it, Asa?

Marriage #7 was a match made in hell. Blair wanted money, while Asa wanted a beautiful young wife to give him another son to carry on the Buchanan name. Little did he know that his bride was popping birth control pills behind his back. When their union went completely sour, Blair worked her husband into an angina attack, then withheld his heart pills. When he got up on his feet again, the ballistic billionaire booted Blair out of the house, and, frankly, she was lucky to get out alive!

Despite stern words of warning from nearly everyone in Llanview, Asa followed his hormones and fell victim to sexy, money-hungry Alex Olanov. To get Asa to make love to her, Alex went as far as to steal Asa's jewels, then climb into his bathtub with them. The only way she'd give them back to him was if he jumped into the tub with her. Asa gave in, they made love, and Alex promptly became the ornery oil tycoon's eighth bride in an outlandish Cleopatra-themed wedding ceremony.

Asa has never had a problem finding a wife. Keeping his brides happy is another matter. The cantankerous cowboy is known to rant, rave, and run roughshod over any woman who crosses his path. The only constant in his life seems to be trusty manservant Nigel Bartholomew Smythe, who finds his master's incessant bellowing quite amusing!

Clint Buchanan

Beneath his gruff, cowboy exterior hides a heart as big as all outdoors. Through marriage, children, divorce, remarriage, and divorce again, Clint's love for Viki has never wavered. A rugged, take-charge kind of guy, Clint Buchanan is always willing to go to great lengths for his loved ones.

Clint Buchanan galloped into town in the fall of 1979, having been brought to town by Viki's dying husband, Joe Riley. Joe had chosen Clint, the editor of an Arizona newspaper, to be his successor as editor of *The Banner* newspaper. The son of Texas oil tycoon Asa Buchanan, Clint left the family fold as a young man, and spent many years estranged from his stubborn father before mending fences with him in Llanview.

Long before they became a romantic pair, Clint exposed Viki Riley to the ways of the West at Asa's rodeo, held on the grounds of the Buchanan clan's Southampton mansion.

$\mathcal{C}$LINT AND VIKI DISCOVERED LOVE IN NEW YORK CITY
1981

VIKI
I think you are a man of inspired genius, and I love the way you are corrupting me.

CLINT
Does that give me a license to further corrupt you?

VIKI
That is a highly debatable point, which we will continue to debate.

CLINT
Okay!

CLINT PROPOSES TO VIKI IN HER PRISON CELL
1982

Clint picked a most unusual time to propose marriage to Viki. While she was serving a 1982 prison sentence for failing to reveal a source, Clint raised Mrs. Riley's spirits by asking her to become his wife.

CLINT
Could I bring up something important?

VIKI
That depends on how important.

CLINT
It's important.

VIKI
Oh, it's that important. Go ahead.

CLINT
Will you marry me?

After a 1985 divorce, Clint and Viki reunited the following year, and remarried to the delight of their family. Just hours before the wedding, Viki thrilled her once-and-future husband with incredible news: she was pregnant!

September 1986 brought Clint and Viki's happiest moment—the birth of Jessica, their first child together.

During his extraordinary journey back in time to 1888, Clint shared a special friendship with little Buddy McGillis, whose family was in jeopardy of losing their farm to Clint's greedy ancestor, cattle baron Buck Buchanan. Clint amazed Buddy with a secret: he was from the future!

Bo Buchanan

Given his unscrupulous father, it's a wonder that Bo's morals are almost always in the right place. Handsome, proud, and sensitive, Bo always tries to do what's right, though his game plan doesn't always succeed. This cowboy's charm lies in his sense of loyalty, his sense of humor, and his perennially hard-luck love life. The crime-solving cowboy lives by the law, but often his freewheeling side finds him playing renegade.

1982

Bo Buchanan has an eye for beautiful women, and a head for business. Over nearly two decades in Llanview, the multi-talented Vietnam vet has owned several radio stations, a record label, produced a popular soap opera, managed country-and-western singers, worked at *The Banner* newspaper, and even driven a Formula 500 race car to victory!

1994

In 1983, Bo fell in love with Delila Ralston, but backed away from their budding relationship after his mother's deathbed confession that Delila's uncle, Yancey Ralston, was his real father. That meant Bo and Delila were cousins! A year later, the truth came out, that Bo was still a Buchanan, not a Ralston. Elated, he finally tied the knot with Delila.

Disillusioned with the ways of his unscrupulous family, Bo sought to find a more "normal" life in 1984. So he went to work in the Lord-Manning factory and, using the fake name "Bill Brady," befriended the working-class O'Neill family.

Long before they were married, Bo and Nora proved they were compatible—at least on the dance floor. On a whim, they entered a jitterbug contest in 1993, and much to their surprise took home the top prize!

When the evil Men of 21 threatened to blow Llanview sky high, Bo underwent a complete makeover, then went undercover as a bomb expert, Major Austin. The disguise called for Llanview's recognizable police commissioner to dye his hair blond and wear ice-blue colored contact lenses. In a race against time, "Major Austin" crawled through an air-shaft tunnel to defuse an explosive device that would have killed his friends and family.

After years of personal tragedy, Bo finally found happiness with a lady lawyer, Nora Gannon, who can handle just about anyone or anything, including Bo's overbearing father. But fishing? Nora's heart bled for her prized catch, and she couldn't bear the thought of eating the poor defenseless creature!

NORA
Honey, you really should be working out at the Police Academy.

BO
You've never complained about my stamina before.

NORA
We're talking about survival in the streets, not between the sheets.

Bo's marriage to Sarah Gordon was chock-full of calamity. In 1989, Sarah rushed to Bo's aid when someone tried to kill him on the campus of Llanview University by dropping a piece of mortar on his head!

$\mathcal{B}$o and Sarah were a storybook couple in so many ways. Once, they even married in a fairy tale wedding atop a mountain in the magical kingdom of Mendorra. Together, Bo and Sarah found something special that has proven elusive to so many—they found paradise. Sadly, Sarah's tragic death brought this fascinating fairy tale to an untimely end.

$\mathcal{W}$hile assuming the role of Llanview's police commissioner in 1994, Bo's first official act was to arrest Dorian Lord for the murder of her husband, Victor. Since then, Llanview's top cop has stamped out violence in the streets.

$\mathcal{B}$o and his fourth-wife-to-be Cassie enjoyed a 1991 pleasure trip to Loon Lake—blissfully unaware that Alex Olanov, obsessed with Bo, was lurking in the shadows with dastardly plans to ruin their romantic outing.

$\mathcal{B}$o traveled to Venice in 1985 to rescue his kidnapped father. Taking a momentary breather from the action-packed journey, he enjoyed the sights of the beautiful Italian city.

The Next Generation

The three original Buchanans have spawned a whole passel of kinfolk who are making history of their own. Three generations of this American dynasty keep Grandpa Asa on his toes. Heaven help the family member who betrays him, or dares to sully the Buchanan name!

Through the years with the Buchanan kids

1987

1990

1991

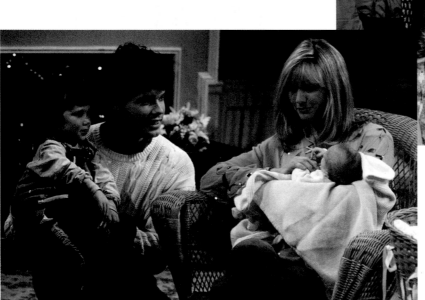

𝒞ord and his three-time wife Tina welcomed a new addition, Sarah, to their family in 1991. Their son, C.J., shared in the excitement.

𝒦evin's then-wife, Lee Ann, brought little Duke Buchanan into the world in 1992, but the cuddly babe couldn't save their sinking marriage. Just days after Duke's birth, Kevin sued for—and won—custody of their newborn son.

The mid-1990s brought a new generation of Buchanan cousins to *One Life to Live*. Here, Bo's son Drew joins Clint's boys, Kevin and Joey, for a family powwow.

Charismatic Joey may be a Buchanan, but he has a penchant for Cramer women. First, Joey fell for the charms of his family's archenemy, Dorian. When their May-December romance went bust, Joey romanced Dorian's niece, Kelly Cramer.

Part Three

Hollywood–Llanview Connection Stars

One Life to Live has been home to many gifted performers who have gained prominence in television and motion pictures since their initial rise to fame on daytime drama. Other already prominent stars, such as Sammy Davis, Jr., have made memorable appearances on the soap. Check out this long line of luminaries who have made the Hollywood–Llanview connection. . . .

Judith Light

Perhaps *One Life to Live*'s best-known alumna, Judith Light won acclaim for her emotional portrayal of the anguished housewife-turned-prostitute, Karen Wolek, a role she played for five years. Judith went on to star in the long-running ABC sitcom *Who's the Boss?*, *Phenom*, and the CBS show *The Simple Life,* and has starred in many TV movies, including 1989's *The Ryan White Story.* Light won two Daytime Emmys for Outstanding Actress, in 1980 and 1981.

Tom Berenger

The ruggedly handsome, blue-eyed Berenger was nominated for an Academy Award for his role as the battle-hardened Sergeant Barnes in Oliver Stone's *Platoon*. He has also starred in such feature films as *The Big Chill*, *Betrayed*, *The Field*, *Shattered*, *Major League*, and *The Gingerbread Man*. As Tim Siegel on *One Life to Live*, his heartwrenching marriage to Jenny Wolek took place on his deathbed.

Laurence Fishburne

At the tender age of twelve, Laurence (then Larry) Fishburne took up temporary residence in the fictional town of Llanview as streetwise Joshua West, who was later adopted by Ed and Carla Hall. Not long after leaving the soap, he spent eighteen months in the Phillipines shooting *Apocalypse Now*. He went on to star on Broadway in "Two Trains Running," and on the silver screen in *What's Love Got to Do With It?*, *Boyz N The Hood*, and *Just Cause*.

Blair Underwood

Though he appeared on *One Life to Live* for less than a year, Blair Underwood made a splash as streetwise Bobby Blue. He rose to TV fame as Jonathan Rollins on *L.A. Law* and in the ABC series, *High Incident*, and has had memorable roles in films, including *Set It Off*, and *Just Cause*.

Soon after leaving *One Life to Live*, Joe Lando landed the lead role of Byron Sully, opposite Jane Seymour, in the prime-time television series, *Dr. Quinn, Medicine Woman*. A fan favorite as the sexy Jake Harrison on *One Life to Live*, Lando was named one of *People* magazine's 50 Most Beautiful People in 1993.

Perhaps the most flattering thing that can happen to an actress is to have a role created for her. That's what happened to Audrey Landers when *One Life to Live*'s writers penned the role of Charlotte Hesser, the clever and spoiled daughter of drug kingpin Carlo Hesser, for the former *Dallas* star.

Richard Grieco

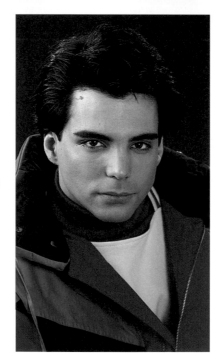

In 1987, Richard Grieco played the contract role of Mari Lynn Dennison's ski-bum boyfriend Rick Gardner. Soon after, he traded in his skis for a gun for the role that brought him teen-idol status—Officer Dennis Booker on *21 Jump Street*.

Phylicia Rashad

Before there was ever a Claire Huxtable on *The Cosby Show*, Phylicia Rashad was Ed Hall's girlfriend, Courtney Wright, on *One Life to Live* in 1983 and 1984. Rashad's real-life sister, Debbie Allen, also guested on the soap in the early 1980s.

Roma Downey

Touched by an Angel star Roma Downey joined the cast of *One Life to Live* in 1988 in the down-to-earth role of Lady Joanna, the sweet daughter of the villainous Lord Henry Leighton. In the story, Joanna could have used some "angelic" intervention when her fiancé, Rob Coronal, dumped her for his ex-wife, Cassie.

Tommy Lee Jones

Soon after graduating from Harvard University, Tommy Lee Jones joined the cast of *One Life to Live*, where he played Dr. Mark Toland for four years. After his character's 1975 murder, Tommy Lee moved on to Hollywood, where he earned rave reviews for his performances as Gary Gilmore in *The Executioner's Song*, and in the highly rated TV miniseries *Lonesome Dove*. Jones starred on the big screen in *Coal Miner's Daughter*, *JFK*, *Men in Black*, and *The Fugitive*, for which he won an Oscar.

Marcia Cross

On *Melrose Place*, Marcia Cross played the devilish Dr. Kimberly Shaw, a role in marked contrast to her *One Life to Live* character, Kate Sanders. During her two-year stint in Llanview, Kate, a brainy archeologist, was as good and decent as Kimberly was malevolent.

Jameson Parker

One half of the long-running prime-time detective team, *Simon and Simon*, Jameson Parker played the role of Jenny Wolek's unscrupulous second husband, Brad Vernon, with sleazy charm.

Ivana Trump

Ivana Trump made a guest appearance on the 6000th episode of *One Life to Live*. Starring as herself, Ivana's scenes took place at the fictitious Ivana's Casino in Atlantic City, where she encountered Luna (pictured here) and Max among others.

"BEING ON THE 6000TH EPISODE OF *ONE LIFE TO LIVE* WAS A LOT OF FUN—ESPECIALLY SINCE THE SCENE THEY ASKED ME TO PLAY TOOK PLACE IN A CASINO—A PLACE I WAS CEO OF FOR MANY YEARS. IT'S A BUSINESS I KNEW A GREAT DEAL ABOUT!"

—IVANA TRUMP

Dr. Ruth

Long before the ficticious Dr. Maude Boylan started doling out sexual advice, Llanviewites were treated to the real thing—Dr. Ruth! In 1992, noted sex therapist Dr. Ruth Westheimer was called upon to turn bumbling Mortimer Bern into the sexy spitting image of his "late" mobster brother, Carlo Hesser. Despite the diminutive doctor's best efforts, the experiment to make a man out of Milquetoast Mortimer failed miserably.

Reba McEntire

Country music superstar and super-soap fan Reba McEntire guest starred on *One Life to Live* in the summer of 1992. In her two-day stint in Llanview, she played herself, an old high-school friend of Luna Moody's.

WHAT A HOOT! I MADE A LOT OF NEW FRIENDS BEHIND THE SCENES IN LLANVIEW. (I EVEN GOT TO MEET BO—HE'S A REAL CUTIE!) I WOULDN'T MIND RETURNING—BUT NEXT TIME I'D LOVE TO BE ONE OF THOSE RICH, POWERFUL PEOPLE WHO LIVES IN A BIG HOUSE ON A HILL. HEY, MAYBE DORIAN HAS ANOTHER SISTER—ONE WHO'S *NOT* CRAZY— WHO SHOWS UP IN LLANVIEW TO CAUSE TROUBLE?

—REBA MCENTIRE

Kurtis Blow

Rap singer Kurtis Blow helped to create an unprecedented "marriage" of rap music and daytime television when he served as special consultant for *One Life to Live*'s own 1991 rap storyline. In the story, struggling musician Kerry Nichols tried to break into the big time. While appearing as himself in several episodes, the thrust of Blow's work was creating and staging the extravagant and intricate rap numbers performed by *One Life to Live*'s rap band, K Funk Mob.

Bill Anderson

When *One Life to Live*'s country-and-western singer, Becky Lee Abbott, made her big debut at Nashville's Grand Ol' Opry, the legendary Bill Anderson joined her on stage. "Whisperin'" Bill made several guest appearances on the soap during the early 1980s.

Roseanne

One Life to Live's macho Buchanan boys—Bo, Clint, and Cord—appeared as themselves in a 1994 episode of *Roseanne*. Roseanne, a longtime fan of the soap, handpicked the handsome guys to star in a soap opera fantasy segment of the long-running sitcom. The three actors were flown to Los Angeles from their base in New York to tape the *Roseanne* scenes.

Arlene Dahl

The ravishing redhead who starred in many MGM movies during the 40s and 50s brought her beauty and glamour to Llanview when she guested on several occasions in the 80s as Mimi King's mother, Miss Lucinda Schenk.

Yasmine Bleeth

Baywatch beauty Yasmine Bleeth rose to soap fame during the 1980s in her role as teenager Ryan Fenelli on ABC's long-running soap, *Ryan's Hope.* In 1991, the brown-haired, blue-eyed actress took on her first adult role as Lee Ann Demerest, a naive Texas lass whose heart was broken by Max Holden, and who gave birth to Kevin Buchanan's son, Duke.

Sammy Davis, Jr.

The incomparable Sammy Davis, Jr., was a huge fan of *One Life to Live.* Davis was known to carry a battery-operated mini-TV with him to rehearsals in Las Vegas, in order not to miss his favorite soap! In the early 1980s, *One Life to Live* extended an offer for him to appear as gambler Chip Warren. Sammy had such a great time that he asked to be written into the plot again and again!

Marsha Mason

Academy Award–winner Marsha Mason guest starred as a New Age priestess who helped perform the long-awaited nuptials of Max and Luna. In the story, the *Goodbye Girl* star assisted Rev. Andrew Carpenter in a non-traditional wedding ceremony, which combined Luna's spiritual beliefs with a more conventional service.

The Beach Boys

Bo Buchanan must have been feeling "good vibrations" when those 1960s surfer dudes, The Beach Boys, appeared on *One Life to Live* in 1988.

Bill Medley
Darlene Love

Righteous Brother Bill Medley and 1960s soul-singer Darlene Love sang the hit duet, "(You're My) Soul and Inspiration" at Tina Roberts's and Cain Rogan's wedding shower in 1994. The Medley/Love duet was also featured on the album, "One Life to Live: The Best of Love."

Little Richard

Good golly!! Rock and roll star Little Richard makes his daytime television debut at the wedding of Bo and Nora. In the memorable 1995 episode, the reluctant bride and groom were persuaded to "dance" down the aisle when Little Richard (a real-life minister) agreed to marry them! Afterward, the legendary rocker serenaded the guests with a rousing medley of his hits.

WHEN ABC FIRST ASKED ME TO BE ON THE SHOW, I THOUGHT, OH, MY GOD, WHAT AM I GOING TO BE DOING? I WASN'T THINKING ABOUT "TUTTI FRUTTI" OR "GOOD GOLLY MISS MOLLY," BUT THAT'S WHAT THEY WANTED. I'M GLAD TO HAVE HAD THE OPPORTUNITY TO DO IT!

—LITTLE RICHARD

Erykah Badu

During the summer of 1997, singer Erykah Badu brought her blend of hip-hop, blues, jazz, and soul to RJ Gannon's Club Indigo, Llanview's hot jazz club.

Frank McCourt

Frank McCourt, the Pulitzer prize–winning author of *Angela's Ashes*, appeared as himself in 1997, and shared a laugh with his real-life brother Malachy, who portrayed the diabolical Irish revolutionary Thomas Kenneally.

Anecdotes
Fan-tastic Tales

Thousands of <u>One Life to Live</u> viewers have had the once-in-a-lifetime opportunity to meet their favorite stars in the flesh. As the cast members of <u>One Life to Live</u> have found, soap fans can be the most passionate of all! Check out their most fan-tastic encounters . . .

Susan Batten (Luna Moody Holden)

When I went back to my hometown, I was surprised to discover that I was suddenly the local celebrity. Thanks to *One Live to Live*, folks back home were lining up for my autograph! At the local farmers' market, I ended up signing my name on dollar bills because no one had any paper!

James DePaiva (Max Holden)

I'll never forget the first time I did a publicity appearance in Chicago, where ABC's really big. There were three tiers of people screaming and going crazy, and we were surrounded by guards onstage. I thought I was looking at a movie about the Beatles.

Lee Patterson (Joe Riley/Tom Dennison)

I started on the show thirty years ago as newsman Joe Riley. Because I like a long vacation now and then, they killed me off at my request in 1970. But the fans missed old Joe so much, I was resurrected in 1972, only to be killed off again in 1979. Then, I returned seven years later as Joe's twin brother. One day, a lady on the street yelled to me, "Hey Patterson, why don't you tell the writers to make you triplets so you can take off again!"

Roger Howarth (Todd Manning)

I meet people on the streets who feel it's important to tell me that Todd is a nice guy. (I guess they feel that my self-esteem is somehow tied up in the character I play.) Well folks, it doesn't hurt my feelings if you think Todd is a dirty SOB. You may like the way I play the role, but you don't have to like Todd. After all, he is the bad guy.

Christopher Douglas (Dylan Moody)

Like Dylan, I always tried to keep a low profile. In fact, I'm still not comfortable with actually being recognized by people. Once, on a plane to LA, I let a flight attendant take my picture, and for the rest of the trip, I was posing with practically everyone on the plane. I guess there are a lot of soap fans in the friendly skies!

Patricia Elliott (Renee Buchanan)

When I served on a grand jury in New York, no one recognized me at first, until I noticed a policeman giving me a long, long look. A few minutes later, the man who oversees the jury came into the courtroom and said loudly, "All right. One of the cops said there's someone here who's on a soap opera." I meekly raised my hand and said, "Okay. Okay. It's me!" Leave it to the police to blow my cover.

Nathan Fillion (Joey Buchanan)

One time, a female fan was a little forward with me. She was making references to my scenes with an older woman–Dorian–then she started running her hands over me. I said, in a friendly manner, "You realize that it's just a show, don't you?" I . . . uh . . . am not sure she did.

Nicholas Walker (Max Holden)

When I first played Max, he skulked around town wearing a shroud to hide his disfigured face. And to help me get into character, I had the makeup department apply a big, fleshy scar to my face every day. On the street, some people gawked at me, others dropped their eyes, and one carload of people slammed on the brakes and just stared. The experience helped me discover a lot about human nature.

Wendee Pratt (Andy Harrison)

I found out firsthand that looking like a cop didn't necessarily help you get a taxi in New York. One day, I went out into the street–in costume–and tried to hail a cab, but they all went whizzing by! I guess the sight of a woman in blue needing a ride was a little strange to them!

James DePaiva (Max Holden)

When my mother came to the United States from Germany, she didn't speak much English. But by watching her "friends" on the soaps every day, Mom picked up the language–and a viewing habit that continues to this day. She used to take me to the local mall to see people like Richard Dean Anderson, who played Dr. Jeff Webber on *General Hospital*. So imagine how funny it was when I started appearing on one of her favorite shows! For my mother, being a soap star is better than being Jack Nicholson.

Holly Gagnier (Cassie Callison)

Let me tell you, stealing your mother's beau can bring on some rather tense moments—offscreen. The day after Cassie seduced Jon, I was shopping in a local store. Suddenly, the sweetest little old woman came over and slugged me! She proceeded to give me the lecture of a lifetime about "respecting your parents" and rather than risk a black eye, I promised I'd take her advice.

Jessica Tuck (Megan Gordon)

I could never get used to being recognized. One day, I couldn't figure out why a little girl was staring at me in an elevator. Was my nose running? Did I use my deodorant? That wasn't it! She knew I was a soap opera star! Now if only I could have remembered that!!

Thom Christopher (Carlo Hesser)

I was waiting to cross the street, when a very attractive woman standing next to me said, "Excuse me, you're Carlo Hesser, aren't you?" I proudly answered, "Yes, I am," and without batting an eyelash she responded, "I want your baby." Slightly taken aback, I quickly replied, "Sorry, I don't do babies on Thursdays," and we both went on our merry way.

Patricia Mauceri (Carlotta Vega)

After taking this role, I was introduced to the huge family of soap opera fans—many of whom can't stand to miss a minute of their favorite daytime dramas. I'll never forget the first time the local TV station here in New York interrupted our show with a late-breaking news bulletin just as the beloved Luna was about to die. The ABC switchboard lit up like a Christmas tree!

Nathan Purdee (Hank Gannon)

Fans of this show are smart! For months, fans were stopping me on the streets to tell me to "keep an eye on Rachel." Hank didn't see her drug problem coming, but the fans did. I'd be standing there on a rainy night, trying to hail a cab, only to hear "Hey Hank. . . . Wise up. Your daughter's an addict!" Frankly, I was thrilled that everyone cared so much.

Michael Storm
(Dr. Larry Wolek)

It was always a pleasure working with Gerald Anthony. For years he played one of the great scoundrels on our show. And Gerry was so convincing. . . . I remember the time, on the street, when a flowerpot came crashing down from above, barely missing him! The woman who dropped it said she was upset because of all the rotten things Marco was doing to Larry! A loyal fan!

Patricia Elliott (Renee Buchanan)

Prior to this role, people on the street rarely recognized me—even though I've been acting for years! Nowadays, folks are always looking at me, and it still takes some getting used to! I always wonder: Are you staring at me because I'm Renee Buchanan or do you just like to stare? Either way, it's a bit unnerving!

Karen Witter (Tina Roberts)

The streets of Llanview were more dangerous than the ones in New York City! When I played Tina, the only person who ever accosted me on the streets of New York was a nine-year-old girl. She walked up and asked me if I was Madonna (of all people) and when I said "no" she hit me and took off. A hit and run!

Robert S. Woods (Bo Buchanan)

Over the years my character has been involved in some pretty dangerous situations, but none as life-threatening as the time I tried to make a simple real-life visit to my local deli for a bite to eat. There I was, just casually munching on a tuna sandwich, when out of nowhere a woman came running at me! Before I could move, she nailed me with a clothesline tackle! I went flying! The tuna went flying! But my tackler just stood up, smiled, and asked for my autpgraph. I just figured the safest thing to do was say yes, but let me tell you, I've been having my sandwiches delivered ever since.

Backstage Tales

Behind the scenes in Llanview, what you see may not always be what you get. Here are some tasty tidbits about the fun and foibles that take place on the set of One Life to Live—along with a few backstage secrets that can now be revealed!

Hillary B. Smith (Nora Buchanan)

Bob Woods and I always try to surprise each other. I always do scenes with him where I'm naked. So I wear foam cups that cover my breasts and I have tape all over them. One day Valerie Pettiford, who played Sheila, wrote "Hi Woodsy" on them, so when I dropped my robe that's what he'd see. We do the scene, I drop my robe, and nothing. Then we do it again—and still nothing. The third time I drop my robe he finally says, "Oh!" I mean, what was he looking at all that time?

Tuc Watkins (David Vickers)

I used to practice my lines by saying them to my dog! You see, I had to make eye contact with someone in order to learn all those words—I couldn't just look at a wall. So I stared straight at my border collie, Blue, who sat there and looked right back at me for as long as it took to get it right.

Sean Moynihan (Powell Lord)

Courtroom scenes used to take hours to tape, but they might have taken days if not for *One Life to Live*'s stage manager, Ray Hoesten. "Ray Jay" saw to it that everything stayed on schedule. Surprisingly, he told me that courtroom scenes were among the easiest scenes for him because everyone was sedate, calm, and solemn. The hardest scenes? Wedding receptions!

Nathan Purdee (Hank Gannon)

Once, I had a courtroom scene with thirteen straight pages of dialogue. And I nearly got through it—that is, until I looked down at my legal pad where Bob Woods had written, "Check your fly before you approach the bench." That was it! I forgot every last one of my lines. But at least my fly was zipped.

Marcia Cross (Kate Sanders)

When we were on location in Argentina, it may have looked romantic, but it was torture. We worked in 110 degree heat, and I pulled off my best Florence Nightingale when my costar, John Loprieno, got seasick between takes in our boating scenes. I had to keep dousing him with water. If I hadn't, you would have seen me romancing a Cord Roberts who was absolutely green, or worse. Acting is such a glamorous life.

James DePaiva (Max Holden)

There was a great scene where I was supposed to hand baby Duke over to his mother, Lee Ann. But just as I handed the baby over to Yasmine Bleeth (Lee Ann) the kid spit up all over her chest! Yasmine didn't flinch though, and they kept the scene. They just had to wipe her shirt off later! It was hilarious! As soon as they said "Cut," everybody cracked up!

Laura Koffman (Cassie Carpenter)

Soap weddings are hard work! At my wedding to Andrew, I couldn't even sit down between takes because I was wearing an eight-foot-long train. While the rest of the cast took a break, all I could do was stand at the altar—for three hours! Still, when Andrew and Cassie recited their vows, I have to admit I was really choked up. All those tears you saw were very real.

Roger Howarth (Todd Manning)

Todd's scar may look real, but of course, it's not. The scar, which looks like an anchovy when it's off, is actually made of latex. It takes about ten minutes for our makeup person to apply it, and the little bugger stays glued on with a combination of spirit gum and eyelash adhesive.

Robert S. Woods (Bo Buchanan)

Man, do we have fun behind the scenes. Over the years, the Buchanan boys have become known for our backstage pranks. Like the joke we always played on one of our leading ladies who liked to write her lines on her hands. Just before taping, one of us would wet our hands and then shake hers—smearing her precious lines!!! We laughed, but she didn't.

Nathan Purdee (Hank Gannon)

For years, Hank was in the midst of a bitter family feud with his bad-seed brother, RJ. Funny thing is, we got along great—offcamera, that is. In fact, Timothy Stickney, who plays RJ, was my dressing-room mate. Which meant I spent twelve hours a day staring at his face in our little cubbyhole of a space in the basement of ABC Studio 17 here in New York City. When you spend that much time with someone day in and day out, you've got to get along.

Michael Storm (Dr. Larry Wolek)

I wasn't the first to play Larry. Before me, the role was played by my real-life brother Jim. When he left, I took over. But they didn't just hand me the part, I had to audition like everyone else! And when I signed back in 1969, I expected to stay for just two years. So much for intentions!

Kassie DePaiva (Blair Manning)

My southern drawl used to disappear when I was in front of the camera because the producers asked me to lose my real Kentucky accent. They thought I sounded too much like another character, Luna. So for years, I talked "refined and dignified." I could just hear my friends back home in Kentucky saying, "Give us a break, Kassie. We know what a redneck you are."

Yorlin Madera (Cristian Vega)

You think it's easy acting on a soap? Think again! Not only do you have to memorize like twenty pages of dialogue, but there's a bunch of technical things to learn like "hitting your mark." You see, they put these little pieces of tape on the studio floor to indicate where you should stand. At first, I had a hard time finding them, but I'm totally into the groove now. If I could get used to getting up at six in the morning, then doing a soap would be a piece of cake.

Marcia Cross (Kate Sanders)

John Loprieno, who played Cord, and I really had a great time working together. We had the most fun learning to do the tango for a romantic scene in Argentina. They say it looked like we'd been dancing for years, but actually we had a private instructor on-set every day for a month teaching us all that intricate footwork.

John Loprieno (Cord Roberts)

Backstage at *One Life to Live*, everyone used to call me Gumby. It all started on a location shoot when I was costumed like Rambo. That mutated to Cordbo, then Gumbo, and finally Gumby. Hey, I've been called worse. . . . as a kid, everyone called me Nailhead!

Doug Wert (Wade Coleman)

Working at Wanda's Diner, Wade helped turn Angel Burgers into a new taste sensation. But if you must know, the burgers that the prop department prepared were anything but tasty. The guys fried them up in the back room in the early afternoon, and sometimes they would sit for hours under the hot lights before we ever took a bite.

Michael Storm (Dr. Larry Wolek)

The hardest thing about playing a physician is trying to memorize all those medical terms. Well, I thought I'd licked the problem the day the script called for me to discuss a complicated case in the hospital cafeteria. I simply wrote my lines on a slip of paper and hid them in my prop coffee cup just before we taped the show. But an extra playing a waitress came by and filled my cup to the brim. I watched in horror as my soggy crib note floated to the top in a sea of java.

Jessica Tuck (Megan Gordon)

James DePaiva played practical jokes with the same zest that he plays mad Max Holden! One day, he got me bad. When I turned my back on Jim during a scene, he poured a cup of salt in my drink! I took a sip and nearly lost my cookies.

Ken Meeker (Rafe Garretson)

I think the most embarrasing moment of my career happened on our set when I had just finished playing a scene in bed with one of my leading ladies. The director yelled, "Cut," I casually threw back the covers, and the crew let out a collective gasp. Well, unbeknownst to me, my realism-seeking costar was topless, and I had just exposed her to the entire studio.

David Ledingham (Suede Pruitt)

I remember Suede had a tattoo—a fake one, but a good one. Everyday, before taping, our makeup artist applied a fresh tattoo to my arm. We had to remember to put it in the same place every time because you couldn't fool those eagle-eyed viewers. One "slip-up" and the letters came pouring in.

Susan Haskell (Marty Saybrooke)

Marty is a very unusual name, but one that fit my character. Our head writer at the time, Michael Malone, relied heavy on symbolism when he named a new character. For instance, Marty was from a very wealthy family, so Michael chose the last name Saybrooke after Old Saybrooke, an upper-crust town in Connecticut, and Marty because it sounds a little boyish and rebellious.

Jessica Tuck (Megan Gordon)

I just loved working with Gerry Anthony (Marco) because we kind of tapped into each other's outrageous behavior. Sometime our scenes were so spontaneous that we surprised ourselves as much as the cameraman and the director! I usually could tell something unplanned was going to happen when Gerry got this twinkle in those little brown eyes of his. Then, watch out!!

Fiona Hutchinson (Gabrielle Medina)

I barely survived Eterna with *One Life to Live*. The five grueling days of shooting the Eterna scenes featured falls, explosions, rock slides, and romance, all in a breathtaking set that was so colossal that it had to be erected in a separate studio. One short week later, I was almost sorry to see the entire structure come tumbling down.

Tonja Walker (Alex Olanov)

I may be the only soap actress on *One Life to Live* who ever had to act with a reptile. And let me tell you, that was not a rubber snake. It was too real. But acting with a snake sure beats the disgusting rats I once had to work with on *General Hospital*!

Michael Palance (Dr. Dan Wolek)

When I played Dan Wolek, doctor, I had no idea what I was doing!! Thank goodness we had someone who did. Whenever I had to "play doctor," the show called in a medical adviser, Annie O'Toole, to help make the scenes look realistic. She told me things like how to hold a scalpel and where to put the stethescope! You know, without Annie's expertise, they might have called the show *One Life to Lose*.

Larry Pine (Roger Gordon)

I risked my life in the underground city of Eterna! That adventure proved to be a frightening experience, not only for me, but also for the ABC Sports Department! During our thrilling escape, the elaborate waterfall constructed in our studio overflowed and flooded their control room—right in the middle of *Wide World of Sports*! I guess we experienced "the thrill of victory" and they felt "the agony of defeat."

Yasmine Bleeth (Lee Ann Demerest)

In a weird way, I felt comfortable walking onto the set of *One Life to Live* for the first time. After being on *Ryan's Hope* for five years, it was nice to have a little piece of the show on *One Life to Live*. You remember Wanda's Place? Well, that set was actually Johnny Ryan's bar reincarnated! Rather than destroy the set, they just moved it to Llanview.

Fabulous Firsts

Who doesn't remember that first day on the job, or the butterflies in the stomach during that first job interview? The cast of One Life to Live *certainly recall exactly what it was like—in the beginning . . .*

Erika Slezak (Viki Carpenter)

It truly seems like yesterday when I walked through those studio doors for the very first time, wide-eyed and eager to please, having never been on TV before in my life! The costume designer, Hazel Roy, came to me just before we started to tape and put a penny in the pocket of my suit jacket and said, "That's for luck." I'm not sure if I saved that penny, but I sure as heck should have, because it was one of the luckiest days of my life.

Sean Moynihan (Powell Lord)

I was especially jittery the first time I worked with Erika Slezak. After all, she'd played Viki for over twenty-three years at the time. Just before our first scene together, Erika took me aside for a little chat and I confessed to her that TV was kind of new to me. She just looked at me and said, "Don't worry. Acting is acting—you can do it." I hope she knows how much those kind words meant to me.

Kirk Geiger (Kevin Buchanan)

Erika Slezak (Viki) bought me a rose on my first day of work and told me, "You're doing wonderfully." When you come in as a recast there's a lot of pressure. All eyes are on you, and you get a little tense. But she was there to ease some of that pressure for me.

Robert S. Woods (Bo Buchanan)

I came to New York to audition for the role of Richard Abbott, but when the casting director asked me to do a screen test with Erika Slezak for the new role of Bo, I reluctantly said, "Okay." But I really wanted to play Richard! It was lucky for me because eighteen years later, where the heck is Richard Abbott?

Kirk Geiger (Kevin Buchanan)

When I first auditioned for Kevin, I really misinterpreted the script. You see, the script had the character in a bar telling his troubles to a bartender named Marty. I'm picturing Marty as this big, burly guy with hairy arms, so you can imagine my shock when, at the end, it said, "Kevin kisses Marty." Hey, wait a minute, I thought. Maybe I better call my agent. As you all know, it turned out Marty was a gorgeous girl with hairy arms. Just kidding, Susan.

Nathan Fillion (Joey Buchanan)

By my first day on the job, I knew everybody's real names. Nah, I'm not psychic. For a few weeks before I started work, I bought every soap opera magazine there was and cut out pictures of the cast of *One Life to Live*. Then I'd tape them in the back of my little notebook and write their real names beside their picture. That way, by my first day on the job, I'd know everybody.

John Viscardi (Father Tony Vallone)

As soon as I learned I'd be playing a priest, I went back to my old Catholic alma mater, Loyola High, to pick up some tips from an old friend, Father Pryor. Then, just before heading to the studio for my first day on the job, I went to confession!! I wanted to start this role with a clear conscience.

Patricia Elliott (Renee Buchanan)

I've enjoyed nearly every second here on the show—that is, except for my first few days. To be honest, those early days were among the most terrifying times I've ever known. You see, I came from the theater, where you had weeks to memorize your lines. Here, you have barely a day! At one point, it got so bad that they practically had to shoot my scenes one line at a time. But I survived, and now, life behind the scenes in Llanview is a pleasure.

Timothy Stickney (RJ Gannon)

During my screen test for the role, I wasn't exactly feeling as cool as RJ. In fact, I was shaking like a leaf. I'd breezed through my first audition, but this one was in front of the cameras. Fortunately, I had worked with Nathan Purdee, who plays Hank, before, but even he couldn't help my nerves. Which only felt worse when my eyes connected with the little red light on the top of the camera. I was talking when all of a sudden the light came on. "Oh, no . . . I'm on!" Somehow I maintained my composure and got the role.

John Loprieno (Cord Roberts)

When I look back to my first week on the show, I still break out in a cold sweat! I put on a stiff pair of cowboy boots and walked right into a "front burner" storyline! It all seems like a blur, but somehow I survived three fights, two love scenes, and forty pages of dialogue each day! By week's end, both my feet and my brain were blistered.

Brenda Brock (Brenda McGillis)

Oh, that first day! I was so nervous!! In my very first scene I had to do a love scene with my leading man, John Loprieno, who was wearing a fake mustache! When we kissed, my sweaty upper lip stuck to his gooey upper lip and they practically had to pull us apart!

Jessica Tuck, (Megan Gordon)

Back then, I just don't think I had "the soap look." Oh, you know the look—big hair and long, luxurious fingernails. And it certainly didn't help my confidence when I went to the casting call and found myself competing against every big-haired blonde in New York! Guess who won? I'll bet they all wanted to claw my eyes out—with those long, luxurious fingernails.

Gina Tognoni (Kelly Cramer)

I'd never watched *One Life to Live* before I auditioned. I screen-tested with a guy named Nathan Fillion, who I thought was there to audition, too. I didn't realize that he was already on the show playing Joey Buchanan. I remember thinking, Wow, look how well he gets along with everybody. Then he came up to me and offered me a danish and I thought, Who the hell does this guy think he is? I was pretty naive, but I got the job!

Hillary B. Smith (Nora Buchanan)

After my audition, I never thought I'd get the role. As originally conceived, Nora was supposed to be a little bit like Katharine Hepburn. But I had my own definite idea of what I wanted her to be—more like Lauren Bacall. So I walked into the audition, and like Sinatra, I did it my way. After I finished my reading, the powers-that-be all sat there with their mouths hanging open. You could hear a pin drop. So, with this experience safely behind me, I headed home, confident that I wouldn't be hearing from *One Life to Live*. But here I am.

James DePaiva (Max Holden)

If I hadn't taken a big risk, I might never have won the role. I was competing with five other actors for the role of Max, and during the screen tests with Tina they were all playing it very safe. So I decided to take a chance! I came running in, picked up Tina, and spun her around three times. She didn't know what hit her! But we hit it off and the part of Max Holden was mine.

Yasmine Bleeth (Lee Ann Demerest)

Lee Ann came to the big city straight from Sweetwater, Texas. As for me, I'd lived my entire life in New York and Paris, so playing a girl from the sticks was kind of a "stretch" for me. Up until the last minute, I didn't even know she had a southern twang. You see, just before my audition, the director said, "By the way, Lee Ann has a southern accent." I thought about it, said, "okay," and like the ad says, I decided to "just do it!"

Allan Dean Moore (Kerry Nichols)

I found myself facing a big problem when I auditioned for the role of rap singer Kerry Nichols. You see, I'm an actor—I'd never performed a rap song in my life! So I called my friend, Grover, who just happened to be a rap composer, and we put together some special material on the spot. It went something like this: "My name is Al, and I'm here to audition, not as an actor, but as a musician." Well, it must have worked because they hired me to front the K Funk Mob.

Grace Phillips (Sarah Buchanan)

When Sarah came back from the dead, she came home to reunite with Bo—and seeing him married to Cassie put her in a state of shock. In real life, my debut on the show was nearly as traumatic! You see, I had recently given up my New York apartment and moved everything I owned to Los Angeles. But then I went and auditioned for *One Life to Live*—which tapes in New York! Wouldn't you know it, I got the part, and had to move everything back East all over again!

Storyline Tales

Is your favorite One Life to Live actor anything like the character he or she portrays? Can you imagine playing the same character day in and day out for years on end? The cast share their thoughts about their characters and the storylines they will always remember. . . . .

Phil Carey (Asa Buchanan)

It's tough to make Asa believable sometimes because he can be such an ass. He's crude, cantankerous, calculating—he's destroyed people's lives. But it doesn't faze him. He just tells his sons, "Do as 1 say, not as 1 do." And 1 gather he must be the greatest stud who's ever lived; every time there's a dull moment, he finds another illegitimate son. He can be very humorous, but he's not a role model.

Kevin Stapleton (Kevin Buchanan)

Almost everyone on this show is more or less like their character. It's hard to do this every day and not be. Some people actually do the work their characters do. But while Kevin Buchanan is rich, I'm not. And 1 don't skulk after married people, because I'm married myself. Otherwise, everything is pretty much the same—except the clothes are different. I'd never dress like him!

Wortham Krimmer (Reverend Andrew Carpenter)

Unlike many soap characters who never seem to go to work, Andrew is always on the job! Even though he wears a collar, both the writers and 1 have always tried our best not to make the Rev-meister a holier-than-thou kind of guy, and that's why 1 was proud when one of the leading magazines chose my character as one of the soaps' "ten most believable professionals." That was quite an honor.

Robert S. Woods (Bo Buchanan)

When the writers were first considering making Bo police commissioner, they came to the guy who knows Bo best, me, to ask if he'd ever done any policework. 1 said, "Oh, sure, Bo used to run a multinational company, so that's like being police commissioner of seventeen countries." Taking me at my word, they gave Bo his new job. What they didn't know is that 1 made the whole thing up!

Andrea Evans (Tina Lord Roberts)

Over the years, Tina did some downright dirty deeds, and people always asked me how she could possibly scheme and keep a clear conscious! Well, it was easy! You see, Tina never meant to do harm to anyone . . . she just went about things in the wrong way! All she ever wanted was to be l-o-v-e-d!

Erika Slezak (Viki Carpenter)

1 must say that some of the most rewarding work I've done was the two weeks that Viki had an extended out-of-body experience while fighting for her life on the operating table. Even though practically every scene had complicated special effects to contend with and 1 had pages and pages of dialogue to learn, 1 loved every touching, challenging moment of it.

Robert S. Woods (Bo Buchanan)

I think one of the reasons for the success of the Buchanans is that we kind of have our own way of communicating. And a lot of what we say, we ad-lib! Credit Clint Richie for saying, "You look like a dying calf in a hailstorm." And Phil Carey [Asa] likes to throw in a few gems of his own, like "Son, you remind me of a horse's patoot."

Reiko Aylesworth (Rebecca Lewis)

I still remember being held hostage by Todd Manning, played with incredible intensity by Roger Howarth. Roger really got into his work, like a scene where Todd was supposed to hold a gun to my head and scream to a couple of cops, "Get out of the way." Instead he screamed, "You get out of the way . . . and you, get a doughnut!"

Roy Thinnes (Sloan Carpenter)

I guess I was one of the few characters who had more than one life to live. Before Sloan, I portrayed an entirely different character—Alex Crown, a devious mobster who was as different as night and day from the law-abiding general I played years later. Funny thing is, Alex had a son, Rob, who married Cassie Callison, and then Sloan's son Andrew married the very same young woman. Strange as it may seem, I suppose I was forever destined to be Cassie's father-in-law.

Erika Slezak (Viki Carpenter)

Viki shared over a decade with Clint Buchanan. But I'll bet you didn't know that "way back when," I was actually supposed to have a relationship with Clint's brother, Bo. However, I left the program for awhile to have a baby, and when I tuned in to see what was going on, there was Bo in a love scene with Pat Ashley! Jokingly, I called the producer and said, 'Hi, its Erika. Not only did you give away my coffee cup, you gave away my boyfriend!'

Michael Palance (Dr. Dan Wolek)

Playing a doctor was a bit of a stretch because in real life, I was only eighteen years old! When I got the role, I rushed right out to the local bookstore and bought the only medical textbook they had in stock—*Every Woman's Guide to Gynecology and Health*! You should have seen the look I got from the saleslady.

Thom Christopher (Carlo Hesser)

I feel fortunate to have played the role for as long as I did. You see, Carlo was only intended to be a bit part—in fact, I only came in to do the character for one day. One day became seven years, and a 1992 Emmy Award, before Carlo's long and lusty life came to an end—for the second time.

Nicholas Walker (Max Holden)

When the show first approached me, I wasn't sure that I wanted to relocate from California to New York, where *One Life to Live* is taped. But my friends kept saying, "You're turning down Max Holden? How can you do that??" Believe me, I heard this enough to realize that Max was one of those special roles—a pivotal, central character who made things happen.

Valerie Pettiford (Sheila Price)

You know, getting the role of Sheila was a thrill for me because I'd been a big fan of *One Life to Live* for years. Early in my career, I was lucky enough to perform as an extra here on *One Life to Live*! This was back when Judith Light and Gerald Anthony were acting out the hottest love-hate relationship in daytime, and I appeared with their characters, Karen and Marco, as a candy striper.

Susan Batten (Luna Moody)

Luna Moody was known to consult her tarot cards more than Cupid to settle matters of the heart. In real life, I'm nowhere near as "celestial" as Luna was, though I have been ruminating lately about the powerful effect that the moon has on our lives. Would you believe that I once knew a woman whose housekeeper worked around the schedule of the moon? That's a heckuva lot of waxing and waning!

Kiss and Tell

Love scenes are always fun to watch, but are they fun to play? Cast members through the years are not afraid to kiss and tell. . . .

Thorsten Kaye (Patrick Thornhart)

In my screen test, I walked in and learned I had to do a kissing scene. Susan Haskell came up to me and said, "I just want to tell you that there'll be no tongues." I thought, Great, because that's what I wanted to do, tongue everybody and go home. It was very awkward; but I like to tease her about it now.

Wortham Krimmer (Reverend Andrew Carpenter)

If I've learned anything, it's that soap opera "sex" isn't always as steamy as it seems. You watch us going at it hot and heavy, but what you are not seeing is Ray, our stage manager, crouching alongside the bed, and reaching up to touch us on the leg so we know when to open our eyes or break the kiss. It's kind of a cue from Cupid!

John Loprieno (Cord Roberts)

I'll never forget the time Tina and Cord had a love scene in a sauna. We taped half the scenes on a Friday, and planned to do the rest on the following Monday—but over the weekend, I picked up a nasty sunburn. So in order to make me look exactly as I did on Friday, they had to cover my tender red body from head to toe with white makeup. [Ouch!]

Laura Koffman (Cassie Carpenter)

As comfortable as I am with Bob Woods [Bo] I must confess that I was nervous before our first kiss. Don't you get nervous when you're going to kiss someone for the first time? And on TV, it's worse because there are twenty crew people watching your every move! Well, after the fact, I was happy to report that my first screen smooch was a delight.

James DePaiva (Max Holden)

The pivotal scene for my character was the first big love scene with Gabrielle. Fiona Hutchison and I sat down and choreographed every movement, every zipper, every hand touch, every kiss. A few things happened spontaneously, but it was very, very well rehearsed. You can't let your fantasies run wild when you're thinking of ideas for these things.

Jensen Buchanan (Sarah Buchanan)

I only ever had two nerve-racking days on *One Life to Live*. The first, understandably, was my first day on the show. But the second was the day of my first screen kiss. Think of it! Millions of people watching you share in one of life's intimate moments! That day, I had an acute case of "quivering lips!" Somehow I got through it, and they tell me it was a hot kiss!

John Loprieno (Cord Roberts)

When Andrea Evans [Tina] and I had our first big passionate love scene, there was soft music, candlelight—very romantic stuff. I picked Tina up in my arms to carry her to the bed and tripped over a lighting cable. The retake was more successful!

Backstage Pass

A peek behind the scenes at some of the people who make <u>One Life to Live</u> happen five days a week, fifty-two weeks a year.

𝒜 twenty-three-year veteran of *One Life to Live*, stage manager Ray Hoesten is always there in a "pinch" for actor James DePaiva (Max Holden.)

𝒢iven the hectic taping schedule, the actors often have to eat on the run. Laura Koffman (Cassie Carpenter) sips some hot soup before rushing upstairs to the set.

*R*odi's Tavern is one of the 100 elaborate sets that are used on *One Life to Live*. The sets are removed each evening and stored in a warehouse thirty-two blocks away.

*T*here is more to Todd Manning's parrot than meets the eye. Ed Richman trains Todd's feathered pal, while actor Ron Gallop provides the voice for the acid-tongued bird.

*B*etween takes, high-school student Erin Torpey (Jessica Buchanan) spends her spare time doing what every teenager must— homework!

*N*athan Purdee (Hank Gannon) unwinds in his dressing room during the midday lunch break. The actors arrive at the studio between 7:00 A.M. and 9:00 A.M. each morning. They rarely leave before 7:00 P.M. in the evening.

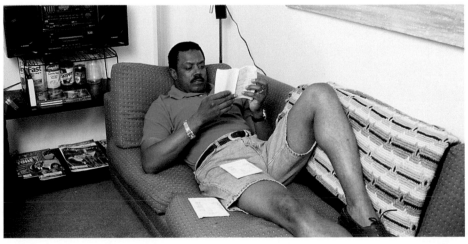

*A*riella and Natalie Jamnik both have "Starr" power. The twins, who share the role of Starr Manning, happily pose with their on-screen grand-mother, Pamela Payton-Wright (Addie Cramer) and Kassie DePaiva (Blair Manning), who is married to her costar, James DePaiva (Max Holden).

*R*obert S. Woods (Bo) enjoys some fresh New York air outside his "home sweet home" away from home—the *One Life to Live* studio. *One Life to Live* moved into the renovated National Guard Armory (which was built in 1901) to accommodate the pro-gram's 1978 expansion to a full hour.

$\mathscr{P}$roducer/director Frank Valentini checks out cameraman Bruce Cooperman's shot. Depending on the complexity of the scene, between three and five cameras are used to tape the action that is seen on air approximately three weeks later.

$\mathscr{S}$tage manager Alan Needleman shares an on-set hug with Erin Torpey, who has grown up before our eyes in the role of Jessica Buchanan.

$\mathscr{W}$ortham Krimmer (Andrew Carpenter) gets a "lift" from *One Life to Live*'s camera crew—Larry Strack, Frank Forsythe, Bruce Cooperman, and Howie Zeidman.

As post-production coordinator and show historian, Margo Husin reads every script and observes the editing of every scene to ensure that the people of Llanview do not do or say anything that might be inconsistent with plot or character.

Robert S. Woods (Bo Buchanan) starts his work day by picking up his dressing room key from long-time security guard David Coleman. The *One Life to Live* contract actors and day players occupy seventeen dressing rooms located one floor below the studio, in the basement of the cavernous *One Life to Live* facility.

Actress Hillary B. Smith (Nora Buchanan) receives the royal treatment from *One Life to Live*'s talented hair and makeup department. From left: makeup artists Dennis Eger and Renate Long, hairstylists Laurie Filippi and Wayne Bilotti, and makeup artist Miriam Meth.

$\mathcal{B}$oom operators Jerry Zeller and Bobby Theodore ensure that viewers can hear—loud and clear—every word spoken by the *One Life to Live* actors.

$\mathcal{T}$he people of Llanview stay on the cutting edge of chic thanks to the talented team of artists who design and maintain the hundreds of costumes in the *One Life to Live* collection, including this emerald green satin cocktail suit, belonging to Dorian Lord. From left: assistant costume designer David Brooks, costume designer Susan Gammie, associate designer Sally Lesser, and wardrobe supervisor Gwyn Martin.

*P*roduction Designer Roger Mooney and Scenic Designers John Kenny and Ruth Wells inspect a model of a set about to be constructed in the ABC scene shop. Mooney and his creative team are responsible for the design and creation of all of the sets seen on the program. Each week, the busy designers introduce an average of five new sets to Llanview.

*T*he phones rarely stop ringing in *One Life to Live*'s always hectic production office. Here, Assistant to the Executive Producer Jennifer Rosen, Production Office Assistant Anthony Wilkinson, Production Associate Diane Rodriguez, and Assistant to the Directors Teresa Anne Cicala tend to the madness!

*A*ssociate head writer Jean Passanante advises scriptwriter Ron Carlivati on some last-minute changes to the *One Life to Live* script. Unlike many daytime writers—who often have offices away from the studio—*One Life to Live*'s scribes are housed in the same building as the cast and crew.

CELEBRATIONS!

𝒯he cast of *One Life to Live* had us seeing red when they gathered in celebration of the 1992 holiday season.

𝒲hen *One Life to Live* turned five in July 1973, the program celebrated with a summer party. Here, creator Agnes Nixon joined cast members Alice Hirson (Eileen Siegel) and Doris Belack to salute the milestone.

$\mathcal{O}$n July 15, 1993, the entire cast donned their formal best to celebrate *One Life to Live*'s silver anniversary.

One Life to Live celebrated the taping of its 7,000th episode on November 20, 1995. During the festivities, five-time Emmy winner Erika Slezak remarked, "If we were in prime time, we'd be in our two-hundred-seventieth year!" The bash also marked the unveiling of the show's new logo and opening.

*T*he cast in 1975, on the occasion of *One Life to Live*'s seventh birthday.

*E*ight of *One Life to Live*'s core players gathered around in 1976 to celebrate the show's expansion from thirty to forty-five minutes.

The cast and crew convened in 1977 to fete producer Charlotte Weil on her birthday.

Cain and Tina's wedding brought the *One Life to Live* cast and crew together in 1994.

The United States turned 220 years old on July 4, 1996. In celebration, *One Life to Live*'s cast gathered to offer hot dogs to their resident Uncle Sam, Thom Christopher (Carlo Hesser).

BACKSTAGE . . .
THROUGH THE YEARS

During the mid-1970s, *One Life to Live* shared a New York studio with *All My Children*. The facility, located at 101 West 67th Street, has since been demolished and replaced with a high-rise apartment building.

The crew shielded Andrea Evans (Tina) from the South American sun in this 1987 photo taken on location in Buenos Aires, Argentina.

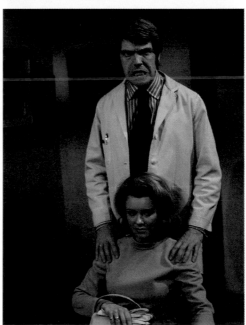

Michael Storm (Larry Wolek) could not resist a bit of backstage clowning in this 1972 on-set shot with his TV wife, Lynn Benesch (Meredith Wolek).

*E*steemed director David Pressman welcomed soap veterans George Reinholt (Tony Lord) and Jackie Courtney (Pat Ashley) to the *One Life to Live* cast in 1975. Before moving to Llanview, the popular actors played lovers Steve and Alice Frame on NBC's *Another World.*

*T*he ABC cameras were on hand to record the 1989 Daisys, *One Life to Live*'s self-styled parody of award shows.

*P*roducer Frank Valentini orchestrated this elaborate 1994 scene in which Blair (Kassie DePaiva), driving Cord's truck, accidentally ran down Luna Moody. Director Jill Mitwell was faced with the daunting task of creating the look of an outdoor car crash in *One Life to Live*'s small studio. To achieve the illusion, production designer Roger Mooney had the entire front end of a car built onto a moving dolly.

Behind the Scenes Facts

$\mathscr{M}$uch of the food consumed by the citizens of Llanview is prepared in the ABC cafeteria. It is often the same food eaten daily by hundreds of ABC employees.

$\mathscr{O}$ne Life to Live premiered on July 15, 1968. The initial storylines focused on a blue-collar Polish family, the Woleks, the blue-blooded Lords, and their Irish, African-American, and Jewish neighbors in Llanview.

$\mathscr{E}$arly morning rehearsals—known as "dry blockings"—are held in a basement room filled with tables and chairs to indicate the actual position of furnishings found on the set.

$\mathscr{O}$ne Life to Live tapes its 8,000th episode in 1999.

$\mathscr{M}$ore than 3,000 sheets of plywood, 1,500 yards of canvas, and 200 gallons of paint are used each year to construct the sets used on One Life to Live.

$\mathscr{E}$arly in 1977, Julia Duffy (Newhart, Designing Women) played the role of Karen Wolek for several weeks. Her stint was temporary; Judith Light joined the cast as the permanent Karen in the spring of 1977.

$\mathscr{F}$ifteen hundred pounds of costumes were shipped from New York to Salzburg, Austria (the actual setting for the fictional city of Mendorra), for six days and nights of remote taping.

$\mathscr{T}$he largest set ever created for daytime drama was One Life to Live's Great Hall of Eterna. The multilevel, thirty-two-foot-high, 360-degree set was so huge that it had to be erected in the TV-1 studio, a separate facility from TV-17, where One Life to Live normally tapes.

$\mathscr{T}$he largest set currently in use is Club Indigo, RJ Gannon's trendy nightspot.

$\mathscr{B}$o Buchanan's experiences as a Vietnam veteran were inspired by Robert S. Woods's actual stint as a special services officer in Southeast Asia.

$\mathscr{G}$etting One Life to Live on the air is a twenty-four-hour operation. At the conclusion of the taping day, a "reset" crew of up to thirty people works throughout the night to set the stage for the next day's program.

$\mathscr{O}$ne Life to Live is the first original soap to air by creator Agnes Nixon.

Back in 1968, *One Life to Live* was a half-hour program. It was expanded to forty-five minutes in 1976 and to a full hour in 1978.

The oldest set currently in use is the Lord Library. This set has been renovated at least four times since 1968, but still retains its original look.

One Life to Live was almost called *Between Heaven and Hell*. The title was changed just before the program went on the air in 1968.

While many weapons used on the program are authentic, the prop department maintains a supply of rubber daggers, rubber guns, and even a rubber sledge hammer!

Every copy of *The Banner* newspaper is designed by the *One Life to Live* Art Department. Only the front and back pages are produced, which are all the viewer ever sees. The inside pages are often back issues of the *New York Times*.

The lag between the taping of an episode and the time it is aired is currently two to three weeks.

Between 2,500 and 3,000 fan letters pour into the production office every month.

On average, *One Life to Live*'s design staff designs and introduces five new sets each week.

Many of the *One Life to Live* sets are repainted, reappointed, and used over and over. For example . . . the beach house used in scenes where Todd was stalking Nora later became Carlo Hesser's penthouse at the Llanview Towers.

The horses in the Buchanan stables are furnished by Chateau Stables in New York City. Many of the horses are the same animals that pull the city's famous hansom cabs.

Clint Buchanan's first name was originally supposed to be Chris. Several days before taping his first show, actor Clint Ritchie convinced the writers to allow him to use his real first time.

Just before airtime, *One Life to Live* hastily changed Ross Harrison's first name to Jake. The last-minute change was prompted by the fact that there were already too many characters named Ross on daytime TV.

The contract actors and day players occupy seventeen dressing rooms located in the basement of the studio.

Each night, a crew works to put down and take up between 3,500 and 5,000 square feet of linoleum and carpet in the *One Life to Live* studio.

The magnificent marble floors in both Llanfair and Asa's mansion, Southampton, aren't really marble at all. The fabulous floors are actually rolls of painted canvas that are stretched out and taped to the cement studio floor.

Wardrobe mistress Gwyn Martin and her staff keep the actors looking spiffy by pressing, cleaning, and altering every article of clothing required for each episode.

Stretch limousines are never used on *One Life to Live,* since they are too big to fit in the studio. Only vehicles smaller than 19.6 feet can make the tight turn from the show's loading dock into the studio.

Christine Jones is the only actor to play three contract roles on *One Life to Live.* The talented actress portrayed nurse Sheila Rafferty, Viki Buchanan (during Erika Slezak's maternity leave), and Pamela Buchanan.

In the late 1960s, *One Life to Live* followed *General Hospital* in ABC's daytime lineup at 3:30 P.M. EST. The program preceded the cult soap opera, *Dark Shadows.*

During the Loon Lake remote, only three characters (Bo, Cassie, and Alex) were seen on camera. However, just out of camera range were three stunt people, a stunt coordinator, two safety divers, an underwater consultant, one camera operator, one underwater camera operator, and ninety crew people!

The longest taping day took place in November 1981. Cast and crew worked from 7:00 A.M. until 4:45 A.M. the following morning to tape scenes involving the burning of Moor Cliffe.

Extreme precautions are taken when fire is incorporated into scenes such as the 1991 burning of Llanfair. Permission must be granted by the New York City Fire Department, and a fire consultant is hired to ensure that the studio has proper ventilation and safety equipment on hand.

A typical one-hour episode of *One Life to Live* features between 300 and 400 separate camera shots.

Every week, *One Life to Live*'s casting department receives more than 500 letters and postcards from aspiring actors hoping for a role.

Actors must memorize all of their lines. Teleprompters and cue cards, still in use on several daytime dramas, were removed from the *One Life to Live* studio in 1988.

One Life to Live sometimes works overtime to tape six shows in five days. Individual scenes from the sixth show are taped over the course of several days and are edited together to make one single episode. This is known behind the scenes as "six-packing."

Emmy Award Winners ®

It stands sixteen inches high, weighs four pounds, and is covered with 24-carat gold plate. Given each year by The Academy of Television Arts and Sciences, the Emmy® Award signifies excellence in daytime drama. Through 1997, One Life to Live has been awarded twenty-three of the prestigious golden statuettes, including Outstanding Individual Directing to David Pressman in 1976, Outstanding Actress honors to Robin Strasser (Dorian Lord) in 1982, and Outstanding Actor honors to Robert S. Woods (Bo Buchanan) in 1983. And on an unprecedented five occasions, Erika Slezak has been chosen as the Outstanding Actress on a Daytime Drama for her riveting portrayal of One Life to Live's First Lady, Victoria Lord Buchanan Carpenter.

Here's to all of the distinguished nominees and winners!

OUTSTANDING LEAD ACTOR IN A DRAMA SERIES
1978–1979
AL FREEMAN, JR. (ED HALL)

One Life to Live's first-ever acting Emmy was awarded to Al Freeman, Jr., for his portrayal of Lt. Ed Hall. Nineteen-seventy-nine was a banner year for the popular actor, who also received a prime-time Emmy nomination for his role in *Roots II*. Freeman received three other Daytime Emmy nominations for his stellar work on *One Life to Live*.

OUTSTANDING LEAD ACTRESS IN A DRAMA SERIES
1979–1980
JUDITH LIGHT (KAREN WOLEK)

"Oh God, I'm so thrilled! I really, really, really wanted this! I really did! Honestly, I have to tell you. And I want to tell you something else, that I am so honored to be included with all of these ladies. I think they are remarkable, and I respect their work enormously as I do all of us that are in daytime, and I really just want to acknowledge us. I want to thank, of course, my mother and father. I want to thank my dear, dear friends. Without their constancy and love, I don't know what I would have done. I want to thank my *One Life to Live* family. Without the directors, the writers—my God, the writers! You know everybody says that they have the best, but I know we've got it. Thank you very much to the Academy. I accept this for all of you!"

∂UTSTANDING LEAD ACTRESS IN A DRAMA SERIES
1980–1981
JUDITH LIGHT (KAREN WOLEK)

Who said "Light"-ning doesn't strike twice? Judith Light disproved the old adage when she took home her second consecutive Emmy Award at the 1981 ceremony. *All My Children*'s James Mitchell (a seven-time Emmy nominee) presented her with a golden bookend.

∂UTSTANDING LEAD ACTRESS IN A DRAMA SERIES
1981–1982
ROBIN STRASSER (DORIAN LORD CALLISON)

At the 1982 annual Emmy celebration, held in the ballroom of New York's Waldorf-Astoria Hotel, Robin Strasser took home the gold for her outstanding portrayal of the multifaceted Dorian Lord. Robin was nominated the previous year, and again in 1983 and 1985.

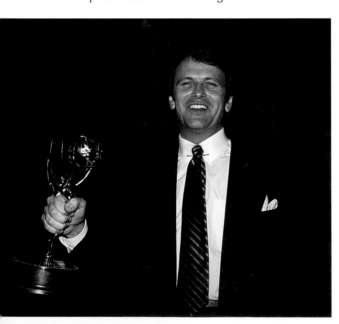

∂UTSTANDING LEAD ACTOR IN A DRAMA SERIES
1982–1983
ROBERT S. WOODS (BO BUCHANAN)

Robert S. Woods received his first nomination and earned his first win at the Tenth Annual Daytime Emmy Awards. Along with Woods, the *One Life to Live* directing team received Emmy Awards for their stellar work during the 1982–83 season.

$\mathcal{O}$UTSTANDING LEAD ACTRESS IN A DRAMA SERIES
1983–1984
ERIKA SLEZAK (VICTORIA LORD BUCHANAN)

Nineteen-eighty-four proved to be a banner year for Erika Slezak. Nominated for the first time the previous year, Erika was honored with her first Outstanding Actress statuette at the Eleventh Annual Daytime Award ceremony, held during the afternoon at New York's Sheraton Center Hotel.

$\mathcal{O}$UTSTANDING LEAD ACTRESS IN A DRAMA SERIES
1985–1986
ERIKA SLEZAK (VICTORIA LORD BUCHANAN)

"I am so honored and so proud. I want to thank the Academy and the Blue Ribbon Panel; and I want to say a very, very special thank you to Mr. Paul Rauch, who is the producer of *One Life to Live*, who gave me a marvelous story for the last year and a half, and who has turned *One Life to Live* into one of the best shows on daytime. I'm so proud to be associated with this show. I really am. I want to thank everyone associated with this show because they all together make it what it is. Thank you to our writers for their wonderful work, and our directors because without them we are absolutely lost. They are wonderful and creative and ingenious and they're marvelous. And, of course, most importantly, are my fellow actors. Without them I would not be here. And I want to thank my husband, Brian, and my sweet children, Michael, and Amanda, because they take such good care of me."

$\mathcal{O}$UTSTANDING SUPPORTING ACTOR IN A DRAMA SERIES
1991–1992
THOM CHRISTOPHER (CARLO HESSER)

The Academy hailed Thom Christopher as the Outstanding Supporting Actor for playing Mob kingpin Carlo Hesser, who was killed off (for the first time!) during the 1992 season. In his acceptance speech, Thom paid special tribute to *One Life to Live*'s veteran stage manager Ray Hoesten, then quipped, "I think I've kind of squelched any critic who says that daytime is about people with hair only!"

$\mathcal{O}$UTSTANDING LEAD ACTRESS IN A DRAMA SERIES
1991–1992
ERIKA SLEZAK (VICTORIA LORD BUCHANAN)

While accepting her third Emmy Award as Outstanding Actress, Erika Slezak honored "my mother and father who taught me to love and to respect the art of acting. And I am extraordinarily proud to have been with *One Life to Live* for twenty-one years. I don't really know of another actress who's had that kind of opportunity. Who has had the opportunity to act as I have for twenty-one years, almost every day? I want to thank all the people who have afforded me that opportunity starting with Agnes Nixon, Joan D'Incecco, and Doris Quinlan, straight through to Paul Rauch and to Linda Gottlieb. I want to thank our writers, headed by Michael Malone, for wonderful work. Our marvelous directors, our whole crew, and everyone at the show. I am truly, truly proud to be associated with them. Thank you!"

OUTSTANDING SUPPORTING ACTRESS IN A DRAMA SERIES
1993–1994
SUSAN HASKELL (MARTY SAYBROOKE)

Susan Haskell distinguished herself in 1993–1994 for her portrayal of *One Life to Live*'s anguished rape victim, Marty Saybrooke. While accepting her award, Susan remembered *One Life to Live*'s viewers when she declared her desire to "share this with the men and women who wrote to me and shared their stories. Thank you so much."

OUTSTANDING YOUNGER ACTOR IN A DRAMA SERIES
1993–1994
ROGER HOWARTH (TODD MANNING)

For his riveting portrayal of a rapist struggling with his tortured psyche, Roger Howarth was chosen 1994's Outstanding Younger Actor. At the conclusion of his speech, Roger sent a special message home to his young son when he said, "Night-night, Jules. I'll try to get Big Bird's autograph for you, and I love you."

OUTSTANDING LEAD ACTRESS IN A DRAMA SERIES
1993–1994
HILLARY B. SMITH (NORA GANNON)

In May 1994, Hillary B. Smith became the seventh *One Life to Live* actress to be chosen as Outstanding Lead Actress. In accepting the honor, Hillary paid homage to her costar, Robert S. Woods. "To Woodsy, thank you for the pleasure and the privilege of riding on your coattails."

OUTSTANDING LEAD ACTRESS IN A DRAMA SERIES
1994–1995
ERIKA SLEZAK (VICTORIA LORD CARPENTER)

For her outstanding work in several rich *One Life to Live* story-lines, Erika Slezak earned her fourth Daytime Emmy at the twenty-second annual awards ceremony, held at New York's Marriott Marquis Hotel. Afterward, a delighted Erika promised to put the statuette "right next to the others—on the top shelf of this big, lovely, antique Welsh dresser in our living room."

OUTSTANDING LEAD ACTRESS IN A DRAMA SERIES
1995–1996
ERIKA SLEZAK (VICTORIA LORD CARPENTER)

Erika Slezak made Emmy history in 1996 by accepting an unprecedented fifth Emmy Award. Taking the stage, she thanked "our extraordinary directors, without whom I would not be here. They did so much. Thank you to an extraordinary cast and crew, in particular, thank you Robin Strasser and Maureen Anderman. And as always, thank you to my wonderful, extraordinary family. I love you all so much. Thank you!"

Complete List of
One Life to Live Emmy
Winners and Nominees

Award Year: 1995-1996

Nominee
Outstanding Drama Series Writing Team
   Michael Malone, Head Writer
   Josh Griffith, Co-Head Writer
   Peggy Sloane, Associate Head Writer
   Jean Passanante, Associate Head Writer
   Richard Backus, Breakdown/Scriptwriter
   Miranda Barry, Breakdown Writer
   Ethel Brez, Breakdown Writer
   David Cherrill, Scriptwriter/Editor
   Neal Bell, Scriptwriter
   Peter Brash, Scriptwriter
   Mike Cohen, Scriptwriter
   Becky Cole, Scriptwriter
   Lloyd Gold, Scriptwriter
   Christopher Whitesell, Scriptwriter
   Lisa Connor, Scriptwriter

Nominee
Outstanding Graphics and Title Design
   Paul Newman, Title Designer
   Billy Pittard, Title Designer

Winner
Outstanding Lead Actress in a Drama Series
   Erika Slezak (Victoria Lord Carpenter)

Nominee
Outstanding Younger Actor in a Drama Series
   Nathan Fillion (Joey Buchanan)

Winner
Outstanding Achievement in Art Direction/Set Decoration/Scenic Design for a Drama Series
    Roger Mooney, Production Designer
    John Kenny, Jr., Art Director
    Ruth Wells, Art Director

Nominee
Outstanding Achievement in Costume Design for a Drama Series
    Susan Gammie, Costume Designer
    Daniel Lawson, Costume Designer
    Sally Lesser, Costume Designer

Nominee
Outstanding Drama Series Directing Team
    Peter Miner, Director
    Jill Mitwell, Director
    Lonny Price, Director
    Gary Tomlin, Director
    Jamie Howarth, Associate Director
    Tracy Casper Lang, Associate Director
    James McDonald, Associate Director
    David Pressman, Director
    Mary Rodden, Associate Director
    Jim Sayegh, Associate Director
    Frank Valentini, Associate Director
    Stan Warnow, Associate Director

Nominee
Outstanding Drama Series Writing Team
    Michael Malone, Head Writer
    Josh Griffith, Head Writer
    Jean Passanante, Associate Head Writer
    Mike Cohen, Writer
    Becky Cole, Writer
    David Cherrill, Writer
    Lloyd Gold, Writer
    Christopher Whitesell, Writer

Winner
Outstanding Lead Actress in a Drama Series
    Erika Slezak (Victoria Lord Carpenter)

Nominee
Outstanding Supporting Actor in a Drama Series
    Roger Howarth (Todd Manning)

Award Year: 1993-1994

Nominee
Outstanding Achievement in Costume Design for a Drama Series
  Susan Gammie, Costume Designer
  Daniel Lawson, Costume Designer
  Sally Lesser, Costume Designer

Winner
Outstanding Drama Series Writing Team
  Michael Malone, Head Writer
  Josh Griffith, Head Writer
  Jean Passanante, Associate Head Writer
  Susan Bedsow-Horgan, Writer
  Christopher Whitesell, Writer
  David Cherrill, Writer
  Becky Cole, Writer
  Lloyd Gold, Writer
  David Smilow, Writer

Nominee
Outstanding Lead Actor in a Drama Series
  Robert S. Woods (Bo Buchanan)

Winner
Outstanding Lead Actress in a Drama Series
  Hillary B. Smith (Nora Gannon)

Nominee
Outstanding Original Song
"He's My Weakness"
  Gloria Sklerov, Composer/Lyricist
  Robin Tapp, Composer/Lyricist

Winner
Outstanding Supporting Actress in a Drama Series
  Susan Haskell (Marty Saybrooke)

Winner
Outstanding Younger Actor in a Drama Series
  Roger Howarth (Todd Manning)

Award Year: 1992-1993

Nominee
Outstanding Lead Actor in a Drama Series
  Robert S. Woods (Bo Buchanan)

Nominee
Outstanding Supporting Actor in a Drama Series
  Thom Christopher (Carlo Hesser/Mortimer Bern)

Nominee
Outstanding Supporting Actress in a Drama Series
  Tonja Walker (Alex Olanov Hesser)

Award Year: 1991-1992

Nominee
Outstanding Achievement in Graphics and Title Design
  Richard Greenberg, Title Designer
  Bruce Schluter, Title Designer

Nominee
Outstanding Drama Series Writing Team
  Michael Malone, Head Writer
  Margaret Depriest, Head Writer
  Craig Carlson, Co-Head Writer
  Josh Griffith, Associate Head Writer
  Alan Bernstein, Breakdown Writer
  Ethel Brez, Breakdown Writer
  Mel Brez, Breakdown Writer
  Jeanne Glynn, Breakdown Writer
  Dorothy Goldstone, Breakdown Writer
  Eleanor Mancusi, Breakdown Writer
  Dorothy Purser, Scriptwriter/Editor
  Jeff Sweet, Script Editor
  Neal Bell, Scriptwriter
  Becky Cole, Scriptwriter
  Lucky Gold, Scriptwriter
  William Hoffman, Scriptwriter
  Juliette Mann, Scriptwriter
  Fran Myers, Scriptwriter
  Roger Newman, Scriptwriter
  Robert Soderberg, Scriptwriter

Winner
Outstanding Lead Actress in a Drama Series
  Erika Slezak (Victoria Lord Buchanan)

Nominee
Outstanding Lead Actress in a Drama Series
  Jessica Tuck (Megan Gordon)

Winner
Outstanding Supporting Actor in a Drama Series
  Thom Christopher (Carlo Hesser)

Nominee
Outstanding Drama Series Writing Team
  S. Michael Schnessel, Head Writer
  Addie Walsh, Associate Head Writer
  Craig Carlson, Co-Head Writer
  Leah Laiman, Co-Head Writer
  Ethel Brez, Associate Head Writer
  Mel Brez, Associate Head Writer
  Lanie Bertram, Writer
  Lloyd Gold, Writer
  Norman Hart, Writer
  Dorothy Purser, Writer

Nominee
Outstanding Original Song
"Here's to the Shows"
  Jonathan Segal, Composer/Lyricist

Award Year: 1988-1989

Nominee
Outstanding Achievement in Makeup for a Drama Series
  Renate Long, Makeup Artist
  Deborah Sperber, Makeup Artist

Nominee
Outstanding Drama Series Directing Team
  Larry Auerbach, Director
  Gary Bowen, Director
  Peter Miner, Director
  David Pressman, Director
  Andrea Rich, Associate Director
  Jim Sayegh, Associate Director

Award Year: 1987-1988

Nominee
Outstanding Achievement in Videotape Editing for a Drama Series
  Carol Wood, Editor
  Leona Ziera, Editor

Nominee
Outstanding Drama Series Directing Team
  Larry Auerbach, Director
  Gary Bowen, Director
  Peter Miner, Director

Lisa Hesser, Associate Director
Susan Pomerantz, Associate Director
David Pressman, Associate Director
Andrea Rich, Associate Director

Nominee
Outstanding Ingenue in a Drama Series
Andrea Evans (Tina Lord Roberts)

Nominee
Outstanding Lead Actress in a Drama Series
Erika Slezak (Victoria Lord Buchanan)

Award Year: 1986-1987

Winner
Outstanding Drama Series Writing Team
Peggy O'Shea, Head Writer
S. Michael Schnessel, Co-Head Writer
Ethel Brez, Associate Head Writer
Mel Brez, Associate Head Writer
Craig Carlson, Associate Head Writer
Lanie Bertram, Associate Writer

Nominee
Outstanding Guest Performer in a Drama Series
Eileen Heckart (Ruth Perkins)

Nominee
Outstanding Supporting Actor in a Drama Series
Al Freeman, Jr. (Ed Hall)
Anthony Call (Herb Callison)

Award Year: 1985-1986

Nominee
Outstanding Achievement in Lighting Direction for a Drama Series
Jo Mayer, Lighting Director
Michael Thornburgh, Lighting Director

Nominee
Outstanding Drama Series Directing Team
Larry Auerbach, Director
Peter Miner, Director
David Pressman, Director
Susan Pomerantz, Associate Director
Stuart Silver, Associate Director

Nominee
Outstanding Lead Actor in a Drama Series
  Robert S. Woods (Bo Buchanan)

Winner
Outstanding Lead Actress in a Drama Series
  Erika Slezak (Victoria Lord Buchanan)

Nominee
Outstanding Supporting Actor in a Drama Series
  Al Freeman, Jr. (Ed Hall)

Nominee
Outstanding Supporting Actress in a Drama Series
  Uta Hagen (Hortense)

Award Year: 1984-1985

Nominee
Outstanding Achievement by a Drama Series Design Team
  Lee Austin, Costume Designer
  Jo Mayer, Lighting Director
  Barry Robinson, Scenic Designer
  Michael Thornburgh, Lighting Director

Nominee
Outstanding Achievement by a Drama Series Technical Team
  Frank Bailey, Tape Sound Mixer
  Albert Forman, Videotape Editor
  Harry Hart, Tape Sound Mixer/Sound Editor
  Charlie Henry, Electronic Camera
  Ken Hoffman, Tape Sound Mixer
  Louis Marchand, Technical Director
  John Morris, Electronic Camera
  Rich Schiaffo, Electronic Camera
  Frank Schiraldi, Electronic Camera
  Doug Schmidt, Technical Director
  Herbert Segall, Senior Video Control
  Howard Zeidman, Electronic Camera
  Leona Zeira, Videotape Editor

Nominee
Outstanding Achievement in Hairstyling
  John Harkins, Hairstylist
  William Kohout, Hairstylist

Nominee
Outstanding Achievement in Makeup
  Paul Gebbia, Makeup Artist
  Renate Long, Makeup Artist

Nominee
Outstanding Direction for a Drama Series
  David Pressman, Director
  Peter Miner, Director
  Larry Auerbach, Director
  Melvin Bernhardt, Director
  John Sedwick, Director
  Ron Lagomarsino, Director
  Susan Pomerantz, Associate Director
  Stuart Silver, Associate Director

Nominee
Outstanding Lead Actress in a Drama Series
  Robin Strasser (Dorian Lord Callison)

Nominee
Outstanding Supporting Actor in a Drama Series
  Anthony Call (Herb Callison)

Award Year: 1983-1984

Nominee
Outstanding Achievement in Any Area of Creative Technical Crafts
Remote: Red Hook
  John Cordone, Electronic Camera

Nominee
Outstanding Achievement in Any Area of Creative Technical Crafts - Directing
Name: The Delila Fantasy
  Raymond Hoesten, Director

Winner
Outstanding Achievement in Technical Excellence for a Daytime Drama Series
  Frank Bailey, Senior Video Engineer
  Albert Forman, Videotape Editor
  Martin Gavrin, Technical Director
  Charlie Henry, Electronic Camera
  Wallace Hewitt, Electronic Camera
  Marianne Malitz, Senior Video Engineer
  Louis Marchand, Technical Director
  John Morris, Electronic Camera

Susan Pomerantz, Associate Director
Rich Schiaffo, Electronic Camera
Frank Schiraldi, Electronic Camera
Herbert Segall, Senior Video Engineer
Stuart Silver, Associate Director
Howard Zeidman, Electronic Camera
Leona Zeira, Videotape Editor

Nominee
Outstanding Actor in a Supporting Role in a Daytime Drama Series
Anthony Call (Herb Callison)

Winner
Outstanding Actress in a Daytime Drama Series
Erika Slezak (Victoria Lord Buchanan)

Nominee
Outstanding Actress in a Supporting Role in a Daytime Drama Series
Christine Ebersole (Maxie McDermot)

Winner
Outstanding Direction for a Daytime Drama Series
Larry Auerbach, Director
George Keathley, Director
Peter Miner, Director
David Pressman, Director

Award Year: 1982-1983

Nominee
Outstanding Achievement in Any Area of Creative Technical Crafts – Lighting Direction
Remote: Silver Springs, Florida
Everett Melosh, Lighting Director

Nominee
Outstanding Achievement in Technical Excellence for a Daytime Drama Series
Frank Bailey, Senior Audio Engineer
Albert Forman, Videotape Editor
Martin Gavrin, Technical Director
Anthony Greco, Videotape Editor
Charlie Henry, Electronic Camera
Ken Hoffman, Senior Audio Engineer
Eugene Kelly, Electronic Camera
Nancy Kriegel, Electronic Camera
Louis Marchand, Technical Director

John Morris, Electronic Camera
Carla Reid, Electronic Camera
Rich Schiaffo, Electronic Camera
Frank Schiraldi, Electronic Camera
Herbert Segall, Senior Video Engineer
Stuart Silver, Associate Director
John Sullivan, Associate Director
Genevieve Twohig, Electronic Camera
John Wood, Electronic Camera
Howard Zeidman, Electronic Camera

Winner
Outstanding Actor in a Daytime Drama Series
   Robert S. Woods (Bo Buchanan)

Nominee
Outstanding Actor in a Supporting Role in a Daytime Drama Series
   Anthony Call (Herb Callison)
   Al Freeman, Jr. (Ed Hall)

Nominee
Outstanding Actress in a Daytime Drama Series
   Erika Slezak (Victoria Lord Buchanan)
   Robin Strasser (Dorian Lord Callison)

Nominee
Outstanding Actress in a Supporting Role in a Daytime Drama Series
   Brynn Thayer (Jenny Janssen)

Nominee
Outstanding Daytime Drama Series
   Joseph Stuart, Producer

Winner
Outstanding Direction for a Daytime Drama Series
   Allen Fristoe, Director
   Norman Hall, Director
   Peter Miner, Director
   David Pressman, Director

Nominee
Outstanding Individual Achievement in Any Area of Creative Technical Crafts - Technical Direction/Electronic Camerawork
Remote: Silver Springs, Florida
   Anthony Gambino, Electronic Camera
   Robert Hoffman, Technical Director

Nominee
Outstanding Writing for a Daytime Drama Series
   Sam Hall, Head Writer
   Peggy O'Shea, Writer
   S. Michael Schnessel, Writer
   Victor Miller, Writer
   Lanie Bertram, Writer
   Craig Carlson, Writer
   Fred Corke, Writer
   Don Wallace, Writer

Award Year 1981-1982

Winner
Outstanding Achievement in Any Area of Creative Technical
Crafts-Lighting Direction
Remote: Gallery Basement
   Everett Melosh, Lighting Director

Nominee
Outstanding Actor in a Supporting Role in a Daytime Drama
Series
   Gerald Anthony (Marco Dane)

Winner
Outstanding Actress in a Daytime Drama Series
   Robin Strasser (Dorian Lord Callison)

Nominee
Outstanding Direction for a Daytime Drama Series
   Norman Hall, Director
   Peter Miner, Director
   David Pressman, Director

Nominee
Outstanding Writing for a Daytime Drama Series
   Sam Hall, Head Writer
   Peggy O'Shea, Writer
   S. Michael Schnessel, Writer
   Lanie Bertram, Writer
   Fred Corke, Writer
   Don Wallace, Writer

Nominee
Outstanding Achievement in Design Excellence for a Daytime Drama Series
  John Anthony, Music Director
  Charles Brandon, Scenic Designer
  Karen Crehan, Hair Designer
  Josephine Foederer, Costume Designer
  Willis Hanchett, Hair Designer
  Tracey Kelley, Makeup Designer
  Jo Mayer, Lighting Director
  Joseph Miller, Costume Designer
  Irving Robbins, Music Director
  Howard Sharrott, Lighting Director
  Jack Urbont, Composer

Nominee
Outstanding Achievement in Technical Excellence for a Daytime Drama Series
  Frank Bailey, Senior Audio Engineer
  Albert Forman, Videotape Editor
  Thomas French, Electronic Camera
  Martin Gavrin, Technical Director
  Anthony Greco, Videotape Editor
  Eugene Kelly, Electronic Camera
  Nancy Kriegel, Electronic Camera
  Louis Marchand, Technical Director
  Earl Moore, Electronic Camera
  John Morris, Technical Director
  Keith Morris, Electronic Camera
  William Phypers, Electronic Camera
  Bill Schloss, Senior Audio Engineer
  Herbert Segall, Senior Video Engineer
  Stuart Silver, Associate Director
  Robert Steinbeck, Videotape Editor
  John Sullivan, Associate Director
  Genevieve Twohig, Electronic Camera
  Richard Westlein, Electronic Camera
  John Wood, Electronic Camera

Winner
Outstanding Actress in a Daytime Drama Series
  Judith Light (Karen Wolek)

Nominee
Outstanding Actress in a Daytime Drama Series
  Robin Strasser (Dorian Lord)

Nominee
Outstanding Direction for a Daytime Drama Series
  Norman Hall, Director
  Peter Miner, Director
  David Pressman, Director

Nominee
Outstanding Writing for a Daytime Drama Series
  Gordon Russell, Head Writer
  Sam Hall, Writer
  Peggy O'Shea, Writer
  Lanie Bertram, Writer
  Fred Corke, Writer
  Don Wallace, Writer

Award Year: 1979-1980

Winner
Outstanding Actress in a Daytime Drama Series
  Judith Light (Karen Wolek)

Nominee
Outstanding Guest/Cameo Appearance in a Daytime Drama
Series
  Sammy Davis, Jr. (Chip Warren)

Nominee
Outstanding Writing for a Daytime Drama Series
  Gordon Russell, Head Writer
  Sam Hall, Writer
  Peggy O'Shea, Writer
  Cynthia Benjamin, Writer
  Lanie Bertram, Writer
  Marisa Gioffre, Writer
  Don Wallace, Writer

Award Year: 1978-1979

Nominee
Outstanding Achievement in Design Excellence for a Daytime
Drama Series
  Charles Brandon, Scenic Designer
  Harry Buchman, Makeup Designer
  Roberto Donzi, Hairstylist
  George Drew, Costume Designer
  Dennis Eger, Makeup Designer
  Donald Gavitt, Lighting Director
  Willis Hanchett, Hairstylist
  Howard Sharrott, Lighting Director

Nominee
Outstanding Achievement in Technical Excellence for a Daytime
Drama Series
   John Anthony, Music Director
   Frank Bailey, Audio
   Albert Forman, Videotape Editor
   Thomas Franch, Cameraperson
   Martin Garvin, Technical Director
   Al Gianetta, Cameraperson
   Anthony Greco, Videotape Editor
   Robert Knudsen, Cameraperson
   Louis Marchand, Technical Director
   Robert Prescott, Jr., Sound Effects
   Irving Robbins, Music Director
   Herbert Segall, Video
   John Sullivan, Associate Director
   Jack Urbont, Composer
   Richard Westlein, Cameraperson

Winner
Outstanding Actor in a Daytime Drama Series
   Al Freeman, Jr. (Ed Hall)

Award Year: 1977-1978

Nominee
Outstanding Actor in a Daytime Drama Series
   Michael Storm (Dr. Larry Wolek)

Nominee
Outstanding Actress in a Daytime Drama Series
   Jennifer Harmon (Cathy Craig)

Nominee
Outstanding Individual Achievement in Daytime Programming
   Charles Brandon, Scenic Director
   Robert Hoppe, Assistant Scenic Director
   Jack Urbont, Music Composer

Award Year: 1976-1977

Nominee
Outstanding Actor in a Daytime Drama Series
   Farley Granger (Dr. Will Vernon)

Nominee
Outstanding Actor in a Daytime Drama Series
Shepperd Strudwick (Victor Lord)

Winner
Outstanding Individual Director for a Daytime Drama Series
David Pressman, Director

Award Year: 1973-1974

Winner
Outstanding Technical Direction and Electronic Camerawork
Gerald Dowd, Technical Director
Louis Marchand, Technical Director
Frank Melchiorre, Cameraperson
John Morris, Cameraperson

Award Year: 1972-1973

Nominee
Outstanding Achievement by Individuals in Daytime Drama
David Pressman, Director

Nominee
Outstanding Program Achievement in Daytime Drama
Agnes Nixon, Producer
Doris Quinlan, Producer

Part Four

Character	Actor	Year
Gwendolyn Abbott	Joan Copeland	1978
Becky Lee Hunt Abbott	Jill Voight	1977
Becky Lee Hunt Abbott Buchanan	Mary Gordon Murray	1979
Richard Abbott	Luke Reilly	1977
Richard Abbott	Keith Langsdale	1980
Richard Abbott	Robert Gribbon	1980
Richard Abbott	Jeffrey Byron	1986
Abuelita	Miriam Colon	1996
Blaine Adams	Kelly Eviston	1991
Judge H. Alden	Brenda Pressley	1992
Sister Amelia	Susan Browning	1989
Audrey Ames	Fia Porter	1988
Amy	R. Koplin	1995
Amy	Julie Nathanson	1995
Andre	Robert Lipton	1985
Arch	William Newman	1990
Eleanor Armitage	Jessica Walter	1996
Ian Armitage	Will Kempe	1997
Guy Armitage	Simon Jones	1997

Character	Actor	Year
Helena Ashley	Augusta Dabney	1979
Maggie Ashley	Jacqueline Courtney	1979
Grace Atherton	Susan Gibney	1994
Bobby Baccala	Jim True	1997
Shirley Bannister	Johann Carlo	1991
Barkus	Tom Toner	1995
Annie Barnes	Rebecca Shaeffer	1985
Bart Baron	Lloyd Hallar	1985
Lisa Baron	Laura Carrington	1985
Susan Barry	Lisa Richards	1974
Babs Bartlett	Carole Shelley	1991
Bass	Victor Slezak	1995
Brian Beckett	Grainger Hines	1984
Lily Beecham	Melody Combs	1990
Joy Behar	Herself	1997
Rafael "Benny" Benitez	Benny Nieves	1997
Connie Bensoncraft	Gloria Biegler	1994
Dr. Mortimer Bern	Thom Christopher	1992
Wilma Bern	Eileen Heckart	1992
Wilma Bern	Elaine Stritch	1993
Frieda Bielin	Marceline Hugot	1995
Bishop	Robert Vaughn	1996
Cornelius Blackwell	Athol Fugard	1988
Ursula Blackwell	Jill Larson	1988
Blade	Ron Eldard	1989
Dr. Alex Blair	Peter Brouwer	1975
Kurtis Blow	Himself	1990
Bobby Blue	Blair Underwood	1985
Michelle Boudin	Dana Barron	1984
Dr. Maude Boylan (Mary Hayes)	Helen Gallagher	1997
Laszlo Braedeker	Walter Slezak	1974
Adam Brewster	John Mansfield	1978
Charlie Briggs	Robert Hogan	1995
Diane Bristol	Mary B. Ward	1986
Earle Brock	Kevin Conway	1973
Dr. Joyce Brothers	Herself	1972
Asa Buchanan	Philip Carey	1979
Austin Buchanan	David Gautreaux	1989
Blaize Buchanan	Loyita Chapel	1988
Bo Buchanan	Robert S. Woods	1979
Clint Buchanan	Clint Ritchie	1979
Baby Duke Buchanan	Adam & Connor O'Brien	1992
Baby Duke Buchanan	Michael & David DeFranco	1993
Drew Buchanan	Keith Bogart	1988

Character	Actor	Year
Drew Buchanan	Victor Browne	1996
Jessica Buchanan	Janelle & Tamara DeMent	1986
Jessica Buchanan	Renee Russo	1987
Jessica Buchanan	Eliza Clark	1990
Jessica Buchanan	Erin Torpey	1991
Joey Buchanan	John Paul Learn	1988
Joey Buchanan	Chris McKenna	1990
Joey Buchanan	Nathan Fillion	1994
Joey Buchanan	Dan Jeffcoat	1997
Kevin Riley (Buchanan)	Morgan K. Melis	1976
Kevin Buchanan	Ryan Janis	1988
Kevin Buchanan	Matthew Vipond	1990
Kevin Buchanan	Joey Thrower	1991
Kevin Buchanan	Kirk Geiger	1992
Kevin Buchanan	Jack Armstrong	1994
Kevin Buchanan	Ken Kenitzer	1995
Kevin Buchanan	Kevin Stapleton	1996
Kevin Buchanan	Timothy Gibbs	1998
Nora Hanen Gannon Buchanan	Hillary B. Smith	1992
Olympia Buchanan (Nicole Bonnard)	Taina Elg	1980
Renee Divine (Buchanan)	Phyllis Newman	1987
Renee Divine Buchanan	Patricia Elliott	1987
Sarah Gordon Buchanan	Jensen Buchanan	1987
Sarah Gordon Buchanan	Grace Phillips	1991
Clint Buckley	Bruce Detrick	1977
Garth Buckley	Alan Coates	1988
Steve Burke	Bernard Grant	1970
Lindsey Butler	Anna Holbrook	1992
Humberto Calderone	Christopher Cousins	1991
Herb Callison	Anthony Call	1978
Calvin	Richard White	1989
Camilla	Opal Alladin	1997
Judge "Killer" Carlin	Tony Roberts	1989
Judge Ronald Carlivati	Michael Lombard	1997
Judge	Philip Bosco	1988
Judge	Frances Sternhagen	1990
Lilith Carlson	Sara Botsford	1997
Philip Carlson	Ron Parady	1992
Bishop John Carpenter	Michael Swan	1996
Cassie Carpenter	Cusi Cram	1981
Cassie Carpenter	Ava Haddad	1983
Cassie Carpenter	Holly Gagnier	1986
Cassie Carpenter	Laura Bonarrigo Koffman	1991
Maggie Carpenter	Crystal Chappell	1995

Character	Actor	Year
Reverend Andrew Carpenter	Wortham Krimmer	1991
Baby River Carpenter	Alex & Zach Blass	1994
Baby River Carpenter	Josh & Justin Cromie	1995
River Carpenter	Ryan Marsini	1996
Sloan Carpenter	Roy Thinnes	1992
Victoria Lord Riley	Gillian Spencer	1968
Victoria Lord Riley	Joanne Dorian	1970
Victoria Lord Carpenter	Erika Slezak	1971
Victoria Lord Riley	Christine Jones	1980
Scott Chandler	Shane McDermott	1996
Laurel Chapin	Janice Lynde	1983
Lee Chapin	Tyrus Cheney	1994
Trent Chapin	David Beecroft	1984
Alana Cheston	Kelly Cheston Young	1992
Chet	Jack Gwaltney III	1993
Choreographer	Mary Jane Houdina	1989
Irene Clayton	Diana Lamar	1994
Ted Clayton (Tom Clarkson)	Keith Charles	1980
Ted Clayton	Mark Goddard	1981
Coco	Nancy Sorel	1989
Judy Cole	Marsha Mason	1969
Wade Coleman	Doug Wert	1987
Astrid Collins	Marilyn McIntyre	1982
Chip Cooper	Cain DeVore	1986
Gary Corelli	Jeff Fahey	1982
Dr. Mario Corelli	Gerald Anthony	1979
Don Leo Coronal	Abe Vigoda	1984
Rob Coronal	Ted Marcoux	1984
Rob Coronal	Mark Arnold	1987
Lord Cove	Vincent Dowling	1996
Anna Craig	Doris Belack	1968
Anna Craig	Kathleen Maguire	1977
Anna Craig	Phyllis Behar	1978
Cathy Craig	Catherine Burns	1969
Cathy Craig	Amy Levitt	1970
Cathy Craig	Jane Alice Brandon	1971
Cathy Craig	Dorrie Kavanaugh	1972
Cathy Craig	Jennifer Harmon	1975
Dr. Jim Craig	Robert Milli	1968
Dr. Jim Craig	Nat Polen	1969
Megan Riley Craig	Kimaree Beyrent	1975
Addie Cramer	Pamela Payton-Wright	1992
Kelly Cramer	Gina Tognoni	1995
Melinda Cramer	Patricia Pearcy	1973
Melinda Cramer	Jane Badler	1977
Melinda Cramer	Sharon Gabet	1987

Character	Actor	Year
Melinda Cramer	Nicole Orth-Pallavicini	1997
Sonya Cramer	Marian Seldes	1998
Beverly Crane	Maeve McGuire	1994
Ethel Crawford	Bethel Leslie	1994
Christine Cromwell	Susan Floyd	1988
Leo Cromwell	Alan Scarfe	1988
Robin Crosley	Linda Watkins	1977
Alex Crown (Coronal)	Roy Thinnes	1984
Chad Cummings	Burke Moses	1990
Gretel Cummings	Linda Dano	1978
Blair Daimler	Mia Korf	1991
Blair Daimler (Manning)	Kassie DePaiva	1993
Marco Dane	Gerald Anthony	1977
Billy Dean	Himself	1994
Death	Mary Kay Adams	1992
Johnny Dee	Anthony Crivello	1990
Neil Delaney	Steve Flynn	1988
Maggie Delekian	Jane Brucker	1986
Tea Delgado	Florencia Lozano	1997
DuAnn Demerest	Lois Smith	1990
DuAnn Demerest	Avril Gentiles	1990
Lee Ann Demerest Buchanan	Yasmine Bleeth	1991
Ruth Ann Demerest	Karen Sillas	1991
Colonel Carlos Demitri	Kabir Bedi	1986
Mari Lynn Dennison	Tammy Amerson	1986
Tom Dennison	Lee Paterson	1986
Aristotle Descamedes	Steven Hill	1984
Desiree	Drenda Sponholtz	1995
Lolly Devore	Marilyn Michaels	1988
Olivia DeWitt	Bridget White	1996
Sabrina	Marsha Mason	1993
Kyle Dickinson	Peter Coleman	1982
Dirk	Walter Gotell	1986
Echo DiSavoy	Kim Zimmer	1983
Nurse Donna	Sandra Guibord	1989
Judge Dory	Ronn Carroll	1997
Dr. Edward Dougherty	Gerry Becker	1997
Billy Douglas	Ryan Phillippe	1992
John Douglas	Donald Madden	1974
Virginia Douglas	Susan Pellegrino	1992
Walter Douglas	Jonathan Hogan	1992
D.A. Tyler Driscoll	Laura Rhodarmer	1995
Johnny Drummond	Wayne Massey	1980
Arte Duncan	John Cullum	1969

Character	Actor	Year
Mr. Dunn	William Wise	1997
Elliott Durbin	Stephen Macht	1996
Mr. Easke	Tom Mardirosian	1997
Doug Eber	Craig Wasson	1991
Jane Eber	Catherine Christianson	1991
Eddie	Tom McBride	1991
Tom Edwards	Joe Gallison	1969
Eli Trager	Geoffrey Wigdor	1997
Greg Ellis	Robert Sedgwick	1990
Laura Jean Ellis	Neith Hunter	1996
Emily	Arija Bareikis	1996
Dr. Emmentaler	Bryon Jennings	1996
Bobby Ever	James Villemaire	1993
Mr. Farinho	Luis Perez	1997
Ben Farmer	Rod Browning	1974
Lydia Farr	Marianne Tatum	1985
Dryve Fast	Adam Storke	1990
Felicia	Florence Anglin	1978
Judge Fitzwater	Novella Nelson	1993
Yousef Franklin	Jonas Chaka	1990
Joelle Frazicr	Diane Erickson	1988
Fred	Bruce Norris	1996
Winslow Freeman	Patrick Breen	1996
Gabriel Lomax	Scott Lawrence	1997
Hank Gannon	Nathan Purdee	1992
Janine Gannon	Kim Staunton	1997
Rachel Gannon	Ellen Bethea	1992
Rachel Gannon	Mari Marrow	1995
Rachel Gannon	Sandra P. Grant	1996
Randall James "RJ" Gannon	Timothy D. Stickney	1994
Rick Gardner	Richard Grieco	1987
Delila Ralston Garretson	Shelly Burch	1988
Rafe Garretson	Ken Meeker	1980
Sammi Garretson	Danielle Harris	1985
Beth Garvey	Dorothy Barton	1993
General Gazi	Tom Mardirosian	1992
Geoffrey	Don Fisher	1987
Jack Gibson	Jim Wlcek	1989
Doc Gilmore	Mario Van Peebles	1983
Billie Giordano	Lisa Peluso	1987
Stacy Giordano	Bonnie Burroughs	1987
Gloria	Harriett D. Foy	1995

Character	Actor	Year
Judge Goldberg	Maggie Burke	1997
Martin Goldman	Peter Davies	1995
Officer Emilio Gonzales	Yancy Arias	1995
Carrie Gordon	Caroline Lagerfelt	1989
Fran Gordon	Willie Burke	1979
Francis Gordon	Barbara Britton	1979
Mick Gordon	James McDonnell	1979
Roger Gordon	Larry Pine	1988
Danton Gordon	Brian Davies	1989
Barbara Graham	Sonia Satra	1998
Bishop Graham	John Franklyn-Robbins	1992
Alicia Grande	Marcia McCabe	1989
Michael Grande	Dennis Parlato	1988
Grant	Anthony DeSando	1996
Dick Grant	A.C. Weary	1978
Sadie Gray	Lillian Hayman	1968
Sadie Gray	Esther Rolle	1971
Griff	Jude Ciccolella	1995
Judge Guernsey	Milo O'Shea	1987
Guilietta	Fabiano Udenio	1985
Gus	Samuel E. Wright	1991
Gus, the plumber	Dan Lauria	1981
Hunter Guthrie	Leonard Stabb	1990
Mrs. Guthrie	Ann Flood	1991
Bulge Hackman	Burke Moses	1992
Capt. Ed Hall	Al Freeman, Jr.	1972
Capt. Ed Hall	David Pendleton	1975
Joshua Hall	Laurence Fishburne	1973
Joshua Hall	Todd Davis	1977
Joshua Hall	Guy Davis	1985
Sondra Hall	Olivia Birkelund	1991
Dr. Ted Hall	Terry Logan	1968
Lee Halpern	Janet Zarish	1987
Len Hanen	Jerry Adler	1995
Selma Hanen	Joan Copeland	1995
Susannah Hanen	Maureen Anderman	1995
Hannah	Helen Stenborg	1997
Dr. Steve Hardy	John Beradino	1969
Bonnie Harmer	Kim Zimmer	1978
Andy Harrison	Bronwen Booth	1989
Andy Harrison	Wendee Pratt	1994
Jake Harrison	Joe Lando	1990
Megan Gordon Harrison	Jessica Tuck	1988

Character	Actor	Year
Harry	Michael Rupert	1996
Joe Hawk	John Gibson	1983
Judge Hawthorne	Paul Hecht	1994
Ian Hayden	Craig Sheffer	1982
Mel Hayes	Stephen Markle	1997
Dorothy Hays	Elisabeth Rohm	1997
Emily Haynes	Kellie Waymire	1993
Neil Hayes	Dick Latessa	1997
Sister Helene	Barbara Eda Young	1996
Rabbi Heller	Camryn Manheim	1995
Alice Henson	Erin O'Brien	1994
Herron	Richard Merrell	1980
Carlo Hesser	Thom Christopher	1990
Charlotte Hesser	Audrey Landers	1990
Stephanie Hobart	Christiann Mills	1991
Stephanie Hobart	Robyn Griggs	1991
Dr. Hoffman	John Gabriel	1993
Prince Raymond Hohenstein	Robert Westenberg	1989
Prince Roland Hohenstein	Joseph Kolinski	1989
Baby Al Holden	Ryan & Sean Buckley	1987
Al Holden	Evan Bonifant	1991
Al Holden	Michael Roman	1993
Al Holden	Jason Alexander Fisher	1997
Gabriella Medina Holden	Fiona Hutchison	1987
Max Holden	Nicholas Walker	1990
Max Holden	James DePaiva	1987
Steve Holden	Russ Anderson	1987
Angela Holliday	Susan Diol	1993
Ina Hopkins	Sally Gracie	1978
Chris Horgan	Richard Paul	1992
Hortense	Uta Hagen	1985
Ben Howard	Albert Hall	1973
Hubcap	Scott Jacoby	1973
Adele Huddleston	Lori March	1978
Greg Huddleston	Paul Joynt	1978
Talbot Huddleston	Byron Sanders	1977
Jeremy Hunter	Jean LeClerc	1991
Ice	David Glass	1995
Ilse	Mari Nelson	1991
Ilse	Heather Ehlers	1991
Isadore	Robert Fields	1991
Ivors	Tony Coleman	1995

Character	Actor	Year
Luther "Luke" Jackson	Pete Matthey	1978
Tracey Jacobs	Barbara McCrane	1995
Tracy James	Kirsten Allen	1985
Dr. Peter Janssen	Jeffrey David Pomerantz	1976
Dr. Peter Janssen	Denny Albee	1980
Dr. Peter Janssen	Robert Burton	1980
Jennifer	Marsha Waterbury	1988
Shelly Johnson	Suzanne Leuffner	1983
Dr. Michael Jonas	Christopher Durham	1992
Jonathan	Bruce McCarty	1992
Julio	Jesse Corti	1991
Heinrich Kaiser	Christopher Cousins	1991
Katrina Karr	Nancy Snyder	1978
Mary Vernon Karr	Deidre Buonaro	1980
Mary Vernon Karr	Regan McManus	1983
Sister Katherine	Robin Groves	1990
Casey Keegan	Rainn Wilson	1997
Keith	Daniel Zelman	1995
Brian Kendall	Stephen Austin	1976
Pat Ashley Lord Kendall	Jacqueline Courtney	1975
Paul Kendall	Tom Fuccello	1979
Thomas Kenneally	Malachy McCourt	1995
Irwin Keyser	Jerry Orbach	1980
Jack Kilgore	Jack Stehlin	1992
Kim	Wai Ching Ho	1984
Bill Kimbrough	Justin McDonough	1968
Hudson King	Christopher Cousins	1991
Mimi King	Kristen Meadows	1979
Faith Kipling	Mary Linda Rapelye	1979
Dr. Ivan Kipling	Jack Betts	1979
Conrad Klein	Patrick Page	1995
Conrad Klein	Evan Handler	1996
Charles Koppleman	Himself	1994
Dr. Kyle	Wendell W. Wright	1997
Kyle	Jaime Harrold	1996
Donald LaMarr	Jared Martin	1987
Gilbert Lange	John Fiedler	1987
Mitchell Laurence	Roscoe Born	1985
Jack Lawson	David Snell	1970
Jack Lawson	Jack Ryland	1972
Layle	Amanda Peet	1995

Character	Actor	Year
Layle	Chelsea Altman	1996
Leicester	Alan Clement	1991
Lord Henry Leighton	Donal Donnelly	1988
Joanna Leighton	Roma Downey	1988
Leonard	Kevin O'Donnell	1991
Lester	Paul Benedict	1996
Edwina Lewis	Margaret Klenck	1977
Miles Lewis	Dex Sanders	1990
Rebecca Lewis	Reiko Aylesworth	1993
Mr. Lima	John Herrera	1997
Lindsey	Anna Holbrook	1993
Kim Soo Ling	Irene Yah Ling Sun	1975
Lucky Lippman	Brian Tarantina	1990
Mary Little	Erin Rourke Corcoran	1987
Prentice Little	Oni Faida Lampley	1997
Dr. Lloyd	Lee Wilkof	1995
Cyndy London	Cynthia Vance	1987
Patrick London	Stephen Meadows	1987
Dorian Cramer Lord	Nancy Pinkerton	1973
Dorian Cramer Lord	Claire Malis	1977
Dorian Cramer Lord	Robin Strasser	1979
Dorian Cramer Lord	Elaine Princi	1990
Eugenia Lord	Lori Match	1987
Powell Lord	Sean Moynihan	1993
Randolph Lord	Larry Pine	1988
Tina Lord	Andrea Evans	1978
Tina Lord	Kelli Maroney	1984
Tina Lord	Marsha Clark	1985
Tina Lord	Karen Witter	1990
Tina Lord	Krista Tesreau	1994
Tony Lord	George Reinholt	1975
Tony Lord	Philip MacHale	1977
Tony Lord	Chip Lucia	1981
Victor Lord	Ernest Graves	1968
Victor Lord	Shepperd Strudwick	1974
Victor Lord	Tom O'Rourke	1985
Victor Lord	Les Tremayne	1987
Victor Lord	Bill Moor	1995
Darlene Love	Herself	1994
Ralph Love	Thomas Hill	1992
Blanchard Lovelace	John Wesley Shipp	1989
Dr. Low	James Salto	1995
Alec Lowndes	Roger Hill	1983
Luis	Rudy Mela	1995

Character	Actor	Year
Madison	Mary Ellen Stuart	1996
Sean Madagan	Michael Louden	1995
Sean Madagan	David Aaron Baker	1996
Evelyn Maddox	Kathy Bates	1984
Lou Maddox	Leo Burmester	1984
Magdalena	Gina Torres	1995
Anthony Makana	Nicolas Coster	1983
Peter Manning	Nick Wyman	1993
Baby Starr Manning	Ariella & Natalie Jamnik	1996
Starr Manning	Meghan Rayder	1998
Todd Manning	Roger Howarth	1992
Det. Nick Manzo	Matt Servitto	1995
Sister Margaret	Dorothy Lyman	1975
Mark	Todd McDurmont	1995
Gloria Marsh	Teresa Blake	1996
Martin	Alvin Lum	1990
Karen Martin Wolek	Niki Flacks	1968
Paul Martin	William Mooney	1978
Tad Martin	Michael E. Knight	1996
Professor Marvel	Wallace Shawn	1992
Gladys Mason	Imogene Coca	1984
Ned Mason	Greg Fiedler	1996
Matt McAllister	Vance Jefferis	1974
M.C.	Steven Stahl	1989
Lana McClain	Jackie Zeman	1976
Maxie McDermott	Christine Ebersole	1983
Molly McDermott	Dody Goodman	1984
O.W. McDermott	Paul Bartel	1992
Reba McEntire	Herself	1992
Brenda McGillis	Brenda Brock	1988
Baby Steven McGillis	Matthew & Michael Pra	1989
May McGillis	Brenda Brock	1988
Tyler "Buddy" McGillis	Braeden Danner	1988
Tyler McGillis	Jeff Bankert	1989
Geoffrey McGrath	Don E. Fischer	1987
Mayor Elizabeth McNamara	Margaret Hall	1992
Jackie McNaughton	Doc Dougherty	1997
Dante Medina	Henry Darrow	1987
Debra Medina	Lucinda Fisher	1989
Julia Medina	Linda Thorson	1989
Jonathan Michaelson	Bruce McCarty	1992
Bill Medley	Himself	1994
Mickey	Angel David	1995
Mickey	Kaleo Griffiths	1995
Buck Miller	Chris Murney	1994

Character	Actor	Year
Hallie Mitchell	Oni Faida Lampley	1994
Rick Mitchell	Joe Fiske	1993
Clay Monroe	Judson Scott	1985
Frank Montagne	Jeff Gendelman	1987
Sandra Montagne	Judith Chapman	1987
Bascomb Moody	Stan Cahill	1993
Charlemagne Moody	Garrett Dillahunt	1993
Dylan Moody	Christopher Douglas	1994
Faye Moody	Anita Keal	1995
Darlene "Luna" Moody Holden	Susan Batten	1991
Maude Moody	Kate Forbes	1996
Tyler "Ty" Moody	Casper Van Dien	1993
Father Moreau	Christopher Cousins	1993
Giles Morgan	Robert Gentry	1983
Bert Mulligan	Shirley Stoler	1993
Moose Mulligan	Richard Bright	1992
Gloria Mundy	Anna Garduno	1990
Helen Murdoch	Marie Masters	1982
Natasha	Shayna Hill	1996
Guy Navarre	Sam Tsoutsouvas	1995
Lt. Jack Neal	Jack Crowder	1969
Lt. Jack Neal	Lon Sutton	1969
Nell	Gina Torres	1996
Kerry Nichols	Allan Dean Moore	1990
Troy Nichols	Terry Alexander	1990
D.A. Tom Nicholson	Chris McKinney	1995
Dr. Kate Nolan	Peggy Wood	1969
Kate Noonan	J. Smith-Cameron	1993
Sheriff Ogilvy	Richard Council	1995
Alex Olanov	Tonja Walker	1990
Nat Olanov	Kip Niven	1990
Olga	Priscilla Lopez	1991
Connie O'Neill	Liz Keifer	1984
Connie O'Neill Vernon	Terry Donahoe	1985
Didi O'Neill Buchanan	Barbara Treutelaar	1987
Harry O'Neill	Frank Converse	1984
Harry O'Neill	Arlen Dean Snyder	1984
Joy O'Neill	Julianne Johnson	1984
Joy O'Neill	Kristen Vigard	1984
Pete O'Neill	James O'Sullivan	1985
Oribe	Himself	1995

Character	Actor	Year
Judge Palmer	Roger Serbagi	1996
Paloma	Chrissy Martinez	1994
Nikos Pappas	Simon Page	1985
Millie Parks	Millee Taggart	1969
Parrot's voice	Ron Gallup	1997
Dr. Pasquin	Geoffrey Ewing	1992
Mark Pemberton	Ed Power	1984
Priscilla Pennyworth	Stephanie Silverman	1995
Dr. Elston Pepper	Orson Bean	1984
Javier Perez	Rene LaVandera	1995
Allison Perkins	Barbara Garrick	1986
Ruth Perkins	Eileen Heckart	1986
Roberta Peters	Roberta Peters	1982
Mrs. Phinney	Robin Miles	1997
Photographer	Gavin Troster	1989
Steve Piermont	Robert Desiderio	1981
Steve Piermont	Richard K. Weber	1981
Dr. Marcus Polk	Donald Moffat	1968
Dr. Marcus Polk	Norman Rose	1969
Dr. Marcus Polk	James Douglas	1985
Fred Porter	David Purdham	1991
Lisa Porter	Danielle DuClos	1990
Dr. Ben Price	Charles Malik Whitfield	1993
Dr. Ben Price	Peter Parros	1994
Rika Price	Vanita Harbour	1990
Sheila Price	Valarie Pettiford	1990
Sheila Price Gannon	Stephanie E. Williams	1994
Jacara Principal	Marva Hicks	1997
Suede (Charles) Pruitt	David Ledingham	1992
Quilligan	Anthony Heald	1995
Quincy	Monté Russell	1991
Quincy	Jesse L. Martin	1995
Sheilah Rafferty	Christine Jones	1975
Drew Ralston	Matthew Ashford	1982
Euphemia Ralston	Grayson Hall	1982
Ray	Scott Cohen	1994
David Renaldi/Reynolds	Michael Zaslow	1983
Little Richard	Himself	1995
Harding Richards	Stephen Joyce	1990
Joe Riley	Lee Patterson	1968
Rita	Rachel York	1996
Rod Riviera	Philip Casnoff	1990

Character	Actor	Year
Dr. Robbins	Kelly Bishop	1996
Al Roberts	Jesse Vent	1986
Clint Roberts (aka Milagro)	Anthony & Victor DeBiase	1988
Baby C.J. (Clint)	Gary & Keith Meredith	1991
C.J. Roberts	Ryan Murphy	1992
C.J. Roberts	Tyler Noyes	1992
Cord Roberts	John Loprieno	1986
Maria Roberts	Barbara Luna	1986
Baby Sarah Roberts	Alexia & Zoe Fisher	1991
Sarah Roberts	Courtney Chase	1993
Sarah Roberts	Hayden Panettiere	1994
Robyn	Sharon Washington	1995
Rick Rodgers	James Rebhorn	1995
Rodi	LaTanya Richardson	1992
Rodi	Cynthia Martells	1992
Cain Rogan	Christopher Cousins	1991
Rick Rogers	James Rebhorn	1995
Jinx Rollins	Elizabeth Burrelle	1984
Rolo	Sherman Howard	1987
Ken Romak	Dean Hamilton	1984
Natasha Romanoff	Natalia Makarova	1993
Ronnie	Stephanie Pope	1995
Rosa	Marina Durrell	1995
Zach Rosen	Josh Philip Weinstein	1992
Rudy	Penn Jillette	1991
Jonathan Russell	Jon Martin	1986
Marcello Salta	Stephen Schnetzer	1980
Charles Sanders	Michael Billington	1986
Charles Sanders	Peter Brown	1986
Elizabeth Sanders	Lois Kibbee	1986
Jamie Sanders	Mark Philpot	1986
Judith Sanders	Louise Sorel	1986
Kate Sanders	Marcia Cross	1986
Dr. Sands	Kathleen Chalfant	1997
Marty Saybrooke	Susan Haskell	1992
Scaggs	Barry Cullison	1990
Lucinda Schenk	Arlene Dahl	1981
Scott	Brian Davies	1983
Carla Gray Hall Scott	Ellen Holly	1968
Dr. Jack Scott	Arthur Burghardt	1978
Sebastian	Michael Cumpsty	1989
Security Guard	Barry Lynch	1989
Judge Selachi	John Horton	1997
Seth	Brad Kane	1991

Character	Actor	Year
Shawna	Kimberly Pistone	1995
Shane	Michael Chaban	1995
Joe Shelby	Kevin Garvanne	1993
Bert Shelly	Herb Davis	1969
Dr. Pamela Shepherd	Kathleen Devine	1978
Sherry	Ellen Foley	1985
Shirley	Johann Carlo	1991
David Siegel	Allan Miller	1968
Eileen Riley Siegel	Patricia Roe	1968
Eileen Siegel	Alice Hirson	1972
Tim Siegel	William Fowler	1969
Tim Siegel	William Cox	1970
Tim Siegel	Tom Berenger	1975
Bert Skelly	Wayne Jones	1969
Skip	Joe Ponazecki	1996
Spring Skye	Sharon Schlarth	1989
Phineas T. Smart	Norman Large	1988
Charlie Smith	Antony Ponzini	1987
Smokey	Richard McWilliams	1991
Pete Smulyan	Bruce MacVittie	1995
Nigel Bartholomew Smythe	Richard Willis	1990
Nigel Bartholomew Smythe	Richard Hunderup	1991
Nigel Bartholomew Smythe	Peter Bartlett	1991
Ernesto Soto	Daniel Faraldo	1997
Linda Soto	Andrea Navedo	1995
Spike	Michael Gaston	1996
Mrs. Spitz	Joan Pape	1992
Matron Spitz	Jennifer Leak	1986
Ellen Spivak	Kathleen Mahoney-Bennett	1995
Jared St. James	W.T. Martin	1990
Dean Stella	Tom Sminkey	1984
Pamela Stewart	Christine Jones	1986
Thomas "Stick" Stickley	Mark Metcalf	1987
Randy Stone	Richard Burgi	1988
Randy Stone	Carl Mueller	1989
Brent Sutton	David Lee Smith	1994
Janice Talbert	Catherine Dent	1997
Tango (Wilton Veneer)	Roderick Cooke	1983
Sister Theresa	Olivia Negron	1996
Patrick Thornhart	Thorsten Kaye	1995
Tico	Sean Thomas	1995
Tiny	Shirley Stoler	1986
Julie Siegel Toland	Lee Warrick	1969
Julie Siegel Toland	Leonie Norton	1974

Character	Actor	Year
Dr. Mark Toland	Tommy Lee Jones	1971
Tonya	Mary Testa	1989
Track	Henry Simmons	1997
Grace Trainor	Frances Foster	1969
Dr. Price Trainor	Peter DeAnda	1968
Dr. Price Trainor	Thurman Scott	1968
Ivana Trump	Herself	1995
Father Tony Vallone	John Viscardi	1990
Arthur Vandenburg	Patrick Horgan	1993
Deborah Van Druten	Nancy Barrett	1979
Sam Vance	Kathleen McNenny	1994
Antonio Vega	Kamar de los Reyes	1995
Carlotta Vega	Patricia Mauceri	1995
Cristian Vega	Yorlin Madera	1995
Sgt. Maggie Vega	Yvette Lawrence	1992
Eddie Velasquez	Jose Soto	1995
Eva Vasquez	Judith McConnell	1983
Mrs. Verdon	Mary Louise Wilson	1990
Jim Vern	Jude Ciccolella	1992
Brad Vernon	Jameson Parker	1976
Brad Vernon	Steve Fletcher	1978
Naomi Vernon	Teri Keane	1976
Samantha Vernon	Julie Montgomery	1976
Samantha Vernon	Susan Keith	1979
Samantha Vernon	Dorian LoPinto	1981
Dr. Will Vernon	Farley Granger	1976
Dr. Will Vernon	Bernie McInerney	1977
Dr. Will Vernon	Anthony George	1977
David Vickers	Tuc Watkins	1994
Leonard Vincent	Kevin O'Connell	1991
Fritz Von Hinkle	Skipp Sudduth	1997
Virgil	John Fiedler	1987
Baroness Helga Von Stoltz	Carole Davis	1990
Marcy Wade	Francesca James	1970
Marcy Wade	Kendall March	1970
Cameron Wallace	Bridget White	1996
Sharon Wallace	Lisa Arrindell Anderson	1996
Simon Warfield	Tim Hart	1983
Chip Warren	Sammy Davis, Jr.	1980
Gary Warren	Ron Palillo	1994
Jason Webb	Mark Brettschneider	1991
Albert West	Gerry Bamman	1997

Character	Actor	Year
Dr. Ruth Westheimer	Herself	1992
Marcus Whitehart	Claude Akins	1992
Eddington Whitfield	Jeffrey Donovan	1995
Georgina Whitman	Ilene Kristen	1982
Georgina Whitman	Nana Tucker Visitor	1982
Jimmy Whitman	Gregory Mark Shaffer	1982
Clover Wilde	Pamela Shoemaker	1985
Jesse Wilde	John Vickery	1984
Dennis Williams	Ron Richardson	1988
Vera Williams	Lorraine Toussaint	1988
Chuck Wilson	Jeremy Slate	1979
Rachel Wilson	Nancy Barrett	1974
Burke Winger	Kelly Kerr	1990
Dan Wolek	Tim Owens (Waldrip)	1983
Dan Wolek	Michael Palance	1989
Danny Wolek	Neail Holland	1974
Danny Wolek	Eddie Moran	1976
Danny Wolek	Steven Culp	1983
Danny Wolek	Ted Demers	1984
Jenny Wolek	Katherine Glass	1975
Jenny Wolek	Brynn Thayer	1978
Karen Wolek	Kathryn Breech	1976
Karen Wolek	Julia Duffy	1977
Karen Wolek	Judith Light	1977
Dr. Larry Wolek	Paul Tulley	1968
Dr. Larry Wolek	Jim Storm	1969
Dr. Larry Wolek	Michael Storm	1969
Meredith Lord Wolek	Trish Van Devere	1968
Meredith Lord Wolek	Lynn Benesch	1969
Vinnie Wolek	Antony Ponzini	1968
Vinnie Wolek	Michael Ingram	1977
Vince Wolek	Jordan Charney	1975
Wanda Webb Wolek	Marilyn Chris	1972
Wanda Webb Wolek	Lee Lawson	1977
"Woody" Woodward	Grant Goodeve	1985
Courtney Wright	Phylicia Ayers-Allen (Rashad)	1983
Ambrose Wyman	David Spielberg	1989
Serena Wyman	Kelly Bishop	1989
Yolana	Janet Sarno	1989
Aida York	Pamela Gien	1985
Zeus	Rob Campbell	1996
Zeus	Connor Trinneer	1996

Photo Credits

All photos and video images are copyright © American Broadcasting Companies, Inc. Photographer credits are as follows:

Page		
16	Owen Franken	
23	Owen Franken	
26	Ann Limongello	
28	Ann Limongello	
30	Ann Limongello	
34	Ann Limongello	
36	Ann Limongello	
38	Ann Limongello	
44	Ann Limongello	
46	Ann Limongello	
50	Ann Limongello	
62	Steve Fenn	
64	Ann Limongello	
65	Ann Limongello	
68	Ann Limongello	
70	Ann Limongello	
72	Ann Limongello	
74	Ann Limongello	
82	Steve Fenn	
92	Ann Limongello	
94	Mike Fuller	
99	Gary Miller	
106	Donna Svennevik	
108	Donna Svennevik	
110	Ann Limongello	
111	Donna Svennevik	
115	Donna Svennevik	
120	Donna Svennevik	
124	Ann Limongello	
128	Craig Sjodin	
132	Donna Svennevik	
135	Ann Limongello	
136	Ann Limongello	
138	Ann Limongello	
140	Ann Limongello	
146	Frank Micelotta	
148	Ann Limongello	
149	Udo Screiber	
150	Kimberly Butler	
152	Ann Limongello	
153	Steve Fenn	
160	Robert Milazzo	
162	Ann Limongello	
165	Steve Fenn	
167	Ann Limongello	
168	Ann Limongello	
170	Ann Limongello	
172	Robert Milazzo	
176	Ann Limongello	
178	Ann Limongello	
180	Ann Limongello	
183	Robert Milazzo	
184	Steve Fenn	
192	Ann Limongello	
194	Donna Svennevik	
196	Ann Limongello	
198	Ann Limongello	
201	Ann Limongello	
206	Ann Limongello	
207	Ann Limongello	
208	Ann Limongello	
209	E. J. Carr	
216	*lower left:* Owen Franken	
217	*left:* Steve Fenn	
219	*top:* Ann Limongello	
220	*all:* Ann Limongello	
221	*bottom:* Donna Svennevik	
222	*top:* Danny Feld	
	center and bottom: Ann Limongello	
223	*all:* Ann Limongello	
224	*all:* Ann Limongello	
226	E. J. Carr	
227	*top:* Donna Svennevik	
	center and bottom: Robert Milazzo	
228	*top:* Donna Svennevik	
229	*top:* Owen Franken	
	bottom: Gary Miller	
230	Robert Milazzo	
231	*all:* Ann Limongello	
232	*center:* Steve Fenn	
	bottom: Ann Limongello	
233	Donna Svennevik	
234	Donna Svennevik	
235	Donna Svennevik	
236	*all:* Steve Fenn	
237	Donna Svennevik	
238	*top:* Robert Milazzo	
	bottom: Mike Ginsburg	
239	Donna Svennevik	
240	*left:* Donna Svennevik	
	right: Robert Milazzo	
241	*all:* Robert Milazzo	
242	*top:* Ann Limongello	
	center: Steve Fenn	
243	*top:* Steve Fenn	
	bottom: Donna Svennevik	
245	*left:* Cathy Blaivas	
	right: Robert Milazzo	
246	Ann Limongello	
247	Ann Limongello	
248	*top:* Ann Limongello	
	center: Owen Franken	
	bottom: Steve Fenn	
249	*top:* Ann Limongello	
	bottom: Steve Fenn	
250	Steve Fenn	
251	*top:* Donna Svennevik	
252	Robert Milazzo	
253	*center:* Donna Svennevik	
	bottom: Robert Milazzo	
254	Ann Limongello	
255	Ann Limongello	
259	Steve Fenn	
260	*left and right:* Ann Limongello	
261	*top:* Ann Limongello	
	bottom: Robert Milazzo	
262	Donna Svennevik	
263	*bottom:* Donna Svennevik	
264	*top:* Cathy Blaivas	
	center: Robert Milazzo	
	bottom: Ann Limongello	
265	*top:* Robert Milazzo	
	bottom: Ann Limongello	
266	*top:* Ann Limongello	
267	Steve Fenn	
268	*all:* Steve Fenn	
269	Donna Svennevik	
270	Ann Limongello	
272	Ann Limongello	
273	*left:* Owen Franken	
	right: Ann Limongello	
274	*bottom:* Kimberly Butler	
275	*top:* Roger Prigent	
276	*left:* Robert Milazzo	
	right: Donna Svennevik	
277	*all:* Ann Limongello	
278	*all:* Ann Limongello	
279	Donna Svennevik	
280	*top:* Robert Milazzo	
	center: Steve Fenn	
	bottom: Ann Limongello	
281	Robert Milazzo	
282	Ann Limongello	
283	*all:* Ann Limongello	
284	Ann Limongello	
285	*all:* Ann Limongello	
286	Ann Limongello	
287	Ann Limongello	
288	*center:* Cathy Blaivas	
289	*all:* Ann Limongello	
290	*all:* Ann Limongello	
292	*top:* Ann Limongello	
	bottom: Donna Svennevik	
293	*all:* Ann Limongello	
294	*all:* Ann Limongello	
295	*all:* Ann Limongello	
296	Ann Limongello	
297	Cathy Blaivas	
298	*all:* Cathy Blaivas	
299	*all:* Cathy Blaivas	
300	Ann Limongello	
301	*all:* Ann Limongello	
302	*all:* Ann Limongello	
303	*left and bottom:* Ann Limongello	
	right: Robert Milazzo	
304	Ann Limongello	
305	*top and center:* Ann Limongello	
	bottom: Danny Feld	
306	*right:* Steve Fenn	
307	*all:* Ann Limongello	
309	*top:* Steve Fenn	
	bottom: Ann Limongello	
310	*all:* Ann Limongello	
311	*left:* Robert Milazzo	
312	Ann Limongello	
314	*top:* Donna Svennevik	
	center: Steve Fenn	
	bottom: Danny Feld	
315	Steve Fenn	
316	*top:* Ann Limongello	
	bottom: Robert Milazzo	
317	*top and bottom:* Ann Limongello	
	center: Mike Fuller	
318	*bottom:* Ann Limongello	
319	*top and center:* Ann Limongello	
	bottom: Cathy Blaivas	
320	Donna Svennevik	
321	*all:* Ann Limongello	
322	*all:* Ann Limongello	
323	*top:* Ann Limongello	
	bottom: Robert Milazzo	
327	*left:* Owen Franken	
	right: Ann Limongello	
328	*center and bottom:* Steve Fenn	
329	*top:* Steve Fenn	
330	*top:* Donna Svennevik	
	center and bottom: Ann Limongello	
331	*top and center:* Ann Limongello	
	bottom: Ida Mae Astute	
332	*top:* Ann Limongello	
	bottom: Dan Cadette	
333	*center:* Robert Milazzo	
334	*all:* Ann Limongello	
335	*top and bottom:* Ann Limongello	
	center: Steve Fenn	
337	*left:* E. J. Carr	
	right: Robert Milazzo	
339	Ann Limongello	
340	Robert Milazzo	
341	*all:* Donna Svennevik	
342	Ann Limongello	
344	Donna Svennevik	
345	Ann Limongello	
346	Ann Limongello	
348	*left:* Steve Fenn	
	right: Donna Svennevik	
351	Ann Limongello	
352	Robert Milazzo	
353	Ann Limongello	
354	Donna Svennevik	
355	*top:* Steve Fenn	
	bottom: Ann Limongello	
356	*all:* Kimberly Butler	
357	*all:* Ann Limongello	
358	*all:* Ann Limongello	
359	*top:* Jim Antonucci	
	center and bottom: Ann Limongello	
360	*top:* Ann Limongello	
362	*top and bottom:* Ann Limongello	
363	*top:* Robert Milazzo	
364	Robert Milazzo	
365	*all:* Ann Limongello	
366	*center and bottom:* Ann Limongello	
367	*top:* Ann Limongello	
	left: Donna Svennevik	
368	*center and bottom:* Ann Limongello	
374	*top:* Ann Limongello	
	bottom: Donna Svennevik	
375	*bottom:* Ann Limongello	
376	*all:* Steve Fenn	
377	*top:* Kimberly Butler	
	bottom: Steve Fenn	
378	*top:* Kimberly Butler	
	center: Dana Belcher	
	bottom: Robert Milazzo	

Index

Characters are in **boldface**.
Page numbers in *italics* refer to illustrations.